R. GUPTA'S®

POPULAR MASTER GUIDE

Indian Air Force

Ground Duty Officers

&

All other Non-Technical Branches

Common Entrance Test (CET)

2012
EDITION

RAMESH PUBLISHING HOUSE, New Delhi

Published by:
O.P. Gupta
for Ramesh Publishing House
Admin. Office: 12-H, New Daryaganj Road,
Opp. Traffic Kotwali,
New Delhi-110002
✆ 23261567, 23275224
Telefax: 011-23275124
EMail: info@rameshpublishinghouse.com
Website: www.rameshpublishinghouse.com
Showroom:
- 4457, Nai Sarak, Delhi-6
✆ 23918938
- 2604/16, Balaji Market,
Nai Sarak, Delhi-6 ✆ 23253720, 23282525

ISBN 978-81-7812-865-8

R-1160

Price: Rs. 140/- only

Printed at:
Rajdhani Offset
Delhi

SCHEME OF EXAMINATION

Common Entrance Test (CET) is a tool to assess the proficiency of the candidate in English and Gendral Awareness, for selection in Ground Duties Branches. CET has two parts, namely:

PART A

Multiple Choice Questions: English and General Awareness (30 Questions) (Duration 20 Minutes).

PART B

Descriptive Test in English: Three Questions—One Comprehension Passage with 5 Questions, one Letter Writing and one Paragraph Writing. (Duration 30 Minutes)

The Test is applicable to all those aspirants who apply for **non-technical branches.**

Note:

1. Candidates who are shortlisted on the basis of CET will be called for Personality Test at one of the Air Force Selection Boards (AFSBs).
2. Medical Examination will be conducted at AFCME, New Delhi or IAM, Bangalore.
3. Onus of meeting eligibility criteria rests with the applicants. Merely undergoing CET/SSB testing would not constitute fulfilment of eligibility requirements.

CONTENTS

Test Paper (Solved)

IAF–GROUND DUTY OFFICERS

COMMON ENTRANCE TEST

Part–A

Directions : *Fill in the blanks by selecting appropriate alternative.*

1. He went to the library .... to find that it was closed.
(*a*) seldom (*b*) never
(*c*) only (*d*) solely

2. I met him only a week ....
(*a*) back (*b*) past
(*c*) ago (*d*) previous

3. Lovely asked me ....
(*a*) why are you angry?
(*b*) why I am angry?
(*c*) why I was angry?
(*d*) why was I angry?

4. He told his wife that .... from Germany.
(*a*) he will like to visit France
(*b*) he was liking to visit France
(*c*) he would like to visit France
(*d*) he is liking to visit France

5. Some people can .... even with murder.
(*a*) get on (*b*) get out
(*c*) get off (*d*) get away

6. Even after repeated warnings, he .... to office on time.
(*a*) never come (*b*) never comes
(*c*) is never coming (*d*) have never come

7. It is time you .... home.
(*a*) go (*b*) went
(*c*) come (*d*) reach

8. Government must .... the rise in prices.
(*a*) cheque (*b*) check
(*c*) cease (*d*) seize

9. There will be a rush for seats when the train ....
(*a*) will arrive (*b*) arrived
(*c*) is arriving (*d*) arrives

10. Diamond mines are located in ....
(*a*) Uttar Pradesh (*b*) Maharashtra
(*c*) Gujarat (*d*) Madhya Pradesh

11. The least populated state in India is ....
(*a*) Goa (*b*) Sikkim
(*c*) Manipur (*d*) Tripura

12. Which state in India ranks first in the production of coffee?
(*a*) Andhra Pradesh (*b*) Kerala
(*c*) Karnataka (*d*) Tamil Nadu

13. Where from Satyameva Jayate is taken?
(*a*) Mundaka Upanishad
(*b*) Mahabharata
(*c*) Thirukkural
(*d*) Arthashastra

14. The climate of India is ....
(*a*) Tropical (*b*) Sulatropical
(*c*) Savanna type (*d*) Latitude

15. 'Ranji Trophy' is associated with the game of ....
(*a*) Hockey (*b*) Football
(*c*) Cricket (*d*) Badminton

16. The world's longest railway platform is at ....
(*a*) Talcher (*b*) New York
(*c*) Kharagpur (*d*) None of these

17. 'Jnanpith Award' is given for excellence in the field of ....
(*a*) Music (*b*) Literature
(*c*) Sports (*d*) Films

18. ELISA test is carried out for detection of ....
(*a*) AIDS (*b*) Typhoid
(*c*) Cancer (*d*) Pregnancy

19. The smallest bone of our body is found in our................ .
(*a*) Ear (*b*) Nose
(*c*) Eye (*d*) Toe

20. India tested its first Nuclear device on ....
(*a*) 15 May, 1972 (*b*) 18 May, 1974
(*c*) 20 May, 1975 (*d*) 26 May, 1976

21. The first woman in space was ....
(*a*) Valentina Tereschkova
(*b*) Kalpana Chawla
(*c*) Junoko Tabei
(*d*) Bachendri Pal

Directions : *Choose the correct* ***antonyms.***

22. SELFISH
(*a*) Selfless (*b*) Unthinking
(*c*) Generous (*d*) Profuse

23. TIGHT
(*a*) Lose (*b*) Loose
(*c*) Loosen (*d*) Untie

24. PERFECT
(*a*) Faulty (*b*) Defective
(*c*) Inadequate (*d*) Imperfect

Directions : *Choose the correct* ***synonyms.***

25. SCOUNDREL
(*a*) poor (*b*) hunter
(*c*) rogue (*d*) vessel

26. APPURTENANCE
(*a*) opportunity (*b*) an accessory
(*c*) legal document (*d*) equipment

27. SCOURGE
(*a*) infliction (*b*) clean
(*c*) misfortune (*d*) polish

Directions : *In each of the following questions, find out which part of the sentence has an error.*

28. Do you know (*a*) / where I have (*b*) / kept my (*c*) / scissor? (*d*)

29. Indian politics (*a*) / is similar as (*b*) / the blind (*c*) / leading the blind. (*d*)

30. Rita and myself (*a*) / are (*b*) / great friends (*c*) / since childhood. (*d*)

ANSWERS

1	2	3	4	5	6	7	8	9	10
(*c*)	(*c*)	(*c*)	(*c*)	(*d*)	(*b*)	(*a*)	(*b*)	(*d*)	(*d*)
11	**12**	**13**	**14**	**15**	**16**	**17**	**18**	**19**	**20**
(*b*)	(*c*)	(*a*)	(*a*)	(*c*)	(*c*)	(*b*)	(*a*)	(*a*)	(*b*)
21	**22**	**23**	**24**	**25**	**26**	**27**	**28**	**29**	**30**
(*a*)	(*a*)	(*b*)	(*d*)	(*a*)	(*b*)	(*a*)	(*d*)	(*b*)	(*b*)

Part-B (Descriptive Type Questions)

Directions : *A passage is given below followed by five questions. Read the passage carefully and answer the questions given below.*

1. Read the following passage and answer briefly the questions that follow :

Almost everyone who is someone possesses a Shahtoosh shawl. As the Persian word 'Shahtoosh' — 'Shah' meaning emperor and 'toosh' meaning nature — denotes, it is a shawl fit for emperors and is procured from nature. Most of the people who collect these shawls, soft and fine enough to go through a ring, are unaware that the Shahtoosh shawl is woven from the wool of Chiru or the Tibetan antelope. Since Chiru is a wild animal found near the snowline in Tibet and China, it is not possible to capture and take its wool. So, those seeking to make a fast buck kill the animal and remove the finest wool from the front of its lower neck and then sell it to the traders and weavers of these exquisite shawls. The hair of the Tibetan antelope is seven times thinner than human hair and the cost of a pure Shahtoosh shawl in the Indian market is close to Rs. 60,000. In the European markets the price of a shawl varies from 2,000 to 10,000 pounds. To weave one shawl the wool of 3 to 4 antelopes is needed. Estimates say that while at the beginning of the century there were a million or more Chiru, today not more than 50,000 to 75,000 Tibetan antelopes are left.

(*a*) Why is a Shahtoosh shawl so expensive?

(*b*) Why is a Shahtoosh shawl considered to be exquisite?

(*c*) Why are Chirus killed though the wool can be taken without killing them?

(*d*) How do we know that Shahtoosh shawls are becoming popular though they are expensive?

(*e*) Find words/phrases from the passage which mean the same as:

(*i*) quick money

(*ii*) taken from

(*iii*) owns

2. You have seen an advertisement in the 'Hindustan Times' calling for applications for the post of a Sales Executive. Write a letter to the Personnel Manager, M/s Rosch Specialities Limited, Munirika, New Delhi, applying for the job with a detailed bio-data of yourself.

3. Write a paragraph of not more than 100 words on the following topic

(*i*) Bandhs—as a way to protest

(*ii*) Capital Punishment

(*iii*) Pleasures of Travel

(*iv*) Importance of celebrating festivals

ANSWERS

1. (*a*) A Shahtoosh shawl is expensive because to weave one shawl the wool of 3 to 4 antelopes is needed. These shawls are so soft, and fine that it can pass through a ring. It is a bit difficult to capture antelope as it is a wild animal. The animal is killed and then the wool is removed from the front of its lower neck and then it is sold to the traders and weavers, and then it is sold further when woven.

(*b*) The Persian word 'Shahtoosh' – 'Shah' means emperor and 'toosh' means nature denotes that it is a shawl which suits emperors and is procured from nature. It gives feeling of superiority as the shawl is very soft and fine. The hair of the Tibetan antelope is seven times thinner than human hair and the shawl made of it is so soft that it can pass through a ring too.

(*c*) Chirus are killed to get the wool of their body because it is not easy to catch them as they are wild animals living near the snowline in Tibet and China. It takes 3 to 4 antelopes to make a shawl, so it would take lots of energy and time to get one shawl made. Those looking forward to make fast money kill these animals.

(*d*) Shahtoosh shawls are becoming popular though they are expensive because these shawls have become a status symbol and people in possession of these shawls feel themselves as superior. The estimates tell that where there were more than a million Chiru at the beginning of the century, now not more than 50,000 to 75,000 Tibetan antelopes are left. These figures show how rapid killing of these animals is done to get the shawls made.

(*e*) (*i*) fast buck

(*ii*) procured from

(*iii*) possesses

2. Ref : VKS/EMP/012 Date: 01.10.2009

M/s Rosch Specialities Ltd
987, Floor 9
Mansarovar Building
Nehru Place
New Delhi - 110019
KA : Mr Sumeet Nangia (Manager Personnel and Administration)
Dear Sir,

Sub : *Appointment in Your Firm as Sales Executive*

JOB CODE : RSL/SALES/2009

This is in reference to the advertisement issued by you in The Hindustan Times dated 30 September, 2009, regarding the post of Sales Executive in your esteemed organisation. I offer my services to your organisation and would like to submit the following details in order to support my claim for the aforesaid post.

I am Vivek, BA (Fine Arts) and MA (English). I am fully computer literate and have thorough exposure to Netscape Navigator, Visual Foxpro, Visual Basic 5.0, Windows 98 as well as MS Office. I am also pursuing my Post-graduate Diploma in Sales Management with ABC Institute of Management, Qutub Institutional Area, New Delhi. This diploma would be over within six months.

Sales is my only passion and result oriented behaviour is the coveted goal of my life. My father is a Sales Manager in a reputed company and I have learned a lot from him about this esteemed profession.

My speciality, as would be clear from my Curriculum Vitae', is in Fast Moving Consumer Goods. I have achieved the highest targets set forth by my management in this wonderful area of growth. I won all the sales battles with flying colours and am ready to take on more challenging assignments in future. I hope you would be able to offer me more difficult challenges in sales career.

Sir, I believe that a salesman never fails in his life. I have a successful record of sales of nearly eight years. I would like to share my experiences with you and would also like to repeat the same feat in your company as well.

My reason for a shift is rather unusual one. It would be very unfair to state that I am not satisfied with my present assignment. I am also being paid well for my sales results and the incentives are also lucrative. However, my company wants me to repeat the sales performance in Rajasthan whereas I am not prepared to go outside my home state which is Delhi.

The reasons emanate from my family background. I have a family to support and my children are too young to be left alone. My wife is also working and hence, she is not able to devote enough time to the children. Further, we are a nuclear family and there is no support from our parents who are living in a remote village of Himachal Pradesh. Hence, my contention for a shift in my job is justified.

Enclosed please find a copy of my Curriculum Vitae' which should be able to give you the requisite information you need. If you need any other information, please ask. I would be pleased to furnish you with more details. Two references have also been enclosed for your scrutiny of my credentials.

Kindly accept my candidature for the aforesaid position and oblige.

Thanking you,
Yours sincerely,

(Vivek Kant Shrivasatava)
Encl : a/a

3. Bandhs—as a way to protest

Bandhs now-a-days have become a popular way to protest in companies. Workers when feel that there demand is been not listened to any want their present condition to be upgraded, they protest by not working. This way of protesting leaves a huge impact on the employers as any no work is performed and there is no production during this period of Bandh. Though it is a very peaceful kind of protest but many a times it gets even hostile too.

GENERAL SCIENCE
GENERAL KNOWLEDGE
SOCIAL SCIENCE

HISTORY OF WORLD

1. Match List I with List II and select the correct answer using the codes given below the lists :

List I

(*a*) Chittagong Armoury Raid
(*b*) Abhinav Bharat
(*c*) Anushilan Samiti
(*d*) Kuka Movement

List II

1. Kalpana Dutt
2. Guru Ram Singh
3. V.D. Savarkar
4. Aurobindo Ghosh

Codes :

	(*a*)	(*b*)	(*c*)	(*d*)
A.	1	3	4	2
B.	1	3	2	4
C.	3	1	2	4
D.	3	1	4	2

2. Abraham Lincon was elected the President of United States in:
   A. 1862 B. 1860
   C. 1875 D. 1855
3. Where is Lake Superior, the largest fresh-water lake in the world, located?
   A. USA B. Brazil
   C. Canada D. Russia
4. D-Day is the day when:
   A. Germany declared war on Britain
   B. US dropped the atom bomb on Hiroshima
   C. Allied Troops landed in Normandy
   D. Germany surrendered to the allies
5. Whose teachings inspired the French Revolution?
   A. Locke B. Rousseau
   C. Hegel D. Plato
6. At a time when empires in Europe were crumbling before the might of Napoleon which *one* of the following Governor-Generals kept the British flag flying high in India?
   A. Warren Hastings
   B. Lord Cornwallis
   C. Lord Wellesley
   D. Lord Hastings
7. Which one of the following statements regarding Fascism in Italy is *not* true?
   A. The Fascists came to power as a result of popular uprising
   B. In 1926, all political parties except Mussolini's party were banned
   C. The Fascists suppressed the Socialist movement
   D. The Fascists were hostile to the Communists
8. The fall of Czar Nicholas-II is known as:
   A. Bloody Sunday
   B. Bolshevik Revolution
   C. February Revolution
   D. October Revolution
9. Industrial Revolution took place first in:
   A. France
   B. Germany
   C. United Kingdom
   D. Japan
10. The British Prime Minister at the outbreak of World War II was
    A. Churchill
    B. Baldwin
    C. Attlee
    D. Chemberlain
11. Some of the rock cut temples, known as the Seven Pagodas, were built by the:
    A. Cauvery
    B. Tungabhadra
    C. Krishna
    D. Godawari
12. The slogan "No taxation without representation" was raised during the:
    A. American War of Independence
    B. Russian Revolution
    C. French Revolution
    D. Indian Freedom struggle
13. In the nineteenth century the people of Europe started moving from the villages to the cities due to the impact of
    A. Epidemics
    B. War
    C. Industrialisation
    D. Population explosion in villages
14. The important cause of the

Civil War in America was:
A. Abolition of slavery
B. Quest for freedom
C. Industrialisation
D. Rebellion by the native Americans

15. Industrial Revolution could not have come about without:
A. Merchant capitalism
B. The Enclosure Movement
C. The services of the proletariat class
D. An agricultural revolution

16. Consider the following statements
The French Revolution came about mainly due to the
1. Extreme poverty of the people
2. Impact of the works of great writers
3. Cruelty of the rulers
4. Impact of impulsive reaction

Which of the above statements are correct?
A. 1, 2 and 4
B. 2 and 3
C. 1, 3 and 4
D. 1, 2, 3 and 4

17. Asia's oldest and largest Buddhist monastery is situated in
A. Tawang (Arunanchal Pardesh)
B. Lhasa (Tibet)
C. Trincomallee (Sri Lanka)
D. Ulan Bator (Mongolia)

18. Who was the main architect of the Russian Revolution?
A. Karl Marx
B. Lenin
C. Stalin
D. Tolstoy

19. V.I. Lenin is associated with
A. Russian Revolution of 1917
B. Chinese Revolution of 1949
C. German Revolution
D. French Revolution of 1789

20. Which one of the following statements is *not* correct?
A. Voltaire believed in Natural Religion
B. Rousseau wrote *Social Contract*
C. Montesquieu authored *The Spirit of Laws*
D. Necker believed in 'General Will'

21. The Nihilists were responsible for the:
A. American Revolution
B. French Revolution
C. Industrial Revolution
D. Russian Revolution

22. The British Prime Minister at the time of India's Independence was :
A. Winston Churchill
B. Clement Attlee
C. Anthony Eden
D. Harold Macmillan

ANSWERS

1	2	3	4	5	6	7	8	9	10
A	C	C	C	B	C	A	C	C	D
11	**12**	**13**	**14**	**15**	**16**	**17**	**18**	**19**	**20**
C	A	C	A	A	D	A	B	A	D
21	**22**								
D	B								

HISTORY OF INDIA

1. 6th April, 1930 is well known in the history of India because this date is associated with..........
   A. Dandi March by Mahatma Gandhi
   B. Quit India Movement
   C. Partition of Bengal
   D. Partition of India
2. Which ruler enforced the system of 'Price Control' in India?
   A. Mohammad Tughlak
   B. Razia Begum
   C. Alauddin Khilji
   D. Sher Shah Suri
3. The concept of 'Din-e-Elahi' was founded by which king?
   A. Dara Shikoh
   B. Akbar
   C. Sher Shah Suri
   D. Shahjahan
4. Who are supposed to be the earliest inhabitants of India? Where did they come from?
   A. Aryans from Central Asia
   B. Dravidians from Mediterranean
   C. Negroids from Africa
   D. Bhils and the Santhals from West Asia
5. The one chief characteristic of temple architecture of the Gupta Age was :
   A. Absence of dome
   B. Huge size
   C. Beautiful carvings
   D. absence of a covered court-yard for the gathering of worshippers
6. The Rigveda consists of :
   A. 1000 hymns
   B. 2028 hymns
   C. 1028 hymns
   D. 1038 hymns
7. The central point in Ashoka's dharma was
   A. royalty to kings
   B. peace and non-violence
   C. respect to elders
   D. religious toleration
8. The social evil which was conspicuously absent during ancient India was :
   A. *Sati*-System
   B. *Devadasi*-System
   C. Polygamy
   D. *Purdah*-System
9. Which, among the following, can be accepted as a novelty introduced by Mughal emperors to their buildings?
   A. Domes
   B. Minarets
   C. Arches
   D. Attached gardens
10. The first ruler of India who defeated Muhammud of Ghur was :
    A. Mularaja II of Gujarat
    B. Prithviraja Chauhan of Delhi
    C. Jayachand of Kannauj
    D. Parmaldeva of Bundelkhand
11. What important event happened in India in 1911?
    A. Bengal was partitioned
    B. Non-Cooperation movement was launched
    C. India's capital was shifted from Calcutta to Delhi
    D. Mahatma Gandhi presided over the Congress session
12. The first phase of the Congress Party (1885-1905) was characterized by its efforts to secure
    A. limited independence
    B. complete freedom
    C. Indianization of services
    D. constitutional reforms
13. The Muslim League demanded a separate homeland for the Indian Muslims openly for the first time at its annual session held in Lahore in the year :
    A. 1931 A.D. B. 1936 A.D.
    C. 1940 A.D. D. 1941 A.D.
14. Under whose governorship did the East India Company secure the Diwani Rights in Bengal, Bihar and Orissa from Emperor Shah Alam?
    A. Lord Cornwallis
    B. Lord William Bentinck
    C. Lord Clive
    D. Lord Wellesley
15. The Simon Commission

was generally boycotted by the Indian political parties. What was the reason for this general non-cooperation?
A. the Commission aimed at dividing the people
B. it was an 'all white' Commission
C. it came after the Jallianwala Bagh carnage
D. it was an eye wash

16. Aligarh Muslim University was founded by :
A. Dr. Saifuddin Kitchlu
B. Mohammad Ali Jinnah
C. Sir Syed Ahmed Khan
D. Maulana Mohammad Ali

17. Ibn Batutah was an African traveller visiting India during the time of :
A. Alivardi Khan
B. Ala-ud-din Khalji
C. Iltutmish
D. Mohammad-bin-Tughlaq

18. The battle of Wandiawash was fought in :
A. 1726 B. 1760
C. 1818 D. 1857

19. The abolition of *Sati* by government regulation was at the time of :
A. Warren Hastings
B. Lord Wellesley
C. Lord Bentinck
D. Lord Ahmerst

20. Pick out the wrong combination :
A. Dilwara Temple ; Mt. Abu
B. Pashupati Temple : Kathmandu
C. Padmanbha Temple : Bangalore
D. Minakshi Temple : Madurai

21. Match the following:
(*a*) Chanhu-daro
(*b*) Kalibangan
(*c*) Lothal
(*d*) Surkotoda
1. Alleged discovery of the skeleton of horse.
2. Bead making.
3. Traces of a dock and ship on seal.
4. Evidence of ploughing the fields.

The Correct code is :

	(*a*)	(*b*)	(*c*)	(*d*)
A.	2	4	3	1
B.	2	1	3	4
C.	1	2	3	4
D.	2	1	4	3

22. Match the Harappan settlements with the banks of rivers on which they were located :

(*a*) Harappa	1. Ravi
(*b*) Mohenjo-daro	2. Indus
(*c*) Ropar	3. Sutlej
(*d*) Kalibangan	4. Ghaggar
(*e*) Lothal	5. Bhogava

Codes :

	(*a*)	(*b*)	(*c*)	(*d*)	(*e*)
A.	1	2	3	4	5
B.	1	2	3	5	4
C.	2	1	3	5	4
D.	2	1	4	3	5

23. The Goddess 'Kannagi' whose many temples were erected during the 'Sangam Age' was the goddess of :
A. Chastity B. Love
C. Prowess D. Wisdom

24. The Jain goal of life is to attain deliverance from the fetters of mudane existence, the way to which lies through three jewels. Which one of the following was not included among the 'three jewels' of Jainism?
A. Right faith
B. Right action
C. Right knowledge
D. Right conduct

25. The most striking feature of the Ashokan pillar is polish. Name the Ashokan pillar which is considered to be the most graceful of all Ashokan pillars.
A. Sarnath
B. Rampurva
C. Laurya-Nandangarh
D. Rummindei

26. Which are the correct statements?
1. The land grants, started in Satavahana period, paved the way for feudal developments in India.
2. Silk and spices were the Chief Indian export articles of Indo-Roman trade.
3. The Guptas issued the largest number of gold coins in ancient India.
4. The first memorial of a 'SATI' dated 510 A.D. is found at Eran in Madhya Pradesh.

A. 1 and 2
B. 1, 3, and 4
C. 1 and 4
D. 1, 2, 3 and 4

27. Who among the following patronised the 'Gandhara' (Indo-Greek style) School of Art?
A. Ashoka, the Great
B. Harsha Vardhana
C. Kanishka
D. Chandragupta

Vikramaditya

28. The Sultanate of Delhi had five ruling dynasties. The dynasty having longest and shortest period were :
A. Ilbari and Khalji
B. Tughlaq and Khalji
C. Tughlaq and Sayyid
D. Ilbari and Lodis

29. Which one of the following events took place at the last during reign of Muhammad-bin-Tughlaq?
A. Introduction of token currency
B. Increase of land-revenue in Doab
C. Transfer of Capital from Delhi to Devagiri.
D. Conquest of Khurasan and Iraq

30. The most learned medieval Muslim ruler who was well versed in various branches of learning including astronomy, mathematics and medicine was :
A. Jalaluddin Khilji
B. Sikander Lodi
C. Ghiyasuddin Tughlaq
D. Muhammad-bin-Tughlaq

31. The 'Sufis' had 12 silsilas. They propounded the idea of Union with God through:
A. Love B. Rituals
C. Fasts D. Prayers

32. Match the following:

(*a*) Peshwa	1. Foreign affairs
(*b*) Panditrao	2. Audit and accounts
(*c*) Amatya	3. Providing grants to scholars
(*d*) Sumant	4. General supervision
	5. Military affairs

Select the correct code :

	(*a*)	(*b*)	(*c*)	(*d*)
A.	2	3	4	5
B.	4	1	2	3
C.	4	3	2	1
D.	3	1	4	2

33. The Regulating Act of 1773 can be regarded as the first measure to :
A. assert the right of British Parliament to legislate for India
B. separate the legislature from the executive
C. separate the judiciary from the executive
D. centralise law-making

34. What was the exact constitutional status of the Indian Republic on 26th January, 1950?
A. A Democratic Republic
B. A Sovereign Democratic Republic
C. A Sovereign Secular Democratic Republic
D. A Sovereign Socialist Secular Democratic Republic

35. When the British obtained the grant of Diwani of Bengal, Bihar and Orissa they acquired the right to :
A. maintain law and order in these territories
B. administer civil justice and collect revenue in these territories
C. collect revenue and establish revenue administration in these territories
D. militarily defend these territories

36. Which of the following were responsible for the growth of nationalism in India during the British rule?
1. Economic exploitation of India.
2. Impact of Western education.
3. Role of the Press.
Select the correct answer using the codes given below :
Codes:
A. 1, 2 and 3 B. 1 and 2
C. 2 and 3 D. 1 and 3

37. Which one of the following nationalist leaders has been described as being radical in politics but conservative on social issues?
A. G.K. Gokhale
B. B.G. Tilak
C. Lala Lajpat Rai
D. Madan Mohan Malviya

38. Provincial Autonomy in British India was envisaged by the :
A. Act of 1909
B. Act of 1919
C. Act of 1935
D. Act of 1947

39. Dyarchy means
A. double government
B. a government in which the centre is very powerful
C. a government based on division of power between centre and provinces
D. None of the above

40. The Indian National Congress observed 'Independence Day' for the first time on 26th January

in :
A. 1920 B. 1925
C. 1930 D. 1947

41. The Ghadar Party was organised in USA by
A. Raja Mahendra Pratap
B. Lala Hardayal
C. Abul Kalam Azad
D. M.A. Jinnah

42. Mahatma Gandhi for the first time practised his Satyagraha in India at :
A. Chauri-Chaura
B. Ahmedabad
C. Champaran
D. Navakholi

43. The non-cooperation movement was suspended by Gandhiji because :
A. The response of the people was poor
B. The Muslims kept aloof from the movement
C. The British government agreed to concede the demands of the Congress
D. Violence broke out at Chauri-Chaura

44. In 1911 the British annulled the partition of Bengal with a view to :
A. provide better administration of the province
B. to placate the Indians
C. to win over the Muslims to its side
D. reduce expenditure on administration

45. There was no Congress representative in the :
A. First Round Table Conference
B. Second Round Table Conference
C. Third Round Table Conference
D. First and Third Round Table Conferences

46. Who among the following transformed the Shivaji and Ganapati festival into a national festival?
A. Lala Lajpat Rai
B. Bal Gangadhar Tilak
C. Veer Savarkar
D. Gopal Krishna Gokhale

47. The Rowlatt Act stood for :
A. compulsory economic support to war efforts
B. imprisonment without trial and summary procedures for trial
C. suppression of Khilafat Movement
D. imposition of restrictions on freedom of the Press

48. Which one of the following finally alienated the Muslims and crystallized the demand for Pakistan?
A. The introduction of separate electorates for the Muslims
B. The establishment of the Muslim League
C. The non-inclusion of Muslims in the provincial governments
D. The federal provisions envisaged under the Government of India Act of 1935

49. At which session of Congress in 1907 the first split in the party occurred?
A. Surat session
B. Pune session
C. Nagpur session
D. Ahmedabad session

50. Consider the following :
1. Ghadar Party
2. Khilafat Movement
3. Dandi March
4. Champaran Satyagraha
The correct chronological sequence is:
A. 4, 1, 2, 3 B. 1, 4, 3, 2
C. 4, 1, 3, 2 D. 1, 4, 2, 3

51. The first effective attempt by the nationalists for drafting the Constitution of Independent India may be traced back to :
A. the Poona Pact
B. Sapru Report
C. Nehru Report
D. Jinnah's Fourteen Points

52. People of the Indus Valley Civilization were
A. warlike
B. vindictive
C. uncompromising
D. None of these

53. The women of Indus Valley Civilization used
A. face powder
B. lip stick
C. elaborate hair styles
D. eye make-up

54. What importance does the year 563 B.C. have in Indian History?
A. Gautam Buddha was born
B. Indus Valley Civilization was made known
C. Chandragupta Maurya came to the throne
D. Rig Veda was written

55. The Great Hindu law given was :
A. Kapil
B. Kautilya
C. Manu
D. None of these

56. Which of the following is not one of the features of the economic regulations of Alauddin Khalji?
A. Use of correct measures
B. Prices fixed being calculated on the basis of production cost
C. Total curbing of black marketing
D. Organisation of separate markets for separate commodities

57. Who among the following was not an exponent of Bhakti movement?
A. Ramananda
B. Kabir
C. Shankaracharya
D. Nanak

58. Consider the following four saints :
1. Kabir
2. Nanak
3. Chaitanya
4. Tulsidas
What is the correct chronological order in which they flourished?
A. 1, 2, 3, 4
B. 2, 3, 4, 1
C. 3, 1, 2, 4
D. 3, 2, 4, 1

59. Brahmo Samaj mainly insisted upon:
A. Abolition of sati
B. Abolition of child marriage
C. Monotheism
D. Reintroduction of converted Hindus

60. Who among the early nationalists worked in England to mobilize public opinion in favour of the Indian National Movement?
A. Gopal Krishna Gokhale
B. D.E. Wacha
C. Lala Lajpat Rai
D. Dadabhai Naoroji

61. Sir Charles Wood despatch of 1854 dealt primarily with:
A. administrative reforms
B. social reforms
C. economic reforms
D. educational reforms

62. The most important feature of the Government of India Act of 1919 was the introduction of:
A. Dyarchy
B. Provincial autonomy
C. Separate electorates
D. Adult franchise

63. The leader of the Young Bengal Movement was:
A. Dwarkanath Tagore
B. Chandrashekhar Deb
C. Ishwar Chandra Vidyasagar
D. Henry Vivian Derozio

64. Indian National Congress found wide acceptance initially among:
A. peasants and working class
B. landlords
C. educated middle class
D. businessmen

65. Arrange the following in chronological order who administered as Governor-Generals in India.
1. Wellesley
2. Cornwallis
3. Warren Hastings
4. Dalhousie
A. 3, 2, 1, 4
B. 1, 2, 4, 3
C. 4, 2, 3, 1
D. 4, 1, 2, 3

66. The Legislative Council can delay the enactment of a Bill passed by the Legislative Assembly for a maximum period of :
A. one month
B. four months
C. six months
D. one year

67. The Sufi Saint, who founded the Chisti order was :
A. Nizamuddin Auliya
B. Khwaja Moinuddin
C. Nasiruddin Chiragh-i-Delhi
D. Homidud-Dini Nagori

68. Akbar's mausoleum is situated at :
A. Agra
B. New Delhi
C. Sikandara
D. Sasaram

69. Who was the founder of the Sunga Dynasty?
A. Agnimitra
B. Divakarmaitra
C. Pushyamitra
D. Vasumitra

70. Where did Babar die?
A. Agra B. Delhi
C. Kabul D. Lahore

71. Jainism differed from Buddhism in which of the following aspects?
A. Doctrine of Ahimsa
B. Faith in Karma
C. Belief in fasting
D. Rejection of Yajna

72. "Go back to the Vedas" was the motto of :
A. Raj Ram Mohan Roy
B. Swami Vivekananda
C. Swami Dayanand Saraswati
D. M.G. Ranade

73. The cutting of forest leads

to :
A. soil erosion and uncontrollable floods
B. desilting denaturation
C. increase of rainfall and humidity
D. None of these

74. Match List I (Name of the revolutionary tried in a conspiracy case) with List II (Name of conspiracy case) and select the correct answer using the codes given below the Lists :

List I
(*a*) Ram Prasad Bismil
(*b*) Surya Sen
(*c*) Aurobindo Ghosh
(*d*) Bhagat Singh

List II
1. Lahore Conspiracy Case
2. Kakori Conspiracy Case
3. Chittagong Armoury Raid
4. Alipore Bomb Case

Codes :

	(*a*)	(*b*)	(*c*)	(*d*)
A.	4	2	3	1
B.	2	3	4	1
C.	3	4	1	2
D.	4	1	2	3

75. The Mathura School of Art was influenced by :
A. Amaravati School of Art
B. Bodh Gaya School of Art
C. Roman School of Art
D. Gandhara School of Art

76. Which one of the following has been the main feature of the South Indian Temple architecture?
A. Sikhara B. Gopuram
C. Vimana D. Mandapa

77. Amir Khusrau was the famous poet in the court of :
A. Akbar
B. Shahjahan
C. Ibrahim Lodi
D. Alauddin Khalji

78. Who among the following, destroyed the "Group of Forty" Nobles?
A. Baharam Shah
B. Iltutmish
C. Sultana Razia
D. Balban

79. Which of the following states was not annexed by Lord Dalhousie under the Doctrine of Lapse?
A. Jammu
B. Oudh
C. Udaipur
D. Nagpur

80. The *Ashtapradhan* was the council of ministers during the reign of :
A. Krishnadeva Rai
B. Tipu Sultan
C. Shivaji
D. Akbar

81. Arrange the following in chronological order:
1. Dandi March
2. Simon Commission
3. Poona Pact
4. Gandhi-Irwin Pact
A. 2, 1, 3, 4 B. 2, 1, 4, 3
C. 4, 3, 1, 2 D. 4, 3, 2, 1

82. Which of the contemporary Muslim writers criticized Alauddin for his disregard of religion :
A. Barani
B. Amir Khusro
C. Al-beruni
D. Minhaj Siraj

83. Which of the following statements is false?
A. The third battle of Panipat sealed the fate of Maratha supermacy in India
B. The foreign invasion in the Punjab failed to suppress the authority of the Sikh Chiefs
C. Guru Arjun Dev developed the Gurumukhi script
D. The Sikh Misls were organised on the principles of autonomy

84. Which of the following Act formally introduced the principle of elections for the first time?
A. The Indian Councils Act, 1909
B. Government of India Act, 1919
C. The 1935 Act
D. India Independence Act, 1947

85. Match the following :
(*a*). C.R. Das
(*b*) Vallabhbhai Patel
(*c*) Khan Abdul Ghaffar Khan
(*d*) Maulana A.K. Azad
1. Bardoli Satygaraha
2. Swarajist
3. Khilafatist
4. Khudai Khidmatgar

	(*a*)	(*b*)	(*c*)	(*d*)
A.	2	1	4	3
B.	2	4	1	3
C.	4	1	3	2
D.	2	1	3	4

86. The object of Alauddin Khalji's economic regulations was mainly :
A. to encourage trade
B. to maintain a strong army
C. to punish shopkeepers
D. the welfare of the people

87. Harihar and Bukka laid the foundation of the Vijayanagar empire under the influence of :
A. Jnaneshvara
B. Tukaram
C. Ramanuj
D. Vidyaranya

88. The practice of 'Jharokha darshan' to the public was stopped by :
A. Jehangir
B. Shahjahan
C. Aurangzeb
D. None of these

89. Who among the following Mughal commanders compelled Shivaji to sign the Treaty of Purandar (1665)?
A. Shayesta Khan
B. Bahadur Khan
C. Mirza Raja Jai Singh
D. Raja Jaswant Singh

90. Which one of the following Mughal emperors gave permission to East India Company to build a factory at Surat?
A. Jehangir
B. Shahjahan
C. Farrukhsiyar
D. Bahadurshah II

91. Which one of the following proved to be Dalhousie's worst political blunder?
A. Annexation of Punjab
B. Occupation of lower Burma
C. 'Doctrine of Lapse'
D. Annexation of Oudh

92. Arrange the following events in chronological order on the basis of codes given below :
1. The Surat Congress
2. March from Sabarmati Ashram to Dandi
3. Rowlatt Act
4. Gandhi-Irwin pact

Codes :
A. 3, 2, 1, 4 B. 1, 3, 2, 4
C. 2, 1, 3, 4 D. 1, 2, 4, 3

93. Which one of the following statements about untouchability is *not* correct?
A. It was widely practised in the Indus Valley civilization
B. The Rigveda does not show any acquaintance with it
C. It is clearly referred to in the Buddhist Jatakas
D. It came to be applied to several castes only in the post-Gupta period

94. The minister in charge of organisation of military contingents in early Delhi Sultanate was known as:
A. Sadrus sudur
B. Rawat-i-arz
C. Naib-i-mumlikat
D. Amir-i-Kohi

95. Alauddin Khalji levied land revenue on the basis of:
A. crop sharing
B. arbitrary assessment
C. measurement
D. a fixed money tribute

96. The revenue department of Vijayanagare Empire was known as:
A. Malkhana
B. Athavana
C. Sangarahni
D. Bhandar

97. Consider the following statements related to the Mansabdari system of the Mughals :
1. Akbar introduced the Mansabdari system.
2. Mansabdars were ranked according to the number of zats and sawars they had.
3. Mansabdars were military officers only.

Which of the above statements are correct?
A. 1, 2 and 3
B. 1 and 2
C. 2 and 3
D. 1 and 3

98. In the Mughal empire, the unit of land revenue assessment was:
A. individual peasant
B. village
C. pargana
D. zamindar

99. The earliest surviving building in India containing a true dome is the:
A. Gol Gumbaz
B. Arhai Din ka Jhopra
C. Tomb of Sultan Garhi
D. Alai Darwaja

100. The Turks brought with them musical instruments:
A. Rabab and Sarangi
B. Sitar and Flute
C. Veena and Tabla
D. Tanpura and Mridanga

101. Zakat under the Mughals signified:
A. a tax on trade amounting to 2½% of value
B. war booty
C. land tax on Muslims amounting to 10% of produce
D. tax imposed on non-Muslims

102. Firoz Tughlaq may be said

to have brought about the decline of the Delhi Sultanate because he:
A. conducted a very large number of military campaigns
B. spent too much money on canals
C. allowed nobility to become hereditary
D. provoked peasant rebellions by his oppression

103. Consider the following events :
1. Cabinet Mission Plan
2. Bombay Plan
3. Wavell Plan
4. Mountbatten Plan
The correct chronological order of these events is
A. 2, 1, 3, 4 B. 2, 1, 4, 3
C. 1, 2, 3, 4 D. 1, 2, 4, 3

104. Consider the following events :
1. Cripps Mission
2. Quit India Movement
3. Individual Satyagraha
4. August Offer
The correct chronological order of these is
A. 4, 3, 2, 1 B. 4, 3, 1, 2
C. 3, 4, 1, 2 D. 3, 4, 2, 1

105. Match List I with List II and select the correct answer using the codes given below the Lists :

List I
(*a*) James Outram
(*b*) John Nicholson
(*c*) Cohn Campbell
(*d*) Hugh Rose

List II
1. Delhi 2. Lucknow
3. Jhansi 4. Kanpur

Codes :

	(*a*)	(*b*)	(*c*)	(*d*)
A.	1	2	3	4
B.	2	1	4	3
C.	2	1	3	4
D.	1	2	4	3

106. Consider the following scripts :
1. Brahmi
2. Kharoshthi
3. Greek
4. Aramaic
Scripts used in Ashokan inscriptions include
A. 3 and 4
B. 1 and 2
C. 1, 2 and 3
D. 1, 2, 3 and 4

107. Which one of the following dynasties was ruling over North India at the time of Alexander's invasion?
A. Nanda B. Maurya
C. Sunga D. Kanva

108. The last major extension of British Indian territory took place during the time of:
A. Dufferin
B. Dalhousie
C. Lytton
D. Curzon

109. The Social System of the Harappans was
A. Fairly egalitarian
B. Slave-Labour based
C. Colour (Varna) based
D. Caste based

110. Which of the following Vedas provides information about the civilisation of the Early Vedic Age?
A. Rigveda
B. Yajurveda
C. Atharvaveda
D. Samaveda

111. The Mughal painting reached its zenith during the reign of:
A. Akbar
B. Jahangir
C. Shahjahan
D. Aurangzeb

112. Permanent Revenue Settlement of Bengal was introduced by:
A. Clive
B. Hastings
C. Wellesley
D. Cornwallis

113. 'Do or die' was one of the most powerful slogans of India's freedom struggle. Who gave it?
A. Gandhiji
B. J.L. Nehru
C. Balgangadhar Tilak
D. Subhash Chandra Bose

114. Primitive man first learnt:
A. to make fire
B. to tame animals
C. to make a wheel
D. to grow grain

115. Which one of the following contains the Gayatri Mantra?
A. Rig Veda
B. Yajur Veda
C. Upanishad
D. Aranyakas

116. The Rajput Clan of Solankis rose to power in :
A. Kannauj
B. Kathiawar
C. Malwa
D. Kashmir

117. Who was the political guru of M.K. Gandhi?
A. Dadabhai Naoroji
B. Gopal Krishna Gokhale
C. Lala Lajpat Rai
D. Lokmanya Tilak

118. An overwhelming majority

of the images of Ajanta are those of:
A. Siva
B. Vishnu
C. The Buddha
D. Durga

119. For the elimination of human misery Gautam Buddha recommended:
A. Syadvada
B. Astangika Marga
C. Kaivalya
D. Triratna

120. Gupta Dynasty was famous for:
A. Art and Architecture
B. Imperialism
C. Revenue and land reforms
D. Patronage of literacy work

121. Permanent Revenue System of Lord Cornwallis proved oppressive to the tenants because they were:
A. Forced to produce more
B. Exploited by the Zamindars
C. Asked to pay yearly revenue in advance
D. Asked to pay under military pressure

122. Gandhiji started Satyagraha movement in 1919 in protest against the:
A. Enactment of Rowlatt Act
B. Champaran Wrongs
C. Simon Commission
D. Colonial exploitation of India

123. In which of the following movements did Mahatma Gandhi make the first use of Hunger Strike as a weapon?
A. Non-Cooperation Movement, 1920-22
B. Rowlatt Satyagraha, 1919
C. Ahmedabad Strike, 1918
D. Bardoli Satyagraha

124. Who started the Saka Era, which is still used by the Government of India?
A. Kanishka
B. Vikramaditya
C. Samudragupta
D. Asoka

125. Who among the following was responsible for the Partition of Bengal in 1905?
A. Lord Minto
B. Lord Lytton
C. Lord Curzon
D. None of the above

126. Which of the following dynasties was the oldest ruling dynasty of ancient India?
A. Rashtrakutas
B. Chalukyas
C. Pallavas
D. Satvahanas

127. Who among the following was the only woman ruler to sit on the throne of Delhi?
A. Chand Bibi
B. Jahan Aara
C. Nur Jahan
D. Razia Sultan

128. Where did the British East India Company open its first factory in India?
A. Madras (Chennai)
B. Surat
C. Calcutta (Kolkata)
D. Bombay (Mumbai)

129. Where was the first session of Indian National Congress held?
A. Bombay (Mumbai)
B. Delhi
C. Madras (Chennai)
D. Calcutta (Kolkata)

130. Which of the following was the most important characteristic of Kanishka's rule?
A. Expansion of Buddhism outside India
B. Re-emergence of Jainism
C. Fourth Buddhist Council at Srinagar
D. Gandhara School of Art

131. The Ajanta caves were built during the period of
A. Guptas
B. Kushans
C. Mauryas
D. Chalukyas

132. The Indus valley people had contacts with the:
A. Egyptians
B. Sumerians
C. Chinese
D. Mesopotamians

133. The court language of Mughals was :
A. Arabic B. Urdu
C. Persian D. Turkish

134. Har Dayal was well-known as the leader of :
A. Anshulian Party
B. Ghadar Party
C. Swaraj Party
D. Hindustan Republican Association

135. Which among the following is the oldest dynasty?
A. Maurya B. Gupta
C. Kushan D. Kanva

136. In which area does the Sabarmati rise?
A. the Satpuras
B. the Vindhyas
C. the Aravallis

D. the Western Ghats

137. Which one of the following pairs of travellers and nationalities is *correctly* matched?
A. Abdur Razzaq : Arab
B. Nicolo Conti : Dutch
C. Nuniz : Italian
D. Domingo Paes : Portuguese

138. Brick platforms used for granaries are seen in the excavation at
A. Rojdi
B. Rangpur
C. Kalibangan
D. Lothal

139. Kapila was the earliest exponent of the
A. Vaisheshika School
B. Mimamsa School
C. Samkhya School
D. Vedanta School

140. Which one of the following Sultans opposed the interference of the Ulema in State affairs?
A. Balban
B. Alauddin Khilji
C. Firoz Shah Tughlaq
D. Bahlol Lodi

141. Match List I with List II and select the correct answer using the codes given below the Lists :

List I
(*a*) Doctrine of Lapse
(*b*) Partition of Bengal
(*c*) Regulating Act
(*d*) Diwani in Bengal, 1765

List II
1. Lord Curzon
2. Warren Hastings
3. Lord Dalhousie
4. Lord Clive

Codes :

	(*a*)	(*b*)	(*c*)	(*d*)
A.	1	3	2	4
B.	3	1	2	4
C.	4	1	3	2
D.	3	4	1	2

142. 'Vedaranyam March' was a part of the:
A. Civil Disobedience Movement
B. Non-Cooperation Movement
C. Temple Entry Movement
D. Swadeshi Movement

143. The word *Varna* is used in the Rig Veda with reference only to:
A. Brahmana
B. Dasa
C. Kshatriya
D. Arya and Dasa

144. Match List I with List II

List I	List II
(*a*) Indra	1. fire
(*b*) Agni	2. light
(*c*) Varuna	3. strength
(*d*) Mitra	4. natural order of the Universe

	(*a*)	(*b*)	(*c*)	(*d*)
A.	3	4	1	2
B.	3	1	4	2
C.	3	2	1	4
D.	3	4	2	1

145. Who ridiculed the INC as representing only "a microscopic minority of the people?"
A. Curzon
B. Kimberly
C. Dufferin
D. George Hamilton

146. First Buddhist Conference after the death of Buddha was presided over by :
A. Mahakashyapa
B. Dharmasen
C. Ajatashatru
D. Nagasen

147. Which one of the following places was known as the 'Shiraz of the East' during the reign of the Sharki Sultans :
A. Agra B. Delhi
C. Jaunpur D. Varanasi

148. 'Depressed Classes League' was established by :
A. Dr. B.R. Ambedkar
B. Babu Jagjivan Ram
C. N.S. Kajrolkar
D. Mahatma Jyotiba Phule

149. Which one of the following emperors had the highest number of Hindu Generals in the Mughal army?
A. Humayun
B. Akbar
C. Jehangir
D. Aurangzeb

150. For the first time the Department of Public Works was established by :
A. Iltutmish
B. Balban
C. Alauddin Khalji
D. Firoz Shah Tughlaq

151. Which of the following occurred last?
A. Annexation Policy
B. Partition of Bengal
C. Permanent Settlement
D. Subsidiary Alliance

152. Which one of the following tombs is called the 'Second Taj Mahal'?
A. Tomb of Anarkali
B. Tomb of Itimad-ud-daula
C. Tomb of Rabia-ud-daurani
D. None of these

153. An anti British outfit 'Abhinava Bharat' was founded by :

A. R.G. Bhandarkar
B. V.D. Savarkar
C. C.R. Das
D. Sardar Bhagat Singh

154. Arrange the following movements in correct chronological order by using the codes given below:

1. Civil Disobedience
2. Khilafat
3. Non-cooperation
4. Quit India

Codes :

A. 1, 2, 3, 4
B. 2, 3, 4, 1
C. 2, 3, 1, 4
D. 3, 1, 4, 2

155. Arrange the following plans in chronological order :

1. Cripps Plan
2. Cabinet Mission Plan
3. Mountbatten Plan
4. Wavell Plan

A. 1, 2, 3, 4
B. 2, 3, 1, 4
C. 3, 4, 1, 2
D. 1, 4, 2, 3

156. The 'Young India' was started as a weekly by :

A. The Home Rule Party
B. The Extremist Party
C. Ghadar Party
D. Swaraj Party

157. The Congress supported the Khilafat Movement mainly for :

1. reinstatement of Caliph
2. removal of Caliph
3. getting the sympathy of the Muslims
4. marginalising Jinnah in the Congress

Select the correct answer from the codes given below:

Codes :

A. 1 and 3 B. 2 and 4
C. 3 and 4 D. 1 and 4

158. Any political party in India can be recognised as National Party if it has State party status in at least :

A. three States
B. four States
C. five States
D. seven States

159. Who presided over the Benares Session of the Indian National Congress in 1905?

A. Surendra Nath Banerji
B. Pheroj Shah Mehta
C. Gopal Krishna Gokhale
D. Dinshaw Wacha

160. Who amongst the following Generals of Alauddin Khilji, ultimately became the first Sultan of Tughlaq dynasty?

A. Ghazi Malik
B. Malik Kafur
C. Zafar Khan
D. Ubigh Khan

161. Who among the following issued the 'Communal Award'?

A. Ramsay Mac Donald
B. Stanley Baldwin
C. Neville Chamberlain
D. Winston Churchil

162. Ellora caves were built by :

A. Pallavas
B. Cholas
C. Rashtrakutas
D. Palas

163. The Brahmo Samaj is based on the principle of :

A. Atheism
B. Monism
C. Monotheism
D. Polytheism

164. Consider the following statements about the Indian National Congress:

1. Sarojini Naidu was the first woman to be the President of the Congress.
2. C.R. Das was in prison when he functioned as the President of the Congress.
3. The first Britisher to become the President of Congress was Alan Octavian Hume.
4. Alfred Webb was the President of the Congress in 1984.

Which of these statements are correct?

A. 1 and 3
B. 2 and 4
C. 2, 3 and 4
D. 1, 2, 3 and 4

165. All India Muslim League was formed in

A. Dhaka B. Lahore
C. Aligarh D. Lucknow

166. Who among the following streamlined the Maratha administration after Sambhaji?

A. Raja Ram
B. Balaji Viswanath
C. Ganga Bai
D. Nanaji Deshmukh

167. The Congress policy of pray and petition ultimately came to an end under the guidance of:

A. Aurobindo Ghosh
B. Bal Gangadhar Tilak
C. Lala Lajpat Rai
D. Mahatma Gandhi

168. Which one of the following ports handled the north

Indian trade during the Gupta Period?
A. Tamralipti
B. Broach
C. Kalyan
D. Cambray

169. Which one of the following was initially the most powerful city state of India in the 6th century B.C.?
A. Gandhar B. Kamboj
C. Kashi D. Magadh

170. The Governor-General who followed a spirited "Forward" policy towards Afghanistan was:
A. Minto B. Dufferin
C. Elgin D. Lytton

171. Consider the following events :
1. Indigo Revolt
2. Santhal Rebellion
3. Deccan Riot
4. Mutiny of the Sepoys
The *correct* chronological sequence of these events is:
A. 4, 2, 1, 3
B. 4, 2, 3, 1
C. 2, 4, 3, 1
D. 2, 4, 1, 3

172. Match List I with List II and select the correct answer using the codes given below the lists :

List I
(Institution of social and religious reform movements)
(*a*) Satya Shodak Samaj
(*b*) Radha Swami Satsang
(*c*) Prarthana Samaj
(*d*) Young Bengal

List II
(Founder)
1. Jyoti B. Phule
2. Shiv Dayal
3. Atma Ram
4. Henry Vivian Derozio

Codes :

	(*a*)	(*b*)	(*c*)	(*d*)
A.	1	2	3	4
B.	2	1	4	3
C.	1	2	4	3
D.	2	1	3	4

173. Lothal was used by the Indus people as a
A. port
B. market
C. capital city
D. permanent settlement by the kings

174. Given below are two statements, one labelled as *Assertion (A)* and the other labelled as *Reason (R)* :
Assertion (A) : Asoka was victorious in the Kalinga War in 269 BC.
Reason (R) : The misery of the Kalinga people depressed him very much.
In the context of the above two statements, which one of the following is *correct*?
A. Both A and R are true and R is the correct explanation of A
B. Both A and R are true and R is not a correct explanation of A
C. A is true but R is false
D. A is false but R is true

175. The person responsible for introducing the concept of Dyarchy in the 1919 Act was:
A. Montagu
B. Tez Bahadur Sapru
C. Lionel Curtis
D. Chelmsford

176. The Sikh military sect 'the Khalsa' was introduced by
A. Guru Har Rai
B. Guru Harkishan
C. Guru Gobind Singh
D. Guru Tegh Bahadur

177. Kalibangan is situated in:
A. Uttar Pradesh
B. Sindh
C. Rajasthan
D. Gujarat

178. The first Sultan of Delhi, who attempted the conquest of South India was:
A. Qutb-ud-din Mubarak
B. Nasir-ud-din Khusrav Shah
C. Ala-ud-din Khilji
D. Jalal-ud-din Firoz

179. Mahabalipuram is an important city that reveals the interest in arts of:
A. Pallavas
B. Cheras
C. Pandyas
D. Chalukyas

180. The Indus people knew the use of Weights and Measures, which is proved by the discovery of the scale at:
A. Kalibangan
B. Harappa
C. Chanhudaro
D. Lothal

181. Who, among the contemporary scholars of Harsha, was the author of Kadambari:
A. Banbhatta
B. Mayur
C. Divakar
D. Jayasena

182. The greatest scholar of medical science during the Gupta Age was :
A. Vaghbhata
B. Bhatti
C. Virahanka

D. Bana

183. Aryans knew:
A. the art of agriculture
B. the use of iron
C. the use of horse
D. the art of writing

184. The literature which the Hindus regard as the revealed word of God is called:
A. Sruti
B. Smriti
C. Brahmanas
D. Upanishadas

185. Which ancient religion prescribed the 'noble-eight-fold path' of virtuous living?
A. Buddhism
B. Jainism
C. Tantricism
D. Vaishnavism

186. Babar defeated Rana Sanga in:
A. 1603 B. 1510
C. 1515 D. 1527

187. The Third and the last Battle of Panipat sealed the fate of Maratha supremacy and Mughal effectiveness. The combined forces of Mughals and Marathas were defeated because of :
A. cowardice of Indian Soldiers
B. bankruptcy of Indian rulers
C. smallness of the Indian armies
D. widespread disunity among the Marathas

188. Which, among the following, did not constitute part of army reforms of Sher Shah?
A. Keeping a large army at the centre
B. Cash payment to the soldiers
C. Introduction of the practices of keeping *Huliya*. Huliya of soldiers and of branding horses
D. Keeping of a swiftly-moving artillery

189. In the Battle of Buxar, Mir Qasim was defeated by the English under the command of :
A. Major Hume
B. Clive
C. Sir Eyre Coote
D. Major Munro

190. Ramsay Macdonald, the British Minister, announced his 'Communal Award' in the year ;
A. 1931 A.D. B. 1932 A.D.
C. 1933 A.D. D. 1934 A.D.

191. Besides being a peerless politician, Tilak was also a fearless journalist and had brought out
A. Poona Samachar
B. Marathawad
C. Kesri
D. Bombay Times

192. Separate electorates were allowed to the Muslims for the first time in 1909 under the .....
A. Minto-Morley Reforms
B. Congress-Muslim League
C. Simon Commission Report
D. Montague-Chelmsford Reforms

193. What immediately preceded the Jallianwala Bagh carnage?
A. Passage of Rowlatt Act
B. Partition of Bengal
C. Mahatma Gandhi's satyagraha
D. Coming of the Simon Commission

194. 'An all party conference was held at Delhi in February, 1928,' to frame a constitution for India acceptable to all Indians. Who, among the following, was elected its Chairman?
A. Moti Lal Nehru
B. Lala Lajpat Rai
C. M.A. Ansari
D. M.K. Gandhi

195. 'Vaishesika' system of philosophy was propounded by
A. Gautam B. Kanda
C. Kapila D. Patanjali

196. The 'Great Bath' was a part of the civilization of:
A. the people of the Indus
B. the people of Aryan Civilization
C. Scythians
D. Huns

197. Aryans had:
A. city culture
B. love for outdoor games
C. simple food and drinking habits
D. fire as God

198. Which, among the following, was not a cause of the decline of Jainism?
A. Lack of religious preachers
B. Absence of royal patronage
C. The division of Jainism in two strong sects
D. Attacks of foreigners

199. What importance does the year 1658 hold in Indian

history?
A. Akbar died
B. Aurangzeb ascended the throne
C. Sikhism was founded
D. Shivaji was born

200. The most magnificent buildings constructed by Akbar are found at :
A. The fort at Agra
B. The fort at Lahore
C. The fort at Allahabad
D. Fatehpur Sikri, 26 miles west of Agra

201. The *Vijaya-Stambha* or the Tower of Victory at Chittor was constructed by its ruler:
A. Rana Hamir Deva
B. Rana Kumbha (Kumbha Karan)
C. Rana Sanga (Sangram Singh)
D. Rana Pratap

202. Which dynasty did Allaud-din Hasan Bahman Shah belong to?
A. Chera B. Chola
C. Bahmani D. Mughal

203. Who, among the following formed the party named as Forward Bloc?
A. Subhash Chandra Bose
B. Sardar Bhagat Singh
C. Chandra Shekhar Azad
D. Jawaharlal Nehru

204. Which, among the following, was the reason of surrendering of his title of 'Sir' by Rabindranath Tagore and of the resignation of Shankar Ram Nagar from the executive council of the Viceroy?
A. The passing of the Rowalatt Act
B. Protest against the Act of 1919
C. To support M.K. Gandhi in his Satyagraha-movement
D. To protest against the event at Jallianwala Bagh and the martial-law imposed in Punjab

205. In 1930, Mahatma Gandhi broke the symbolic salt laws (after launching the famous Dandi March). This was also a call for:
A. violent activity
B. seizure of English goods
C. civil disobedience
D. complete unity among Congressmen

206. The Social System of the Harappans was:
A. Fairly egalitarian
B. Slave-Labour based
C. Colour (Varna) based
D. Caste based

207. Which of the following Vedas provides information about the civilisation of the Early Vedic Age?
A. Rigveda
B. Yajurveda
C. Atharvaveda
D. Samaveda

208. The first Indian ruler, who established the supremacy of Indian Navy in the Arabian Sea, was:
A. Rajaraja I
B. Rajendra I
C. Rajadhiraja I
D. Kullottunga I

209. The Mughal painting reached its zenith during the reign of:
A. Akbar
B. Jahangir
C. Shahjahan
D. Aurangzeb

210. Permanent Revenue Settlement of Bengal was introduced by:
A. Clive
B. Hastings
C. Wellesley
D. Cornwallis

211. Through which principle or device did Gandhi strive to bridge economic inequalities?
A. Abolition of machinery
B. Establishment of village industries
C. Trusteeship theory
D. None of the above

212. Who was the founder of the Divine Life Society?
A. Ramakrishna Paramahansa
B. Swami Sivananda
C. Swami Vivekananda
D. Mother Teresa

213. During the early Vedic period, the society was divided on the basis of:
A. Birth
B. Occupation
C. Religion
D. Wealth

214. During whose viceroyalty was India's capital shifted from Calcutta to New Delhi?
A. Lord Minto II
B. Lord Curzon
C. Lord Hardinge
D. Lord Irwin

215. Who amongst the following was the founder of the Vijayanagara kingdom?
A. Akbar
B. Sultan of Bahmani
C. Krishna Devaraya
D. Harihara

216. The first European sailor to land on the western coast of India belonged to:
A. England B. France
C. Portugal D. Spain

217. Which of the following classes did not participate in the Revolt of 1857?
A. Agricultural labourers
B. Peasants
C. Zamindars
D. Moneylenders

218. The Alwars of South India were:
A. Warriors
B. Merchants
C. Saints
D. Sculptors and painters of idols

219. The Sangam works in Tamil are assignable to:
A. The period from 5th to 8th century AD
B. The early centuries of the Christian era
C. The period from the 5th to the 3rd century BC
D. The period from the 9th to the 11th century BC

220. Consider the following :
1. Samhitas
2. Brahmanas
3. Aranyakas
4. Upanishads
Which of these formed a part of the Vedas?
A. 1, 2 and 3
B. 1, 2 and 4
C. 1, 3 and 4
D. 2, 3 and 4

221. Consider the following events:
1. Civil Disobedience Movement.
2. Nehru Report
3. Communal Award
The correct chronological sequence of these events is
A. 2, 1, 3 B. 1, 3, 2
C. 3, 2, 1 D. 2, 3, 1

222. Eminent lawyers in the INA Defence Committee included:
A. Bhulabhai Desai, Tej Bahadur Sapru and Asaf Ali
B. Tej Bahadur Sapru, Kailashnath Katju and Pandit Nehru
C. Bhulabhai Desai, Pandit Nehru and M.A. Jinnah
D. Asaf Ali, Tej Bahadur Sapru and Pandit Nehru

223. Who was called the pioneer of the Panchayati Raj for introducing local self government in British India?
A. Warren Hastings
B. Lord William Bentinck
C. Lord Canning
D. Lord Ripon

224. Which one of the following was the greatest contribution of Alauddin Khilji in the field of agrarian administration?
A. He brought the peasant in direct relation with the State
B. He tried to curb and control the intermediaries
C. He was the first to introduce the system of measurement of land for the assessment of revenue
D. The records of the village accountant were audited

225. Who was the founder of the first Sufi order in India?
A. Khwaja Qutab-ud-din Bakhtiar Kaki
B. Sheikh Nizam-ud-din Auliya
C. Khwaja Moinud-din-Chisti
D. Sheikh Nasir-ud-din Mahmud

226. The founder of the Vikramsila University was
A. Devapala
B. Harshavardhana
C. Sasanka
D. Dharmapala

227. Simon Commission visited India during the:
A. Civil Disobedience Movement
B. Non-Cooperation Movement
C. Swadeshi Movement
D. Quit India Movement

228. "Din-i-Ilahi" was founded by:
A. Guru Nanak
B. Kabir
C. Akbar
D. Shahjahan

229. The following persons came to India at one time or another :
1 Fahien
2. I-Tsing
3. Megasthenese
4. Hiuen-Tsang
The correct chronological sequence of their visits is
A. 3, 1, 2, 4 B. 3, 1, 4, 2
C. 1, 3, 2, 4 D. 1, 3, 4, 2

230. "It made its proposals in May. It still wanted a united India. There was to be a Federal Union composed of British provinces."
The above quotation is

related to:
A. Simon Commission
B. Gandhi-Irwin Pact
C. Cripps Mission
D. Cabinet Mission

231. Which one of the following Viceroys of India utilised for the first time local self-government as the basis of election?
A. Lord Bentinck
B. Lord Cornwallis
C. Lord Lansdowne
D. Lord Ripon

232. Match List I with List II and select the correct answer using the codes given below the lists:

List I
(Year)
(*a*) 1775 (*b*) 1780
(*c*) 1824 (*d*) 1838

List II
(Event)
1. First Anglo-Burmese War
2. First Anglo-Afghan War
3. First Anglo-Maratha War
4. Second Anglo-Mysore War

Codes :

	(*a*)	(*b*)	(*c*)	(*d*)
A.	4	3	2	1
B.	4	3	1	2
C.	3	4	1	2
D.	3	4	2	1

233. The first venture of Gandhi in all India Politics was the
A. Non-Cooperation Movement
B. Rowlatt Satyagraha
C. Champaran Movement
D. Dandi March

234. The term 'Aryan' denotes
A. An ethnic group
B. A nomadic people
C. A speech group
D. A superior race

235. The Finance Minister during the Mughal Rule was
A. Diwan-i-Ala
B. Sadr
C. Emperor
D. Mir-i-Bakshi

236. Which one of the following pair is *not* correctly matched?
A. Jahangir : William Hawkins
B. Akbar : Sir Thomas Roe
C. Shahjahan : Travernier
D. Auranzeb : Manucci

237. Wnich sect of Buddhism spread over India, Japan, China, Tibet and Central Asia?
A. Hinayana
B. Bodhisatva
C. Sarvastivada
D. Mahayana

238. The Jama Masjid of Delhi was built by:
A. Akbar
B. Humayun
C. Jahangir
D. Shahjahan

239. The Non-Cooperation Movement was withdrawn in 1922 because
A. The Government accepted all the demands of the movement leaders
B. The people turned hostile towards it
C. Of the Chauri-Chaura incident
D. It could not be sustained

240. Who among the following was the temporary President of the first session of the Constituent Assembly of India?
A. H.V. Kamat
B. S. Nijalingappa
C. Dr. Rajendra Prasad
D. Sachidananda Sinha

241. Consider the following persons :
1. John Marshal
2. S.R. Rao
3. R.D. Banerji
4. Dayaram Sahani

Who among these were associated with the first excavations carried out at Harappa and Mohenjodaro?
A. 1, 2 and 3
B. 2, 3 and 4
C. 1, 3 and 4
D. 1, 2 and 4

242. The Chinese traveller Fa-hien visited the court of which Indian King when he was in India?
A. Asoka
B. Chandragupta I
C. Chandragupta II
D. Samudragupta

243. Where are the Dilwara Temples located?
A. Shravana Belagola
B. Parasnath Hills
C. Indore
D. Mt. Abu.

244. Who founded the Mohammedan Anglo-Oriental College at Aligarh?
A. Sir Syed Ahmed Khan
B. Badruddin Tayabji
C. Maulana Abul Kalam Azad
D. Mohammad Ali Jinnah

245. Which from of *Prakrit* was uniformly used by Asoka in all his inscriptions?
A. Ardh-Magadhi
B. Suraseni

C. Magadhi
D. Angika

246. Which of the following materials was mainly used in the manufacture of Harappan seals?
A. Terracota B. Bronze
C. Copper D. Iron

247. Buland Darwaza was built to commemorate Akbar's victory on:
A. Malwa B. Deccan
C. Bengal D. Gujarat

248. Who from the following led the uprising of 1857 in Lucknow?
A. Kunwar Singh
B. Tantia Tope
C. Rani Lakshmibai
D. Hazrat Mahal

249. Who among the following was *not* associated with the Indian National Army?
A. Subhas Chandra Bose
B. Rash Behari Bose
C. Mohan Singh
D. Bhagat Singh

250. Why was Non-Cooperation Movement suspended?
A. Ill-health of Gandhiji
B. Differences between Hindus and Muslims
C. Differences between the leaders
D. Violent incident at Chauri-Chaura

251. The Salt Satyagraha was started in the year:
A. 1930 B. 1932
C. 1928 D. 1931

252. Which among the following States was forced to merge itself with the Union of India after 1947?
A. Hyderabad
B. Kashmir
C. Patiala
D. Mysore

253. Who established the Chishti Order in India?
A. Nizammudin Auliya
B. Salim Chishti
C. Shaikh Moinuddin Chishti
D. Halimuddin Nagauri

254. Which type of pottery marked the beginning of Second Urbanisation in India?
A. Painted grey ware
B. Northern black polished ware
C. Ochre coloured pottery
D. Black and red ware

255. For which of the following acts was Bhagat Singh and his colleagues Rajguru and Sukhdev were hanged on March 23, 1931?
A. For the murder of Saunders at Lahore in 1928
B. Kakori Conspiracy Case
C. For throwing a bomb in the Central Legislative Assembly on April 18, 1929
D. Lahore Conspiracy Case

256. At which place did Gandhiji make salt during freedom struggle?
A. Sevagram
B. Wardha
C. Dandi
D. Sabarmati

257. Consider the following places :
1. Lumbini
2. Bodh Gaya
3. Sarnath
4. Kushinagar
In the context of the life of Buddha, the *correct* chronological sequence of these places is
A. 1, 2, 3, 4
B. 1, 2, 4, 3
C. 2, 1, 3, 4
D. 2, 1, 4, 3

258. Bhagavatism centred around the worship of
A. Siva B. Bhagvati
C. Skanda D. Vishnu

259. Match List I with List II and select the *correct* answer using the codes given below the lists :

List I
(*a*) Iltutmish
(*b*) Quli Qutbshah
(*c*) Sher Shah
(*d*) Akbar

List II
1. Mausoleum at Sasaram
2. Agra Fort
3. Charminar
4. Qutub Minar

Codes :

	(*a*)	(*b*)	(*c*)	(*d*)
A.	3	4	2	1
B.	4	3	1	2
C.	4	3	2	1
D.	3	4	1	2

260. Rani Durgawati was fought against Akbar in 1564 ruled over
A. Awadh
B. Golconda
C. Gondwana
D. Malwa

261. Consider the following native rulers :
1. Kunwar Singh
2. Nana Sahib
3. Scindhia of Gwalior
4. Nizam of Hyderabad
Who among these native rulers did *not* participate in

the Revolt of 1857?
A. 1, 2 and 4
B. 2 and 3
C. 3 and 4
D. 1, 2, 3 and 4

262. Aligarh Movement was started by
A. Mohammed Ali Jinnah
B. Sir Syed Ahmed Khan
C. Dr. Zakir Hussain
D. Sir Muhammad Iqbal

263. Consider the following nationalists :
1. Bal Gangadhar Tilak
2. Gopal Krishna Gokhale
3. Bipin Chandra Pal
4. Lala Lajpat Rai
Who among them were referred to as 'militant' nationalists of the freedom movement?
A. 1, 2 and 3
B. 2 and 4
C. 1, 3 and 4
D. 1, 2, 3 and 4

264. A token copper currency was introduced by :
A. Alauddin
B. Sher Shah
C. Muhammad-bin Tughlaq
D. Firoz Shah Tughlaq

265. Who was the first Indian lady to preside over the Congress?
A. Raj Kumari Amrit Kaur
B. Annie Besant
C. Vijayalakshmi Pandit
D. Amrita Sher-Gil

266. The greatness of Sher Shah lies in his :
A. victories against Humayun
B. superior generalship
C. administrative reforms
D. secular attitude

267. The Sultan who made a successful attempt to free himself from the control of the ulemas was :
A. Balban
B. Alauddin
C. Firoz Shah
D. Jalaluddin

268. The Indian Civil Service was introduced during the rule of :
A. Dalhousie
B. Curzon
C. Bentinck
D. Cornwallis

269. The original aim of East India company was :
A. colonization
B. trade
C. exploitation of raw materials
D. To find a market for her manufactured goods

270. Which metal was first used by the vedic people?
A. Silver B. Gold
C. Iron D. Copper

271. Mahatma Gandhi's first experience with mass movement in India was at :
A. Champaran
B. Bardoli
C. Chauri Chaura
D. Dandi

272. The rulers of which dynasty started the practice of granting tax-free villages to Brahmanas and Buddhist Monks?
A. Satavahanas
B. Mauryas
C. Guptas
D. Cholas

273. The Bandung Conference was a major milestone in the history of:
A. The Non-aligned movement
B. Indo-Chinese relationship
C. U.S.-Vietnam War
D. Creation of ASEAN

274. On September 20, 1932, Mahatma Gandhi began a fast unto death in Yervada Jail against
A. British repression of the Satyagrahis
B. Violation of the Gandhi-Irwin Pact
C. Communal award of Ramsay MacDonald
D. Communal riots in Calcutta

275. Match List I with List II and select the correct answer using the codes given below the Lists :

List I
(*a*) French
(*b*) English
(*c*) Dutch
(*d*) Portuguese

List II
1. Calicut
2. Masulipattam
3. Pondicherry
4. Hoogly

Codes :

	(*a*)	(*b*)	(*c*)	(*d*)
A.	3	4	1	2
B.	3	4	2	1
C.	4	3	1	2
D.	4	3	2	1

276. The monopoly of Indian trade of the East India Company was abolished by the:
A. Regulating Act, 1773
B. Charter Act, 1813
C. Charter Act, 1853
D. Government of India Act, 1858

277. The temple of Somnath which was destroyed by Mahmud Ghazni was dedicated to Lord:

A. Vishnu B. Siva
C. Surya D. Ganapati

278. Match List I with List II and select the *correct* answer using the codes given below the lists :

List I

(*a*) Ibadatkhana
(*b*) Jama Masjid of Delhi
(*c*) Adhai Din Ka Jonpada
(*d*) Vijay Stambha of Chittor

List II

1. Qutubuddin Aibak
2. Rana Kumbha
3. Shahjahan
4. Mehmud Begda
5. Akbar

Codes :

	(*a*)	(*b*)	(*c*)	(*d*)
A.	5	3	1	2
B.	5	3	4	2
C.	2	4	5	1
D.	3	5	1	4

279. Match List I with List II and select the *correct* answer using the codes given below the Lists :

List I (*Dynasty*)	List II (*State*)
(*a*) Kadamba	1. Orissa
(*b*) Kharavela	2. Karnataka
(*c*) Chalukya	3. Bengal
(*d*) Pala	4. Gujarat

Codes :

	(*a*)	(*b*)	(*c*)	(*d*)
A.	1	2	4	3
B.	1	2	3	4
C.	2	1	3	4
D.	2	1	4	3

280. Consider the following observations :

1. Taxes in India are very light.
2. The highways are not safe for travellers.
3. People do not lock their houses while going out.
4. Taxes and laws are very oppressive.

Which of these observations were made by Fahien, the Chinese traveller who visited India?

A. 3 and 4 B. 1 and 2
C. 1 and 3 D. 2 and 4

281. Which *one* of the following is a special feature of the Chola Policy?

A. Autonomous village Panchayats
B. Division of kingdom into the Mandalas
C. Monarchical system
D. Enlightened Council of Ministers

282. Consider the following statements : In the reign of Jehangir, Kandahar could not be recaptured due to:

1. inefficiency of Mughal army.
2. refusal of Khurram to proceed to that place.
3. difficulties in organising an expedition.
4. severe cold in Afghanistan.

Which of these statements are *correct*?

A. 1, 2 and 3
B. 2, 3 and 4
C. 1 and 4
D. 1, 2, 3 and 4

283. Which *one* of the following Sultans was advised by Qazi Mughisuddin to act according to the laws of Shariat, but the Sultan rejected his advice?

A. Jalaluddin Khilji
B. Alauddin Khilji
C. Mohd-bin-Tughlaq
D. Firoz Tughlaq

284. Consider the following statements : *Madad-i-maash* grants were awarded to:

1. men of learning.
2. religious devotees.
3. persons of noble lineage.
4. destitute persons incapable of earning a livelihood.

Which of these statements are *correct*?

A. 1, 2 and 3
B. 2, 3 and 4
C. 1 and 4
D. 1, 2, 3 and 4

285. Whose did not participate in the first war of independence in 1857?

A. Tatya Tope
B. Rani Lakshmi Bai
C. Bahadur Shah Zafar
D. Bhagat Singh

286. When was 'Quit India' movement launched?

A. 1947 B. 1942
C. 1935 D. 1929

287. How many years ago was the 'Khalsa Panth' Launched?

A. 150 B. 300
C. 200 D. 400

288. The Mughal Emperor in India who gave Surat to the British East India Company was :

A. Babur
B. Akbar
C. Jehangir
D. Aurangzeb

289. Chandranagore was a

trading centre of the :
A. English
B. French
C. Dutch
D. Portuguese

290. The most important aspect in Queen Victoria's Proclamation was :
A. The Governor of Bengal came to be called as Governor General
B. Provincial autonomy was accorded
C. Property qualifications were prescribed for franchise
D. The administration in India was taken over by the Crown

291. What is the correct chronological order of the following events in 1919?
1. Jallianwala Massacre
2. Rowlatt Act
3. Khilafat Movement

Select the correct answer using the codes given below:
Codes :
A. 2, 1, 3 B. 2, 3, 1
C. 1, 2, 3 D. 1, 3, 2

292. The Saka era was founded in the year :
A. B.C. 57
B. A.D. 78
C. A.D. 319
D. A.D. 248

293. Which of the following factors helped in the growth of Indian nationalism in the 19th century?
1. Western education
2. Racial arrogance of the British
3. Russophobia
4. Economic exploitation of India
5. Pro-Muslim attitude of the British'

Choose the correct by using the codes given below :
Codes :
A. 1, 2, 3, 4 and 5
B. 1, 2 and 5
C. 3, 4 and 5
D. 1, 2 and 4

294. Which of the following was/were responsible for the rapid spread of Buddhism in India after its origin?
1. Teachings of the Buddha
2. Use of Pali language
3. Dislike for the Brahmanas
4. Monastic organisation

Select the correct answer from the codes given below:
Codes :
A. 1 alone
B. 1 and 2
C. 2, 3 and 4
D. 1, 3 and 4

295. The Vikramasila monastery was founded by :
A. Shashanka
B. Dharmapala
C. Devapala
D. Lakshmanasena

296. Rice cultivation is associated with which one of the following Harappan sites?
A. Harappa
B. Lothal
C. Kalibangan
D. Kot Diji

297. The salient feature of the Rigvedic religion was worship of :
A. Trimurties
B. Nature
C. Pashupati
D. Mother Goddess

298. 'Tripitakas' are the sacred books of the :
A. Hindus
B. Muslims
C. Jains
D. Buddhists

299. Which of the following was the main aim of Mahmud Ghaznvi's expeditions in India?
1. Spread the Islamic religion
2. Gaining fame
3. Plundering the wealth of country
4. Establishing his empire over whole of northern India

Select the correct answer using the codes given below:
Codes :
A. 1, 2 and 3
B. 3 alone
C. 1, 3 and 4
D. 1, 2, 3 and 4

300. The correct chronological sequence of the entry of the given alien power in India is:
A. Indo-Greeks, Scythians, Kushanas, Hunas
B. Indo-Greeks, Hunas, Kushanas, Scythians
C. Scythians, Kushanas, Hunas, Indo-Greeks
D. Scythians, Kushanas, Indo-Greeks, Hunas

301. "They used to live outside the cities and whenever they entered the cities they had to walk by sounding the sticks."
The above statements was

made by
A. Fahien
B. Heinen Tsang
C. I'tsing
D. Marco Polo

302. The Vernacular Press Act of 1878, adopted by Lord Lytton, intended to :
A. help English newspapers
B. promote freedom of the Press
C. restrain newspapers published in Indian languages
D. curb freedom of the Press in general

303. The most important thing in the minting of coins was:
A. weight
B. size
C. punch mark
D. shape

304. What is false of Buddhist Mahayana?
A. They believed in numerous Bodhisattvas.
B. They believed in images.
C. Prakrit was their language.
D. It rose under Kanishka

305. Which of the following is correctly matched?
A. *Chausa* : Humayun and Sher Shah
B. *Haldighati* : Akbar and Jai Singh
C. *Panipat* : Shah Jahan and Aurangzeb
D. *Kalinjar* : Sher Shah and Humayun

ANSWERS

1	2	3	4	5	6	7	8	9	10
A	C	B	C	D	C	B	D	D	B
11	**12**	**13**	**14**	**15**	**16**	**17**	**18**	**19**	**20**
C	D	C	C	B	C	D	B	C	C
21	**22**	**23**	**24**	**25**	**26**	**27**	**28**	**29**	**30**
A	A	A	B	C	D	C	B	B	D
31	**32**	**33**	**34**	**35**	**36**	**37**	**38**	**39**	**40**
A	C	A	B	B	A	B	C	A	C
41	**42**	**43**	**44**	**45**	**46**	**47**	**48**	**49**	**50**
B	C	D	B	D	B	B	C	A	A
51	**52**	**53**	**54**	**55**	**56**	**57**	**58**	**59**	**60**
C	D	A	A	C	D	C	A	C	D
61	**62**	**63**	**64**	**65**	**66**	**67**	**68**	**69**	**70**
D	B	D	C	A	B	B	C	C	A
71	**72**	**73**	**74**	**75**	**76**	**77**	**78**	**79**	**80**
B	B	A	B	D	B	D	D	A	C
81	**82**	**83**	**84**	**85**	**86**	**87**	**88**	**89**	**90**
B	A	C	A	A	B	D	C	C	A
91	**92**	**93**	**94**	**95**	**96**	**97**	**98**	**99**	**100**
D	B	A	B	C	B	B	C	D	A
101	**102**	**103**	**104**	**105**	**106**	**107**	**108**	**109**	**110**
A	C	A	B	B	D	A	B	A	A
111	**112**	**113**	**114**	**115**	**116**	**117**	**118**	**119**	**120**
B	D	A	A	A	C	B	C	B	A
121	**122**	**123**	**124**	**125**	**126**	**127**	**128**	**129**	**130**
B	A	C	A	C	D	D	B	A	C
131	**132**	**133**	**134**	**135**	**136**	**137**	**138**	**139**	**140**
A	B	C	B	A	C	A	C	C	B

141	142	143	144	145	146	147	148	149	150
B	D	D	B	C	A	C	A	D	D
151	152	153	154	155	156	157	158	159	160
B	B	B	C	D	A	A	B	C	B
161	162	163	164	165	166	167	168	169	170
A	C	C	B	A	B	B	A	D	D
171	172	173	174	175	176	177	178	179	180
D	A	A	D	A	C	C	C	A	C
181	182	183	184	185	186	187	188	189	190
A	A	A	A	A	D	D	D	D	B
191	192	193	194	195	196	197	198	199	200
C	A	A	C	B	A	B	D	B	D
201	202	203	204	205	206	207	208	209	210
B	C	A	D	C	A	A	A	B	D
211	212	213	214	215	216	217	218	219	220
B	B	B	C	D	C	D	C	B	A
221	222	223	224	225	226	227	228	229	230
C	A	D	C	A	D	A	C	A	D
231	232	233	234	235	236	237	238	239	240
D	C	A	A	A	B	D	D	C	D
241	242	243	244	245	246	247	248	249	250
C	C	D	A	C	A	D	D	D	D
251	252	253	254	255	256	257	258	259	260
A	A	C	B	D	C	A	D	B	C
261	262	263	264	265	266	267	268	269	270
C	B	C	C	B	C	B	D	B	D
271	272	273	274	275	276	277	278	279	280
A	A	A	C	B	B	B	A	D	C
281	282	283	284	285	286	287	288	289	290
A	D	B	D	D	B	B	C	B	D
291	292	293	294	295	296	297	298	299	300
A	B	D	D	B	B	B	D	B	A
301	302	303	304	305					
A	C	C	C	A					

GEOGRAPHY

1. ....is situated near the banks of Sabarmati River
   A. Bhavnagar
   B. Aurangabad
   C. Ahmedabad
   D. Rajkot
2. Sericulture is:
   A. science of the various kinds of serum
   B. artificial rearing of fish
   C. art of silkworm breeding
   D. study of various cultures of a community
3. The leading producers of groundnut in India are :
   A. Tamil Nadu and Karnataka
   B. Deccan Plateau and Gujarat
   C. Bihar and Haryana
   D. Punjab and Gujarat
4. Indian Standard Time is based on:
   A. 80°E longitude
   B. 82½°E longitude
   C. 110°E longitude
   D. 25°E longitude
5. Tides in the oceans are caused by :
   A. Gravitational pull of the moon on the earth's surface including sea water
   B. Gravitational pull of the sun on the earth's surface only and not on the sea water
   C. Gravitational pull of the moon and the sun on the earth's surface including the sea water
   D. None of these
6. Nagarjunasagar Project is situated on the river:
   A. Tungabhadra
   B. Cauvery
   C. Krishna
   D. Godavari
7. The difference between the Indian Standard Time and the Greenwich Mean Time is:
   A. – 3½ hours
   B. + 3½ hours
   C. – 5½ hours
   D. + 5½ hours
8. Which of the following dams is not on Narmada river?
   A. Indira-Sagar Project
   B. Maheshwar Hydel Power Project
   C. Jobat Project
   D. Koyna Power Project
9. Which of the following statements is **not true** about the availability of water on the earth, the crisis for which is going to increase in the years to come?
   A. About 97.5 per cent of the total volume of water available on the earth is salty
   B. 80 per cent of the water available to us for use comes in bursts as monsoons
   C. About 2.5 per cent of the total water available on the earth is polluted water and cannot be used for human activities
   D. Possibility is that some big glaciers will melt in the coming ten-fifteen years and sea level will rise by 3-4 metres all over the earth
10. Which of the following is **not** a cash crop?
    A. Jute
    B. Paddy
    C. Cashewnut
    D. Sugarcane
11. Through which States does Cauvery River flow?
    A. Gujarat, M.P., Tamil Nadu
    B. Karnataka, Kerala, Tamil Nadu
    C. Karnataka, Kerala, Andhra Pradesh
    D. M.P., Maharashtra, Tamil Nadu
12. Indian Standard Time is the local time of 82½°E which passes through :
    A. Guntur B. Delhi
    C. AllahabadD. Kolkata
13. The 17th parallel defines the boundary between:
    A. North and South Korea
    B. USA and Canada
    C. North and South Vietnam

D. China and Russia

14. During the period of south-west monsoon, Tamil Nadu remains dry because:
A. the winds do not reach this area
B. there are no mountains in this area
C. it lies in the rain shadow area
D. the temperature is too high to let the winds cool down

15. Which country does top in producing cocoa?
A. Ghana
B. Brazil
C. Ivory Coast
D. Nigeria

16. The biggest reserves of thorium are in :
A. India
B. China
C. The Soviet Union
D. U.S.A.

17. The Girnar Hills are situated in which of the following states?
A. Gujarat
B. Karnataka
C. Madhya Pradesh
D. Maharashtra

18. During December 22nd the sun is vertically over:
A. Tropic of Cancer
B. Tropic of Capricorn
C. The Equator
D. None of the above

19. Photosphere is described as the :
A. Lower layer of atmosphere
B. Visible surface of the sun from which radiation emanates
C. Wavelength of solar spectrum
D. None of the above

20. Broadly, there are three layers of the earth of the crust, the mantle and the core. The crust forms what percentage of the volume of the earth?
A. 0.5% B. 2.5%
C. 7.5% D. 12.5%

21. The grassland of Argentina is known as :
A. Pampas
B. Campos
C. Savanna
D. None of the above

22. Different seasons are formed because
A. Sun is moving around the earth
B. of revolution of the earth around the Sun on its orbit
C. of rotation of the earth around its axis
D. All of the above

23. Eskers and Drumlins are features formed by:
A. underground water
B. running water
C. the action of wind
D. glacial action

24. Match List I and List II and select the correct answer using the codes given below the Lists :

List I
(Rivers)
(*a*) Ghaghara
(*b*) Brahmaputra
(*c*) Narmada
(*d*) Sabarmati

List II
(Towns)
1. Lucknow
2. Hoshangabad
3. Ahmedabad
4. Guwahati
5. Ayodhya

	(*a*)	(*b*)	(*c*)	(*d*)
A.	4	5	1	2
B.	5	4	2	3
C.	5	4	3	1
D.	3	5	2	1

25. Match List I with List II and select the correct answer using the codes given below the Lists :

List I
(Item in the Constitution of India)
(*a*) Chapter on Fundamental Rights
(*b*) India as 'a Union of States' with more powers to the Union
(*c*) Parliamentary privileges and procedure of law making
(*d*) Concurrent List in Union-State relations

List II
(Country from which derived)
1. United Kingdom
2. Australia
3. Ireland
4. United States of America
5. Canada

Codes :

	(*a*)	(*b*)	(*c*)	(*d*)
A.	3	4	1	2
B.	3	4	1	5
C.	4	5	1	2
D.	2	4	5	3

26. The world is divided into :
A. 12 time zones
B. 20 time zones
C. 24 time zones
D. 36 time zones

27. The 'Kiel' canal links the :
A. Pacific and Atlantic Oceans
B. Mediterranean Sea and

Red Sea
C. Mediterranean Sea and Black Sea
D. North Sea and Baltic Sea

28. Match the following :

(*a*) Himadri	1. Outer Himalayas
(*b*) Shivalik	2. Inner Himalayas
(*c*) Himachal	3. Middle Himalayas
(*d*) Sahyadri	4. Western Ghats

	(*a*)	(*b*)	(*c*)	(*d*)
A.	1	2	3	4
B.	4	2	3	1
C.	2	1	3	4
D.	1	2	3	4

29. The term 'Regur' refers to:
A. Laterite soils
B. Black Cotton soils
C. Red Soils
D. Deltaic Alluvial Soils

30. Location of sugar industry in India is shifting from north to south because of:
A. cheap labour
B. expanding regional market
C. cheap and abundant supply of power
D. high yield and high sugar content in sugarcane

31. Consider the following statements :
1. Ozone is found mostly in the Stratosphere.
2. Ozone layer lies 55-75 km above the surface of the earth.
3. Ozone absorbs ultra-violet radiation from the Sun.
4. Ozone layer has no significance for life on the earth.

Which of the above statements are correct?
A. 1 and 3 B. 2 and 4
C. 2 and 3 D. 1 and 4

32. Match List I with List II and select the correct answer using the codes given below the Lists :

List I (*Crops*)	**List II** (*Producer*)
(*a*) Banana	1. Colombia
(*b*) Cocoa	2. Ghana
(*c*) Coffee	3. Jamaica
(*d*) Tea	4. Kenya

Codes :

	(*a*)	(*b*)	(*c*)	(*d*)
A.	2	3	1	4
B.	3	2	1	4
C.	3	2	4	1
D.	2	3	4	1

33. Darjeeling and Dharamsala would be the right places to visit if one wanted to get a clear view respectively of
A. Kanchanjunga and Dhauladhar ranges
B. Nandadevi and Dhauladhar ranges
C. Kanchanjunga and Nandadevi ranges
D. Nandadevi and Nanga Parbat

34. Atmosphere exists because:
A. The Gravitational force of the Earth
B. Revolution of the Earth
C. Rotation of the Earth
D. Weight of the gases of atmosphere

35. Victoria lake is located in the continent:
A. Africa
B. Asia
C. North America
D. South America

36. The famous Lagoon Lake of India is :
A. Dal Lake
B. Chilka Lake
C. Pulicat Lake
D. Mansarover

37. Where are most of the earth's active volcanoes concentrated?
A. Europe
B. Pacific Ocean
C. Africa
D. South America

38. Through which of the following states does the river Chambal flow?
A. U.P., M.P., Rajasthan
B. M.P., Gujarat, U.P.
C. Rajasthan, M.P., Bihar
D. Gujarat, M.P., U.P.

39. Which country is called the sugar bowl of the world?
A. Cuba
B. India
C. Argentina
D. USA

40. The area covered by forest in India is about:
A. 46% B. 33%
C. 23% D. 21%

41. In India, there are three crop seasons. Two of them are Kharif and Rabi, name the third one?
A. Barsati B. Garama
C. Zaid D. Khari

42. In India agriculture of Jute is maximum on which Delta area?
A. Ganga
B. Mahanadi
C. Brahamputra
D. Godawari

43. The natural vegetation of Savana consists of:
A. Tall grass

B. Scrub jungle
C. Short grass
D. Trees

44. The zone of excessively dry climate with very cold temperature throughout the year correspond to:
A. Arctic deserts
B. Tundra
C. Alpine meadouss
D. Antarctica

45. The International Date Line is represented by:
A. 100° Meridian
B. 0° Meridian
C. 180° Meridian
D. 90° Meridian

46. Adam's bridge connects:
A. Israel and Jerusalem
B. Amman and Damascus
C. Persian Gulf and Gulf of Oman
D. Dhanushkodi (Rameswaram) and Talaimannar

47. In May-June each year, the monsoon winds approach the southern tip of India from:
A. Northly direction
B. North-easterly direction
C. North-westerly direction
D. South-westerly direction

48. Sahyadri is the traditional name of the:
A. Western Ghats
B. Eastern Ghats
C. Aravallis
D. Barabar and Nagarjun hills

49. The fertility of the soil can be increased by growing:
A. Cereals
B. Fibre Crops
C. Legumes
D. Root Crops

50. India's Oil bearing areas are mostly associated with the:
A. Plutonic rocks
B. Volcanic rocks
C. Sedimentary rocks
D. Metamorphic rocks

51. Which one of the following pairs is *not* correctly matched?

	Places	**Minerals**
A.	Kudremukh	Iron Ore
B.	Singhbhum	Manganese
C.	Hazaribagh	Silver
D.	Khetri	Copper

52. The much discussed Tehri Dam Project is located in which of the following states?
A. Madhya Pradesh
B. Rajasthan
C. Haryana
D. Uttarakhand

53. Which of the following States has abundant black soil?
A. Karnataka
B. Maharashtra
C. Tamil Nadu
D. Kerala

54. Match the following

I
(*a*) Kumaon Himalayas
(*b*) Nepal Himalayas
(*c*) Punjab Himalayas
(*d*) Assam Himalayas

II
1. Between Indus and Sutlej
2. Between Kali and Tista
3. Between Tista and Brahmaputra
4. Between Sutlej and Kali

	(*a*)	(*b*)	(*c*)	(*d*)
A.	1	2	3	4
B.	2	3	1	4
C.	4	2	3	1
D.	4	2	1	3

55. The largest irrigation canal in India is the:
A. Yamuna Canal (West)
B. Indira Gandhi Canal
C. Lower Ganga Canal
D. Upper Ganga Canal

56. Laterite soil develop as a result of:
A. deposits of alluvial
B. deposition of loess
C. leaching
D. continued vegetation cover

57. Which of the following countries is the largest gold-producing country in the world?
A. Mexico
B. USA
C. South Africa
D. Canada

58. On which of the following rivers is Almatti Dam located?
A. Mahanadi B. Cauvery
C. Krishna D. Penganga

59. Ursa Minor is
A. the name of a satellite
B. the name of an island
C. a group of stars that form the little dipper in the most northern constellation
D. the name of a disease in USA

60. Which of the following is a block mountain?
A. Rocky B. Vosgas
C. Alps D. Andes

61. Which is the shortest route from Moscow to San Francisco?
A. via Canada
B. over land
C. over to South Pole
D. over to North Pole

62. Cash crops of India include:
A. paddy and jawar
B. maize, jawar and paddy
C. cotton and sugarcane
D. bajra and paddy

63. The equator is a parallel or latitude of:
A. 23½° B. 0^2
C. 66½° D. 90^2

64. To complete one revolution in its orbit, the earth takes:
A. one month
B. two years
C. 6 months
D. 12 months

65. Which strait separates Europe from Africa?
A. Bosperus
B. Gibraltar
C. Dover
D. Bering

66. The beneficiary States of Sardar Sarovar Project are :
A. Gujarat, Maharashtra, MP and Rajasthan
B. AP, MP, Gujarat and Maharashtra
C. Orissa, MP, Gujarat and Maharashtra
D. MP, Gujarat, Karnataka and Maharashtra

67. 'Horn of Africa' consists of:
A. Algeria, Morocco and West Sahara
B. Libya, Sudan and Egypt
C. Somalia, Ethiopia and Djibouti
D. Zimbabwe, Botswana and Angola

68. The coldest place on the earth is :
A. Halifax
B. Chicago
C. Siachen
D. Verkhoyansk

69. Match List I with List II and select the correct answer from the code given below:

List I *(Town)*	**List II** *(River)*
(*a*) Berlin	1. Tiber
(*b*) Lahore	2. Hudson
(*c*) New York	3. Ravi
(*d*) Rome	4. Spree

Codes :

	(*a*)	(*b*)	(*c*)	(*d*)
A.	1	2	3	4
B.	4	3	2	1
C.	3	4	1	2
D.	1	4	2	3

70. The Kullu Valley is situated between the mountain ranges of :
A. Dhauladhar and Pir Panjal
B. Ranjoti and Nagtibba
C. Ladakh and Pir Panjal
D. Middle Himalayas and Sivalik

71. Which one of the following towns is nearest to the Tropic of Cancer?
A. Agartala
B. Gandhinagar
C. Jabalpur
D. Ujjain

72. Which one of the following pairs is not correctly matched?
A. Kota—Chambal
B. Bhubaneshwar—Mahanadi
C. Jabalpur—Narmada
D. Surat—Tapti

73. The first three largest sugar producing States in India are :
A. Bihar, UP, Maharashtra
B. UP, Maharashtra, Karnataka
C. UP, Maharashtra, Tamil Nadu
D. Bihar, UP, Andhra Pradesh

74. Indira Gandhi Canal has its source at :
A. Gandhi Sagar Dam
B. Bhakra Dam
C. Harike Barrage
D. Govind Ballabh Sagar

75. Consider the following statements :
1. Tides are of great help in navigation and fishing.
2. High tide enables big ships to enter or leave the harbour safely.
3. Tide prevents siltation in the harbours.
4. Kandla and Diamond Harbour are tidal ports.

A. 1 and 4
B. 2, 3, and 4
C. 1, 2 and 3
D. 1, 2, 3 and 4

76. Which of the following countries is not a South American country?
A. Argentina B. Bolivia
C. Colombia D. Mexico

77. Which of the following is the biggest fresh water lake in India?
A. Dal Lake
B. Sukhna Lake
C. Loktak Lake
D. None of these

78. Which of the following rivers is not a tributory of the Indus?
A. Sutlej
B. Jhelum
C. Bhagirathi
D. Chenab

79. Which of the following pairs of the river dam project and the State in which it is located, is **not** correct?

A. Gandhi Sagar–Madhya Pradesh
B. Tungabhadra–Tamilnadu
C. Bhakra Nangal–Punjab
D. Hirakud–Orissa
E. All are correct

80. If it is 10.00 a.m. I.S.T., then what would be the local time at Shillong on 92°E longitude?

A. 9.38 a.m.
B. 10.38 a.m.
C. 10.22 a.m.
D. 9.22 a.m.

81. Match List I with List II and select the *correct* answer using the codes given below the Lists :

List I
(Rivers)
(*a*) Cauvery
(*b*) Krishna
(*c*) Narmada
(*d*) Chambal

List II
(Dams)
1. Alamatti
2. Mettur
3. Gandhi Sagar
4. Sardar Sarovar

Codes :

	(*a*)	(*b*)	(*c*)	(*d*)
A.	1	4	2	3
B.	2	1	4	3
C.	2	1	3	4
D.	1	3	4	2

82. The Brahmaputra empties into:

A. Ganga
B. Jamuna
C. Bay of Bengal
D. None of these

83. The State which produces the largest quantity of wheat is:

A. Haryana
B. Rajasthan
C. Uttar Pradesh
D. Punjab

84. Which State of India has maximum percentage of land under forest?

A. Meghalaya
B. Arunachal Pradesh
C. Himachal Pradesh
D. Mizoram

85. When does the moon come between the sun and the earth?

A. Lunar eclipse
B. Solar eclipse
C. Sidereal day
D. Full moon day

86. Which of the following statements about Kharif and Rabi is *not* correct?

A. Kharif season begins with the onset of monsoon season and is harvested in late Spring
B. Kharif season begins with the onset of monsoon season and is harvested in Autumn
C. Rabi season begins in Autumn after the rains and harvested in late Spring
D. Important Kharif crops are rice, millets, jute, maize and cotton; important Rabi crops are wheat, gram, barley and linsead

87. Raniganj Coal Mine is situated in:

A. Jharkhand
B. Madhya Pradesh
C. West Bengal
D. Maharashtra

88. The latitude of a place is expressed by its angular distance in relation to:

A. Equator
B. South Pole
C. Axis of the Earth
D. North Pole

89. The southern tip of India is:

A. Cape Camorin
B. Point Calimere
C. Indira Point in Nicobar Islands
D. Kovalam in Trivandrum

90. Which is India's largest lake?

A. Nainital
B. Sambhar
C. Sishram
D. Chilka

91. During winter, the northern half of India is warmer than areas of similar latitudinal location by 3° to 8° because:

A. India is essentially a tropical country
B. The surface wind blows in a particular direction in one season
C. The Great Himalayas check the penetration of cold polar air into India effectively
D. Of winter rains

92. When rivers carrying a load enter the sea, their flow gets checked, and much of the material so carried is deposited off shore. Such deposits result in the formation of :

A. An atoll
B. A delta
C. A harbour
D. A lake

93. Turpentine oil used in

medicine is obtained from :
A. Acacia
B. Chir pin
C. Myrobalans
D. Kusum

94. Which country is known for the most frequent earthquakes?
A. Italy B. Japan
C. China D. Iran

95. Which of the following statements is wrong?
A. Maize is grown as Rabi crop in almost all the states of India.
B. Maize is raised in those areas which are free from frost for 4½ months.
C. Sugarcane crop occupies the fields for a period ranging from 10 to over 12 months.
D. All of the above

96. Which of the following mountain systems is the oldest?
A. Himalayas
B. Aravalli
C. Satpura
D. Nilgiri
E. None of these

97. In determining the Indian climate, major role played by Himalayas is/are :
A. The east-west extension of the Great-Himalayas does not permit the summer monsoon to cross it and thus keeps its sojourn restricted to India
B. They direct the summer monsoon towards the north-west
C. During the winter they stop the southward penetration of the cold and dry polar air
D. All of the above

98. The highest percentage share of groundnut production in India is contributed by:
A. Andhra Pradesh
B. Gujarat
C. Karnataka
D. Maharashtra

99. The strait that separates USA and Russia where they are nearest in:
A. Hudson B. Davis
C. Bering D. Bosporus

100. Which river is flowing near Ayodhya?
A. Ganga B. Yamuna
C. Saryu D. Krishna

101. Which of the states in the largest producer of silver?
A. Maharashtra
B. Karnataka
C. Bihar
D. Rajasthan

102. Which river is flowing through Amesterdam?
A. Amstel B. Rhine
C. Clide D. Thames

103. Which of the following is cold stream?
A. Curasia
B. Labrador
C. Gulf of Stream
D. Hakuna Hatata

104. High velds are the temperate grasslands of :
A. Africa
B. South Australia
C. Europe and Asia
D. South America

105. Narmada flows through :
A. Gujarat, Madhya Pradesh and Orissa
B. Karnataka and Tamil Nadu
C. Madhya Pradesh and Gujarat
D. Madhya Pradesh and Orissa

106. The rock material carried by a glacier is called...........
A. alluvium B. meanders
C. nodules D. moraines

107. In which of the following type of clouds does the 'halo' of moon occur?
A. Cumulus B. Cirrus
C. Nimbus D. Stratus

108. Match List I with List II and find out the correct answer from the codes given below the Lists :

List I
(Thermal Power Plants)
(*a*) Kahalgaon
(*b*) Farakka
(*c*) Ramagundam
(*d*) Gandhar

List II
(Locations)
1. West Bengal
2. Bihar
3. Gujarat
4. Andhra Pradesh

Codes :

	(*a*)	(*b*)	(*c*)	(*d*)
A.	1	2	3	4
B.	4	3	1	2
C.	2	1	4	3
D.	3	2	1	4

109. Solar eclipse takes place when:
A. The moon comes between the sun and the earth
B. The earth comes between the sun and the moon
C. The sun comes between

the moon and the earth
D. None of the above

110. The Suez Canal connects:
A. Baltic Sea and the Caspian Sea
B. Mediterranean Sea and the Red Sea
C. Red Sea and the Caspian Sea
D. Mediterranean Sea and the North Sea

111. Krishna Raja Sagar Dam is built across the river:
A. Cauvery
B. Tungabhadra
C. Krishna
D. Godavari

112. India leads the world in the export of:
A. Cofee
B. Cotton
C. Manganese
D. Mica

113. Which of the following States has rich forests of sandalwood?
A. Andhra Pradesh
B. Karnataka
C. Kerala
D. Madhya Pradesh

114. Which of the following is the smallest ocean of the world?
A. Pacific B. Indian
C. Atlantic D. Arctic

115. The country where most inhabitants are confined to seven cities is:
A. Brazil B. Australia
C. China D. Russia

116. Which kind of power accounts for the largest share of power generation in India?
A. Hydroelectricity
B. Nuclear
C. Thermal
D. Solar

117. Light Year is a unit of:
A. Intensity of light
B. Distance
C. Time
D. Planetary motion

118. Which of the following statements about the total goods traffic (in terms of gross tonne km.) carried by the Indian Railways is correct?
A. Steam and electric locomotives together haul about 50% of the traffic
B. Diesel and electric locomotives together haul about 95% of the traffic
C. Steam locomotive alone haul about 40% of the traffic
D. Steam and diesel locomotives haul about 60% of the traffic

119. Who is referred to in the following statements?
"Contrary to the existing notions, he suggested that the earth revolves around the sun and rotates on its axis".
A. Aryabhatta
B. Brahmagupta
C. Bhaskara
D. None of the above

120. The Tropic of Cancer does *not* pass through:
A. Gujarat
B. Orissa
C Tripura
D. West Bengal

121. The States of India having Common border with Myanmar are :
A. Mizoram, Manipur, Nagaland, Arunachal Pradesh
B. Mizoram, Manipur, Tripura, Meghalaya
C. Mizoram, Tripura, Meghalaya, Assam
D. Assam Manipur, Tripura, Arunachal Pradesh

122. International Date line lies on:
A. Greenwich meridian
B. 90° East meridian
C. 90° West meridian
D. 180° EW meridian

123. The common elements of 'NIFE' layer of the earth include:
A. Silicon and magnesium
B. Nickel and iron
C. Silver and tungsten
D. Silicon and aluminium

124. Match List I and List II and select the correct answer using the codes given below the Lists :

List I
(Ocean currents)
(*a*) Kuroshio
(*b*) Gulf Stream
(*c*) Agulhas
(*d*) Benguela

List II
(Country)
1. Namibia
2. Mozambique
3. Australia
4. U.S.A.
5. Japan

Codes :

	(*a*)	(*b*)	(*c*)	(*d*)
A.	4	5	2	3
B.	5	3	4	1
C.	1	4	3	2
D.	5	4	2	1

125. Match List I with List II and

select the correct answer using the codes given below the Lists :

List I

(*a*) Troposphere
(*b*) Stratosphere
(*c*) Ionosphere
(*d*) Exosphere

List II

1. Dust particles
2. Ozone layer
3. Meteors
4. Aurora

Codes :

	(*a*)	(*b*)	(*c*)	(*d*)
A.	1	2	4	3
B.	1	2	3	4
C.	2	1	4	3
D.	2	1	3	4

126. States of four major power plants labelled 1, 2, 3 and 4 are shown on the given map of India. Match the leads with following names of places :

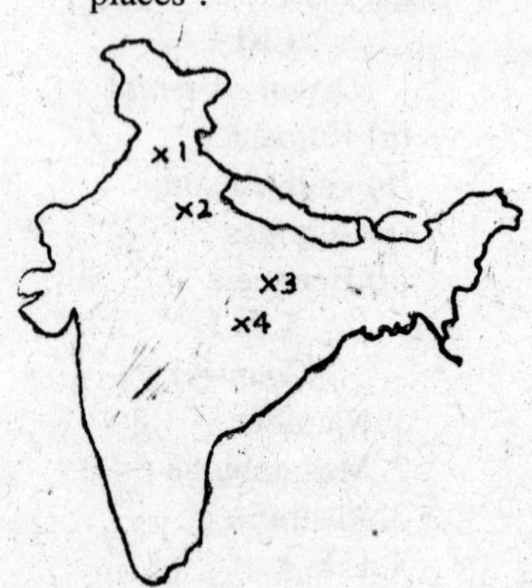

(*a*) Bhakra
(*b*) Narora
(*c*) Rihand
(*d*) Amarkantak

Select the correct answer using the codes given below:

Codes :

	(*a*)	(*b*)	(*c*)	(*d*)
A.	2	1	3	4
B.	4	3	1	2
C.	1	2	3	4
D.	4	1	3	2

127. Which of the following is correctly matched?
A. Teak : J & K
B. Deodar : M.P.
C. Sandalwood : Karnataka
D. Palm : Himachal Pradesh

128. When it is 8 P.M. in Allahabad, the time in London is?
A. 2.30 P.M. B. 3.30 P.M.
C. 4.30 P.M. D. 5.30 P.M.

129. The Nagarjunsagar project is on the river:
A. Sutlej B. Narmada
C. Krishna D. Kaveri

130. The oldest oil refinery in India is at:
A. Digboi (in Assam)
B. Haldia (near Kolkata)
C. Koyali (near Baroda)
D. Noonmati (in Assam)

131. The longest highway in India runs from
A. Kolkata to Jammu
B. Jammu to Kanyakumari
C. Ambala to Nagarcoil
D. Varanasi to Kanyakumari

132. The tropic of cancer passes through the middle part of India. As a result, the
A. Southern half of the country has a tropical climate
B. Northern half of the country has a temperate climate
C. Southern half of the country has a temperate climate
D. Northern half of the country has a tropical climate

133. The planets are kept in motion in their respective orbits by the:
A. Rotation of the sun on its axis
B. Gravitation and centrifugal forces
C. Great size and spherical shape
D. Rotation and the density of the planets

134. The greatest depth of water surface is about 11,000 metres at Mariana trench. It is located in the:
A. Atlantic Ocean
B. Pacific Ocean
C. Indian Ocean
D. Antarctica Ocean

135. The point, at which an object travelling in an elliptical orbit around the sun is closest to the sun, is:
A. Apogee B. Perigee
C. PerihelionD. Aphelion

136. All vital atmospheric processes leading to various climatic and weather conditions take place in the:
A. Troposphere
B. Ionosphere
C. Exosphere
D. Stratosphere

137. Match List I with List II and select the correct answer using the codes given below the lists :

List I

(*a*) Cotton
(*b*) Flax
(*c*) Sugarbeet
(*d*) Jute

List II

1. Rainfall 1000-1500 m.m.; Temperature 40°-60°C
2. Rainfall 1500-2000 m.m.; Temperature 25°-35°C
3. Rainfall 600-800 m.m.; Temperature 5°-18°C
4. Rainfall 500-1000 m.m.; Temperature 18°-22°C
5. Rainfall 500-600 m.m.; Temperature 18°-22°C

Codes :

	(a)	(b)	(c)	(d)
A.	1	3	4	2
B.	2	3	5	4
C.	4	5	2	1
D.	4	3	5	2

138. Meghalaya is an exclusive tribal State of which of the following groups of tribals?
A. Khasis, Usharis and Lakhris
B. Khasis, Jaintias and Garos
C. Jaintias, Garos and Kurkis
D. Garos, Pangs and Hmars

139. Which is the State of India where the sex ratio (number of females per thousand males) is above 1000?
A. Tamil Nadu
B. Kerala
C. Karnataka
D. Andhra Pradesh

140. The greatest diversity of animal and plants species occurs in:
A. temperate deciduous forests
B. tropical moist forests
C. heavily polluted rivers
D. desert lands

141. The highest volcano of the world is:
A. Mt. Fujiyama
B. Mt. Cotapaxi
C. Mt. Etna
D. Mt. Kilimanjaro

142. The cold oceanic current passing through the coast of North America is known as:
A. Kuroshio Current
B. Gulf Stream
C. Labrador Current
D. Falkland Current

143. Which of the following soil is very hard to cultivate?
A. Alluvial
B. Red
C. Black
D. Sandy

144. Time difference between extreme eastern and western points of India is:
A. 1 hr. 30 minutes
B. 2 hrs. 15 minutes
C. 2 hrs.
D. 3 hrs. 45 minutes

145. Which of the following are both seaports and oil-refining centres?
A. Visakhapatnam, Chennai and Mumbai
B. Kolkata, Quilon and Kandla
C. Kozhikode, Cuttack and Haldia
D. Mangalore, Haldia and Visakhapatnam

146. The Hirakud Project is on which of the following rivers?
A. Godavari
B. Mahanadi
C. Damodar
D. Kosi

147. The name of the galaxy in which Earth is a planet is:
A. Andromeda
B. Ursa Major
C. Ursa Minor
D. Milky way

148. Consider the following statements :
1. Relief and the distance from the sea are the two factors that control the distribution of rainfall in India.
2. Most parts of India receive an average annual rainfall of 150 cm to 200 cm.
3. Jammu & Kashmir receives snowfall during winter due to the influence of cyclones in the Mediterranean sea.
4. All branches of the Arabian sea branch of south-west monsoon give heavy rainfall.

Which of these statements are *correct*?
A. 1, 2 and 4
B. 1, 3 and 4
C. 2, 3 and 4
D. 1 and 3

149. Consider the following statements :
1. The first modern steel producing unit was established at Kulti.
2. Bhilai steel plant was established during the First Five Year Plan.
3. Bokaro steel plant was established in the Third Five Year Plan.
4. Rourkela steel plant was established with the collaboration of the then Soviet Union.

Which of these statements are *correct*?

A. 1, 2 and 4
B. 1, 3 and 4
C. 1 and 3
D. 2 and 3

150. Which one of the following States has the highest percentage of tank irrigation to the total irrigated area?

A. Andhra Pradesh
B. Karnataka
C. Orissa
D. Tamil Nadu

151. Which one of the following major ports of India handles maximum traffic?

A. Cochin
B. Kandla
C. Mumbai
D. Vishakhapatnam

152. What is meant by the term "cirrus"?

A. A low cloud
B. A rain-bearing cloud
C. A high-cloud
D. A hail-bearing cloud

153. Most of the weather phenomena take place in the:

A. stratosphere
B. troposphere
C. tropopause
D. ionosphere

154. Which national park is known for the Great Indian one-horned Rhinoceros?

A. Dudwa
B. Rhinoceros
C. Kaziranga
D. Gir

155. The famous Ghana Bird Sanctuary is located at :

A. Jorhat
B. Barpeta
C. Nainital
D. Bharatpur

156. From which part of the plant is jute obtained?

A. flower B. fruit
C. stem D. leaf

157. The deposits of the ancient Tethys Sea were folded to form the:

A. Himalayas
B. Rockies
C. Andes
D. Alps

158. The largest irrigation canal in India is called the:

A. Yamuna Canal
B. Sirhand Canal
C. Indira Gandhi Canal
D. Upper Bari Doab Canal

159. Atmospheric pressure exerted on earth is due to:

A. rotation of earth
B. revolution of earth
C. gravitational pull
D. uneven heating of earth

160. Pruning is an essential part in cultivation of:

A. Rubber B. Tobacco
C. Coffee D. Tea

161. The tip of South America is:

A. Cape Catoche
B. Cape of Good Hope
C. Cape Horn
D. Cape Cod

162. Consider the following rivers :

1. Ganga
2. Brahmaputra
3. Godavari
4. Krishna

Which of these rivers build a common delta?

A. 1 and 4 B. 1 and 3
C. 1 and 2 D. 3 and 4

163. Which *one* of the following planets is known for its main seven rings made up of icy particles?

A. Jupiter B. Mercury
C. Saturn D. Venus

164. At the Equator, the Sun will lie overhead on:

A. March 18 and Sept. 20
B. March 19 and Sept. 21
C. March 20 and Sept. 22
D. March 21 and Sept. 23

165. Crop rotation refers to the practice of cultivating:

A. one crop in one season followed by a different crop in the next season
B. more than one crop in the same field in different seasons
C. the same crop in different fields in different seasons
D. many crops in the same field in one season

166. What is the rank of the earth in the solar system in the terms of size?

A. Third B. Fourth
C. Fifth D. Sixth

167. Consider the data given in the following table :

Country	*Standard Meridian*
India	82.30 E
UK	00.00
Japan	135.00 E
Pakistan	70.00 E
Thailand	102.00 E

Which *one* of the following inferences can be drawn from the data given in the table?

When the standard time in India is:

A. 10.00 a.m., it is 1.30 p.m. in Japan.

B. 11.00 a.m., it is 10.00 a.m. in Pakistan.
C. 4.00 p.m., it is 10.00 a.m. in U.K.
D. 2.00 p.m., it is 1.00 p.m. in Thailand.

168. Match List I with List II and select the *correct* answer using the codes given below the Lists :

List I
(*a*) Fujiyama
(*b*) Vesuvius
(*c*) Mouna Loa
(*d*) Krakatoa

List II
1. Indonesia
2. USA
3. Italy
4. Japan

Codes :

	(*a*)	(*b*)	(*c*)	(*d*)
A.	3	4	1	2
B.	3	4	2	1
C.	4	3	1	2
D.	4	3	2	1

169. The circulation of ocean water occurs:
A. only laterally
B. only vertically
C. both laterally and vertically
D. neither laterally nor vertically

170. Match List I with List II and select the *correct* answer using the codes given below the Lists :

List I
(Storm)
(*a*) Cyclone
(*b*) Hurricane
(*c*) Typhoon
(*d*) Willy-Willy

List II
(Country of Occurrence)
1. China 2. Australia
3. India 4. USA

Codes :

	(*a*)	(*b*)	(*c*)	(*d*)
A.	3	4	2	1
B.	4	3	2	1
C.	3	4	1	2
D.	4	3	1	2

171. Which *one* of the following regions has the maximum intensity of shipping routes?
A. Atlantic Ocean
B. Indian Ocean
C. North Pacific Ocean
D. South Pacific Ocean

172. Where does Chambal river originate from?
A. Bhind B. Ratlam
C. Mhow D. Ujjain

173. Which one of the following rivers flows towards the west?
A. Ganga B. Narmada
C. Godavari D. Yamuna

174. Which state is the leading producer of Soyabean in India?
A. Maharashtra
B. Punjab
C. Kerala
D. Madhya Pradesh

175. Which is called the "Tiger State"?
A. Rajasthan
B. Madhya Pradesh
C. Uttar Pradesh
D. Jammu and Kashmir

176. What is 'Jhum'?
A. A folk Dance
B. The name of a river valley
C. A tribe
D. A type of cultivation

177. In which months is the Rabi crop sown?
A. March-April
B. June-July
C. October-November
D. January-February

178. Which Indian sea-port is important as the chief-exporter of iron ore as well as a naval base?
A. Cochin
B. Kandla
C. Chennai
D. Vishakhapatnam

179. Which one of the following rivers is known as "Sorrow of Bihar"?
A. Damodar B. Gandak
C. Kosi D. Sone

180. Given below are two statements, one labelled as *Assertion (A)* and the other labelled as *Reason (R)* :

Assertion (A) : One of the movements of the surface water of ocean is known as ocean current.

Reason (R) : Ocean currents are caused mainly due to planetary winds and the difference in temperature and density of water.

In the context of the above two statements, which one the following is correct?
A. Both A and R are true and R is the correct explana-tion of A
B. Both A and R are true but R is not a correct explanation of A
C. A is true but R is false
D. A is false but R is true

181. Consider the following statements about the earthquake:
1. earthquake usually originates from the sudden adjustments in

the crust of the earth

2. it may be of tectanic or volcanic origin
3. Most servere earthquakes are associated with fault lines which of the following statements are correct?

A. 1, 2 and 3
B. 1 and 2
C. 2 and 3
D. 2 and 4

182. Changes in the weather conditions occur in which one of the following layers of the atmosphere?

A. Troposphere
B. Stratosphere
C. Ozonosphere
D. Exosphere

183. Tsunamis are huge sea waves caused by :

A. Earthquakes
B. Volcanoes
C. Winds
D. Icebergs

184. Which of the following pairs of states and their important crops are correctly matched?

1. Kerala : Tapioca
2. Maharashtra : Cotton
3. W. Bengal : Jute
4. Gujarat : Groundnut

Select the correct answer using the codes given below:

Codes :

A. 1, 2 and 3
B. 1, 3 and 4
C. 1, 3 and 4
D. 2, 3 and 4

ANSWERS

1	**2**	**3**	**4**	**5**	**6**	**7**	**8**	**9**	**10**
C	C	B	B	C	C	D	D	D	B
11	**12**	**13**	**14**	**15**	**16**	**17**	**18**	**19**	**20**
B	C	C	C	A	A	A	B	B	A
21	**22**	**23**	**24**	**25**	**26**	**27**	**28**	**29**	**30**
A	B	D	B	C	C	D	C	B	D
31	**32**	**33**	**34**	**35**	**36**	**37**	**38**	**39**	**40**
A	B	A	A	A	B	B	A	A	D
41	**42**	**43**	**44**	**45**	**46**	**47**	**48**	**49**	**50**
C	A	A	A	C	D	D	A	C	C
51	**52**	**53**	**54**	**55**	**56**	**57**	**58**	**59**	**60**
C	D	B	D	B	C	C	C	B	B
61	**62**	**63**	**64**	**65**	**66**	**67**	**68**	**69**	**70**
A	C	B	D	B	A	C	D	B	D
71	**72**	**73**	**74**	**75**	**76**	**77**	**78**	**79**	**80**
B	A	C	A	D	D	D	C	B	B
81	**82**	**83**	**84**	**85**	**86**	**87**	**88**	**89**	**90**
B	A	C	D	B	A	C	A	C	D
91	**92**	**93**	**94**	**95**	**96**	**97**	**98**	**99**	**100**
C	B	B	B	A	B	D	B	C	C
101	**102**	**103**	**104**	**105**	**106**	**107**	**108**	**109**	**110**
B	B	B	A	C	D	B	C	A	B
111	**112**	**113**	**114**	**115**	**116**	**117**	**118**	**119**	**120**
C	C	B	B	B	A	B	B	A	B
121	**122**	**123**	**124**	**125**	**126**	**127**	**128**	**129**	**130**
A	D	B	D	B	C	C	A	C	A
131	**132**	**133**	**134**	**135**	**136**	**137**	**138**	**139**	**140**
B	A	B	B	C	A	D	B	B	B

141	142	143	144	145	146	147	148	149	150
B	C	B	C	A	B	D	B	C	A
151	**152**	**153**	**154**	**155**	**156**	**157**	**158**	**159**	**160**
C	C	B	C	D	C	A	C	C	D
161	**162**	**163**	**164**	**165**	**166**	**167**	**168**	**169**	**170**
C	C	C	D	B	C	A	D	C	C
171	**172**	**173**	**174**	**175**	**176**	**177**	**178**	**179**	**180**
A	A	B	D	B	D	C	D	C	C
181	**182**	**183**	**184**						
A	A	A	D						

ECONOMICS

1. A closed economy is the one which :
   A. does not permit emigration or immigration
   B. permits emigration but no immigration
   C. engages in no foreign trade
   D. engages in no foreign and domestic trade or transit
2. In a developed economy the major share of employment originates in the :
   A. primary sector
   B. tertiary sector
   C. secondary sector
   D. any of the above
3. The Economic and Social Commission for Asia and Pacific (ESCAP) is located at
   A. Bangkok
   B. Kuala Lumpur
   C. Manila
   D. Singapore
4. Commercial vehicles are not produced by which of the following companies in India?
   A. TELCO
   B. Ashok Leyland
   C. DCM Daewoo
   D. Birla Yamaha
5. In India, the Public Sector is most dominant in:
   A. transport
   B. steel production
   C. commercial banking
   D. organised term-lending financial institutions
6. The main argument advanced in favour of small scale and cottage industries in India is that:
   A. cost of production is low
   B. they require small capital investment
   C. they advance the goal of equitable distribution of wealth
   D. they generate a large volume of employment
7. The most serious economic problems of India are:
   A. Poverty and unemployment
   B. Stagnation, not poverty
   C. Unemployment, not poverty
   D. Underdevelopment, not poverty
8. Which of the following is not one of the three central problems of an economy?
   A. What to produce
   B. How to produce
   C. When to produce
   D. For whom to produce
9. If saving exceeds investment, the national income will:
   A. fall
   B. rise
   C. fluctuate
   D. remain constant
10. In which of the following industries in India are the maximum number of workers employed?
    A. Sugar
    B. Jute
    C. Textiles
    D. Iron and Steel
11. Terrace Cultivation is practiced mostly:
    A. in urban areas
    B. on slopes of mountains
    C. on tops of hills
    D. in undulating tracts
12. Which of the following is a selective Credit Control method?
    A. Bank Rate
    B. RBI directives
    C. Cash Reserve Ratio
    D. Open market operations
13. Which of the following taxes is not shared by the Central Government with the States?
    A. Union excise duties
    B. Customs duty
    C. Income tax
    D. Estate duty
14. ICICI is the name of a:
    A. Financial Institution
    B. Chemical Industry
    C. Cotton Industry
    D. Chamber of Commerce and Industry
15. Structural Unemployment arises due to
    A. Deflationary conditions
    B. Heavy industry bias
    C. Shortage of raw material
    D. Inadequate productive

capacity

16. Which of the following is the largest single source of the government's earning from tax revenue?
A. Excise duties
B. Customs duties
C. Corporation tax
D. Income tax

17. The largest public sector bank in India is:
A. Central Bank of India
B. Punjab National Bank
C. State Bank of India
D. Indian Overseas Bank

18. Which of the following statements best explains the term contraband goods?
A. Goods produced only for exports
B. Goods produced in joint sector only
C. Goods for the trading of which licence is not required
D. Goods that are forbidden, from export, import or even possession, by law.

19. Price in the market is fixed by:
A. Stock exchange rates
B. The demand and supply ruling in the market at a particular time
C. The Finance Minister
D. None of the above

20. Devaluation of currency helps to promote:
A. National Income
B. Savings
C. Imports at lower cost
D. Exports

21. Balanced economic growth can be achieved only if:
A. All the sectors of economy grow at the same rate
B. Population growth is arrested
C. All the inter dependent sectors grow in harmony
D. Basic and heavy industries are assigned highest priority

22. Which one of the following contributes most to the National Income in India?
A. Agricultural Sector
B. Industrial Sector
C. Foreign Trade Sector
D. Tertiary Sector

23. 'MODVAT' stands for:
A. Ad Valorem tax on output
B. Deduction of cost of inputs from the value of output
C. Reduction in import duties
D. Imposition of tax on professions

24. Largest revenue in India is obtained from:
A. Direct tax
B. Excise duties
C. Raiiways
D. None of the above

25. The term 'devaluation' means:
A. Reducing the value of a currency in terms of another currency
B. Increasing the value of a currency
C. Revising the value of a currency
D. None of the above

26. Per capita net availability of pulses has shown a tendency of:
A. Increase over time
B. Decrease over time
C. Constant over time
D. First increase then decrease

27. National Income is the same as:
A. Net national product at market price
B. Net domestic product at market price
C. Net national product at factor cost
D. Net domestic product at factor cost

28. Which one of the following is not an example of indirect tax?
A. Sales tax
B. Excise duty
C. Customs duty
D. Expenditure tax

29. The major aim of devaluation is to:
A. encourage imports
B. encourage exports
C. encourage both exports and imports
D. discourage both exports and imports

30. Structural unemployment arises due to:
A. deflationary conditions
B. heavy industry bias
C. shortage of raw materials
D. inadequate productive capacity

31. When was the Family Planning Programme officially started in India?
A. 1950 B. 1952
C. 1956 D. 1962

32. When was the Reserve Bank of India nationalised?
A. 1947 B. 1949
C. 1950 D. 1951

33. Which of the following is

not a feature of the Indian economy?
A. High rate of population growth
B. Disguised unemployment
C. Lowest rate of adult literacy
D. High rate of exports

34. The 'Relative Deprivation' approach for measuring poverty has been adopted by:
A. developing countries
B. developed countries
C. under-developed countries
D. None of the above

35. 'Disinvestment' means selling the shares of the public sector units to the:
A. workers or other companies (public or private)
B. workers only
C. MNC's only
D. private sector only

36. Sustainable economic development means an increase in the rate of growth of real:
A. total and per capita product
B. total and per capita product and level of literacy rate
C. total and per capita product and life expectancy at birth
D. total and per capita product, taking into account the cost of degradation of the quality of environment in this process

37. Functional unemployment occurs when:
A. unemployed have no qualification for job
B. people frequently change their job
C. people were thrown out from job due to recession
D. None of these

38. Which among the following does **not** have a 'free trade zone'?
A. Kandla
B. Mumbai
C. Vishakhapatnam
D. Thiruvanantpuram

39. Sun Belt of USA is important for which one of the following industries?
A. Cotton textile
B. Petrochemicals
C. Hi-tech electronics
D. Food Processing

40. Commercial banking system in India is
A. unit banking
B. branch banking
C. mixed banking
D. None of the above

41. The Duburi Thermal Power Plant Project approved by the Cabinet Committee on Foreign Investment will be set up in which of the following States?
A. Tamil Nadu
B. Orissa
C. Andhra Pradesh
D. Karnataka

42. Which one of the following states produce about 50 per cent of the total silk textiles in India?
A. West Bengal
B. Assam
C. Karnataka
D. Jammu and Kashmir

43. Gilt-edged market means:
A. Bullion market
B. Market of Government securities
C. Market of Guns
D. Market of pure metals

44. Which of the following is not a financial institution?
A. IDBI B. ICICI
C. FICCI D. HDFC

45. Private banks in India account for what share of the total banking sector?
A. 4% B. 8%
C. 12% D. 20%

46. Division of Labour is limited by
A. hours of work
B. the number of workers
C. extent of the market
D. working space

47. The First paper mill of the country was started in 1832. Where was it located?
A. Nepanagar in Madhya Pradesh
B. Mumbai in Maharashtra
C. Sehrampore in West Bengal
D. **Yamunanagar in Haryana**

48. "World Development Report" is an annual publication of
A. United Nations Development Programme
B. World Trade Organisation
C. International Monetary Fund
D. International Bank of Reconstruction and Development.

49. The theory of distribution relates to
A. the distribution of assets
B. the distribution of income

C. the distribution of factor payments
D. equality in the distribution of income and wealth

50. Movement along the same demand curve is known as
A. Extension and contraction of demand
B. Increase and Decrease in Demand
C. Increase of supply
D. Contraction of supply

51. Who amongst the following launched a new scheme named as "Dhana Lakshmi?"
A. Life Insurance Corporation of India
B. General Insurance Corporation of India
C. National Assurance Corporation
D. Unit Trust of India

52. RBI does *not* transact the business of which of the following State Governments?
A. Nagaland
B. Assam
C. Rajasthan
D. Jammu and Kashmir

53. Which of the following is *not* a rural development programme?
A. TRYSEM
B. DWACRA
C. CRY
D. RLEGP

54. Persons below the poverty line in India are classified as such based on whether:
A. they are entitled to a minimum prescribed food basket.
B. they get work for a prescribed minimum number of days in a year.
C. they belong to agricultural labourer household and the scheduled caste/tribe social group.
D. their daily wages fall below the prescribed minimum wages.

55. Which one of the following statements regarding the levying, collecting and distribution of Income Tax is *correct*?
A. The Union levies, collects and distributes the proceeds of income-tax between itself and the States
B. The Union levies, collects and keeps all the proceeds of income-tax of itself
C. The Union levies and collects the tax but all the proceeds are distributed among the States
D. Only the surcharge levied on income-tax is shared between the Union and the States

56. Consider the following statements :
Industrial development in India, to an extent, is constrained by
1. Lack of adequate entrepreneurship and leadership in business.
2. lack of savings to invest.
3. lack of technology, skills and infrastructure.
4. limited purchasing power among the larger masses.

Which of the above statements are *correct*?
A. 1, 2 and 3
B. 1, 3 and 4
C. 2, 3 and 4
D. 1, 2 and 4

57. There was no independent development of industries in India during British rule because of the:
A. absence of heavy industries.
B. scarcity of foreign capital.
C. scarcity of natural resources.
D. preference of the rich to invest in land.

58. Consider the following statements : Small-scale industries are, in most cases, not as efficient and competitive as the large-scale ones. Yet the Government provides preferential treatment and reservations in a range of products to the small firms because small-scale industries:
1. provide higher employment on a per unit capital deployment basis.
2. Promote a regional dispersion of industries and economic activities.
3. Have performed better in export of manufactured products than the large scale ones.
4. provide jobs to low-skill workers, who otherwise may not find employ-

ment avenues elsewhere.
Which of the above statements are *correct*?
A. 1 and 4 B. 1 and 2
C. 2 and 3 D. 3 and 4

59. Since 1980, the share of the tertiary sector in the total GDP of India has:
A. shown an increasing trend
B. shown a decreasing trend
C. remained constant.
D. been fluctuating.

60. The philosophy of *Laissez faire* is identified with:
A. Welfare State
B. Socialist State
C. Gandhian State
D. Industrial State

61. What is dual pricing?
A. wholesale price and retail pricing
B. pricing by agent and pricing by retailers
C. price fixed by Government and price in open market
D. daily prices and weekly prices

62. The largest share in our imports is from:
A. North America
B. European Community
C. OPEC (Organisation of Petroleum Exporting Countries)
D. African and Asian Developing Countries.

63. Which of the following would not tend to increase the population of a country?
A. an increase in the birth rate
B. a fall in the death rate
C. an increase in the average age at marriage
D. an increase in immigration

64. The statement "India is a rich country inhabited by poor people" means :
A. Government owns much gold but the people are poor
B. there are considerable income inequalities
C. country has rich, vast resources but they are not properly exploited
D. None of the above

65. The national debt :
A. constitutes a burden on future generations who will have to pay it
B. differs greatly from private debt because 'we owe it to ourselves'
C. represents wasteful expenditure because all government spending is wasteful
D. None of the above

66. In India, principal source of State revenue is :
A. gains from government companies/enterprises
B. grants/foreign aid from other countries
C. taxes and loans
D. loan from foreign governments and international agencies

67. Inflation is caused by :
A. increase in money supply
B. increase in production
C. decrease in production
D. both (*a*) and (*c*)

68. Development expenditure of the Central Government does not include :
A. expenditure on social and community services
B. grants-in-aid to States and Union Territories
C. interest payments
D. expenditure on economic services

69. Which of the following is not a cause of low productivity in Indian agriculture?
A. cooperative farming
B. inadequate inputs availability
C. sub-division and fragmentation of land holdings
D. poor finance and marketing facilities

70. Kudremukh is situated in :
A. Gujarat
B. Karnataka
C. Maharashtra
D. Tamil Nadu

71. Chotanagpur plateau is the centre of industries because:
A. it possesses copper
B. it possesses coal
C. it has cheap labour
D. abundant subsidies available there

72. What is the main reason for occurrence of structural unemployment?
A. inflation
B. inclination towards heavy industry
C. shortage of raw material
D. inadequate production capacity

73. Which of the following is not the characteristic of the Indian economy?
A. poor quality of human capital
B. occupational pattern is primary producing

C. prevalence of high level of technology
D. under-developed nature of the economy

74. The largest area covered by HYV (high yielding varieties) seeds is under :
A. rice B. wheat
C. sugarcane D. oil seeds

75. An agricultural (land) holding which is just sufficient to provide employment as well as livelihood to a family of, say, five persons is called :
A. a family holding
B. an optimum holding
C. an economic holding
D. large holding

76. Which factor among the following, creates obstacle in measuring correct estimate of national income?
A. Inflation
B. Under-employment
C. Existence of non-monetised sector
D. Low rate of savings

77. Which among the following taxes, has been the most elastic source of tax revenue in India?
A. Excise duty
B. Service tax
C. Custom duty
D. Corporation tax

78. When too much money is chasing too few goods, the situation is known as
A. deflation
B. recession
C. inflation
D. stagflation

79. Consider the following events :
1. conversion of Imperial Bank of India into SBI.
2. establishment of NABARD.
3. setting up of RRBs.
4. nationalisation of RBI.
The correct chronological sequence of these events is:
A. 4, 1, 2, 3
B. 4, 1, 3, 2
C. 1, 4, 3, 2
D. 1, 4, 2, 3

80. Barter System refers to a system where :
A. one man sells goods to many individuals
B. where one individual exchanges the commodity against money
C. goods are sold at a price
D. goods are exchanged against goods

81. When the price of a substitute of commodity X falls, the demand for X
A. rises
B. falls
C. remains unchaged
D. Any of these

82. Which of the following is *not* the instrument of fiscal policy?
A. bank rate
B. government expenditure
C. taxes
D. licence fees

83. Which one of the following is *not* an example of fixed cost?
A. rent of land
B. insurance charge
C. interest on machinery
D. raw materials used in production

84. A 45° supply curve represents:
A. perfectly elastic supply
B. unit elastic supply
C. less than unit elastic supply
D. perfectly inelastic supply

85. What is the percentage of the total workforce employed in Agriculture sector in India?
A. about 50%
B. about 56%
C. about 60%
D. about 52%

86. Purchase of a tractor by a farmer is:
A. final consumption
B. fixed investment
C. inventory investment
D. intermediate consumption

87. Major food-crop of India in terms of production is:
A. wheat B. barley
C. rice D. jowar

88. Which *one* of the following regions is the most important trading partner of India?
A. Asia and Oceania
B. North-west Europe
C. North America
D. Commonwealth of Independent States

89. Indian economy is most appropriately described as a:
A. capitalist economy
B. mixed economy
C. socialist economy
D. None of the above

90. In recent years the Indian economy has been characterised as a
A. backward economy

B. developed economy
C. developing economy
D. None of these

91. Which year is known as the "Year of the Great Divide" with regard to population growth in India?
A. 1921
B. 1947
C. 1931
D. None of these

92. What is NABARD's primary role?
A. To provide term loans to state co-operative banks
B. To assist state governments for share capital contribution
C. To act as re-finance institution
D. All of the above

93. Which of the following cities of Gujarat has the largest concentration of diamonds 'cutting' and polishing units in the world
A. Kathiawar
B. Porbandar
C. Ahmedabad
D. Surat

94. Which one of the following situations makes a firm most efficient?
A. Falling average costs
B. Rising average costs
C. Constant average costs
D. Lowest average costs

95. A country generally resorts to devaluation of its currency to :
A. convert deficit in her balance of payments
B. eliminate surplus in her balance of payments
C. satisfy the conditions laid down by the I.M.F.
D. increase her overall imports

ANSWERS

1	2	3	4	5	6	7	8	9	10
C	B	A	D	D	D	A	C	D	C
11	**12**	**13**	**14**	**15**	**16**	**17**	**18**	**19**	**20**
B	B	B	A	D	A	C	D	B	D
21	**22**	**23**	**24**	**25**	**26**	**27**	**28**	**29**	**30**
C	A	A	B	A	D	C	D	B	D
31	**32**	**33**	**34**	**35**	**36**	**37**	**38**	**39**	**40**
B	B	D	A	A	D	B	D	D	C
41	**42**	**43**	**44**	**45**	**46**	**47**	**48**	**49**	**50**
B	C	B	C	B	B	C	D	D	D
51	**52**	**53**	**54**	**55**	**56**	**57**	**58**	**59**	**60**
A	D	C	A	A	C	D	B	A	D
61	**62**	**63**	**64**	**65**	**66**	**67**	**68**	**69**	**70**
C	B	C	C	B	C	D	C	A	B
71	**72**	**73**	**74**	**75**	**76**	**77**	**78**	**79**	**80**
B	D	C	B	A	C	D	C	A	D
81	**82**	**83**	**84**	**85**	**86**	**87**	**88**	**89**	**90**
B	A	D	B	D	B	C	B	B	C
91	**92**	**93**	**94**	**95**					
A	D	D	D	A					

INDIA'S FIVE-YEAR PLANS

1. The Five Year Plans are reviewed and approved by the..........
   A. Union Cabinet
   B. Planning Commission
   C. National Development Council
   D. Lok Sabha and Rajya Sabha

2. Which of the following States in India has done pioneering work in 'decentralised planning' by decentralisation and devolution of authority and funds and has obtained positive results?
   A. Kerala
   B. Maharashtra
   C. Goa
   D. None of these

3. Which of the following is the most important objective of Indian planning?
   A. Reducing price instability
   B. Increasing capital formation
   C. Reducing inequality of income and wealth
   D. Increasing per capita income

4. Which of the following were the principle aims of First Five Year Plan?
   1. Self-sufficiency in foodgrain production.
   2. Rehabilitate Indian economy shattered by second war and partition.
   3. Development of basic and heavy industries.
   4. Minimum Needs Programme.

   A. 1 and 2 only
   B. 3 and 4 only
   C. 1, 2 and 3 only
   D. 1, 2, 3 and 4 only

5. Planning Commission is an:
   A. Advisory body
   B. Constitutional Body
   C. Stable Committee
   D. (A) and (B)

6. The Planning Commission of India was established in:
   A. 1942 B. 1947
   C. 1950 D. 1951

7. Duration of the Eleventh Five Year Plan is:
   A. 1990-95 B. 1991-96
   C. 2007-12 D. 1993-98

8. The strategy of Rolling Plan was adopted during the prime ministership of:
   A. V.P. Singh
   B. Rajiv Gandhi
   C. Morarji Desai
   D. Lal Bahadur Shastri

9. Which of the following is the most important objective of Indian Planning?
   A. Reducing price instability
   B. Increasing capital formation
   C. Reducing inequality of income and wealth
   D. Increasing per capita income

10. Minimum Needs Programme was introduced during the:
   A. Sixth Plan
   B. Eighth Plan
   C. Third Plan
   D. No such programme was introduced

11. Under which plan did the Government introduce an agricultural strategy which gave rise to Green Revolution?
   A. Sixth Five Year Plan (FYP)
   B. Second FYP
   C. Fourth FYP
   D. Third FYP

12. Which statement is correct for Indian Planning Commission?
   A. It is not defined in Indian Constitution
   B. Members and Vice-Chairman of it do not have fixed working duration
   C. Member do not require any minimum education
   D. All of these

13. Which Indian Five Year Plan ensured higher growth rate as compared with targeted growth rate?
   A. Fifth Plan
   B. Fourth Plan
   C. Second Plan
   D. Eighth Plan

14. Since the advent of Planning era in India, the share of agriculture sector in GDP has :
A. continued to decline
B. continued to rise
C. first increased and then declined
D. first declined and then increased

15. Since the start of Planning in India, the total number of years not covered by any Five-Year Plans is :
A. 6 B. 7
C. 5 D. 3

16. NABARD was established in—
A. Fourth Plan
B. Sixth Plan
C. Eighth Plan
D. Fifth Plan

17. The government's efforts to fight the menace of unemployment continue since the :
A. First Plan
B. Second Plan
C. Fifth Plan
D. Seventh Plan

18. When was the Fourth Five Year Plan launched?
A. 1953 B. 1956
C. 1962 D. 1969

19. Economic Planning is in—
A. Union list
B. Concurrent list
C. State list
D. Not any specified list

20. 'Food for Work Programme' was introduced during which one of the following Five-Year-Plans?
A. I B. II
C. V D. IX

ANSWERS

1	2	3	4	5	6	7	8	9	10
C	D	D	A	A	C	C	B	D	A
11	**12**	**13**	**14**	**15**	**16**	**17**	**18**	**19**	**20**
D	D	D	C	A	B	A	B	B	A

Indian Constitution

1. Who gives recognition to political parties in India?
   A. Parliament
   B. President
   C. Supreme Court
   D. Election Commission
2. The Quorum of the Legislative Council is :
   A. one-fourth of its total membership or 10
   B. one-fourth of its membership
   C. one-tenth of its membership or ten whichever is greater
   D. 25
3. The Indian Constitution is:
   A. federal
   B. unitary
   C. a happy mixture of the federal and unitary
   D. federal in normal times and unitary in times of emergency
4. Universal adult franchise implies a right to vote to all:
   A. adult residents of the State
   B. adult male citizens of the State
   C. residents of the State
   D. adult citizens of the State
5. When a resolution prefering a charge against the President has been passed by a specified majority in the House, it is sent to the other House for investigation. If, as a result of such an investigation, a resolution is passed through a specified majority by the other House, declaring that the charge has been sustained, the President shall leave his office. The specified special majority must not be less than :
   A. two-third of the members present and voting
   B. one-third of the members present and voting
   C. three-fourth of the members present and voting and two-third of the total membership
   D. two-third of the total membership
6. Which one of the following judicial powers of the President of India has been *wrongly* listed?
   A. he appoints the Chief Justice and other judges of the Supreme Court
   B. he can remove the judges of the Supreme Court on grounds of misconduct
   C. he can consult the Supreme Court on any question of law or fact which is of public importance
   D. he can grant pardon, reprieves and respites to persons punished under Union Law
7. The Vice-president of India can be removed from his office before the expiry of his term if :
   A. the Rajya Sabha passes a resolution by a majority of its members and the Lok Sabha agrees with the resolution
   B. if the Supreme Court of India recommends his removal
   C. the President so desires
   D. None of the above
8. The Chief Justice of a High Court in India is appointed by the :
   A. Governor of the State
   B. Prime Minister of India
   C. Chief Justice of the Supreme Court
   D. President of India
9. Which of the following statements is constitutionally not true about the passing of the Union Budgets, Railway Budgets and Finance Bill in India?
   1. Under the law, Finance Bill should be adopted by both the Houses of the Parliament within 45 days of its introduction.
   2. If the Finance Bill is not adopted within specified

period, the government loses its authority to levy the taxes proposed in the budgets.
3. In the absence of full budget, a vote-on-account gives the power to the government to spend.
4. Government cannot raise revenues without a proper approval of the Finance Bill

A. Only 2
B. Only 3
C. Only 4
D. Only 1, 2 and 3

10. Normally, on whose advice the President's Rule is imposed in a State?
A. Chief Minister
B. Legislative Assembly
C. Governor
D. Chief Justice of High Court

11. Which Article of the Indian Constitution deals with Amendment procedure?
A. Article 368
B. Article 358
C. Article 367
D. All of these

12. Government is the agency through which the will of :
A. the state is expressed
B. the people is expressed
C. the head of the state is expressed
D. the majority is expressed

13. In a unitary system of government :
A. The centre is all powerful
B. The centre is weaker than the states
C. The centre and states stand at par
D. The states and centre are supreme in their respective spheres

14. In Cabinet system of Government the real executive authority rests with :
A. The Council of Ministers
B. The Prime Minister
C. The Constitution
D. The Parliament

15. The Head of the State under a parliamentary government:
A. is an elected representative
B. is a hereditary person
C. is a nominated person
D. may be any one of the above

16. In the event of a ministerial proposal being defeated on the floor of the legislature, under the parliamentary system :
A. the government waits for a general no-confidence motion
B. the minister concerned is taken to task by the Prime Minister
C. the minister is forced to resign
D. the whole Council of Ministers resign

17. The "due process of law" is an essential characteristic of the judicial system of:
A. UK B. France
C. USA D. India

18. Under the Constitution it is :
A. obligatory for the President to accept the advice of the Council of Ministers but is not obliged to follow it
B. obligatory for the President to accept the advice of the Council of Ministers
C. not obligatory for the President to seek or accept the advice of the Council of Ministers
D. obligatory for the President to seek the advice of the Council of Ministers if his own party is in power

19. Which one of the following statements is correct?
A. the Presiding Officer of Rajya Sabha is elected every year
B. the Presiding Officer of Rajya Sabha is elected for a term of two years at a time
C. the Presiding Officer of Rajya Sabha is elected for a term of six years
D. the Vice-President of India is the ex-officio Presiding Officer of Rajya Sabha

20. The introduction of "no confidence" motion in the Lok Sabha requires the support of at least:
A. 50 members
B. 70 members
C. 60 members
D. 80 members

21. The High Court comes under :
A. State List
B. Union List
C. Concurrent List
D. None of the above

22. Which one of the following

has been wrongly listed as a Fundamental Duty of the Indian citizens?

A. to develop scientific temper, humanism and spirit of inquiry and reform

B. to work for raising the prestige of the country in the international sphere

C. to protect and improve the natural environment

D. to strive towards excellence in all spheres of individual and collective activity

23. Which one of the following is not a Fundamental Duty as outlined in Article 51A of the Constitution?

A. to abide by the Constitution and respect its ideals

B. to defend the country and render national service when called upon to do so

C. to work for the moral upliftment of the weaker sections of society

D. to preserve the rich heritage

24. The main characteristics of the Directive Principles of State Policy given in the Indian Constitution are :

A. not enforceable by any court

B. fundamental in the governance of the country

C. 'Like instruments, instructions, political manifesto and a code of moral precepts which have to guide governors of the country'

D. no law can be passed, which is opposed to these principles

25. Of the following which are true?

A. In a State, the Legislative Council is dominant with regard to non-financial bills and the Legislative Assembly with regard to financial (money) bills

B. Vidhan Parishad can virtually block legislation even if the same is passed by the Vidhan Sabha

C. In case of a tie between the two Houses, the Governor is duty-bound to call a joint session of the two Houses to have the issue settled on a majority verdict

D. If a Bill is twice approved by the Vidhan Sabha, it becomes law even if rejected by the Vidhan Parishad

26. Which one of the following types of emergency can be declared by the President?

A. Emergency due to threat of war, external aggresion or internal disturbances

B. Emergency due to break-down of constitutional machinery in a State.

C. Financial emergency on account of threat to the financial credit of India

D. all the three emergencies

27. Which of the following taxes is not levied by the Union Government?

A. Wealth Tax

B. Excise Duty

C. Profession Tax

D. Income Tax

28. Fiscal policy is connected with:

A. issue of currency

B. exports and imports

C. public revenue and expenditure

D. None of these

29. Deficit financing is spending:

A. by getting foreign aid

B. less than what is needed

C. in excess of revenue

D. by borrowing from abroad

30. If the Speaker of the State Legislative Assembly decides to resign, he should submit his resignation to the:

A. Judges of the High Court

B. Deputy Speaker

C. Chief Minister

D. Finance Minister

31. The Constitution of India provides for the nomination of two members of Lok Sabha by the President to represent:

A. the Parsis

B. men of eminence

C. the business community

D. the Anglo-Indian community

32. India is a Federal State because of:

A. dual judiciary

B. dual citizenship prevalent here.

C. share of power between the Centre and the States

D. written Constitution

33. Residuary Subjects are those subjects which are :

A. contained in the State list

B. contained in the Union list

C. contained in the Concurrent list

D. not covered by any of the three lists

34. Which of the following writs can be issued, by the Supreme Court, to enforce Fundamental Rights?

A. writ of Habeas Corpus

B. writ of Mandamus

C. writ of Quo Warranto

D. All of these

35. When the offices of both the President and the Vice-President of India are vacant, who will discharge their functions?

A. Prime Minister

B. Home Minister

C. Chief Justice of India

D. The Speaker

36. The Supreme Court tenders advice to the President of India on a matter of law or fact:

A. on its own

B. only when such advice is sought

C. only if the matter relates to some basic issue

D. only if the issue poses a threat to the unity and integrity of the country

37. Six months shall **not** intervene between two sessions of the Indian Parliament because :

A. it is the customary practice

B. it is the British convention followed in India

C. it is an obligation under the Constitution of India

D. None of the above

38. The States of the Indian Union can be recognised or their boundaries altered by:

A. the Union Parliament by a simple majority in the ordinary process of legislation

B. two-thirds majority of both the Houses of Parliament

C. two-thirds majority of both the Houses of Parliament and the consent of the legislatures of concerned States

D. an executive order of the Union government with the consent of the concerned State governments

39. The Basic Feature theory of the Constitution of India was propounded by the Supreme Court in the case of :

A. Minerva Mills Vs. Union of India

B. Golaknath Vs. State of Punjab

C. Maneka Gandhi Vs. Union of India

D. Keshavananda Vs. State of Kerala

40. Which one of the following writs is issued by a court in case of illegal detention of a person?

A. Habeas corpus

B. Mandamus

C. Certiorari

D. Quo-warranto

41. Sharda Act deals with

A. Widow remarriage

B. Child marriage

C. Inter-caste marriage

D. Polygamy

42. The Vice-President discharges the duties of the President during his illness for a maximum period of:

A. three months

B. six months

C. one year

D. Indefinitely

43. Which one of the following courts can a citizen move for the enforcement of Directive Principles of State Policy?

A. The Supreme Court

B. The High Court

C. Both A and B

D. None of these

44. The party system in India can be described as:

A. Single Party

B. Bi-Party

C. Multi-Party

D. a mixture of all these

45. The Chief Minister:

A. should not be a member of the State Legislature

B. must be a member of the State Legislature

C. must be a member of the Legislative Council

D. must be a member of the Legislative Assembly

46. The Constitution of India was created:

A. a very weak centre

B. a very strong centre

C. a centre which is weak in normal times but very strong during emergencies
D. None of these

47. The recommendations of the Finance Commission are:
A. binding on the President
B. not binding on the President
C. generally accepted as a matter of convention
D. accepted or rejected by the Governments according to its convenience

48. Consider the following statements about the Attorney General of India :
1. He is appointed by the President of India.
2. He must have the same qualifications as are required for a Judge of the Supreme Court.
3. He must be a member of either House of Parliament.
4. He can be removed by impeachment by Parliament.

A. 1 and 2
B. 1 and 3
C. 2, 3 and 4
D. 3 and 4

49. The Parliament can make any law for the whole or any part of India for implementing International treaties:
A. with the consent of all the States
B. with the consent of the majority of States
C. with the consent of the States concerned
D. without the consent of any State

50. Eighth Schedule of the Constitution contains:
A. Fundamental Rights
B. List of religions
C. Laws placed beyond the Jurisdiction of courts
D. List of 22 official languages

51. Who is a non-member but can participate in the business of either of the houses of Parliament?
A. Vice-President
B. Solicitor-General
C. Attorney-General
D. Chief Justice

52. In Indian Republic the real executive authority rests with the:
A. Prime Minister
B. President
C. Bureaucrats
D. Council of Ministers

53. The mind and ideals of the framers of Indian Constitution are reflected in:
A. The Preamble
B. The Fundamental Rights
C. The Directive Principles of State Policy
D. The Independent Judiciary

54. Who can dissolve the Lok Sabha before the expiry of its normal term of 5 years?
A. the Prime Minister
B. the President at his own
C. the President on the recommendation of the Prime Minister
D. the President on the recommendation of the Speaker

55. How many times has the Preamble of the Constitution of India been amended?
A. Once B. Twice
C. Thrice D. Never

56. Reasonable restrictions on Fundamental Rights can be imposed by:
A. The Parliament
B. The President
C. The Supreme Court
D. The Prime Minister

57. What is the meaning of the word 'Secular' as used in the Preamble to the Constitution?
A. Monotheism
B. Polytheism
C. Abnegation of all religions
D. Freedom of religion and worship to all citizen

58. The Parliament is not empowered to vote on the expenditure charged on the 'Consolidated Fund of India' which includes the emoluments and allowances of:
A. Prime Minister and his Council of Ministers
B. President of India
C. Secretaries of Various Ministries
D. Armed Forces of India

59. The control of the preparation of electoral rolls for Parliament and Legislatives in India, vests with:
A. Cabinet
B. Prime Minister
C. President
D. Election Commission

60. Which one of the following Articles lays down that the State shall take steps to organise village panchayats?
A. Article 40
B. Article 26
C. Article 57
D. Article 58

61. Which language is not specified in the 8th Schedule of the Indian Constitution?
A. Sanskrit B. Sindhi
C. Urdu D. Rajasthani

62. The Governor of State is:
A. Free from the control of the Centre
B. Controlled by the Centre and he is the agent of the President
C. Not an agent of the President
D. Not free to act in discretion in certain matters

63. Which of the following exercised the most profound influence in framing the Indian Constitution?
A. British Constitution
B. US Constitution
C. Irish Constitution
D. The Government of India Act, 1935

64. Which can be the maximum interval between two sessions of Parliament?
A. Three months
B. Four months
C. Six months
D. Nine months

65. Separation of the Judiciary from the Executive has been provided in which one of the following parts of the Indian Constitution?
A. The Preamble
B. The Fundamental Rights
C. The Directive Principles of State Policy
D. The Seventh Schedule

66. A Money Bill passed by Lok Sabha is deemed to have been passed by Rajya Sabha also when no action is taken by the Upper House within:
A. 10 days B. 14 days
C. 20 days D. 30 days

67. What is the total number of seats reserved for the Scheduled Castes and the Scheduled Tribes in Lok Sabha?
A. 69 and 30 respectively
B. 79 and 40 respectively
C. 89 and 50 respectively
D. None of these

68. The Judges of the Supreme Court hold office till the age of:
A. 62 years B. 65 years
C. 68 years D. 60 years

69. Election Commission is a/an:
A. legal body
B. constitutional body
C. executive committee
D. informal body

70. The greatest hallmark of personal liberty is :
A. Mandamus
B. Certiorari
C. Quo warranto
D. Habeas Corpus

71. Which one of the following Fundamental Rights has been a subject of maximum controversy and litigation?
A. right to freedom of speech
B. right to property
C. right to Constitutional remedies
D. right to religion

72. How many members can be nominated to the Rajya Sabha by the President?
A. none B. 10
C. 12 D. two

73. The framers of the Constitution borrowed the idea of judicial review from the Constitution of:
A. France
B. USA
C. United Kingdom
D. all three

74. The Electoral System in India is based on:
A. adult franchise
B. separate electorate
C. indirect election system
D. multi-vote system

75. The guardian of the Constitution of India is the:
A. Indian Parliament
B. Supreme Courts of India
C. Prime Minister of India
D. High Courts of States

76. The basic tenet of secularism as enshrined in the Constitution of India is:
A. propagation of all religions by the State
B. propagation of atheism
C. non-propagation of any religion by the State
D. None of the above

77. The word 'secular' in the Preamble of the Indian Constitution was incorporated by the:
A. 42nd amendment
B. 62nd amendment
C. 44th amendment
D. 41st amendment

78. The Directive Principles of

State Policy is contained in .... of the constitution.
A. Part V B. Part III
C. Part IV D. Part VI

79. The President of India takes oath or affirmation in the presence of the:
A. Vice-President
B. Prime Minister
C. Chief Justice of India
D. None of these

80. 'Zero hour' is:
A. mentioned in the rules of the Parliamentary procedure
B. mentioned in the Constitution
C. coined by the press
D. dependent upon the mercy of speaker

81. To recognise a party as national or all India party, it has to obtain how many per cent of the total valid votes polled in the previous general election?
A. 10 per cent
B. 4 per cent
C. 12 per cent
D. 3 per cent

82. The sitting of the House of the People may be terminated by :
A. adjournment
B. prorogation
C. dissolution
D. All the above

83. Which Article of the Indian Constitution empowers Parliament to make law for giving effect to international agreements :
A. Article 249
B. Article 250
C. Article 252
D. Article 253

84. Money Bill has been defined by the Constitution under Article :
A. 109
B. 110
C. 111
D. Both B and C

85. Zonal Councils have been created by :
A. Constitution
B. Act of Parliament
C. Government Resolution
D. National Development Council

86. The main object of the Article 13 of the Indian Constitution is to secure the paramountcy of the Constitution in regard to :
A. Directive Principles of State Policy
B. Fundamental Rights
C. Fundamental Duties
D. All the above

87. Which of the following is the subject matter of 79th Amendment Act?
A. continued use of English as an Associate Language
B. land reforms
C. reservation of seats for women in Legislatures
D. extension of reservation for SC/STs up to 2010

88. With the passage of the Depositories Related Laws Bills after amendment by the Parliament, public sector banks can take up which of the following activities?
A. Merchant Banking
B. Portfolio Management
C. Underwriting jobs
D. Paperless trading

89. Consider the following statements about the Attorney General of India :
1. He is appointed by the President of India.
2. He must have the same qualifications as are required for a judge of the Supreme Court.
3. He must be a member of either House of Parliament.
4 He can be removed by impeachment by Parliament.
A. 1 and 2
B. 1 and 3
C. 2, 3 and 4
D. 3 and 4

90. Consider the following functionaries :
1. Cabinet Secretary
2. Chief Election Commissioner
3. Union Cabinet Ministers
4. Chief Justice of India
Their correct sequence in order of Preference is
A. 3, 4, 2, 1 B. 4, 3, 1, 2
C. 4, 3, 2, 1 D. 3, 4, 1, 2

91. The primary function of the Finance Commission in India is to
A. distribute revenue between the Centre and the States
B. prepare the Annual Budget
C. advise the President on financial matters
D. allocate funds to various ministries of the Union and the State Governments

92. The State which has the

largest number of seats reserved for the Scheduled Tribes in the Lok Sabha is:

A. Bihar
B. Gujarat
C. Uttar Pradesh
D. Madhya Pradesh

93. 84th Amendment Bill gives reservation for which of the following categories?

A. Women in Parliament
B. Anglo - Indians, Scheduled Castes and Scheduled Tribes
C. Freedom of Press
D. Freedom of Religion

94. Article 370 of the Indian Constitution deals with which of the following?

A. Fundamental Rights
B. Special status of Jammu and Kashmir
C. National Emergency
D. Impeachment of the President

95. The President of India can nominate how many members from the Anglo-Indian community to the Lok Sabha?

A. Two B. Five
C. Ten D. Twelve

96. The Constitution of India recognises:

A. only religious minorities
B. only linguistic minorities
C. religious and linguistic minorities
D. religious, linguistic and ethnic minorities

97. Consider the following statements :

An amendment of the Constitution of India can be initiated by the

1. Lok Sabha
2. Rajya Sabha
3. State Legislatures
4. President

Which of the above statements is/are *correct*?

A. 1 alone
B. 1, 2 and 3
C. 2, 3 and 4
D. 1 and 2

98. The amount of security deposit required to be paid by a candidate for contesting election to the office of the President of India is:

A. Rs. 2,500
B. Rs. 5,000
C. Rs. 10,000
D. Rs. 15,000

99. The minimum number of votes required for proposing an independent candidate for election to a Parliamentary or Assembly constituency is:

A. 1 B. 5
C. 10 D. 15

100. Who among the following can be removed from the office without impeachment?

A. President of India
B. Chief Justice of India
C. Governor of a State
D. Chief Election Commissioner

101. After their retirement, the Judges of the Supreme Court are *not* permitted to practice:

A. for ten years
B. before the Supreme Court
C. before the High Court
D. before any court in India

102. The provisional President of the Constituent Assembly was

A. Sachchidananda Sinha
B. Dr. Rajendra Prasad
C. Dr. B.R. Ambedkar
D. Pt. Jawaharlal Nehru

103. The Chairman of the Finance Commission is appointed by:

A. the President
B. the Prime Minister
C. the Cabinet
D. the Parliament

104. Articles 74 and 75 of Indian Constitution deal with matters of:

A. the Council of Ministers
B. the Speaker of Lok Sabha
C. the President of India
D. the Cabinet Ministers

105. The Chairman of the Drafting Committee of the Indian Constitution was:

A. Pt. Jawaharlal Nehru
B. Dr. Rajendra Prasad
C. Mahatma Gandhi
D. Dr. B.R. Ambedkar

106. Fourth Estate is referred to:

A. Public Opinion
B. Chamber of Commerce
C. the Newspaper
D. Political Parties

107. Rajya Sabha being a permanent house:

A. one-third of its members retire every two years
B. one-half of its members retire every three years
C. one-fifth of its members retire every year
D. one-sixth of its members retire every year

108. Fundamental Rights granted to the Indian Citizens:

A. cannot be suspended

B. can be suspended
C. can never be suspended under any circumstances
D. None of the above is correct

109. The Joint Session of both the Houses of Parliament is summoned by:
A. Speaker of the Lok Sabha
B. President
C. Prime Minister
D. Chairman of Rajya Sabha

110. In a federal government the states enjoy:
A. original powers
B. powers delegated by the Centre
C. powers given by the Constitution
D. powers given by the people

111. A candidate for election as President must be:
A. not more than seventy-five years of age
B. at least twenty years old
C. not less than thrity-five years of age
D. at least eighteen years of age

112. Which one of the following statements is *incorrect*?
A. the President is an integral part of the Parliament
B. the President is not a part of the Parliament
C. the President can summon each House of Parliament
D. the President can dissolve the Lok Sabha

113. The fundamental rights granted to Indian citizens by the Constitution are :
A. absolute
B. justiceable
C. a check on the possible tyranny of the majority
D. those rights which are considered essential for the realization of the highest good of the citizens

114. The Council of Ministers can be removed from office:
A. by the President at his discretion
B. by the Rajya Sabha if it passes a resolution to this effect
C. by the Lok Sabha if it passes a vote of no-confidence against it
D. by the Lok Sabha and the Rajya Sabha jointly by passing a vote of no-confidence against it

115. Which one of the following executive functions of the Council of Ministers has been *wrongly* listed?
A. it formulates the executive policy of the country
B. it coordinates the policies, programmes and activities of the various departments
C. it plays an important role in filling up various political, judicial and ambassadorial assignments
D. it plays an important role in the election of the President

116. The Attorney General of India is appointed by:
A. The Chief Justice of Supreme Court
B. The Minister of Law
C. The President
D. The Comptroller and Auditor General

117. Which of the following rights **does not** belong to the Right of Freedom?
A. To assemble peacefully
B. To form association or Unions
C. To establish denominational institutions
D. To reside in any part of India

118. It is said in Indian Constitution that Hindi:
A. will be national langauge of India
B. will be communication language between State Governments
C. will be official language of Indian Union
D. will be communication language between Central Govt. and State Govt.

119. How many languages so far has been included in Eighth Schedule of our Constitution?
A. 14 B. 15
C. 16 D. 22

120. What is the minimum age required to become the President of India?
A. 25 years B. 30 years
C. 35 years D. 40 years

121. Which part of Indian Constitution emphasises the welfare aspect of the State?
A. Preamble to the Constitution
B. Fundamental Rights
C. Directive Principles of

State Policy
D. Schedule Seven appended to the Constitution

122. Which one of the following categories of members are not included in the Legislative Council?
A. members elected by municipalities, district boards and other local authorities in the States
B. representatives of temples, churches and mosques
C. representatives of persons engaged in teaching in institution not lower in standard than secondary schools
D. members nominated by the Governor from amongst persons having special knowledge of literature, science, art, co-operative movement and social service

123. The overall objective of Fundamental Rights is to ensure :
A. democratic government
B. individual liberty
C. judicial independence
D. secularism

124. The President can vacate his office by addressing his resignation to :
A. the Vice-President
B. the Speaker of Lok Sabha
C. the Prime Minister
D. the Chief Justice of India

125. Which one of the following has been *wrongly* listed as a qualification for membership of the Legislative Assembly?
A. must be citizen of India
B. must be more than 30 years of age
C. must not hold any office of profit
D. must possess such other qualifications as may be prescribed by a law Parliament

126. The Supreme Court of India enjoys :
A. only original jurisdiction
B. only appellate jurisdiction
C. only advisory jurisdiction
D. all the above types of jurisdictions

127. A money bill duly passed by the Lok Sabha can be held up by the Rajya Sabha for a maximum of:
A. two years
B. six months
C. three months
D. fourteen days

128. The Governor is responsible to the :
A. state legislature
B. state legislative assembly
C. President
D. Prime Minister

129. Agriculture, presently a State subject, can be shifted to the Concurrent List under which of the following Articles of the Indian Constitution?
A. 357 B. 368
C. 375 D. 328
E. Cannot be shifted

130. Article 254 of the Indian Constitution describes which of the following?
A. The Parliament has the power to increase the number of judges
B. The Union and States have concurrent powers to legislate on any matter enumerated in List III
C. In case of any conflict between Union laws and State laws, the Union laws shall prevail
D. The Union has exclusive power to make laws on any matter not enumerated in the Concurrent List or State List

131. A British citizen staying in India *cannot* claim right to:
A. Freedom of trade and profession
B. Equality before the Law
C. Protection of life and personal liberty
D. Freedom of religion

132. Which of the following items is contained in the Union List?
A. Politce
B. Census
C. Land revenue
D. Public health and sanitation

133. The Constitution of India describes India as a:
A. Confederation
B. Union of States
C. Federation
D. None of these

134. Which of the following Articles of our Constitution

gives special status to Jammu & Kashmir?
A. Article 326
B. Article 352
C. Article 356
D. Article 370

135. In India the voting age was reduced from 21 years to 18 years in:
A. 1988 B. 1989
C. 1990 D. 1991

136. The Constitution of India draws its authority from
A. the Indian Independence Act, 1947
B. the Constituent Assembly which represented all sections of People of the Society
C. the people of India
D. the President and the Supreme Court

137. Under which *one* of the following Articles of the Constitution of India, is the 'Annual Financial Statement' of the economy to be laid by the Government on the table of the Parliament before 31st March, every year?
A. Article 16
B. Article 31
C. Article 124
D. Article 112

138. Which *one* of the following States has a separate Constitution?
A. Assam
B. Jammu & Kashmir
C. Arunachal Pradesh
D. Sikkim

139. Given below are two statements one labelled as *Assertion (A)* and the other labelled as *Reason (R)* :

Assertion (A) : The Right to Property in the Constitution of India ceased to be a Fundamental Right but it continues to exist as a Constitutional Right.

Reason (R) : Forty-fourth Amendment deleted Article (19) (f) and Article 31 from Part III and added a new Article 300-A, in Part XII.

In the context of the above two statements which one of the following is *correct*?
A. Both A and R are true and R is the correct explanation of A
B. Both A and R are True but R is not the correct explanation of A
C. A is true but R is false
D. A is false but R is true

140. Generally the Prime Minister is :
A. the seniormost member of the Parliament
B. the leader of the majority party in the Lok Sabha
C. A close friend of the President
D. not a member of Parliament

141. Who decides whether a bill is a money bill or not?
A. Speaker of the Lok Sabha
B. The President
C. The Prime Minister
D. None of these

142. In the Rajya Sabha, the States have been provided:
A. equal representation
B. representation on the basis of population and size
C. representation on the basis of population
D. representation on the basis of size

143. The Legislative Council in a State can be abolished by Parliament on the recommendation of :
A. The Governor
B. The State Legislative Assembly
C. The President
D. None of these

144. What is the period within which a proclamation of national emergency made by the President is to be placed before each house of the Parliament for approval?
A. Within one month
B. Within two months
C. Within four months
D. Within six months

145. Which Writ is issued by a High Court or Supreme Court to compel an authority to perform a function that is it was not performing?
A. Writ of Certiorari
B. Writ of Habeas Corpus
C. Writ of Mandamus
D. Writ of Quo Warranto

146. In case of a disagreement between the two Houses of Parliament over a non-money bill:
A. the bill will lapse
B. the President may sign it into a law
C. the President may call a joint sitting of both the Houses to consider it
D. the President may ask

both the Houses to reconsider it

147. Which of the following articles of the Indian Constitution is related to the protection of the interest of minorities?
A. Article 256
B. Article 29
C. Article 370
D. Article 354

148. How many members are nominated by the President of India to the Rajya Sabha?
A. 2 B. 5
C. 6 D. 12

149. The normal duration of the Lok Sabha in India is:
A. 4 years
B. 5 years
C. 5 year 6 months
D. 6 years

150. Which one of the following statements regarding the Vice-President of India officiating as President, is *correct*?
A. He shall continue to be the Chairman of the Council of States
B. He shall cease to be the Chairman of the Council of States
C. He shall nominate the next seniormost member of the House to be the Chairperson of Council of States
D. None of the above

151. Consider the following statements : The creation of a new State in India, from an existing State, involves the consent of the:
1. Supreme Court
2. Legislature of the State concerned.
3. President.
4. Parliament.
Which of these statements are *correct*?
A. 1, 2 and 3
B. 2, 3 and 4
C. 1 and 4
D. 1, 2, 3 and 4

152. The provisions relating to Fundamental Rights in the Constitution of India:
A. cannot be amended
B. can be amended by a simple majority in Parliament
C. can be amended by a two-thirds majority in Parliament
D. can be amended by a two-thirds majority of the members present and voting in Parliament and ratified by a majority in the State Legislatures

153. Which one of the following options is **not** available to the President in the event of the Prime Minister losing majority support in Lok Sabha?
A. Dissolving the Lok Sabha
B. Inviting the leader of another party to form a government
C. Seeking advisory opinion of the Supreme Court on the question of dissolution
D. Nominating the Speaker of the Lok Sabha as new Prime Minister

154. Which of the following words were added to the Preamble to the Constitution of India under the 42nd Amendment?
A. Democratic Republic
B. Democratic Socialist
C. Sovereign Secular
D. Socialist Secular

155. Given below are two statements, one labelled as *Assertion (A)* and the other labelled as *Reason (R)* :
Assertion (A) : The chapter of the 'Directive Principles of State Policy' has been made the part of the Constitution of India.
Reason (R) : It reflects the concepts of welfare State and the creation of the socialist pattern of society.
In the context of the above two statements, which one of the following is correct?
A. Both A and R are true and R is the correct explanation of A
B. Both A and R are true but R is not a correct explanation of A
C. A is true but R is false
D. A is false but R is true

156. Given below are two statements, one labelled as *Assertion (A)* and the other labelled as *Reason (R)* :
Assertion (A) : Centre giving directions to the States is not desirable but could not be altogether avoided in practice.
Reason (R) : The Union government is empowered to give such directions to

the States as may appear to the government of India to be necessary to ensure compliance with the laws made by the Parliament.
In the context of the above two statements, which one of the following is correct?
A. Both A and R are true and R is the correct explana-tion of A
B. Both A and R are true but R is not the correct explanation of A
C. A is true but R is false
D. A is false but R is true

157. Who among the following non-members can take part in the proceedings of the Indian Parliament without the right to vote?
A. Ex-Speaker of Lok Sabha
B. Attorney General of India
C. The Chief Justice of India
D. Comptroller and Auditor General of India

158. Who among the following have the right to vote in the elections to both the Lok Sabha and the Rajya Sabha?
A. Elected members of the Lower House of the Parliament
B. Elected members of the Upper House of the Parliament
C. Elected members of the Upper House of the State Legislature
D. Elected members of the Lower House of the State Legislature

159. Agricultural tax is assigned to the state governments by:
A. The Finance Commission
B. The National Development Council
C. The Inter-State Council
D. The Constitution of India

ANSWERS

1	2	3	4	5	6	7	8	9	10
D	C	D	D	A	B	A	D	C	C
11	**12**	**13**	**14**	**15**	**16**	**17**	**18**	**19**	**20**
A	A	A	A	D	D	C	B	D	A
21	**22**	**23**	**24**	**25**	**26**	**27**	**28**	**29**	**30**
B	B	C	B	D	D	C	C	C	B
31	**32**	**33**	**34**	**35**	**36**	**37**	**38**	**39**	**40**
D	C	D	D	C	B	C	A	D	A
41	**42**	**43**	**44**	**45**	**46**	**47**	**48**	**49**	**50**
B	D	D	C	B	B	C	A	D	D
51	**52**	**53**	**54**	**55**	**56**	**57**	**58**	**59**	**60**
C	C	A	C	A	A	D	B	D	A
61	**62**	**63**	**64**	**65**	**66**	**67**	**68**	**69**	**70**
D	D	D	C	C	B	B	B	B	D
71	**72**	**73**	**74**	**75**	**76**	**77**	**78**	**79**	**80**
B	C	A	A	B	C	A	C	C	C
81	**82**	**83**	**84**	**85**	**86**	**87**	**88**	**89**	**90**
B	D	D	B	B	B	D	A	A	C
91	**92**	**93**	**94**	**95**	**96**	**97**	**98**	**99**	**100**
A	D	B	B	A	C	D	C	C	C
101	**102**	**103**	**104**	**105**	**106**	**107**	**108**	**109**	**110**
D	A	A	A	D	C	A	B	B	C

111	112	113	114	115	116	117	118	119	120
C	B	D	C	D	C	C	A	D	C
121	122	123	124	125	126	127	128	129	130
C	B	B	A	B	D	D	C	B	C
131	132	133	134	135	136	137	138	139	140
B	B	B	D	B	C	D	B	A	B
141	142	143	144	145	146	147	148	149	150
A	C	B	A	C	C	B	D	B	B
151	152	153	154	155	156	157	158	159	
B	C	D	D	A	A	B	D	D	

EVERYDAY SCIENCE

1. Name the instrument with the help of which a sailor in a submarine can see the objects on the surface of the sea.
   A. Telescope
   B. Periscope
   C. Gycroscope
   D. Stereoscope
2. 'HEMOPHILLIA' is the disease of ....
   A. liver B. blood
   C. brain D. bones
3. Vitamin A is abundantly found in ....
   A. Brinjal B. Tomato
   C. Carrot D. Cabbage
4. .... is not soluble in water.
   A. Vitamin A
   B. Vitamin B
   C. Vitamin C
   D. Vitamin D
5. The blood vessels with the smallest diameter are called ....
   A. capillaries
   B. arterioles
   C. venules
   D. lymphatics
6. Out of the following .... has the greatest elasticity.
   A. steel
   B. rubber
   C. aluminium
   D. annealed copper
7. Cooking gas is a mixture of which of the following two gases?
   A. Carbon Dioxide and Oxygen
   B. Butane and Propane
   C. Carbon Monoxide and Carbon Dioxide
   D. Methane and Ethylene
   E. None of these
8. The substance most commonly used as a food preservative is:
   A. sodium carbonate
   B. tartaric acid
   C. acetic acid
   D. benzoic acid
9. Normally, the substances that fight against diseases in human systems are known as:
   A. dioxyribonucleic acids
   B. carbohydrates
   C. enzymes
   D. antibodies
10. The SI unit of temperature is ....
    A. Kelvin
    B. Celsius
    C. Fahrenheit
    D. None of the above
11. One of the common fungal diseases of man is :
    A. plague B. ringworm
    C. cholera D. typhoid
12. A clear sky is blue because:
    A. red light is scattered more than blue
    B. ultra violet light has been absorbed
    C. blue light is scattered more than red
    D. blue light has been absorbed
13. Jenner introduced the method of making people immune to :
    A. small pox B. rabies
    C. cholera D. polio
14. The largest cell in the human body is :
    A. Nerve cell
    B. Live cell
    C. Muscle cell
    D. Kidney cell
15. What is the device that steps up or steps down the voltage?
    A. Dynamo
    B. Conductor
    C. Inductor
    D. Transformer
16. The protein deficiency disease is known as :
    A. Kwashiorker
    B. Cirrhosis
    C. Eczema
    D. Clycoses
17. Iron deficiency causes :
    A. rickets B. anaemia
    C. cirrhosis D. goitre
18. Blood group of an individual is controlled by :
    A. Haemoglobin
    B. Shape of RBC
    C. Shape of WBC
    D. Genes
19. In a normal man the amount of blood pumped out by the heart per minute is about :
    A. 1 litre B. 3 litres

C. 4 litres D. 5 litres

20. Red/green colour blindness in man is known as :
A. Protanopia
B. Deutetanopia
C. Both A and B above
D. Marfan's syndrome

21. The blue colour of the water in the sea is due to :
A. Reflection of the blue light by the impurities in sea water.
B. Reflection of the blue sky by sea water and scattering of blue light by water molecules
C. Absorption of other colours by water molecules
D. None of the above

22. The image formed on the retina of the eye is :
A. upright and real
B. larger than the object
C. small and inverted
D. enlarged and real

23. If the surface water in a lake is just going to freeze, what will be the temperature of water at the bottom?
A. 0°C
B. more than 4°C
C. 4°C
D. less than 4°C

24. Oil rises up the wick in a lamp :
A. because oil is volatile
B. due to the capillary action phenomenon
C. due to the surface tension phenomenon
D. because oil is very light

25. The 'stones' formed in human kidney consist mostly of :
A. calcium oxalate
B. sodium acetate
C. magnesium sulphate
D. calcium

26. We hear the sound later, while the light is seen earlier:
A. because light's speed is more than that of sound
B. because lights travel in a straight direction while sound in a zigzag direction
C. because sound's frequency is lower than light
D. All of the above

27. Which part of an eye is transplanted?
A. Cornea B. Retina
C. Iris D. Sciera

28. The Universal donor group of blood is:
A. O B. A
C. B D. AB

29. The green colour of the leaf is due to
A. Presence of Chloroplast
B. Presence of Chromium
C. Presence of Nicoplast
D. Presence of excess of oxygen

30. How many calories of energy is yielded by a cup of tea?
A. 4 B. 400
C. 40 D. 1000

31. Camel uses its hump for
A. storing water
B. storing fat
C. for balancing the body
D. temperature regulation

32. A man standing in a free falling lift releases a ball from his hand. The ball would be :
A. moving down
B. moving up
C. stationary
D. moving up and down

33. Which one of the following substances is used for preservation of food gains?
A. Sodium benzoate
B. Vinegar
C. Sodium chloride
D. Potassium permanganate

34. The disease caused by Asbestos is:
A. Emphysema
B. Paralysis
C. Diarrhoea
D. Dysentery

35. The universal law of gravitation was propounded by :
A. Kepler
B. Galileo
C. Newton
D. Copernicus

36. Bats can fly in the dark because :
A. they have a better vision in the dark
B. the pupils of their eyes are very big
C. they are guided by ultrasonic waves produced by them
D. any bird can do so

37. Blood is formed in the human adult by the :
A. heart
B. spleen
C. kidney
D. bone marrow

38. Pencil 'lead': is made up of:
A. graphite
B. charcoal
C. lead oxide
D. lampblack

39. The deficiency of which one

of the following vitamin. leads to bleeding of gums and loosening of teeth?
A. Vitamin D
B. Vitamin C
C. Vitamin B
D. Vitamin A

40. How much blood does a normal person have in his body?
A. 8 litres
B. 4 to 5 liters
C. 10 liters
D. 2 liters

41. Which colour of light has the longest wave length?
A. Yellow B. Blue
C. Red D. Green

42. Petrol fire can be extinguished by:
A. Water
B. Carbon dioxide
C. Sand
D. None of these

43. Which of the following is nearest to earth?
A. Sun
B. Moon
C. Mercury
D. None of the above

44. What is the name of the instrument that measures the speed of wind?
A. Lactometer
B. Hydrometer
C. Anemometer
D. None of the above

45. Moon has no atmosphere because:
A. its surface is not smooth
B. it is quite far off
C. it does not have any living being
D. root mean square velocity of all gases is more than their escape velocity on moon's surface

46. Which one of the following is present in tobacco?
A. Nicotine B. Heroin
C. Marijuana D. Cocaine

47. Normal temperature of human body is :
A. 36.8°C B. 94.8°F
C. 98.6°F D. 49.8°C

48. The unit of distance used in navigation is :
A. nautical mile
B. kilometer
C. light year
D. yard

49. If the reading in a barometer shows an abrupt fall, the chances are that the weather will be :
A. very cool
B. very stormy
C. full of rains
D. calm and quiet

50. The gas which is used in cold storage plants for refrigeration is known as :
A. Chlorine
B. CO_2
C. Amonia
D. Hydrogen

51. In the Fahrenheit scale, the number 32 corresponds to:
A. 100°C B. 23°C
C. 32°C D. 30°C

52. The term 'global warming' means:
A. quick melting of polar ice sheets
B. depletion of ozone layer
C. high temperature in torrid zone
D. general rise in temperature due to carbon dioxide

53. The pond appears shallower than it actually is, due to:
A. reflection
B. refraction
C. mirage
D. dispersion

54. The disease dropsy affects:
A. stomach
B. spinal cord
C. liver
D. kidney

55. The drug obtained from the bark of cinchona, was used for treating malaria. The synthetic drug which replaced the natural product is :
A. Chloromycetin
B. Chloroquine
C. Tetracycline
D. Ampiciline

56. When there is a decrease in the concentration of oxygen in the blood, the rate of breathing :
A. decreases
B. increases
C. does not change
D. first decreases, then increases

57. These days yellow lamps are frequently used as street light. Which one of the following is used in these lamps :
A. Sodium B. Neon
C. Hydrogen D. Nitrogen

58. The age of a tree, in years, can be ascertained by :
A. its weight
B. its height
C. the number of its annular rings
D. length of its root

59. Which one of the following instruments is used for locating submerged objects

in an ocean?
A. Audiometer
B. Galvanometer
C. Sextant
D. SONAR

60. Match List I and II and select your answer from the codes given below :

List I
(*a*) Hi-Tec City
(*b*) Science City
(*c*) Rocket Launching Centre
(*d*) Central Drug Research Institute

List II
1. Lucknow 2. Thumba
3. Kolkata 4. Hyderabad

Codes :

	(*a*)	(*b*)	(*c*)	(*d*)
A.	1	2	3	4
B.	4	3	2	1
C.	2	3	4	1
D.	1	4	2	3

61. The computer hardware which is of silica can store plenty of data. It is called :
A. Disk
B. Chip
C. Magnetic Tape
D. File

62. What is the function of a pace maker :
A. It decreases the heart beat
B. It regulates the heart beat
C. It increases the heart beat
D. It accelerates blood supply to heart

63. Which of the following is not a name associated with computer manufacturing?
A. HCL B. WIPRO
C. Oracle D. INDAL

64. Which of the following gases is used for purification of water?
A. Oxygen
B. Ammonia
C. Chlorine
D. Carbon dioxide

65. The 'stones' formed in human kidney consist mostly of :
A. calcium oxalate
B. sodium acetate
C. magnesium sulphate
D. calcium

66. Most of the explosions in mines occur due to the mixing of:
A. Hydrogen with oxygen
B. Oxygen with acetylene
C. Methane with air
D. Carbon dioxide with ethane

67. Match List I (Diseases) with List II (Types of disease) and select the correct answer using the codes given below the lists :

List I
(*a*) Haemophilia
(*b*) Diabetes
(*c*) Rickets
(*d*) Ringworm

List II
1. Deficiency disease
2. Genetic disease
3. Hormonal disorder
4. Fungal infection

Codes :

	(*a*)	(*b*)	(*c*)	(*d*)
A.	2	3	4	1
B.	2	3	1	4
C.	3	2	1	4
D.	3	2	4	1

68. The blood glucose level is commonly expressed as:
A. Millimeter of Hg.
B. Milligram per decilitre
C. Parts per million
D. Grammes per litre

69. Match List I (Endocrine glands) with List II (Hormones secreted) and select the correct answer using the codes given below the lists :

List I
(*a*) Gonads
(*b*) Pituitary
(*c*) Pancreas
(*d*) Adrenal

List II
1. Insulin
2. Progesterone
3. Growth hormones
4. Cortisone

Codes :

	(*a*)	(*b*)	(*c*)	(*d*)
A.	3	2	4	1
B.	2	3	4	1
C.	2	3	1	4
D.	3	2	1	4

70. Which one of the following materials is very hard and very ductile?
A. Carborundum
B. Tungsten
C. Cast iron
D. Nichrome

71. Soft drinks such as colas contain significant quantities of:
A. Caffeine B. Nicotine
C. Tannin D. Renin

72. Which one of the following does a TV remote control unit use to operate a TV set?
A. Light waves
B. Sound waves
C. Microwaves
D. Radio waves

73. The deficiency of which of the following vitamins

causes eye diseases?

A. B B. A
C. C D. K

74. Which of the following is *not* a type of broadband internet connection?

A. Cable B. DSL
C. Satellite D. Dial-up

75. Which of the following is considered as a good source of vitamin 'A'?

A. Wheat B. Rice
C. Pulses D. Carrot

76. Barometer is used to measure which of the following?

A. Quantity of heat
B. Electric current
C. Density of liquids
D. Atmospheric pressure

77. Which of the following is *not* caused by bacteria?

A. Tetanus
B. Whooping Cough
C. Pneumonia
D. Rabies

78. At what temperature the readings in the Centigrade and Fahrenheit thermometers will be exactly same?

A. 40 degrees
B. 0 degree
C. Minus 40 degrees
D. None of these

79. The largest known vertebrate is:

A. Elephant
B. Whale
C. Giant Squid
D. Tiger

80. Dialysis is used for the treatement of:

A. Heart
B. Kidneys
C. Lungs
D. None of these

81. The Earth is almost spherical in shape was first stated by:

A. Ptolemy
B. Aryabhatta
C. Pythagoras
D. Copernicus

82. Match List I with List II and select the *correct* answer using the codes given below the lists :

List I

(*a*) Summer Solstice
(*b*) Autumn Equinox
(*c*) Winter Solstice
(*d*) Vernal Equinox

List II

1. March 21 2. June 21
3. Sept. 23 4. Dec. 22

Codes :

	(*a*)	(*b*)	(*c*)	(*d*)
A.	1	4	2	3
B.	2	1	3	4
C.	2	3	4	1
D.	3	2	4	1

83. In any calender year, the *correct* sequence of seasons in the Northern Hemisphere is:

A. autumn, spring, summer, winter
B. spring, autumn, winter, summer
C. summer, autumn, spring, winter
D. winter, spring, summer, autumn

84. The difference in latitude between the Tropic of Cancer and the Tropic of Capricorn is:

A. 23 degrees
B. 47 degrees
C. 66 degrees
D. 90 degrees

85. Across the International Date Line

A. Alaska and Siberia have the same date.
B. Alaska's date is ahead of Siberia's date.
C. Alaska's date is behind Siberia's date.
D. Alaska's date is ahead or behind Siberia's date in alternate years.

86. Consider the following peaks :

1. Kanchanjunga
2. K2
3. Nanga Parbat
4. Nanda Devi

The *correct* sequence of these peaks in *descending* order of their heights is

A. 2, 3, 1, 4 B. 2, 1, 3, 4
C. 1, 2, 3, 4 D. 1, 3, 4, 2

87. Match the List I with List II and select the *correct* answer using the codes given below the lists :

List I
(Mineral areas)

(*a*) Bailadila
(*b*) Bhandara
(*c*) Zawar
(*d*) Hazaribagh

List II
(Mineral deposits associated with these areas)

1. Zinc
2. Iron ore
3. Manganese
4. Mica

Codes :

	(*a*)	(*b*)	(*c*)	(*d*)
A.	2	3	4	1
B.	2	3	1	4
C.	3	2	1	4
D.	3	2	4	1

88. Air coolers are more

suitable for:
A. hot and humid climate
B. hot and dry climate
C. cool and humid climate
D. cool and dry climate

89. Which of the following *does not* provide any energy?
A. Fats
B. Proteins
C. Vitamins
D. Carbohydrates

90. If there is a circular hole in a metal plate, what happens to the radius of the hole when the plate is heated?
A. Increases
B. Decreases
C. Unchanged
D. Depends upon the metal

91. The number of heart-beats on an average in an adult human is in the range of:
A. 60-65 B. 66-70
C. 71-80 D. 85-90

92. The SI unit of heat is ....
A. calorie
B. kilocalorie
C. watt
D. joule

93. Which of the following produces more severe burns?
A. Boiling water
B. Steam
C. Hot air
D. Sun rays

94. Oxygen was discovered by ....
A. Cavendish
B. Scheele
C. Priestley
D. Rutherford

95. Which of the following is not an insect?
A. Butterfly
B. Mosquito
C. Spider
D. Cockroach

96. Air sacs of birds :
A. keep body warm
B. facilitate blood circulation
C. reduce body weight
D. maintain body temperature

97. The total number of bones in the body of man is :
A. 205 B. 206
C. 216 D. 236

98. Liquefied Petroleum Gas is essentially a mixture of:
A. Carbon monoxide and Carbon dioxide
B. Butane and Propane
C. Ethylene, Propylene, Butane and a number of other hydrocarbons roughly in equal proportions
D. Methane and Ethylene

99. Which one of the following is known as the virility vitamin?
A. Vitamin A
B. Vitamin C
C. Vitamin E
D. Vitamin K

100. If a patient advised to include more of yellow fruits, carrots and butter in his food, he is evidently suffering from:
A. Beri-Beri
B. Night blindness
C. Rickets
D. Scurvy

101. What is measured by Hygrometer?
A. Relative density of liquids
B. Pureness of milk
C. Relative humidity
D. Atmospheric pressure

102. Which among the following gives maximum energy?
A. Fats B. Protein
C. Vitamins D. Sugar

103. In coffee .... is the main stimulator.
A. Brussene
B. Cafine
C. Cafeine
D. Phenalyaniline

104. The hardest form of carbon is ....
A. coke B. graphite
C. diamond D. charcoal

105. Consider the following inventions in the textile industry :
1. Spinning Jenny.
2. Power-loom.
3. Water frame
4. Cotton gin.
The correct chronological sequence of these inventions is
A. 1, 3, 2, 4 B. 3, 1, 4, 2
C. 3, 1, 2, 4 D. 1, 3, 4, 2

106. Which of the following instruments is used for recording "Earthquake waves"?
A. Barograph
B. Hydrograph
C. Pantograph
D. Seismograph

107. Who invented aeroplane?
A. Orville & William Wright
B. Benry Ford
C. Boeing
D. Karl Benz

108. In the Kerosene lamp there are holes below the chimney so that:
A. they give way to the escape of smoke

B. the stem is viewed from below
C. supply of oxygen is maintained
D. the heat generated is dissipated through

109. Camels live in deserts without water for a few days. They do so by:
A. using the water stored in their muscles
B. using the fat stored in the hump
C. reducing their metabolic activity
D. reducing water use

110. Average human body temperature is:
A. 40.5°C B. 36.9°C
C. 98.4°C D. 82.4°F

111. Which vitamin participates in blood clotting?
A. D B. A
C. C D. K

112. What is measured by a sling psychrometer?
A. temperature
B. humidity
C. vapour pressure
D. absolute humidity

113. Human nerve cells originate from the embryonic
A. endoderm
B. ectoderm and mesoderm
C. ectoderm
D. mesoderm

114. Common Salt is:
A. sodium Chloride
B. sodium Bicarbonate
C. magnesium Carbonate
D. calcium Carbonate

115. Lime Water contains:
A. sodium hydroxide
B. calcium hydroxide
C. sodium carbonates
D. calcium chloride

116. Chemically, dry ice is:
A. ice formed from pure distilled water
B. solid carbon dioxide
C. solid sulphur dioxide
D. a mixture of ice and common salt

117. A catalyst is a substance which:
A. stops a chemical reaction
B. helps initiate a reaction
C. increases the speed of a reaction
D. decreases the speed of a reaction

118. 'ELISA' test is employed to diagnose:
A. Polio virus
B. AIDS antibodies
C. Tuberculosis bacterium
D. Cancer

119. The gas used for artificial fruit ripening of green fruit is:
A. Ethylene
B. Acetylene
C. Ethane
D. Methane

120. The three elements most needed in common fertilisers are:
A. Sulphur, Phosphorus and Sodium
B. Nitrogen, Potassium and Phosphorous
C. Phosphorous, Sodium and Nitrogen
D. Calcium, Phosphorous and Potassium

121. Which of the following is the lightest gas?
A. Hydrogen B. Helium
C. Nitrogen D. Oxygen

122. Which of the following is considered a good source of Vitamin D?
A. Citrus fruits
B. Wheat
C. Sunlight
D. Cheese

123. Which of the following is considered as a non-conventional source of energy?
A. Coal
B. Hydro electricity
C. Natural Gas
D. Wind power

124. Match List I with List II and select the *correct* answer using the codes given below the lists :

List I
(Names)
(*a*) S.N. Bose
(*b*) S. Chandrasekhar
(*c*) S. Ramanujam
(*d*) Aryabhatta

List II
(Contribution)
1. Theory of numbers
2. Elementary
3. Astronomy
4. Theory of black holes

Codes :

	(*a*)	(*b*)	(*c*)	(*d*)
A.	2	1	4	3
B.	4	3	2	1
C.	2	4	1	3
D.	3	1	4	2

125. Nights are cooler in the deserts than in the plains, because:
A. sand radiates heat more quickly than Earth
B. in deserts the sky remains clear most of time
C. sand absorbs heat more quickly than Earth
D. None of the above

126. What is the average rate of heart beats per minute in a healthy adult person?
A. 86 B. 98
C. 72 D. 64

127. At what level of noise can a person become deaf
A. 25 decibel
B. 45 decibel
C. 95 decibel
D. None of the above

128. It is harmful to sleep under a tree at night because the tree releases :
A. Oxygen
B. Carbon dioxide
C. Carbon mono-oxide
D. Sulphur dioxide

129. Which of the following is not a symptom of heart attack?
A. Chest pain
B. Nausea and Sweating
C. Numbness and aching of arms
D. Pain in legs

130. Which is the gas inside an electric bulb?
A. Oxygen
B. Air
C. Carbon dioxide
D. None of the above

131. Which one of the following apparatuses is used for measuring blood pressure?
A. Sphygmomanometer
B. Pyrometer
C. Manometer
D. Hygrometer

ANSWERS

1	2	3	4	5	6	7	8	9	10
B	B	C	A	A	A	B	D	D	A
11	**12**	**13**	**14**	**15**	**16**	**17**	**18**	**19**	**20**
B	C	A	A	D	A	B	D	D	A
21	**22**	**23**	**24**	**25**	**26**	**27**	**28**	**29**	**30**
B	B	B	B	A	A	A	A	A	C
31	**32**	**33**	**34**	**35**	**36**	**37**	**38**	**39**	**40**
B	A	A	A	A	C	D	A	B	B
41	**42**	**43**	**44**	**45**	**46**	**47**	**48**	**49**	**50**
C	B	B	C	D	A	C	A	B	C
51	**52**	**53**	**54**	**55**	**56**	**57**	**58**	**59**	**60**
C	D	B	D	B	B	A	C	D	B
61	**62**	**63**	**64**	**65**	**66**	**67**	**68**	**69**	**70**
B	B	D	C	A	C	B	B	C	D
71	**72**	**73**	**74**	**75**	**76**	**77**	**78**	**79**	**80**
A	D	B	D	D	D	D	C	B	B
81	**82**	**83**	**84**	**85**	**86**	**87**	**88**	**89**	**90**
B	C	D	B	C	B	B	B	C	A
91	**92**	**93**	**94**	**95**	**96**	**97**	**98**	**99**	**100**
C	D	B	C	C	C	B	B	C	B
101	**102**	**103**	**104**	**105**	**106**	**107**	**108**	**109**	**110**
C	B	B	C	A	D	A	C	B	B
111	**112**	**113**	**114**	**115**	**116**	**117**	**118**	**119**	**120**
D	B	C	A	B	B	C	B	B	B
121	**122**	**123**	**124**	**125**	**126**	**127**	**128**	**129**	**130**
A	C	D	C	A	C	D	B	D	D
131									
A									

CULTURAL SCIENCE

1. Match List I with List II and select the correct answer using the codes given below the Lists :

List I

(*a*) Vishakhadatta
(*b*) Shudraka
(*c*) Kalidasa
(*d*) Vatsyayana

List II

1. Mrichhakatika
2. Ritusamhara
3. Kamasutra
4. Devichandraguptam

Codes :

	(*a*)	(*b*)	(*c*)	(*d*)
A.	1	4	2	3
B.	4	1	3	2
C.	1	4	3	2
D.	4	1	2	3

2. In which one of the following langauges is the *Dalit* writing more conspicuous?
A. Punjabi
B. Assamese
C. Marathi
D. Oriya

3. The first writer to use Urdu as the medium of poetic expression was:
A. Amir Khusrau
B. Mirza Ghalib
C. Bahadur Shah Zafar
D. Faiz

4. The religious text of the Zoroastrians is named as:
A. Torah
B. The Analects
C. Tripatika
D. Zend Avesta

5. Name the music duo which composed music for Raj Kapoor's film 'Bobby'?
A. Laxmikant Pyarelal
B. Shankar Jaikishen
C. Kalyanji Anandji
D. Nadeem Shravan

6. Raja Harishchandra, an early Indian film, was produced by :
A. D.G. Phalke
B. Ashok Kumar
C. Ardeshir Irani
D. None of the above

7. All films are certified by .... before they are publicly exhibited :
A. Films Division
B. National Film Development Corporation (NFDC)
C. Directorate of Advertising and Visual Publicity (DAVP)
D. Central Board of Film Certificate (CBFC)

8. Who among the following is the director of the film 'Taal'?
A. Gulzar
B. Shekhar Kapoor
C. Satish Shah
D. Subhash Ghai

9. Who amongst the following actresses has played the leading role in the film Elizabeth, which was very famous?
A. Gwyneth Paltrow
B. Cate Blanchett
C. Simi Garewal
D. Kim Basinger

10. The film 'Train to Pakistan' is based on the novel of the same name, written by:
A. Bhishma Sahani
B. Khushwant Singh
C. Amrita Pritam
D. Khwaja Ahmed Abbas

11. Most of the odissi performances are based on a famous 12th century poem, Geet Govind, written by
A. Chaitanya
B. Surdas
C. Vidyapati
D. Jaidev

12. The first feature film (talkie) to be produced in India was:
A. Hatimtai
B. Alam Ara
C. Pundalik
D. Raja Harishchandra

13. Who directed the film "Bombay"?
A. Shyam Benegal
B. Meera Nair
C. Shekhar Kapoor
D. Mani Ratnam

14. Late Iftekhar Ahmad was famous in which of the following fields?
A. Acting
B. Singing
C. Music
D. Literature

15. Who among the following is the director of the film 'Kaho Na Pyar Hai'?
A. Subhash Ghai
B. Shekhar Kapoor
C. Ramesh Sippy
D. Rakesh Roshan

16. The character played by Jim Carrey in the movie *Man on Moon* is based on:
A. Andy Kaufman
B. Edwin Aldrin
C. John Glenn
D. Neil Armstrong

17. A popular Hindi film-based on the famous Sanskrit play *Mrichhakatika*, was titled:
A. *Meghadoot*
B. *Amrapali*
C. *Utsav*
D. *Shakuntala*

18. Who composed the song 'Zara Yad Karo Kurbani'?
A. Javed Akhtar
B. Pradeep
C. Nusrat Fateh Ali Khan
D. Raghupati Sahay 'Firaq'

19. Who was the producer of the serial 'Mahabharat'?
A. Shyam Benegal
B. B.R. Chopra
C. Ramanand Sagar
D. Mani Ratnam

20. Which of the following is a folk dance of Rajasthan?
A. Garba B. Dandya
C. Jhumar D. Kathak

21. The famous dancer Mamata Sankar is the daughter of :
A. Ravi Sankar
B. Sachin Sankar
C. Uday Sankar
D. Moni Sankar

22. Which is Maharashtra's well known folk form of musical theatre?
A. Lavni B. Nautanki
C. Tamasha D. Goatha

23. The classical Indian Music has its origin in which of the following :
A. Atharvaveda
B. Rigveda
C. Samaveda
D. Yajurveda

24. Teratali is the folk dance of:
A. Kerala
B. Rajasthan
C. Madhya Pradesh
D. Tamil Nadu

25. 'Karagam', a religious folk dance is associated with:
A. Tamil Nadu
B. Kerala
C. Andhra Pradesh
D. Karnataka

26. Consider the following statements regarding the Chakiarkoothu form of dance :
1. It is performed by Chakiar caste.
2. It cannot be traditionally witnessed by the higher caste Hindus.
3. Mizhavu is the accompanying instrument.
4. Its theatre form is called Koothambalam.

Which of these statements are correct?
A. 1, 3 and 4
B. 1, 2 and 3
C. 2, 3 and 4
D. 1, 2 and 4

27. Which of the following is a classical dance form of Kerala?
A. Kathak
B. Kuchipudi
C. Bharat Natyam
D. Kathakali

28. Which one of the following pairs of folk dance forms and states is *not* correctly matched :
A. Korku : Maharashtra
B. Jhummar : Haryana
C. Thali : Himachal Pradesh
D. Mukna : Manipur

29. Maestro Kishan Maharaja was associated with
A. Shehnai B. Tabla
C. Santoor D. Flute

30. Sitar, Sarangi and Tabla became popular from the period of:
A. The Mughals
B. The Delhi Sultanate
C. The Vardhanas
D. The Guptas

31. Lavani is a:
A. Marathi folk song
B. Musical instrument
C. Well known player of flute
D. Treatise on percussion instruments

32. .... is associated with 'Kathakali' dance.
A. Andhra Pradesh
B. Kerala
C. Uttar Pradesh
D. Tamil Nadu

33. Which one of the following is essentially a solo dance?
A. Kuchipudi
B. Kathak
C. Manipuri
D. Mohiniattam

34. Which one of the following dance forms is associated with Samyukta Panigrahi?
A. Kathakali
B. Mohiniattam
C. Kathak
D. Odissi

35. Which of the following is the folk dance of Meghalaya?
A. Khasi
B. Loho
C. Bamboo Dance
D. Khantum

36. Kuchipudi is a dance drama of which of the following States?
A. Andhra Pradesh
B. Kerala
C. Karnataka
D. Tamil Nadu

37. Which one of the following pairs is not correctly matched?
A. Poor Man's Kathakali : *Ottanthullal*
B. Heir to Devadasi Dance : *Odissi*
C. Dance Form of Urban Origin in Karnataka : *Yakshagana*
D. Manipuri Dance : Related to Vaishnavism

38. Which one of the following pairs is *not* correctly matched?
A. Bharatanatyam : Tamil Nadu
B. Mohiniattam : Orissa
C. Kuchipudi : Andhra Pradesh
D. Bhangra : Punjab

ANSWERS

1	2	3	4	5	6	7	8	9	10
D	C	A	D	A	A	D	D	B	B
11	**12**	**13**	**14**	**15**	**16**	**17**	**18**	**19**	**20**
D	B	D	A	D	D	C	B	B	C
21	**22**	**23**	**24**	**25**	**26**	**27**	**28**	**29**	**30**
C	A	C	B	C	B	D	A	B	B
31	**32**	**33**	**34**	**35**	**36**	**37**	**38**		
A	B	D	D	A	A	C	B		

SPORTS

1. 'The Colonel' is the nickname of which Indian Test Cricketer?
   A. Colonel C.K. Naidu
   B. Rahul Dravid
   C. Mohinder Amarnath
   D. Dilip Vengsarkar
2. The term 'Grandmaster' is used in which of these games?
   A. Judo B. Chess
   C. Bridge D. Karate
3. The term "Derby" is related with which of the following?
   A. Polo
   B. Swimming
   C. Racing
   D. Horse Racing
4. With which game is Geet Sethi associated?
   A. Basketball
   B. Chess
   C. Snooker
   D. Tennis
5. The First Olympic Games were held Olympic (Greece) in the year:
   A. 300 BC
   B. 872 BC
   C. 776 BC
   D. 205 AD
6. Match List I with List II and select the correct answer using the codes given below the Lists :

List I	List II
(*a*) Basketball	1. Lob
(*b*) Bridge	2. Revoke
(*c*) Golf	3. Pivot
(*d*) Tennis	4. Bunker

Codes :

	(*a*)	(*b*)	(*c*)	(*d*)
A.	2	3	1	4
B.	2	3	4	1
C.	3	2	1	4
D.	3	2	4	1

7. How many players are there in each side in the game of Netball?
   A. 11
   B. 6
   C. 9
   D. 7
8. Match the following
   (*a*) Deodhar Trophy
   (*b*) Durand Cup
   (*c*) Davis Cup
   1. Volleyball
   2. Football
   3. Cricket
   4. Tennis

	(*a*)	(*b*)	(*c*)
A.	3	2	4
B.	3	1	4
C.	2	3	1
D.	1	2	4

9. Which of the following is called 'Grand Slam'?
   A. Winning the highest number of medals in the Olympic games
   B. Winning the men's singles title in Wimbledon Championship
   C. Winning the Wimbledon Singles title successively for two years
   D. Winning all thirteen tricks of a deal at one time in the card games of Bridge
10. With which game is the term 'butterfly stroke' associated?
    A. Swimming
    B. Cricket
    C. Gliding
    D. Skiing
11. Who is the first Indian to win the 'International Grand Master' title in Chess?
    A. Anupama Abhayankar
    B. Bhagyashree Sathe Thipsay
    C. Vishwanathan Anand
    D. D.V. Prasad
12. Arjuna Award has been instituted for outstanding contribution in the field of:
    A. social service
    B. literature
    C. art and music
    D. games and sports
13. The term 'Tee' is associated with which of the following sports?
    A. Golf
    B. Table Tennis
    C. Polo
    D. Judo
14. 'Straight from the Heart' is the autobiography of whom among the following?
    A. Imran Khan

B. Kapil Dev
C. Richard Hadlee
D. Ian Botham

15. In which year the Olympic Games were revived at Athens?
A. 1905 B. 1896
C. 1801 D. 1856

16. Which of the following is *not* associated with the game of Hockey?
A. Nehru Trophy
B. Agha Khan Cup
C. Duleep Trophy
D. Dhyan Chand Trophy

17. Baron Pierre de Coubertin, father of the modern Olympic Games, belongs to:
A. Greece B. USA
C. France D. Italy

18. In which continent the Olympic Games have *not* been organised a single time till now?
A. Asia
B. Australia
C. Africa
D. None of these

19. Which village of Jalandhar district of Punjab is called the 'Nursery of Hockey Players'?
A. Makaragaon
B. Sansarpur
C. Belgharia
D. Chakdah

20. Which team won the FIFA 2010 World Cup
A. India
B. Spain
C. England
D. Pakistan

21. Match List I (Player) with List II (Game/Sport) and select the correct answer using the codes given below the Lists:

List I *(Player)*
a. Marat Safin
b. Gopi Chand
c. Michael Owen
d. Nari Contractor

List II *(Game/Sport)*
1. Badminton
2. Football
3. Lawn Tennis
4. Cricket

	(a)	*(b)*	*(c)*	*(d)*
A.	3	2	1	4
B.	4	1	2	3
C.	3	1	2	4
D.	4	2	1	3

22. Abhinav Bindra is a distinguished athlete in which of the following games?
A. Swimming
B. Weightlifting
C. Shooting
D. Archery

23. Cricket was an Olympic event at which of the following Olympics?
A. London, 1908
B. Amsterdam, 1928
C. Paris, 1900
D. Melbourne, 1956

24. In the game of Baseball, distance between each base in a Diamond shaped ground is:
A. 90 ft B. 80 ft
C. 72 ft D. 56 ft

25. Sportsmen and the sports in which they attained world-wide distinction are listed below. Which one is not correct?
A. KD Singh : Hockey
B. Venus Williams : Tennis
C. Pale : Chess
D. Don Bradman : Cricket

26. Davis Cup is associated with the sport of
A. Cricket B. Football
C. Tennis D. Hockey

27. Who was the captain of the Indian official Cricket Test Series against England in 1932?
A. Ranjit Singh Ji
B. The Yuvraj of Patiyala
C. The Maharaja of Porbandar
D. Raja of Baroda

28. Who among the following has not taken more than 500 wickets in Test Cricket?
A. Courtney Walsh
B. M. Murlitharan
C. Shane Warne
D. Richard Hadlee

29. The first winner of "Rajiv Khel Ratna Award" was
A. Geet Sethi
B. Sachin Tendulkar
C. Viswanathan Anand
D. Karnam Malleswari

30. Rovers Cup is associated with which game?
A. Football
B. Boating
C. Rowing
D. Cricket

31. What is the national game of the USA?
A. Cricket
B. Soccer
C. Baseball
D. Billiards

32. Which of the following international tennis tournaments is held on grass court?
A. US Open

B. French Open
C. Wimbledon
D. Australian Open

33. Melbourne is associated with which sport?
A. Cricket
B. Footboll
C. Polo
D. Chess

34. 'Merdeka Cup' is associated with ....
A. Golf
B. Football
C. Squash
D. Hockey

35. Which of the following terms is associated with the game of 'Wrestling'?
A. Revoke
B. Bogey
C. Mallet
D. Half nelson

36. The "Dronacharya Award" is associated with
A. Eminent Surgeons
B. Famous Artists
C. Sport Coaches
D. Expert Engineers

37. Which Cricketer nicknamed 'Jumbo'?
A. Venkatesh Prasad
B. Anil Kumble
C. Glenn McGrath
D. Shane Warne

38. Who among the following has become the first woman in the world to swim across seven seas?
A. Bula Chaudhary
B. Shikha Tandon
C. Amanda Beard
D. Arti Saha

39. Which Indian sportsman is known as Hockey wizard throughout the world?
A. A.B. Subbiah
B. Jude Felix
C. Dhyanchand
D. Ajitpal Singh

40. Number of players on each side of Volley ball, Basket ball and Baseball game are respectively?
A. 5, 6, 9　B. 6, 5, 9
C. 6, 9, 5　D. 6, 5, 7

41. Which of the following teams won the first one-day Cricket World Cup held in 1975?
A. England
B. West Indies
C. Australia
D. Pakistan

ANSWERS

1	2	3	4	5	6	7	8	9	10
D	B	E	C	C	D	D	A	D	A
11	12	13	14	15	16	17	18	19	20
C	D	A	B	B	C	C	C	B	B
21	22	23	24	25	26	27	28	29	30
C	C	C	A	C	C	C	D	C	A
31	32	33	34	35	36	37	38	39	40
C	C	A	B	D	C	B	A	C	B
41									
B									

UNO AND WORLD

1. Which of the following countries is not a member of North Atlantic Treaty Organisation?
   A. Norway
   B. United Germany
   C. Portugal
   D. Australia
2. Khmer Rouge is a dictatorial party of :
   A. Cambodia
   B. Indonesia
   C. Malaysia
   D. Thailand
3. Which country is *not* a member of SAARC?
   A. China
   B. Bangladesh
   C. Nepal
   D. Pakistan
4. The headquarters of WTO is located at :
   A. Geneva
   B. Paris
   C. The Hague
   D. Washington
5. The main function of the World Trade Organisation (WTO) is:
   A. enforcing of Uruguay Round Agreements
   B. facilitating multi-lateral trade relations of member countries and reviewing trade policies
   C. administering trade dispute settlement procedures
   D. None of the above
6. The Secretary-General of the UNO is appointed by the:
   A. General Assembly
   B. Security Council
   C. Trusteeship Council
   D. World Bank
7. The United Nations officially came into existence in 1945 on :
   A. November 24
   B. October 14
   C. October 24
   D. November 14
8. Which one of the following is true of the International Court of Justice?
   A. The Judges of the Court are appointed according to the discretion of the Secretary General
   B. No two Judges may belong to the same country
   C. The Court consists of 20 Judges
   D. The statute of the International Court of Justice is not an integral part of the UN Charter
9. Which of the following was *not* among the six founding countries of the European Community?
   A. Belgium B. France
   C. Germany D. UK
10. The smallest country in South America is:
    A. Ecuador B. Guyana
    C. Surinam D. Uruguay
11. In which year "Human Rights Resolution" was adopted by the U.N.?
    A. 1945 B. 1946
    C. 1947 D. 1948
12. Where is the headquarters of INTERPOL located?
    A. Berlin
    B. California
    C. Lyons
    D. Montreal
13. Parliament of which of the following countries is known as Great People's Khural?
    A. Malaysia
    B. Mongolia
    C. Thailand
    D. Indonesia
14. 'SAPTA' is related to—
    A. Trade
    B. Education
    C. Security
    D. Environment
15. When is the UN Day celebrated?
    A. October 24
    B. January 24
    C. June 24
    D. September 24
16. The charter of the UN was signed on June 26, 1945 at:
    A. San Francisco
    B. Geneva
    C. California
    D. Paris
17. The members of the NAFTA include:

A. USA, Canada and Mexico
B. USA, Canada, Mexico and UK
C. USA, UK, Russia and Mexico
D. USA, Canada and Brazil

18. Which institution is know as 'Soft loan window' of the World Bank?
A. IDA
B. IFC
C. IMF
D. None of these

19. Which of the following countries is being criticised as it failed to pay its dues to the United Nations Organisation (U.N.O.) in full?
A. France
B. Germany
C. Britain
D. USA

20. The headquarter of OPEC is at—
A. Viena
B. Kuwait City
C. Algeria
D. Tehran

21. The headquarters of World Intellectual Property Organisation (WIPO) is located in which of the following cities?
A. Paris
B. Madrid
C. New York
D. Geneva

22. Which of the following is the headquarters of the World Bank?
A. The Hague
B. Washington
C. Paris
D. Geneva

23. Green Index has been developed by:
A. World Bank's environmentally and socially sustainable development division
B. United Nations development programme
C. Kyoto Protocol
D. United Nations environment programme

24. Match List I with List II and select *correct* answer using the codes given below the Lists :

List I
(*a*) WTO
(*b*) IDA
(*c*) IMF
(*d*) IBRD

List II
1. Provides loans to address short-term balance of payment problems.
2. Multilateral trade negotiation body.
3. Sanction of soft loans.
4. Facilitating lendings and borrowings for reconstruction and development.

Codes :

	(*a*)	(*b*)	(*c*)	(*d*)
A.	2	3	4	1
B.	2	3	1	4
C.	3	2	4	1
D.	3	2	1	4

25. Which Indian nationalist leader looked upon a war between Germany and Britain as a godsent opportunity which would enable Indians to exploit the situation to their advantage?
A. C. Rajagopalachari
B. M.A. Jinnah
C. Subhash Chandra Bose
D. Jawaharlal Nehru

26. World Intellectual Property Organisation (WIPO) was formed in the year:
A. 1965
B. 1976
C. 1968
D. 1967

27. Name of the currency of Itlay is—
A. Pounds
B. Lira
C. Dollar
D. Lats

28. International Criminal Court was established in the year:
A. 1995
B. 1996
C. 1997
D. 1998

29. Which country from the following is a permanent member of the UN Security Council?
A. Switzerland
B. People's Republic of China
C. Japan
D. Ukraine

30. The Indian National Army (Azad Hind Fauj) fought in the Second World War against:
A. Germany
B. Japan
C. Italy
D. Great Britain

31. The Headquarters of the International Monetary Fund is located at:
A. Paris
B. Vienna

C. Washington D.C.
D. Geneva

32. Bosnia-Herzegovina formed the part of:
A. Czechoslovakia
B. Yugoslavia
C. Bulgaria
D. Azerbaijan

33. The Sparatly Islands over which Vietnam, Brunei, Malaysia, the Philippines and Taiwan have claims are in the:
A. South China Sea
B. Java Sea
C. Sea of Japan
D. Berino Sea

34. Where is the Headquarters of Asian Development Bank?
A. Washington
B. Paris
C. Manila
D. Canberra

35. The old name of which country was Abissinia?
A. Ethiopia B. Albania
C. Ghana D. Ukraine

36. Which is 'Country of Golden Fleece'?
A. Scotland B. Australia
C. Denmark D. Thailand

37. United Nations World Conference against Racism was held in September, 2001 in
A. New York B. Algiers
C. Harare D. Durban

38. The United Nations University is located in which of the following cities?
A. Geneva
B. New York
C. Paris
D. Tokyo

39. Which of the following countries is *not* a member of the South Asian Association for Regional Cooperation (SAARC)?
A. Bhutan
B. Maldives
C. Bangladesh
D. Myanmar

40. The six official languages of the UN are Russian, Chinese, English, French Spanish and
A. Hindi B. Urdu
C. Arabic D. Japanese

41. Consider the following statements about European Union :
1. The European Union was known early as the European Community.
2. The Single European Act (1986) and the Maastricht Treaty were milestones in its formation.
3. Citizens of the European Union countries enjoy dual citizenship.
4. Switzerland is a member of this European Union.

Which of the above statements are correct?
A. 2 and 4 B. 1 and 3
C. 3 and 4 D. 1, 2 and 3

42. The language spoken by the largest number of people in the world is:
A. Hindi B. English
C. Mandarin D. Spanish

43. Which is the capital of mongolia?
A. Ulan-Bator
B. Doha
C. Hanoi
D. Beirut

44. *Majlis* is the parliament of which country?
A. Israel B. Iraq
C. Egypt D. Iran

45. Which country is known as the 'Land of Thousand Lakes'?
A. Norway B. Finland
C. Canada D. Ireland

46. The headquarters of UNESCO is situated at
A. The Hague
B. Washington
C. New York
D. Paris

47. In the United Nations, the five Big Powers enjoy the right to Veto in the:
A. General Assembly
B. Security Council
C. Economic and Social Council
D. Trusteeship Council

48. 'MFN clause' is one of the main pillars on which
A. WTO is based
B. IMF is based
C. IBRD is based
D. IDA is based

49. Which *one* of the following pairs takes care of the trade and economic interests of the developing countries at the international level?
A. G-15 and G-7
B. G-15 and G-77
C. G-7 and G-24
D. G-77 and G-24

50. Which of the following is the smallest country of the world?
A. Uganda
B. Bhutan

C. Vatican City
D. Sri Lanka

51. Which of the following is *not* an agency of United Nations Organisation?
A. UNDP
B. OPEC
C. WTO
D. UNHCR

52. In which one of the following countries is the "Head of the State" hereditary?
A. Pakistan
B. Japan
C. Canada
D. Bangladesh

53. Given below are two statements, one labelled as *Assertion (A)* and the other labelled as *Reason (R)* :
Assertion (A) : India is a member of G-77.
Reason (R) : India is a member of SAARC.
In the context of the above two statements, which one of the following is correct?
A. Both A and R are true and R is the correct explanation of A
B. Both A and R are true but R is not a correct explanation of A
C. A is true but R is false
D. A is false but R is true

54. W.T.O. came into existence in :
A. January 1995
B. January 1996
C. January 1997
D. January 1990

ANSWERS

1	2	3	4	5	6	7	8	9	10
D	A	A	A	B	A	C	B	D	C
11	**12**	**13**	**14**	**15**	**16**	**17**	**18**	**19**	**20**
A	C	B	A	A	A	A	A	D	A
21	**22**	**23**	**24**	**25**	**26**	**27**	**28**	**29**	**30**
D	B	D	B	C	D	B	D	B	D
31	**32**	**33**	**34**	**35**	**36**	**37**	**38**	**39**	**40**
C	B	A	C	A	B	D	D	D	C
41	**42**	**43**	**44**	**45**	**46**	**47**	**48**	**49**	**50**
D	C	A	D	B	D	B	A	B	C
51	**52**	**53**	**54**						
B	B	B	A						

BOOKS AND AUTHORS

1. Who is the author of the book 'PRISON DIARY'?
   A. Bal Gangadhar Tilak
   B. Rajendra Prasad
   C. Jai Prakash Narayan
   D. Jawahar Lal Nehru
2. Who is the author of 'Satanic Verses'?
   A. Lewis Carrol
   B. Salman Rushdie
   C. Parry Mason
   D. Mulk Raj Anand
3. Who wrote 'Gitanjali'?
   A. Kalidas
   B. Gopal Das 'Neeraj'
   C. Rabindra Nath Tagore
   D. Jawahar Lal Nehru
4. Who, among the following, scholars flourishing during the Gupta Age, was the author of *Dasakumara-Charita?*
   A. Asanga B. Dignaga
   C. Dandina D. Bhattin
5. The author of *Gitagovinda* was:
   A. Halayudha
   B. Jayadeva
   C. Kalhana
   D. Jona-raja
6. "Ingenious Pain" is a book/novel written by :
   A. Andrew Miller
   B. Santa Monica
   C. Ben Johnson
   D. Bill Gates
7. Who amongst the following is the author of the famous book "An Equal Music"?
   A. Salman Rushdie
   B. Shasthivrata
   C. Vikram Seth
   D. Kamla Markandeya
8. The famous Moorti Devi Award is given for excellence in which of the following fields?
   A. Medicine
   B. Science & Technology
   C. Social Service
   D. Journalism
9. Who has written "Devdas"?
   A. Tarasankar Bandyopadhyay
   B. Bankim Chandra Chattopadhyay
   C. Rabindranath Tagore
   D. Sarat Chandra Chattopadhyay
10. "Ain-i-Akbari" is written by:
    A. Todar Mal
    B. Abul Fazal
    C. Sheikh Saadi
    D. Mirza Ghalib
11. "Alice in Wonderland" is written by :
    A. Lewis Carrol
    B. Chester Bowles
    C. Charles Dickens
    D. Jonathan Swift
12. "Mrichchhakatikam" is written by :
    A. Vishakhadatta
    B. Vatsyayana
    C. Sudraka
    D. Bana Bhatt
13. "My Experiments with Truth" is written by :
    A. Jawaharlal Nehru
    B. M.K. Gandhi
    C. Abul Kalam Azad
    D. Rajendra Prasad
14. Who wrote the book "India Wins Freedom"?
    A. Maulana Abul Kalam Azad
    B. Mahatma Gandhi
    C. Sir Mohammad Iqbal
    D. Abdul Gaffar Khan
15. Match List I with List II and select the correct answer using the codes given below the Lists :

    List I
    (*a*) *Condition of India*
    (*b*) *Mother India*
    (*c*) *Farewell to India*
    (*d*) *Passage to India*

    List II
    1. Edward Thompson
    2. E.M. Forster
    3. India League
    4. Katherine Mayo

    Codes :

	(*a*)	(*b*)	(*c*)	(*d*)
A.	2	1	4	3
B.	3	4	1	2
C.	3	1	2	4
D.	4	2	1	3
16. 'Poverty and Un British Rule in India' written by:
    A. R.C. Dutt
    B. J.L. Nehru
    C. D.B. Naoroji
    D. S.N. Sen

17. Name the author of the book *A Passage to England:*
A. E.M. Forster
B. Nirad C. Choudhuri
C. Vikram Seth
D. Eric Segal

18. The author of the book 'The Struggle in My Life' is:
A. Mandela
B. J.L. Nehru
C. Tilak
D. Gokhale

19. Who amongst the following is the author of the book 'The White Tiger'?
A. Arvind Adiga
B. Arundhati Roy
C. Michael Portillo
D. Bon Okri

20. Which of the following books is not written by Salman Rushdie?
A. The Satanic Verses
B. Shame
C. Naked Face
D. Midnight's Children

21. Who is the author of the book 'My Frozen Turbulence in Kashmir'?
A. Anita Desai
B. Kushwant Singh
C. Arun Shourie
D. Jagmohan

22. Who is the author of the book, *The God of Small Things*?
A. Mrinal Pandey
B. Shekhar Kapur
C. Arundhati Roy
D. Arun Shourie

23. *Harshcharita* was written by :
A. Banbhatt
B. Harsha Vardhan
C. Kalidas
D. Jaidev

24. Who is the author of *A Tale of Two Cities*?
A. D.H. Lawrence
B. R.L. Stevenson
C. Charles Dickens
D. William Shakespeare

25. *Long Walk to Freedom* is the autobiography of:
A. Martin Luther King
B. Nelson Mandela
C. Fidel Castro
D. Farookh Abdullah

26. "The Arctic Home of the Vedas" was written by :
A. Acharya Vinobha Bhave
B. Minoo Masani
C. S. Radhakrishnan
D. Bal Gangadhar Tilak

27. 'Neel Darpan', is a play written by:
A. Din Bandhu Mitra
B. Harish Ch. Mukherji
C. Tagore
D. Bankim Chandra

28. Who is the author of the book *'Business at the Speed of Thought'*?
A. Bill Gates
B. Robert Whiting
C. T.R. Reid
D. Peter Drunker

29. Mr. Dario Fo is the author of which of the following books?
A. News of Kidnapping
B. Taming the Waters
C. Beach Boy
D. Accidental Death of an Anarchist

30. Match the List I with List II and select the *correct* answer using the codes given below the Lists :

List I
(Books)
(*a*) *The First Indian War of Independence*
(*b*) *Anand Math*
(*c*) *Life Divine*
(*d*) *Sadhana*

List II
(Authors)
1. Rabindranath Tagore
2. Sri Aurobindo
3. Bankim Chandra Chatterji
4. Vinayak Damodar Savarkar

Codes :

	(*a*)	(*b*)	(*c*)	(*d*)
A.	4	3	2	1
B.	3	4	1	2
C.	4	3	1	2
D.	3	4	2	1

31. "In Custody" an English novel, is written by which one of the following?
A. V.S. Naipaul
B. Vikram Seth
C. Anita Desai
D. Shobha De

32. The *Tunnel of Time* is the autobiography of:
A. I.K. Gujral
B. Vishwanath Pratap Singh
C. Chandrashekhar
D. R.K. Laxman

33. *Half A Life* is the autobiography of
A. Amrita Pritam
B. V.S. Naipaul
C. Khushwant Singh
D. Dominique Lappierre

34. Who is the author of the book *Wings of Fire*?
A. Vikram Seth
B. A.P.J. Abdul Kalam

C. Arundhati Roy
D. M.J. Akbar

35. Who is the author of the lyric poetry 'Gitagovinda'?
A. Vyas
B. Lord Krishna
C. Jayadev
D. Adi Sankaracharya

36. Which of the following is not a book written by Nobel Laureate V.S. Naipaul?
A. An Area of Darkness
B. A Wounded Civilisation
C. A Bend in the River
D. Against the Grain

37. Which one of the following statements is not correct?
A. 'Neel Darpan' was a play based on the exploitation of the indigo farmers
B. The author of the play 'Ghasiram Kotwal' is Vijay Tendulkar
C. The play 'Navanna' by Nabin Chandra Das was based on the famine of Bengal
D. Urdu theatre was used to depend heavily on Parsi theatre

38. The book *Adha Likha Dastavej* is written by
A. Indira Goswami
B. Kedarnath Singh
C. Nirmal Verma
D. Giriraj Kishore

39. The Book 'Shadow of a Princess' is a first-hand account of Princess Diana's life. It is written by
A. Patrick Jepson
B. Byron Lord
C. Clive Ponting
D. James Jeans

40. Match the following List I with List II and select the correct answer from the code below :

List I
(Authors)
(*a*) Mahatma Gandhi
(*b*) Ram Manohar Lohia
(*c*) Dr. Rajendra Prasad
(*d*) Abul Kalam Azad

List II
(Books)
1. India Divided
2. India Wins Freedom
3. Hind Swaraj
4. The Wheel of the History

Codes :

	(*a*)	(*b*)	(*c*)	(*d*)
A.	1	3	4	2
B.	4	3	2	1
C.	3	4	1	2
D.	2	3	4	1

41. Anand Math was written by:
A. Rabindranath Tagore
B. Bankim Chandra Chattopadhyay
C. Aurobindo
D. Madhusudan Dutta

42. Who amongst the following is the author of the famous book "The Dark Side of Chameleot"?
A. Seymour Hersh
B. Salman Rushdie
C. Nirad C. Chaudhuri
D. Shobha De
E. None of the above

43. The book "Doctor Zhivago" is written by
A. John Gray
B. Boris Pasternak
C. Dean Ornish
D. Ardeshir Vakil

44. "A Brush with Life: An Autobiography" is written by
A. M.F. Hussain
B. Satish Gujral
C. Sudhir Dar
D. R.K. Laxman

45. Who has written 'Hind Swaraj'?
A. Bal Gangadhar Tilak
B. Vinoba Bhave
C. Chandra Shekhar Azad
D. Mahatma Gandhi

46. Whose work is 'Bijak'?
A. Surdas
B. Kabir
C. Ravidas
D. Peepaji

47. Who wrote the novel 'Mrignayani'?
A. Vrandavan Lal Verma
B. Acharya Chatursen
C. Amrat Lal Nagar
D. Bhagwati Charan Verma

48. Who among the following wrote "Unhappy India"?
A. Lala Lajpat Rai
B. Maulana Abul Kalam Azad
C. Annie Besant
D. Mahatma Gandhi

ANSWERS

1	2	3	4	5	6	7	8	9	10
C	B	C	C	B	A	C	D	D	B

11	12	13	14	15	16	17	18	19	20
A	C	B	A	B	C	B	A	A	C
21	**22**	**23**	**24**	**25**	**26**	**27**	**28**	**29**	**30**
D	C	A	C	B	D	A	A	D	A
31	**32**	**33**	**34**	**35**	**36**	**37**	**38**	**39**	**40**
A	D	B	B	C	D	D	A	A	C
41	**42**	**43**	**44**	**45**	**46**	**47**	**48**		
B	A	B	B	D	B	A	A		

PERSONS

1. The different schools of modern socialism derive their strength primarily from the writings of ....?
   A. Joseph Stalin
   B. Leo Tolstoy
   C. Mao Tse-tung
   D. Karl Marx
2. Baba Amte was famous as a ....
   A. Painter
   B. Singer
   C. Politician
   D. Social Worker
3. Who is the first Indian to join the Formula One League?
   A. Narain Karthikeyan
   B. Karun Chandok
   C. Kasam Khan
   D. N. Anbu
4. Who was the political guru of Gandhiji?
   A. Dadabhai Naoroji
   B. Bal Gangadhar Tilak
   C. Lala Lajpat Rai
   D. Gopal Krishna Gokhale
5. Sundarlal Bahuguna, a famous environmentalist, is associated with :
   A. Chipko Movement
   B. Narmada Bachao
   C. Satyagraha
   D. Anti-corruption
6. Mother Teressa's native place was :
   A. Albania B. France
   C. Greece D. Italy
7. The live polio vaccine which can be taken by mouth was developed by :
   A. Albert Sabin
   B. Edward Jenner
   C. Jonas Salk
   D. Selman Waksman
8. Which one of the following authors put forth the theory of the Drain of India's resources to England?
   A. Raja Rammohan Roy
   B. Bankim Chandra Chatterjee
   C. G.G. Agarkar
   D. Dadabhai Naoroji
9. The "Last Supper" is a famous renaissance painting. It was a master-piece of :
   A. Michael Angelo
   B. Leonardo da Vinci
   C. Titian
   D. Raphael
10. Dhyanchand is associated with which sports?
    A. Badminton
    B. Hockey
    C. Tennis
    D. Football
11. 'Man is born free, yet every where he is in chains'. This was said by:
    A. Voltaire
    B. John Stuart Mill
    C. Rousseau
    D. Karl Marx
12. Who among the following was a prominent social reformer?
    A. Baba Gurmukh Singh
    B. Raja Mahendra Pratap
    C. Bipin Chandra Pal
    D. Jotiba Govind Phule
13. Lord Hunt, was associated with which of the following fields?
    A. Politics
    B. Music
    C. Economics
    D. None of these
14. Who was known as "Man of Destiny"?
    A. Napoleon
    B. Nehru
    C. Hitler
    D. Mussolini
15. Who discovered that mosquito served as a carrier of malaria?
    A. Jonas Salk
    B. Ronald Ross
    C. Louis Pasteur
    D. Robert Koch
16. Who was the first woman Governor of an Indian State?
    A. Sushila Nayar
    B. Sucheta Kripalani
    C. Sarojini Naidu
    D. Sulochana Modi
17. Who among the following founded the Bhartiya Jana Sangh?
    A. Deen Dayal Upadhyaya
    B. Veer Savarkar
    C. Dr. Ram Manohar Lohia
    D. Dr. Shyama Prasad Mukherjee

18. Who among the following President of India held his office for two successive terms?
A. V.V. Giri
B. Dr. Rajendra Prasad
C. Dr. S Radhakrishnan
D. None of these

19. Ustad Amjad Ali Khan is an exponent of:
A. Flute B. Sitar
C. Sarod D. Tabla

20. Who is the first non-Indian to receive the Bharat Ratna?
A. Martin Luther King
B. Zubin Mehta
C. Mother Teressa
D. Khan Abdul Ghaffar Khan

21. Who among of the following was an extremist?
A. Bal Gangadhar Tilak
B. Mahatma Gandhi
C. G.K. Gokhale
D. Dadabhai Nauroji

22. Who among the following Congress leaders was called the 'Grand Old Man' of India?
A. Mahatma Gandhi
B. Bal Gangadhar Tilak
C. Dadabhai Naoroji
D. Madan Mohan Malaviya

23. The first UN Secretary General was:
A. Javier Perez de Cuellar
B. U Thant
C. Tryguve Lie
D. Kurt Waldheim

24. The pioneer of Bhakti Movement in India was:
A. Kabir
B. Ramananda
C. Shankaracharya
D. Ramanuj

25. In which of the following did Sardar Vallabhbhai Patel play a leading role?
A. Bijolia Movement
B. Dandi March
C. Textile Mill workers strike at Ahmedabad
D. Bardoli Satyagraha

26. One-time associate of Mahatma Gandhi, broke off from him and launched a radical movement called 'self-respect movement'. Who was he?
A. P. Thyagaraja Shetu
B. Chhatrapati Maharaj
C. E.V. Ramaswamy Naicker
D. Jyotirao Govindrao Phule

27. Who among the following is renowned in Hindustani classical music (vocal)?
A. Shovana Narayan
B. M.S. Subbulakshmi
C. Pt. Jasraj
D. M.S. Gopalakrishnan

28. Who among the following won the Nobel Prize twice?
A. Winston Churchill
B. Madame Curie
C. Octavio Paz
D. George Choupak

29. MK Gandhi was born on October 2. Another famous Indian leader also born on this day was:
A. Lal Bahadur Shastri
B. Sardar Patel
C. Rajendra Prasad
D. J.L. Nehru

30. Name the person who became the first woman, the first Asian and the first Muslim to head (Secretary-General) the human rights watchdog, Amnesty International.
A. Ikno Hirayana
B. Irene Zubaida Khan
C. Gloria Arroya
D. Dame Silvia

31. Anna Hazare is known for :
A. Watershed Development
B. Rural Education
C. Tribal Development
D. Co-operative Development

32. Jayadeva, the lyricist of the Gita Govinda, adorned the court of :
A. Dharmpala
B. Devapala
C. Vijayasena
D. Lakshmansena

33. Adi Shankar who later on became Shankaracharya was born in :
A. Kashmir
B. Kerala
C. Andhra Pradesh
D. West Bengal

34. Pt. Shiv Kumar Sharma is a maestro of which one of the following instruments?
A. Sitar B. Tabla
C. Flute D. Santoor

35. The first writer to use Urdu as the medium of poetic expression was:
A. Amir Khusrou
B. Mirza Ghalib
C. Bahadur Shah Zafar
D. Faiz

36. Match *List I* with *List II* and select the correct answer using the codes given below the Lists :

List I

(*a*) Pandit Vishnu Digamber Paluskar

(*b*) Venkatamahi
(*c*) Shyama Shastri
(*d*) Amir Khusrou

List II

1. Introduced the scheme of *Raga* classification of Indian music
2. Proponent of Carnatic music
3. Proponent of the *Khayal* form of Hindustani music
4. Wrote the music for the song *Vande Mataram*

Codes :

	(*a*)	(*b*)	(*c*)	(*d*)
A.	4	1	3	2
B.	4	1	2	3
C.	1	4	3	2
D.	1	4	2	3

37. The Sufi Saint who maintained that devotional music was one way of coming close to God was:
A. Moin-ud-din Chisti
B. Baba Farid
C. Saiyyad Muhammad Gesudaraz
D. Shah Alam Bukhari

38. Match List I with List II and select the correct answer using the codes given below the lists :

List I

(*a*) T. Balasaraswathi
(*b*) Uma Sharma
(*c*) Indrani Rahman
(*d*) Raja and Radha Reddy

List II

1. Kuchipudi
2. Odissi
3. Kathak
4. Bharatanatyam

Codes :

	(*a*)	(*b*)	(*c*)	(*d*)
A.	3	4	2	1
B.	2	1	4	3
C.	4	3	2	1
D.	1	2	4	3

39. Who amongst the following is associated with "Microsoft"?
A. Andrew Grove
B. Bill Gates
C. Ted Turner
D. Rupert Murdoch

40. 'Royal Asiatic Society' was founded by:
A. Sir William Jones
B. Sir John Marshall
C. R.D. Banerjee
D. Sir William Bentinck

41. Who was the Guru of Kabir?
A. Ramanuja
B. Ramananda
C. Vallabhacharya
D. Namadeva

42. The reputed musician duo, Tansen and Baiju Bawra, flourished during the reign of:
A. Jehangir
B. Bahadur Shah Zafar
C. Akbar
D. Shah Jahan

43. The headquarters of the establishment of Dalai Lama is:
A. Bodh Gaya
B. Dharamshala
C. Sanchi
D. Periyar

44. Tiger Woods, the famous Golf player is from which country?
A. Australia
B. USA
C. Canada
D. England

45. Who among the following personalities from the field of music is associated with Violin?
A. Pt. Bhimsen Joshi
B. Pt. V.G. Jog
C. Pt. Shiv Kumar Sharma
D. M.S. Subbulakshmi

46. "Non-violence is the law of our species as violence is the law of the brute. But where there is only a choice between cowardice and violence, I would rather have India resort to violence to defend her honour than that she should, in a cowardly manner become or remain a helpless witness to her own dishonour." This was said by:
A. Jawaharlal Nehru
B. Subhash Chandra Bose
C. Mahatma Gandhi
D. Bal Gangadhar Tilak

47. Dr. M.S. Subbulakshmi had distinguished herself in the field of:
A. Kathak
B. Bharatha Natyam
C. Playing Violin
D. Vocal Music

48. The Khalsa Panth was founded by:
A. Guru Nanak Dev
B. Guru Teg Bahadur
C. Guru Hargobind
D. Guru Gobind Singh

49. 'Abinava Bharat' a secret society of revolutionaries was organised by:
A. Khudiram Bose
B. V.D. Savarkar
C. Prafulla Chaki
D. Bhagat Singh

50. Match List I with List II and select the correct answer using the codes given below the lists :

List I
(Persons)
(*a*) Shyamji Krishna Varma
(*b*) Madame Bhikaji Cama
(*c*) Annie Besant
(*d*) Aurobindo Ghosh

List II
(Journals)
1. *Bande Mataram*
2. *Indian Sociologist*
3. *The Talwar*
4. *Commonwealth*

Codes :

	(*a*)	(*b*)	(*c*)	(*d*)
A.	2	3	4	1
B.	3	2	1	4
C.	2	3	1	4
D.	3	2	4	1

51. Who won the Man Booker Prize for a 16th Century story 'Wolf Hall'?
A. J.M. Caetzee
B. Simon Mawer
C. Hilary Mantel
D. A.S. Byatt

52. The Greek philosopher who wrote nothing Yet (who) is the most famous and that greatest figure in the world, he was
A. Marcus Aurelius
B. Plato
C. Aristotle
D. Socrates

53. Who compiled the first Guru Granth Sahib?
A. Guru Ram Das
B. Guru Teg Bahadur
C. Guru Har Kishan
D. Guru Arjun Dev

54. Match List I with List II and select the correct answer using the codes given below the lists :

List I
(*a*) Mahatma Gandhi
(*b*) Bal Gangadhar Tilak
(*c*) Subhash Chandra Bose
(*d*) Swami Vivekananda

List II
1. "Dilli Chalo"
2. "Tilak and Non-violence are my God".
3. "Swaraj is my birth right"
4. "Arise, Awake"

Codes :

	(*a*)	(*b*)	(*c*)	(*d*)
A.	1	2	4	3
B.	2	1	4	3
C.	2	4	3	1
D.	2	3	1	4

55. Who amongst the following is the first to win a Nobel Prize?
A. Rabindranath Tagore
B. Rudyard Kipling
C. Dr. C.V. Raman
D. Prof. Amartya Sen

56. Who amidst the following has distinguished as a carnatic musician (vocal)?
A. T.N. Krishnan
B. Dr. N. Rajam
C. B. Krishnamurthi Shastrigal
D. T.R. Mahalingam

57. The *Sati* system was abolished mainly because of the efforts of:
A. the British
B. Raja Ram Mohan Roy
C. the Missionaries
D. Maharishi Karve

58. Maoze Dong was the leader of the Communist Movement of:
A. Myanmar
B. Malaysia
C. China
D. Mongolia

59. "Swaraj is my birth right and I shall have it." Who said it?
A. Aurobindo Ghose
B. Mahatma Gandhi
C. Subhash Chandra Bose
D. Bal Gangadhar Tilak

60. Who had discovered North America in 1497?
A. John Cabot
B. Vasco de Gama
C. Columbus
D. James Cook

61. Who amongst the following is renowned in the field of painting?
A. Parveen Sultana
B. Prof. T.N. Krishnan
C. Ram Kinkar
D. Raja Ravi Varma

62. *Dhrupad Dhamar* style of singing was started by:
A. Amir Khusro
B. Raja Man Singh Tomar
C. Tansen
D. Vishnu Digambar Paluskar

63. Match List I with List II and select the *correct* answer using the codes given below the Lists :

List I
(*a*) W.C. Banerjee
(*b*) Annie Besant
(*c*) Madanlal Dhingra
(*d*) Motilal Nehru

List II
1. Home Rule Movement
2. Indian Revolutionary
3. Swaraj Party
4. First President of Indian National Congress

Codes :

	(*a*)	(*b*)	(*c*)	(*d*)
A.	1	4	3	2
B.	1	4	2	3

C. 4 1 3 2
D. 4 1 2 3

64. Who is Medha Patkar?
A. Singer
B. Dancer
C. Painter
D. Social Activist

65. Which one of the following is *not* correctly matched?
A. Ravi Shankar–Sitarist
B. M.F. Hussain–Tabla Player
C. R.K. Narayan–Novelist
D. Kaifi Azmi–Poet

66. Who said, "You give me blood, I will give you freedom"?
A. Mahatma Gandhi
B. Bal Gangadhar Tilak
C. Subhash Chandra Bose
D. Bhagat Singh

67. Which one of the following is contrary to the basic teachings of Mahatma Gandhi?
A. Politics devoid of religion is immoral
B. That government is best which governs the least
C. Ends justify means
D. Economic equally can be practised only through trusteeship

ANSWERS

1	**2**	**3**	**4**	**5**	**6**	**7**	**8**	**9**	**10**
D	D	A	D	A	A	A	D	B	B
11	**12**	**13**	**14**	**15**	**16**	**17**	**18**	**19**	**20**
C	D	D	A	B	C	D	B	C	D
21	**22**	**23**	**24**	**25**	**26**	**27**	**28**	**29**	**30**
A	C	C	D	D	C	B	B	A	B
31	**32**	**33**	**34**	**35**	**36**	**37**	**38**	**39**	**40**
D	D	B	D	A	B	A	C	B	A
41	**42**	**43**	**44**	**45**	**46**	**47**	**48**	**49**	**50**
B	C	B	B	B	C	D	D	B	A
51	**52**	**53**	**54**	**55**	**56**	**57**	**58**	**59**	**60**
C	D	D	D	B	C	B	C	D	A
61	**62**	**63**	**64**	**65**	**66**	**67**			
D	B	D	D	B	C	C			

HONOURS AND AWARDS

1. Which of the following prizes is given by the UNESCO for popularisation of Science?
   A. Visvesvarayya Award
   B. UNESCO Peace Prize
   C. Shanti Swaroop Bhatnagar Award
   D. Kalinga Prize
2. Dr. C.V. Raman was awarded Nobel Prize in:
   A. Chemistry
   B. Physics
   C. Literature
   D. Medicine
3. Famous 'Oscar Awards' are presented by the:
   A. American Motion Pictures Association
   B. Academy of Motion Pictures Arts and Sciences
   C. World Film Society
   D. American Film Society
4. Who among the following was the first recipient of the Rajiv Gandhi Khel Ratna Award?
   A. Viswanathan Anand
   B. Dhanraj Pillai
   C. Homi Motivala
   D. Bahadur Prasad
5. The award which is an equal to Nobel Prize in Architecture is:
   A. Pulitzer Prize
   B. Pitzker Prize
   C. Abel Prize
   D. None of the above
6. Who among the following has not been honoured with Bharat Ratna posthumously?
   A. Vallabh Bhai Patel
   B. Pandit Madan Mohan Malviya
   C. Lok Nayak Jayaprakash Narayan
   D. Vinoba Bhave
7. Professor Amartya Sen has been honoured with the:
   A. UNESCO Peace Prize
   B. Nobel Prize in Economics
   C. Bharat Ratna
   D. Both B and C
8. Dhanvantari Awards are given for the best performance in the field of:
   A. Space Research
   B. Nuclear Sciences
   C. Economics
   D. Medical Sciences
9. Nobel Prizes are *not* given for which of the following fields?
   A. Physics
   B. Chemistry
   C. Peace
   D. Music
10. Which of the following awards is *not* given for excellence in the field of sports and games?
    A. Rajiv Gandhi Award
    B. Dhyan Chand Award
    C. Vyas Samman
    D. Arjun Awards

ANSWERS

1	2	3	4	5	6	7	8	9	10
D	B	B	A	B	B	D	D	D	C

MISCELLANEOUS–DAYS, COMMISSIONS (WOMEN, CHILDREN ETC.)

1. Which of the following is observed as AIDS Day?
   A. 1st December
   B. 11th December
   C. 21st December
   D. 31st December
2. Which of the following is observed as "International Disabled Day"?
   A. 2nd December
   B. 12th December
   C. 22nd December
   D. None of these
3. When is the "International Women's Day" observed?
   A. March 8
   B. February 14
   C. May 10
   D. October 2
4. Pick out the wrong combination :
   A. Flag Day : December 7
   B. Children's Day : November 14
   C. Martyrs' Day : January 30
   D. Teachers' Day : December 10
5. 'National Science Day' is observed every year on:
   A. February 28
   B. April 5
   C. November 19
   D. October 2
6. Which of the following places is known as the Mecca of temple architecture?
   A. Ajanta B. Khajuraho
   C. Konark D. Gaya
7. On which of the following days the World Human Rights Day is celebrated?
   A. December 3
   B. December 10
   C. December 17
   D. December 25
8. Match List I with List II and select the correct answer using the codes given below:

   List I
   (*a*) World T.B. Day
   (*b*) World AIDS Day
   (*c*) Anti Leprosy Day
   (*d*) International Ozone Day

   List II
   1. December 1
   2. January 30
   3. September 16
   4. March 26

   Codes :

	(*a*)	(*b*)	(*c*)	(*d*)
A.	4	1	2	3
B.	3	4	1	2
C.	2	3	4	1
D.	1	2	3	4

9. Minorities Rights Day in India is observed on—
   A. December 15
   B. December 25
   C. December 18
   D. None of these
10. Which of the following days is observed as World Food Day?
    A. September 23
    B. September 15
    C. October 23
    D. October 16
11. Which of the following is not a Computer language?
    A. Windows 2007
    B. PASCAL
    C. C++
    D. FORTRAN
12. When you call frequently "May-Day"?
    A. Day of Happiness
    B. Sign of Danger
    C. New Year
    D. First May
13. OTIS is brand name of:
    A. Software
    B. Shoes
    C. Lift and elevators
    D. Chemical and Paints
14. Dove is a symbol of :
    A. Mourning B. Peace
    C. War D. Joy
15. Who is the Supreme Commander of the Armed Forces?
    A. President
    B. Prime Minister

C. General
D. Field Marshal

16. There is a traditional flower arrangement called Athapoo. In which festival is this used?
A. Onam
B. Rath Yatra
C. Teej
D. Pongal

17. Which day is celebrated as the International Labour Day?
A. 1st January
B. 21st July
B. 31st December
D. 1st May

18. The World Health Day is observed on:
A. 24th October
B. 5th September
C. 4th November
D. 7th April

19. "The International Day of the Disabled" is observed on which of the following days?
A. 30th January
B. 8th December
C. 14th November
D. None of these

ANSWERS

1	2	3	4	5	6	7	8	9	10
A	D	A	D	A	C	B	A	C	D
11	12	13	14	15	16	17	18	19	
A	D	C	B	A	A	D	D	D	

General English

TENSE

1. The tense of a verb shows the time of an action or event. It also indicates the state of an action.
2. The following are the principal tenses of verb in the English language.
   (*a*) The Present Tense
   (*b*) The Past Tense
   (*c*) The Future Tense
3. Each of these three tenses has four forms. They are:
   (*a*) Indefinite
   (*b*) Continuous
   (*c*) Perfect
   (*d*) Perfect Continuous

PRESENT TENSE

4. To describe repeated actions or habits.
   Ex: I always speak the truth.
   She reads the newspaper everyday.
5. To describe facts which are true of all times.
   Ex: The sun rises in the east.
   The earth moves round the sun.
   Honesty is the best policy.
6. To make general statements.
   Ex: She speaks English better than she writes it.
   People speak English all over the world.
7. To express a future planned action.
   Ex: He leaves for U.S.A. next week.
8. In exclamatory sentences beginning with here or there.
   Ex: There she goes?
   Here comes the train?
9. In clauses after conjunctions of times or Condition, when the main clause is in the future.
   Ex: She will come if you invite her.
   You will not pass if you do not work hard.
10. When reference is made to an author's writings, whether the author is dead or alive.
    Ex: Keats says: A thing of beauty is a joy for ever.
11. In radio commentaries on, for instance, football and cricket matches.
    Ex: Ram passes the ball to Syam, dashes forward, passes again, gets it back again, and kicks it up the field.
12. To summarise a play or story, or describe a past event in a vivid or dramatic manner.
    Ex: When the scene opens, Mr. Ram Bahadur is sitting on a chair at the left corner of the hall. The phone rings: He takes it up. Just then the door opens and his wife enters.

The Present Continuous Tense is used in the following ways:

13. For an action going on at the time of speaking.
    Ex: They are playing football.
    It is raining.
14. To express an action going on over a period of time including the present, but which may not be going on actually at the moment of speaking.
    Ex: She is learning to drive.
    I am writing a novel.
15. For an action that is planned or arranged to take place definitely in the near future.
    Ex: He is going to Nepal tomorrow.
    She is coming tomorrow.
16. To express the speaker's disliking or disapproval of an action that happens often.
    Ex: She is always bothering me with her silly questions.
    We are becoming lazy every day.

    Note: There are some verbs which are not normally used in the continuous tense. These are:
    (*a*) *Verbs of possession:* own, possess, contain, consist of, belong to, etc.
    (*b*) *Verbs of thinking:* think, suppose, believe, agree, disagree, doubt, imagine, forget, know, mean, mind, recognise, understand, trust, remember, recollect, and so on.
    (*c*) *Verbs of emotion:* hope, wish, want, desire, like, love, hate, refuse, prefer, dislike, please, forgive and so forth.
    (*d*) *Verbs of perception:* see, hear, notice, smell, etc.
    (*e*) *Verbs of appearing:* appear, look, seem, etc.

The Present Perfect Tense is used in the following ways:

17. To indicate an action just finished.

Ex: She has gone out.

He has finished his work.

Note: (*a*) In the present perfect tense, the time of the action is neither given nor implied.

(*b*) It amply deserves to be noted with due care that the present perfect tense is never used when some expression of past time is given or implied.

18. To denoted an action beginning at some time in the past and continuing up to the present moment.

Ex: I have known her for many years.

He has lived here for over five years.

19. To describe an action that is referred to as an experience gained from events that happened in the past.

Ex: She has helped me many times.

He has seen the Taj Mahal in moonlight.

20. To describe a past action, the time of which is not given.

Ex: I have received a letter from my wife.

The train has just arrived.

21. With so far and yet, to describe an action that is still unfinished.

Ex: The meeting has not started yet.

The servant has not watered the plants so far.

22. To denote a future indefinite tense, when preceded by after-before, as soon as, till, until, etc.

Ex: She will play after she has finished her work.

The Present Perfect Continuous Tense is used in the following ways:

23. To express an action that began at some time in the past, and is still continuing. The action should be continuing at the time of speaking.

Ex: It has been raining for four hours.

I have been writing books for thirty years.

She has been wasting her time since morning.

Note: (*a*) This sentence is often used when time expression with for or since is given.

(*b*) For is used when period of time is given, e.g. four months, six hours, five days, a long time, etc.

(*c*) Since is used when point of time is given, e.g. four o'clock, yesterday, Friday, the 4th September, 1998, etc.

24. To emphasise the uninterrupted and continued nature of an action even though it is completed.

Ex: I have been writing all day.

He has been doing his home work the whole morning.

Note: There are some verbs, such as wait, live, etc. which express a state, and carry the idea of continuity. In the cases of such verbs, the present perfect and the present perfect continuous mean one and the same thing. Look at the two sentences named below:

(*i*) He has lived in Calcutta for five years.

(*ii*) He has been living in Calcutta for five years.

These two sentences mean exactly the same thing. There is no difference in meaning of the said sentences.

PAST TENSE

The Past Indefinite Tense is used in the following ways:

25. To describe an action completed in the past. In such a case, some expression of past time is usually given or implied.

Ex: He saw a movie last night.

She lived in Hyderabad six years ago.

He left for Chennai yesterday.

26. To express an action which was habit or more regularly performed in the past.

Ex: She met me twice a day during the summer holidays.

He attended temple every Tuesday.

I always carried an umbrella.

27. To describe an event or action which occupied a period of time in the past which is now completed.

Ex: I taught in this college for ten years.

Note: (*a*) We can also use 'used to' + verb in place of the past indefinite tense to express actions which were habits, or a continuing state of thing in the past, especially when the time is not clearly indicated.

Ex: She used to feed ten poor widows every day.

I used to attend Hanuman Temple regularly when I was a young man.

She used to visit me every Sunday.

(*b*) The expression used to does not have present tense form.

The Past Continuous Tense is used in the following ways:

28. To express an action that was going on at some time in the past. The time of the action may or may not be indicated.

Ex: He was looking into the matter.

I was having my lunch at 2 o'clock yesterday.

What were you doing all the morning yesterday?

29. To show gradual development of a happening.

Ex: It was getting dark.

The girl was growing like a plant.

30. To denote an action that was in progress when another action took place.

Ex: I was writing a letter when Rita came.

He was sleeping when the phone rang.

31. To express irritation or disapproval on a frequently repeated past action.

Ex: She was continually asking for money.

He was constantly asking foolish questions.

They were always quarrelling with one another.

Note: In such cases, the adverbs always, constantly, continually etc. are used.

The Past Perfect Tense is used in the following ways:

32. To describe an action that was completed before another action took place in the past.

Ex: The patient had died before the doctor arrived.

I went to school after the rain had stopped.

33. To describe an unfulfilled condition in the past.

Ex: If I had early, I would have caught the train.

If she had worked hard, she would have passed.

If he had asked me, I would have helped him.

34. With the verbs want, wish, hope, intend to show that the intention or hope or wish was not fulfilled.

Ex: She had wished to become a doctor.

I had hoped to win a medal.

He had intended to send his son to U.K.

35. To show the result of some action.

Ex: The girl had grown into a woman.

36. When the simple sentence contains such words as already, before etc.

Ex: I had seen him before

He had already caught the thief.

The Past Perfect Continuous Tense is used in the following ways:

37. To show an action which continued in the past for a given period of time before another past action.

Ex: She had been living in Mumbai for five years before 1998.

He had been playing for two hours before he went to bed.

FUTURE TENSE

The Future Indefinite Tense is used in the following ways:

38. By using the present indefinite tense.

Ex: Their wedding is on Monday next.

The meeting starts at 4.30 p.m.

39. By using is/am/are + about to + first form of the verb.

Ex: The train is about to leave the station.

The plane is about to take off.

The meeting is about to start.

Note: Bear in mind that the use of this pattern expresses an action or event which is on the point of taking place, that is, which is likely to happen almost immediately.

40. By using is/am/are + to + first form of the verb.
Ex: I am to meet her tomorrow.
He is to wait for me at the bus-stop.

41. By using going to + first form of the verb.
Ex: I am going to buy a car this week.
This wall is going to collapse soon.

42. By using shall/will + first form of the verb.
Ex: She will be ten next month.
He will be in Calcutta next month.
I shall leave as soon as the rain stops.
She will meet me this evening.

The Future Continuous Tense is used in the following ways:

43. To denote an action which will be going on at a given point of time in the future.
Ex: I shall be playing in the evening.
We shall be taking our test tomorrow at 10.30 a.m.

44. To refer to an event that is expected to take place in the normal course. It suggests something that is expected to happen.
Ex: I shall be meeting her tomorrow.
The train will be arriving soon.

The Future Perfect Tense is used in the following ways:

45. To denote an action which will be completed by some point of time in the future.
Ex: He will have come back home by 5.30 p.m.
I shall have finished my work before you come.
The train will have left by the time you reach the station.

The Future Perfect Continuous Tense is used in the following ways:

46. To denote an action which will be in progress even after a given point of time in the future.
Ex: By the end of this month, he will have been living in Mumbai for ten years.
By the end of this week, I shall have been learning Hindi for three years.

CORRECT USE OF ARTICLES

1. A, An and The are the three articles in the English Language.

2. A and an are called the indefinite articles. The is called the definite article.

3. Neither a nor an points out any definite or particular person, place or thing.

4. These two articles — a and an — are the same for all genders.

5. The choice between a and an wholly depends upon the sound of the word before which a or an is to be used.

6. A or an is used before a singular countable noun.

Note: (*a*) A countable noun has both a singular and a plural form. A singular countable noun must have a determiner, such as a, an, the, my, his, her, etc. in front of it.
(*b*) An uncountable noun has only one form.

7. The is called the definite article. It refers to some particular or definite place, person or thing. The is the same for singular and plural, and for all genders. It is used with both countable and uncountable nouns.

8. The indefinite article a is used before:
(*a*) a word beginning with a consonant having a consonant sound.
Ex: a boy, a man, a book, etc.
(*b*) a word that begins with a vowel (especially) with the sound of wa.
Ex: a one-rupee note, a one-eyed man, etc.
(*c*) a word beginning with u or eu giving the consonant sound of yu.
Ex: a university, a usage, a union, a unit, a utensil, a useful book, a uniform, a eulogy, a European, and so on.

9. The indefinite article an is used before:
(*a*) a word beginning with a vowel (a, e, i, o, u) having a vowel sound.

Ex: an apple, an egg, an umbrella, an idiot, and so forth.

(*b*) a word beginning with a silent h.

Ex: an heir, an hour, an honest man, an honourable person, etc.

(*c*) an abbreviation, the first letter of which begins with a consonant having a vowel sound.

Ex: an M.A., an M.P., an M.L.A., an S.D.O., an F.R.S., an X-mas gift, etc.

10. A or an is not used before:

(*a*) plural nouns.

(*b*) uncountable nouns.

(*c*) a noun preceded by the expression kind of.

Ex: What kind of flower is it?

(*d*) names of meals.

Ex: He was at dinner at 8.30 p.m.
She gave me breakfast at eight.

Note: An indefinite article can be used before names of meals when these are preceded by an adjective.

Ex: She gave me a good breakfast at eight.
He was invited to a sumptuous dinner.

11. A or an is used in the following ways:
Before the word most when it is used in the sense of very or very much or exceedingly.

Ex: Mridula is a most intelligent girl.
This is a most unfortunate event.

12. In the sense of every.

Ex: I pay her five hundred rupees a month.
He earns two hundred rupees a week.

13. In the sense of one.

Ex: I bought a book.
She will buy an umbrella.

14. In the sense of some, any or single.

Ex: I have a great regard for her.
She did not say a word against me.
He is an honest man.

15. Before a singular countable noun which is used as an example to represent a class.

Ex: A cow is a useful animal.

Note: It must be borne in mind that man or woman, when used in a general sense to represent mankind or womankind as a whole, never takes an article.

Ex: Man is mortal.
Woman is the ornament of the home.
Woman is man's better half.

16. With a noun complement. This includes names of professions.

Ex: He is an actor.
It was an earthquake.
She is a good dancer.

17. In the sense of the same.

Ex: They are much of an age.
Birds of a feather flock together.

18. In certain phrases.

Ex: a bad cold, at a loss, a severe pan, on an average, a sore throat, make a noise, as a rule, make a mess, make an effort, make a mistake, etc.

19. With certain numbers.

Ex: a hundred, a thousand, a million, etc.

20. Before the word half it follows a whole number.

Ex: One and a half kilograms.
One kilogram and a half.

Note: (*a*) 1/2 kilogram (kg.) = half a kg. In such an expression, a must not be used before half.

(*b*) A + half + noun is sometimes possible.

Ex: a half-holiday, a half-portion, a half-share etc.

21. With expression such as 1/3 (one-third), etc.

Ex: a third, a quarter, and so on.

22. In expressions of price, speed, ratio, etc.

Ex: Fifty kilometres an hour, ten times a day, at Rs. 10/- a kg, at Rs. 100/- a metre.

23. In exclamations before singular nouns.

Ex: Such a long queue.

24. A can be used before Mr./Miss/Mrs. + surname.

Ex: a Mr. Bose, a Miss Bose, A Mrs. Bose, etc.

Note: (*a*) A Mr. Bose, denotes a person who is called Bose, and implies that he is a strange to the speaker.

(*b*) Mr. Bose, without a, implies that the speaker knows Mr. Bose, or knows of his existence.

25. Before a proper noun to make it a common noun.
 Ex: Ram Nath a Newton. (a great scientist)
 Alok Gupta is a Shakespeare. (a great dramatist)

26. Before certain uncountable nouns preceded by nouns + of.
 Ex: a piece of advice, a bit of news, a drop of water, etc.

27. After the words many, rather, such, quite, etc.
 Ex: She has many a boy-friend.
 Everybody will welcome such a chance.
 It is rather a pity that you were ill.

28. After an adjective preceded by so, as, too, how, quite, etc.
 Ex: He is not so big a fool as you think.
 This is too heavy a box for me to carry.

The is used in the following ways:

29. To indicate that, what is expressed by the noun, has already been mentioned, and to refer back to it.
 Ex: I saw a boy and a girl in the park. The boy was fat and short. The girl was slim and tall.

30. Before a noun denoting a hospital, temple, school, college, prison, etc. if its purpose or use is not referred to.
 Ex: He has gone to the hospital to visit a friend who is employed there.

31. With noun modified in such a way that uniqueness is indicated.
 Ex: the top, the bottom, the left side, the right side, the front of the house, the year in which I was born etc.

32. Before an adjective in the superlative degree.
 Ex: He is the tallest of all the boys in the class.

33. Before abstract and material nouns of they are used with an adjunct which makes them definite.
 Ex: The gold we use in India is all imported.
 The joy he experienced was almost overwhelming.

34. The can be used before a member of a certain group of people.
 Ex: The small shopkeepers finds life increasingly difficult.

35. With national adjectives ending in ch or sh.
 Ex: the Dutch, the Spanish, the Welsh, etc.

36. Before a noun which by locality can represent only one particular thing.
 Ex: My son is in the garden. (the garden of this house)

37. In place of a possible adjective before the names of parts of the body.
 Ex: I struck him on the (not his) head.

38. Before same.
 Ex: This is the same building.

39. After all, both and half.
 Ex: Both the sons are intelligent.
 All the people of this colony are rich.
 Half the mangoes are ripe.

40. Before a common noun to give it the meaning of an abstract noun.
 Ex: At last, the father in him was throughly aroused for his son.
 In this sentence, the father in him denotes the fatherly affection or love in him.

41. Before an adjective used to denote an abstract quality.
 Ex: I love the beautiful.
 She loves the good.
 He loves the pure.

42. Before musical instruments.
 Ex: Mohni can play the piano very-well.

43. Before the names of well-known historical events.
 Ex: the Sepoy Mutiny of 1857, the Battle of Panipat, the World War of 1914, the Quit India Movement.

44. Before the proper names of certain well-known or sacred books.
 Ex: the Mahabharat, the Ramayana, the Gita, the Bible.
 Note: If the title of the book is the name of a person, or if the author's name if given in the possessive case, no article is used.
 Ex: Balmiki's Ramayana, Firdausi's Shah Nama, Julius Caesar.

45. Before the names of certain countries, each of which is a union of smaller units.
 Ex: He has gone to the United States of America.

46. Before proper names consisting of noun + of + noun.
Ex: the Bay of Bengal, the Cape of Good Hope, the United States of America.

47. Before the adjectives east, west, etc. + noun in certain names.
Ex: the West Indies, the East End, the North Pole.
Note: The is not used before certain names.
Ex: South Africa, North America, West Germany, etc.

48. The is used with names of people, but it has a very limited use.
The + plural surname can be used to mean the ..... family.
Ex: the Guptas = Mr. and Mrs. Gupta, and children.

49. The is used before titles.
Ex: the King of ....., the Nawab of ....., the Maharaja of ..... .

50. Before the names of political parties.
Ex: the National Congress, the Communist Party of India.

51. Before the name of a nation, race, community, etc.
Ex: the Indians, the Hindus, the Jains, the Brahmins, etc.

52. Before certain collective nouns.
Ex: the army, the navy, the police, the jury, etc.

53. Before the names of ships, well-known trains, etc.
Ex: the Taj Express, the Vikrant, the Flying Queen, etc.

54. Before titles of rank and honour.
Ex: the Hon'ble Mr. K.R. Narayanan, President of India, is an crudite scholar.

55. Before names of certain canals.
Ex: the Suez Canal, the Panama Canal, etc.

56. Before names of certain chains of mountains.
Ex: the Himalayas, the Alps, etc.

57. Before names of newspaper, magazines, etc.
Ex: the Hindustan Times, the Statesman, the Shama, the Sushma, etc.

58. Before certain countries, cities, etc.
Ex: the Yemen, the Sudan, the Hague, etc.

59. Before the dates of months.
Ex: the 4th April, 1993, the 15th August, 1947, etc.

The is omitted in the following ways:

60. The is omitted before a common noun used in its widest sense.
Ex: Woman is tender-hearted.
Man is not immortal.

61. Usually before proper nouns.
Ex: Delhi is the Capital of India.
Who was Kalidas?

62. Before languages and diseases.
Ex: I am learning Hindi.
She is scared of malarial fever.

63. Before the words father, mother, aunt, uncle.
Ex: Father is not at home.
Aunt has come to see me.

64. Before plural nouns which are used to denote a class.
Ex: Historians love to study old books.
Boys go to school at 9.30 a.m. .
Camels are useful animals.
Note: But it is correct to say:
The boys, who go to school at 9.30 a.m., return at 4 p.m.
The Camels of Saudi Arabia are very strong.
It amply deserves to be noted with due care that here particular boys and Camels are meant.

65. Before the names of meals.
Ex: I had lunch at 1.30 p.m.
She had breakfast at 8.30 a.m.
Note: The can be used when meals are preceded by an adjective.
Ex: What is about the wedding dinner?

66. Before a common noun in the vocative case.
Ex: Come here, boy.

67. Before a common noun which is used to denote an institution, a hospital, etc. named after some particular person.
Ex: He is employed in Prem Kumar Hospital.
She is a student of Bharat Ram College.

68. In certain phrases consisting of a transitive verb followed by its object.
Ex: to catch fire, to take breath, to cast anchor, to send word, to give ear, to set sail, to lose heart, to leave home, to take offence, etc.

69. In certain phrases consisting of a preposition followed by its object.

Ex: at home, in hand, in debt, by day, at sunrise, at noon, on demand, by land, by train, on foot, at ease, from top to bottom, from head to foot, etc.

70. Before the names of days, months, countries, cities, towns, etc.

71. After a possessive adjective.

Ex: It is my book.

72. Sometimes (not always) before parts of the body and articles of clothing.

Ex: Raise your right hand.
He took off his coat.

73. Before names of subjects.

Ex: Do you like History?
He teaches Chemistry.

74. After expressions, such as sort of, type of, kind of, manner of, etc.

Ex: What sort of person is he?
What type of house do you live in?

An article, a, an, or the can be repeated in the following ways:

75. When two or more adjectives qualify the same nouns, the article is used along the first adjective only.

Ex: He has a black and white goat.

This sentence means a goat that is partly black and partly white.

76. When two or more adjectives qualify different nouns, the article is used before each adjective.

Ex: He has a black and a white goat.

This sentence denotes two goats, one black and the other white.

77. In expressing a comparison, if two nouns refer to the same person or thing, the article is used before the first noun only.

Ex: He is a better electrician than clerk.

This sentence denotes one person who is both an electrician and a clerk. He knows both the jobs. But his work as an electrician is better than that as a clerk.

78. If two nouns refer to different persons or things, the article must be used with each noun.

Ex: He is a better electrician than a clerk.

This sentence refers to two persons. One of them is an electrician, and the other is a clerk. The comparison is between these two persons. Here it is implied that the clerk also knows the job of an electrician. But the electrician's work is better than that of the clerk.

An article a, an, and the is used or omitted in the following ways:

79. English = the English language.
the English = the English nation (People).

80. He went to sea = He became a sailor.
He went to the sea = He went on a voyage.

81. She has got headache = She has got chronic headache.
She has got a headache = She has got an attack of headache.

82. He is Newton = He is Newton himself.
He is a Newton = He is a scientists as great as Newton.

83. He goes to school = He goes to study.
He goes to the school = He goes to a particular school, not for studying but for some other purpose.

84. He has gone to market = He has gone to make purchases.
He has gone to the market = He has gone to the place where there is a market, but not to make purchases.

85. She is a member of society = She has not cut off all connections with the world.
She is a member of a (or the) society = She is a member of a particular society.

86. To see light = to look at light.
To see the light = to be born.

87. The emeny is in possession of the General = The enemy has the General in keeping.
The enemy is in the possession of the General = The general has the enemy in keeping.

88. He works in wood = He is a carpenter.
He works in the wood = He is a woodcutter, or he does some other work in the forest.

89. She kept house for a long time = She managed house for a long time.
She kept the house for a long time = She remained indoors for a long time.

CORRECT USE OF PREPOSITIONS

1. At, by, for, of, on, in, out, off, up, to, till, with, after, from, through, etc. are called Simple Prepositions.
2. Along, amid, among, amongst, around, amidst, across, about, above, beyond, between, beside, beneath, below, before, behind, inside, outside, without, within, underneath, etc., are called Compound Prepositions.
3. From among, from under, from beneath, out of, from within, etc. are called Double Prepositions.
4. Barring, considering, concerning, during, pending, regarding, respecting, not withstanding, owing, etc. are called Participal Prepositions.
5. Along with, according to, away from, because of, by means of, by dint of, by virtue of, by way of, by reason of, instead of, in consequence of, in addition to, in the course of, in place of, in lieu of, in spite of, in accordance with, in favour of, in front of, in order to, in regard to, in compliance with, on account of, owing to, for the sake of, with a view to, with reference to, with regard to, etc. are called Phrase Prepositions.

   Note: Let us observe the following three expressions:

   (*a*) o'clock: of clock.

   (*b*) thrice a week: thrice in a week.

   (*c*) a hunting: on hunting.

   Of, in and on in said expressions are prepositions. When prepositions are used in this way, they are called Disguised Prepositions.
6. The noun or noun — equivalent (pronoun, adverb, gerund, infinitive, adverbial phrase or adverbial clause) before which the preposition is placed is called its object.

   Ex: The book is *on* the table. (*Noun*)
   I depend *on* her. (*Pronoun*)
   Go away *from* here. (*Adverb*)
   He is fond *of* playing. (*Gerund*)
   The boat is *about* to sink. (*Infinitive*)
   She was well *till* a few days ago. (*Adverbial phrase*)
   I shall sell it *for* what it is worth. (*Adverbial clause*)

   The italicised noun or noun-equivalents in the sentences named above one objects to the prepositions on, from, of, about, till, and for.
7. A preposition is usually placed before a noun or noun-equivalent it governs.

   Ex: She died of cancer.
8. A preposition is placed at the end of a sentence in the following ways:

   (*a*) When the relative pronoun is that.

   Ex: The child tore the paper that I was writing on.
   Here is the pen that you were looking for.

   (*b*) If a preposition governs a relative pronoun.

   Ex: This is the girl whom I spoke about.

   (*c*) When the relative pronoun is understood.

   Ex: This is the man he spoke to. (whom is understood)

   (*d*) If a preposition governs an interrogative pronoun or an interrogative adverb.

   Ex: What are you looking at?
   Where are you going to?

   (*e*) When the preposition is used with the infinitive placed at the end of the sentence.

   Ex: Do you have a chair to sit on?
   I have no money to help you with.
9. Sometimes the object governed by the preposition is placed first/before the preposition for the sake of emphasis.

   Ex: This I insist on.
   He is known all the world over.
10. A preposition can also be used at the beginning of an interrogative sentence.

    Ex: In which house do you live?
    To whom are you referring?
11. There are occasions when the prepositions for, on, etc. are omitted before nouns of place or time.

    Ex: Wait a minute (= Wait for a minute).
    He cannot walk a kilometre (= he cannot walk for a kilometre).
    She did it last month (= She did it in last month).

12. There are many words which can be used as prepositions or as adverbs. The most important of these are about, above, across, along, before, below, behind, besides, by, down, in, near, on, off, over, past, round, through, under, up, and so on.

Ex:

Preposition	**Adverb**
He was here before ten.	He has done this sort of work before.
She is behind us.	She is long way behind.
He climbed over the wall.	You will have to climb over too.
He ran up the stairs.	He went up in the lift.
He got off the bus at the corner.	He got off at the corner.
The shop is just round the corner.	Come round and see me this evening.

13. There are some words with prepositions which require gerunds after them.

Ex:

abstrains from drinking	hinder from visiting
aim at doing	refrain from hurting
addicted to gambling	prevent from working
bent upon doing	persist in disobeying
excel in dancing	succeed in doing
averse to playing	disqualified from holding
desist from talking	knack of getting things done
capable of teaching	prohabit from entering
desirous of going	tired of writing
fond of playing	pretext for delaying
insist on going	thought of eluding.

14. Some words, which differ slightly in form and meaning and are formed from the same origin, take different prepositions after them.

Ex:

according to	but	in accordance with.
confidence in	but	confident of.
desire for	but	desirous of.
affection for	but	affectionate to.
negligent for	but	neglectful of.
ambition for	but	ambitious of.
fond of	but	fondness for.
dislike to/of	but	liking for.
alternate with	but	alternative to.
derogate from	but	derogatory to.
descend from	but	descendant of.
equal to	but	equality with/of.
except for	but	exception to.
hinder from	but	hindrance to.
infatuate with	but	infatuation for.
partial to	but	partiality for.
prejudice against	but	prejudicial to.
prepare for	but	preparatory to.
pursuant to	but	in pursuance of.
qualify for	but	disqualify from.
result of	but	resulted from.
respect for	but	rspectful to.
sensible of	but	insensible to/of.
consequent on/ upon	but	in consequence of.
trust in	but	distrust of.
want of	but	wanting in.

15. The verbs, which are placed immediately after prepositions, are usually in the gerund form.

Ex: Bindu insisted on buying a dictionary.
He left without paying his bill.

16. Some words with prepositions can take the gerund as well as the infinitive.

Ex: He is afraid of going out alone at night.
I am not afraid to go out alone at night.

17. Certain verbs usually take the infinitive after them.

Ex: I refused to refuse her earnest request.
I agree to disagree with you on this point.
He hopes to succeed in the examination.

18. Some intransitive verbs became transitive by placing prepositions after them.

Ex: laugh at, listen to, depend on/upon, prevail on/upon, etc.

19. Sometimes prepositions are profixed to verbs in order to form new verbs.

Ex: Outbid, outnumber, overcome, overflow, overlook, undergo, undertake, uphold, upgrade, withdraw, withhold, withstand, etc.

20. In and Within.

(*a*) In refers to the end of a period of time usually in the future.

Ex: He will return in a month. (at the end of one month)

(*b*) Within means before the end of a period of time.

Ex: He will return within a month. (before the end of the month)

21. In and Into.

(*a*) In indicates rest or motion inside anything.

Ex: She is in the garden. (rest, inside)
She is walking in the garden (motion, inside)

(*b*) Into means motion towards the inside of anything.

Ex: I walked into the garden.
Thieves broke into his house.

22. On and Upon.

(*a*) On is used:

(*i*) in speaking of things at rest.

Ex: He sat on a big stone.
The book in on the table.

(*ii*) Before the names of days and dates.

Ex: On Friday, on the 2nd of August, etc.

(*iii*) To denote support and concern.

Ex: He lives on his maternal uncle.
I write books on politics.

(*iv*) To express a condition or situation.

Ex: He is on the verge of stravation.

(*b*) Upon is Used:
In speaking of things in motion.

Ex: The tiger sprang upon the goat.

23. Beside and Besides.

(*a*) Beside means:

(*i*) by the side of.

Ex: She sat beside her mother.

(*ii*) Out of.

Ex: He was beside himself with joy.
She was beside herself with anger.

(*b*) Besides means in addition to or moreover.

Ex: Besides being fined, he was imprisoned by the magistrate.
There will be five of us for dinner, besides Mohini.

24. Between and Among.

(*a*) Between is used for two persons of things.

Ex: Distribute these apples between these two beggars.

(*b*) Among is used for more than two persons of things.

Ex: I distributed ten rupees among ten poor children.

25. Above means:

(*a*) higher than some thing.

Ex: The water came above our knees.

(*b*) higher in rank, position or importance then sb/sth.

Ex: A captain in the Navy ranks above a captain in the Army.

(*c*) greater in number, price, weight, etc. than sth.

Ex: Yesterday, the temperature was above the average.

(*d*) more than sb/sth.

Ex: A soldier must value honour above life.

(*e*) beyond the reach of sth.

Ex: She is above suspicion.

(*f*) too good, etc. for sth.

Ex: He is above deceit, *i.e.*, not deceitful.

26. Over is used to mean:

(*a*) resting on the surface of and partly or completely covering sb/sth.

Ex: Spread a cloth over the table.
Put your hand over her mouth.

(*b*) In or to a position higher than but not touching sb/sth.

Ex: They held a large umbrella over her.
The sky is over our heads.

(*c*) across.

Ex: There is a bridge over the river.
He looked over the hedge.

(*d*) On the for or opposite side of sth.

Ex: Lalita Devi lives over the road.

(*e*) so as to cross sth, and be on the other side.

Ex: He climbed over the wall.
I jumped over the stream.

(*f*) in or across every part or most ports of sth/a place.

Ex: Sangeeta is famous all over the world.

(*g*) more than.
Ex: Kamini is over two metres tall.
The road is over ten kilometres long.
I am over twenty.
(*h*) indicating control, authority, command, etc.
Ex: Akbar, the Great, ruled over a great empire.
She has only the director over her.
(*i*) during; while eating, doing, etc.
Ex: We shall discuss it over lunch.
I had a pleasant chat with her over a cup of tea.
(*j*) throughout a period; during.
Ex: He stayed in Culcutta over Durga Pooja.
(*k*) because of sth.
Ex: There was an argument over money between those two boys.
(*l*) transmitted by sth.
Ex: We heard it over the radio.
She told me everything over the phone.
Note: Over and above is an idiom. It means besides; in addition to.
Ex: The waiters get good tips over and above their wages.

27. With is used to mean:
(*a*) despite; in spite of.
Ex: With all her faults, I love her very dearly.
(*b*) considering one fact in relation to another.
Ex: With no hope of a holiday, life is very depressing.
(*c*) indicating separation from sb/sth.
Ex: We can't disperse with the formalities.
I can never part with this ring.
(*d*) as a client or an employee.
Ex: We are with the same bank.
I hear he is with Ramesh Publishing House.
(*e*) including sth.
Ex: The meal with pudding came to fifty rupees each.
(*f*) in the company of sb.
Ex: Rajni lives with her parents.
(*g*) in the charge, care or possession of sb.
Ex: She left a message for me with my secretary.
The keys are with reception.
(*h*) having or carrying sth.
Ex: I saw a girl with red hair.
He looked at her with a hurt expression.
(*i*) indicating the tool or instrument used.
Ex: He cut it with a knife.
I shall feed her with a spoon.
(*j*) indicating the material or item used.
Ex: Fill the bucket with water.
(*k*) because of sth; on account of.
Ex: She trembled with fear.
(*l*) indicating the manner, etc. in which sth is done, or takes place.
Ex: I shall do it with pleasure.
I welcomed her with open arms.
(*m*) in the same direction as sth.
Ex: The shadow moves with the sun.
Swim with the tide.
(*n*) because of.
Ex: Skill comes with experience.
(*o*) in regard to, concerning or towards sb/sth.
Ex: He is angry with his eldest daughter.
(*p*) as regards sb/sth.
Ex: It is a very busy time with us at the moment.
(*q*) agreeing with or supporting sb/sth.
Ex: I am with you all the way.
She had a row with him.

28. By is used to mean:
(*a*) according to; from the evidence of.
Ex: By my watch, it is two o'clock.
Judging by appearances can be misleading.
(*b*) to denote the doer of an action in the passive voice.
Ex: The thief was beaten by the policeman.
(*c*) at the side of; near; beside.
Ex: She came and sat by me.
Our house is by the Hanuman Temple.
(*d*) across; along; passing through.
Ex: He entered by the back door.
I travelled to Culcutta by Patna.
(*e*) past sb/sth.
Ex: I walked by her without speaking.
I go by the temple every morning on my way to work.
(*f*) not later than; before.
Ex: You should finish the work by tomorrow.

(*g*) during or in sth.
Ex: He sleeps by night.
The view is best seen by moonlight.
(*h*) through the action power or work of sb/sth.
Ex: This is a play by Tagore.
(*i*) in successive units, groups of degrees.
Ex: He is improving day-by-day.
(*j*) to the extent of.
Ex: The bullet missed him by two inches.

29. Off, as a preposition, means:
(*a*) down or away from a position on sth.
Ex: The boy fell off the tree.
Keep off the grass.
The ball rolled off the table.
(*b*) at some distance from sth.
Ex: There is a big house off the street.

30. Of means the following:
(*a*) Belonging to sb/sth.
Ex: She is a fast friend of mine.
The handle of the umbrella is broken.
(*b*) Created by.
Ex: The works of Tagore are highly lauded by all.
(*c*) About sb/sth.
Ex: I have never heard of him.

31. Until/Till
Until and till, as prepositions, mean one and the same thing, and are used to denote the following:
(*a*) Up to a specified time.
Ex: It may last till Friday.
Nothing happened until (*i.e.*, before) 5 o'clock.

32. For
The preposition for is used to mean the following:
(*a*) Indicating the person intended to receive sth.
Ex: Here is a letter for you.
All these presents are for her.
(*b*) As the price, reward or penalty of sth.
Ex: I bought this pen for ten rupees.
He got a medal for bravery.
You can go to prison for dangerous driving.
(*c*) Meaning sth.
Ex: What is the A for in A. Hasham?
Shaking you head for No is not universal.
(*d*) Indicating a distance.
Ex: The road goes on for ten miles.

33. At is used to denote the following:
(*a*) Indicating a point in space.
Ex: I shall be at home all morning.
She works at the hospital.
(*b*) Indicating a point of time.
Ex: I left school at the age of 15.
She got married at 45.
(*c*) To show a price, rate, speed, etc.
Ex: He bought sugar at ten rupees per kg.
He was driving at 60 miles per hour.
(*d*) Before town and villages.
Ex: He lives at Meerut.

34. In is used to mean the following:
(*a*) To indicate place
Ex: Children are playing in the street.
I read about it in the newspaper.
(*b*) During a period of time.
Ex: In 1993, in April, in summer, in the morning, etc.
(*c*) To indicate medium, means, material, etc.
Ex: Please speak in English.
Say it in a few works.
Write it in ink.

35. From is used to mean the following:
(*a*) To indicate the place or direction from which sb/sth starts.
Ex: The train from Patna has arrived.
She comes home from work at 7 p.m.
(*b*) To show the lower limit of a range of numbers, prices, etc.
Ex: I write from 5 to 8 letter daily.
Tickets cost from ten rupees to twelve rupees.
(*c*) To indicate the reason, cause or motive.
Ex: She felt sick from tiredness.
He suffers from cold and hunger.

36. Since is used to denote from a specified time in the past till a later past time, or till now.
Ex: I have not eaten since breakfast.
He has been wearing glasses since he was ten.
Note: Since is used with present perfect, past perfect and perfect continuous tenses.

CORRECT USE OF ACTIVE VOICE AND PASSIVE VOICE

The steps to change an active voice to passive voice are as follows:

1. Only transitive verbs can be used in the passive voice.

2. As an intransitive verb has no object, it cannot be used in the passive voice.

3. The active voice is used when the doer of the action is to be made prominent.

4. The passive voice is used when the person or thing which receives the action is to be made prominent.

5. Some transitive verbs have both a direct object and an indirect object in the passive voice. In such an event, any of the two objects may be used as the subject of the passive verb. And the other object is retained.

Ex: He gave me a pen. *(Active Voice)*

I was given a pen by him. *(Passive Voice)*

or

A pen was given to me by him. *(Passive Voice)*

6. Certain transitive verbs, even in active form, are sometimes used in a passive sense.

Ex: The flowers smell sweet (..... are sweet when they are smelt).

These mangoes taste sour (..... are sour when they are tasted).

7. The Passive verb is formed by using the appropriate tense of the helping verb to be with the past participle of the main verb.

Ex: I have written a letter. *(Active Voice)*

A letter has been written by me. *(Passive Voice)*

8. When a verb is changed from the active into the passive voice:

(*a*) the object in the active voice becomes the subject in the passive voice;

(*b*) the subject in the active voice becomes the object in the passive voice, and is preceded by the proposition by; and

(*c*) the main verb is changed to past participle which is preceded by the proper form of the helping verb to be according to the tense of the main verb in the active voice and the number of the new subject.

9. The tense of the verb is not to be changed. Only the form of the verb is to be changed.

10. The preposition by must be used with the doer of the action in the passive voice, when it helps to complete the sense.

11. Out of the twelve forms of the tenses of verbs, only eight can be expressed in the passive voice.

It amply deserves to be noted with due care that none of the following four forms of the tenses admits of the use of a verb in the passive voice.

(*a*) Present Perfect Continuous

(*b*) Past Perfect Continuous

(*c*) Future Perfect Continuous

12. An intransitive verb, connected with a preposition, can sometimes be used in the passive voice. The preposition must be retained.

Ex: She laughed at me. *(Active Voice)*

I was laughed at by her. *(Passive Voice)*

13. Bear in mind that only the object, not the objective complement, can become the subject of the verb in the passive voice.

Ex: They elected me president. *(Active Voice)*

I was elected president by them. *(Passive Voice)*

In the first sentence above, me and president are the object and the objective complement respectively.

This is why the object me has become the subject of the verb in the passive voice.

14. Sometimes an intransitive verb also possesses an object which is called cognate object. (Cognate means having the same source or origin as another one).

Ex: (*a*) She sings a sweet song. (*Active Voice*)
A Sweet song is sung by her. (*Passive Voice*)

Song in the first sentence at (*a*) above, originates from the verb sing. The meaning of song is implied in the verb sing.

15. When the verb expresses a command, advice, request, etc. and happens to be in the second person, the word let is used to begin the sentence in the passive voice. Be is used before the past participle of the main verb.

Ex: Do this work. (*Active Voice*)
Let this work be done. (*Passive Voice*)

16. The past participle of the main verb must always be used after the appropriate form of the helping verb.

Ex: She has done this job. (*Active Voice*)
This job has been done by her. (*Passive Voice*)

17. Am, is or are is used before the past participle of the main verb in the present indefinite tense.

Ex: I help her. (*Active Voice*)
She is helped by me. (*Passive Voice*)
She loves me. (*Active Voice*)
I am loved by her. (*Passive Voice*)
He praises you. (*Active Voice*)
You are praised by him. (*Passive Voice*)

18. Is being, am being, or are being is used before the past participle of main verb in the present continuous tense.

Ex: I am reading a book. (*Active Voice*)
A book is being read by me. (*Passive Voice*)

19. Has been or have been is used before the past participle of the main verb in the present perfect tense.

Ex: He has done this work. (*Active Voice*)
This work has been done by him. (*Passive Voice*)

20. Was or were is used before the past participle of the main verb in the past indefinite tense.

Ex: She rebuked him. (*Active Voice*)
He was rebuked by her. (*Passive Voice*)

21. Was being or were being is used before the past participle or the main verb in the past continuous tense.

Ex: He was reading a book. (*Active Voice*)
A book was being read by him. (*Passive Voice*)

22. Had been is used before the past participle of the main verb in the past perfect tense.

Ex: You had written a letter. (*Active Voice*)
A letter had been written by you. (*Passive Voice*)

23. Will be or shall be is used before the past participle of the main verb in the future indefinite tense.

Ex: She will love you. (*Active Voice*)
You will be loved be her. (*Passive Voice*)

24. Will have been or shall have been is used before the past participle of the main verb in the future perfect tense.

Ex: He will have helped you. (*Active Voice*)
You will have been helped by him. (*Passive Voice*)

25. Be is used with should, must, can, could, ought to, may or might.

Ex: Can you speak the truth? (*Active Voice*)
Can the truth be spoken by you. (*Passive Voice*)
You must help him. (*Active Voice*)
He must be helped by you. (*Passive Voice*)

The passive voice is restricted to the following uses:

26. When the doer or performer of the action in a sentence is unknown or difficult to name or identify.

Ex: His mother was killed in a road times.
She was warned several times.
Every shop must be closed for one day in a week.
Let the door be kept open.

27. The passive form is preferred when the subject in the active voice is quite clear from the context.

Ex: He was sentenced to ten years' imprisonment in a murder case. Here it is quite apparent from the context that the judge sentenced him..... .

28. When it is unnecessary to state who the doer of the action is.

Ex: This book was printed in Calcutta.

29. When we wish to draw attention to the receiver, but not to the doer of the action.
Ex: The thief was caught red-handed.

30. When it is desirable for reasons of secrecy, fact or modesty not to mention the doer of the action.
Ex: It has been decided that ..... .
It has been fully proved that ..... .

31. When we start the sentence with very important words in it.
Ex: A favourable impression has been created by the prompt action taken by the government.

Note: Unknown or vague active voice subjects, such as somebody, someone, everyone, everybody, they, people, etc. are usually not required in the passive voice.
Ex: Somebody has picked his pocket. *(Active Voice)*
His pocket has been picked. *(Passive Voice)*

CORRECT USE OF NARRATION (DIRECT AND INDIRECT SPEECH)

1. The technique of reproducing the exact words spoken by a person is called the use of the direct speech.
Ex: Ragini says, "I am very intelligent."
2. When the words spoken by a person are reproduced or rewritten in our own words by changing the tense and the person whenever necessary, it is called the indirect speech.
Ex: Ragini says that she is very intelligent.
3. In a direct speech, the actual words used by the speaker are placed within inverted commas (" "). These words are called the reported speech.
The words which are outside the inverted commas are called the reporting speech. It has a subject and a verb. The verb is called the reporting verb.
4. The reported speech is separated from the reporting verb by a comma.
5. The first word of the reported speech begins with a capital letter.

Indirect Speech:

6. Inverted commas are not used.
7. The comma separating the reporting verb from the reported speech is removed.
8. The conjuction that is usually used after the reporting verb.
9. The tense of the reporting verb is never changed.
10. Sometimes the reporting verb is changed according to the sense of the reported speech.
11. There is a change in the person of the pronouns used in the reported speech.
12. The verbs and the tense used in the reported speech are changed.
13. There is a change in the words expressing nearness in time or place in the reported speech.
14. A sentence in the indirect speech contains one principal clause, and one or more subordinate clauses.

Change of Tense

15. If the reporting verb is in the present tense or in future tense, the tense of the verb in the reported speech is not changed.
Ex: Anita says, "I am out of sorts (unwell)." *(Direct)*
Anita says that she is out of sorts. *(Indirect)*
16. If the reporting verb is in the past tense, the tense of the verbs in the reported speech is also changed into its corresponding past tense in the following ways:
(*a*) Simple present becomes simple past.
Ex: Sita said, "I am unwell." *(Direct)*
Sita said that she was unwell. *(Indirect)*
(*b*) Present continuous becomes past continuous

Ex: He said, "I am working hard." (*Direct*)
He said that he was working hard. (*Indirect*)

(*c*) Present perfect becomes past perfect.

Ex: She said, "I have penned a letter." (*Direct*)
She said that she had penned a letter. (*Indirect*)

(*d*) Present perfect continuous becomes past perfect continuous.

Ex: He said, "It has been raining for two hours." (*Direct*)
He said that it had been raining for two hours. (*Indirect*)

(*e*) Past indefinite becomes past perfect.

Ex: He said, "I came in the morning." (*Direct*)
He said that he had come in the morning. (*Indirect*)

(*f*) Past continuous becomes past perfect continuous.

Ex: Rita said, "I was reading a book." (*Direct*)
Rita said that she had been reading a book. (*Indirect*)

Note: The past perfect and the past perfect continuous of the verbs in the reported speech remain unchanged.

(*g*) In future tense, shall/will becomes would.

Ex: He said to me, "I shall help you." (*Direct*)
He said to me that he would help me. (*Indirect*)

17. If the reported speech expresses a universal truth or a habitual fact, the present tense of the verbs in the reported speech is not changed.

Ex: He said, "The earth moves round the sun." (*Direct*)
He said that the earth moves round the sun. (*Indirect*)
He said, "I go for a walk every morning." (*Direct*)
He said that he goes for a walk every morning. (*Indirect*)

18. If the reported speech states a part historical event, the past indefinite tense of the verb in the reported speech is not changed.

Ex: He said, "Mahatma Gandhi opposed the British Government." (*Direct*)
He said that Mahatma Gandhi opposed the British Government. (*Indirect*)

19. If the reported speech expresses two actions that took place at the same time, the past indefinite tense or the past continuous tense in the reported speech remains unchanged.

Ex: Usha said, "I sang while Nisha danced." (*Direct*)
Usha said that she sang while Nisha danced. (*Indirect*)

20. If the reported speech expresses on imagined condition, its tense remains unchanged.

Ex: She said, "I would build a school if I won a lottery." (*Direct*)
She said that she would build a school if she won a lottery. (*Indirect*)

Change of Pronouns in the Indirect Speech

21. A pronoun of the first person in the reported speech is changed to that of the same person as the subject of the reporting verb.

Ex: He said, "I am honest and sagacious." (*Direct*)
He said that he was honest and sagacious. (*Indirect*)

22. A pronoun of the second person is changed to that of the same person as the object of the reporting verb.

Ex: He said to me, "You are polite." (*Direct*)
He said to me that I was polite. (*Indirect*)

23. When the pronoun you is used in the sense of one, it is not changed.

Ex: She said, "You can always bank upon a true friend." (*Direct*)
She said that you could always bank upon a true friend. (*Indirect*)

24. A pronoun of the third person in the reported speech is not changed.

Ex: I said to him, "She is gentle." (*Direct*)
I said to him that she was gentle. (*Indirect*)

25. When the pronoun we indicates mankind, it is not changed.

Ex: Mamta says, "We are mortals." (*Direct*)
Mamta says that we are mortals. (*Indirect*)

26. When the pronoun we stands for any ruling authority or the author of a book, etc., it is changed into he or she according to the sense.

Ex: The author says, "We have explained everything." *(Direct)*
The author says that he has explained everything. *(Indirect)*

27. When we stands for a newspaper on magazine, it is changed into it.

Ex: The Bengal Times writes, "We are grieved to learn of his sad and sudden demise." *(Direct)*
The Bengal Times writes that it is grieved to learn of his sad and sudden demise. *(Indirect)*

28. When a personal pronoun of the third person in the Indirect speech is repeated, some ambiguity is likely to surface.
This is why we should avoid it by putting the noun within brackets after the pronoun.

Ex: Rajni said to Mohini, "I do not understand what you say. *(Direct)*
Rajni said to Mohini that she (Rajni) did not understand what she (Mohini) said. *(Indirect)*

29. Gender should be changed with the person of the pronoun.

Ex: Bhagwan said to her, "You look very attractive." *(Direct)*
Bhagwan said to her that she looked very attractive. *(Indirect)*

30. The words expressing nearness in time or place in the direct speech are changed into words expressing distance in the indirect speech.

Words of this type are named below:

Ago	is changed into	before
Here	is changed into	there
Now	is changed into	then
These	is changed into	those
Hither	is changed into	thither
Hence	is changed into	thence
Come	is changed into	go
Hereby	is changed into	thereby
This	is changed into	that
Today	is changed into	that day
Tonight	is changed into	that night
Tomorrow	is changed into	the next day
Next day	is changed into	the following day
Yesterday	is changed into	the previous day or the day before
Last night	is changed into	the previous night or the night before
Last week	is changed into	the previous week
Last month	is changed into	the previous month
Next week	is changed into	the following week
Henceforth	is changed into	thence forth
Next month	is changed into	the following month
Next week	is changed into	the following week
Last week	is changed into	the previous week
The day	is changed into	the day before
Before yesterday	is changed into	previous day

Ex: She said to me, "I met you two days ago." *(Direct)*
She told me that she had met you two days before. *(Indirect)*
He said, "I was there yesterday." *(Direct)*
He said that he was there the previous day. *(Indirect)*

Note: There are exceptions to the rule mentioned above. If this, now, here, etc. in the direct speech refer to the objects, which are present at the time of reporting the speech, or at the place or time at which the speech is reported, they remain unchanged.

Ex: He said, "This is my book." *(Direct)*
He said that this (the book before the speaker or in his hand) was his book. *(Indirect)*

To change an assertive sentence from Direct into Indirect Speech

31. The reporting verb is not changed if it is not followed by an object.

32. If the reporting verb is followed by an object, "It is changed into told or some other suitable verb, such as replied, pleaded, assured, asserted, remarked, added, stated, informed, reminded, complained, reported, threatened, explained, observed, denied, answered, mentioned, declared, narrated, affirmed, confessed, warned, alleged, acknowledge, told" etc.

33. The comma is removed.

34. The inverted commas are replaced by the conjuction that. It is used to connect the reported speech with the principal clause.

35. All the general rules are followed.

Ex: He said to me, "I escaped in the guise of a woman." (*Direct*)

He informed me that he had escaped in the guise of a woman. (*Indirect*)

To change an interrogative sentence from Direct into Indirect Speech

36. The reporting verb is changed into some verb of enquiry, such as ask, enquire, demand, etc.

37. If the question begins with an interrogative word, such as who, whom, what, which, when, where, why, how, whose, etc., no conjuction is used to introduce the indirect speech.

38. The conjuction if or whether should be used to introduce the indirect speech, if the question begins with are, is, was, were, do, has, have, shall, will, can, etc. In other words, if or whether should be used when the question may have yes or no for an answer.

39. The reported speech is changed from the interrogative form to the assertive form. The mark of interrogation is replaced by a full stop.

40. The general rules are observed.

Ex: He said, "Is Kamini at home?" (*Direct*)

He asked if Kamini was at home. (*Indirect*)

She said to me, "Why have you beaten my daughter?" (*Direct*)

She demanded of me why I had beaten her daughter. (*Indirect*)

To change an imperative sentence from Direct into Indirect Speech

41. The reporting verb is changed into a verb signifying a request, command, advice, etc. The verb should be suited to the sense or context. Suitable verbs that can go with imperative sentences are:

(*a*) *Command:* direct, instruct, command, shout, threaten, summon, require, order, tell, bid, ordain, etc.

(*b*) *Request:* beg, ask, request, entreat, plead, beseech, invite, implore, solicit, and so on.

(*c*) *Advice:* suggest, urge, offer, prompt, persuade, exhort, advise and so forth.

(*d*) *Prohibition:* forbid, prevent, prohibit, etc.

42. The vocatives are changed into objects of the reporting verb.

43. The verb of the reported speech is changed into an infinitive.

44. No conjunction is generally used to introduce the reported speech.

45. If the command or advice is negative, the reporting verb is changed into forbid.

46. The general rules should be followed.

Ex: She said to me, "Please sit down." (*Direct*)

She requested me to sit down. (*Indirect*)

The teacher said, "Boys work hard and steadily." (*Direct*)

The teacher advised the boys to work hard and steadily. (*Indirect*)

To change optative sentences from Direct into Indirect Speech

47. The reporting verb is changed into wish, prayer, blessing, and so on, to denote approximately the feeling or idea expressed in the reported speech.

48. The conjunction that is used to introduce the reported speech.

49. The vocative is changed into the object of the reporting verb.

50. The sentence is changed from optative form into assertive form.

51. The general rules should be complied with
Ex: She said to me, "May you live long?" (*Direct*)
She prayed that I might live long. (*Indirect*)
I said to her, "May you be happy?" (*Direct*)
I wished that she might be happy. (*Indirect*)

To change exclamatory sentences from Direct into Indirect Speech

52. The reporting verb is changed into such verbs or expressions as exclaim, applaud, confess, approve, cry out, yell, pray or any other verb which conveys the feeling of exclamation.
53. All interjections and exclamations are omitted. Their sense is conveyed by means of expressions like with joy, with regret, with sorrow, with delight, with contempt, with impatience, etc.
54. If necessary, new words should be introduced to express the full force by exclamation.
55. The conjunction that may be used to introduce the reported speech.
56. Omit all vacatives and make them the objects of the reporting verb.
57. If an exclamatory sentence begins with words, such as how or what, omit them is the indirect form of speech. Express their sense by using the words great, big, very, etc.
58. The exclamatory expressions "How beautiful!", "What a good idea!" are changed into very beautiful and a very good idea, as and if necessary.
59. Remove the commas and the inverted commas.
60. Change the sentence from exclamatory form to assertive form.
61. All the general rules should be complied with.
Ex: He said, "How beautiful she is!" (*Direct*)
He exclaimed with delight that she was very beautiful. (*Indirect*)
She said, "Alas! I am ruined." (*Direct*)
She exclaimed with sorrow that she was ruined. (*Indirect*)
62. A table showing different feelings expressed by certain exclamations and interjections is given below:

	Exclamations	Feeling
(*a*)	Bravo! Hear! Hear! Well done	Approval
(*b*)	Look! Hark! Lo! Hush!	Attention
(*c*)	Pooh! Pshaw!	Contempt
(*d*)	Hurrah! Hah! Hah! Hah!	Joy
(*e*)	Alas! Alack! Ah! Ah me!	Sorrow
(*f*)	Fie! For shame!	Reproof
(*g*)	What! Oh! Good heavens!	Surprise

SYNONYMS AND ANTONYMS

S = Synonym, A = Antonym, N = Noun, V = Verb, Adj = Adjective

Words Beginning With A

ABANDON

S: discard, desert, discontinue, renounce, relinquish, abnegate, forsake, surrender, give up, quit.

A: retain, maintain, uphold, stay, remain.

ABATE

S: lessen, decrease, diminish, subside, slacken, subside, allay, reduce, curtail.

A: increase, enlarge, heighten, intensify, raise.

ABBREVIATE

S: shorten, abridge, compress, curtain, condense,

contract, prune, truneate, reduce.

A: enlarge, expand, lengthen, extend, elongate, prolong, protract.

ABILITY

S: competence, aptitude, capability, talent, intelligence, cleverness, capacity.

A: inability, incompetence, incapacity, incapability, inaptitude.

ABLE

S: capable, competent, intelligent, talented, efficient, skilful.

A: unable, incapable, inefficient, incompetent.

ABRUPT

S: sudden, curt, steep, hasty, unexpected, disconnected, disjointed, brusque, rough.

A: expected, anticipated, gradual, courteous, smooth.

ABSURD

S: illogical, irrational, inconsistent, silly, inane, unreasonable, funny, ridiculous, laughable, ludicrous, nonsensical, fatuous.

A: logical, reasonable, rational, consistent, sensible, sound, proper, sane.

ACCURATE

S: exact, precise, correct, actual, just, right, correct.

A: incorrect, inexact, improper, fallacious, inaccurate, misleading, erroneous.

ADEQUATE

S: ample, abundant, enough, sufficient, plentiful, copious.

A: inadequate, insufficient, meagre, scant, scantly, skimpy.

AFFABLE

S: urbane, polite, friendly, courteous, amiable, suave, good-tempered.

A: impolite, unfriendly, discourteous, haughty.

AKIN

S: kindred, similar, allied, cognate, alike, related, analogous.

A: dissimilar, unrelated, unallied, unconnected, different, unlike, separate.

ALERT

S: wary, vigilant, watchful, attentive, heedful, cautious, lively, fully awake.

A: unwatchful, sluggish, relaxed, quiet, restful.

ABNORMAL

S: unusual, irregular, anomalous, unnatural, odd, strange, erratic.

A: usual, regular, natural, normal, customary,

ACTIVE

S: brisk, energetic, lively, nimble, agile.

A: inactive, indolent, sluggish, lazy, passive, torpid.

ACTUAL

S: real, genuine, authentic, true, concrete, factual, existing.

A: unreal, implied, assumed, false, imaginary, fictitious.

AMBIGUOUS

S: vague, uncertain, undecided, undefined, obscure, doubtful, indistinct, dubious, perplexing.

A: lucid, plain, clear, obvious, unambiguous, unmistakable, indisputable.

APT

S: appropriate, apposite, suitable, fitting, pertinent, germane, relevant, congruent, harmonious, congruous.

A: inapt, inappropriate, incongruous, improper, unsuitable, inapposite, irrelevant.

ARDENT

S: fervid, fervent, warm, impassioned, plowing, intense, eager, earnest, passionate, hearty, cordial, enthusiastic.

A: cool, indifferent, apathetic, nonchalant, unimpassioned.

ATROCIOUS

S: nefarious, heinous, cruel, outrageous, beastly, horrible, horrendous.

A: noble, humane, honourable, laudable, admirable, moral.

AUDACIOUS

S: bold, daring, fearless, impudent, brash, rash, reckless, impertinent, madcap, insolent, brave, disrespectful, intrepid.

A: cowardly, timid, fearful, meek, humble, afraid, frightened, scared, different, panicky, apprehensive, shy, mousy, timorous, fidgety.

AUTHENTIC

S: genuine, real, trustworthy, true, reliable, accurate, authoritative, sound, tangible, definite, actual, precise, exact, correct, factual, veritable, sterling.

A: apocryphal, unreliable, spurious, false, fictitious, fake, sham, imaginary, counterfeit, baseless, untrue.

Words Beginning With B

BEAUTIFUL

S: catching, prepossessing, fetching, cute, enticing, engaging, attractive, charming, fascinating, captivating, alluring, tempting, lovely, bewitching, reductive, pretty, enchanting, winning, comely.

A: ugly, unattractive, unprepossessing, repulsive, gaunt, haggard, unpleasing, revolting, hideous.

BITTER

S: tart, harsh, pungent, unpalatable, acrid, spiteful, cutting, stinging, sour, unpleasant, sarcastic, resentful, biting, sardonic, caustic, severe, acrimonious, poignant, distasteful.

A: tasty, toothsome, tasteful, palatable, pleasant, delicious, warm.

BRIGHT

S: brilliant, shining, luminous, lustrous, radiant, sparkling, quick-witted, cheerful, clever, resplendent, flashing, lucid, limpid, sagacious, keen, astute, shrewd, brainy, intelligent.

A: dull, ignorant, cheerless, imbecite, murky, dark, gloomy, sullen.

BRIEF

S: compendious, concise, short, terse, laconic, curt, succinct, condensed, compact, pithy.

A: long, lengthy, prolonged, protracted, elongated, lengthened, extended, detailed, prolix, verbose, wordy.

BRUTAL

S: atrocious, savage, beastly, brutish, fiendish, devilish, barbarous, cruel, ruthless, merciless, crude, ferocious, bestial, heinous.

A: humane, gentle, civilised, merciful, polished, sympathetic, tender, liberal, considerate, good-natured.

Words Beginning With C

CANDID

S: frank, outspoken, sincere, impartial, honest, artless, ingenuous, straightforward.

A: sly, wily, insincere, reserved, unfair, evasive.

CAPRICIOUS

S: unpredictable, impulsive, fickle, changeable, inconstant, whimsical.

A: constant, firm, steadfast, unswerving.

CARELESS

S: heedless, inattentive, indifferent, negligent, remiss, lax, unmindful.

A: cautious, vigitant, careful, mindful, attentive.

CERTAIN

S: indisputable, reliable, sure, definite, undisputed, unmistakable, positive, absolute.

A: uncertain, disputable, doubtful, indefinite, ambiguous, dubious, questionable.

CHEEK

S: impudence, impertinence, effrontery, gall, temerity, audacity, insolence, sauce, sass.

A: politeness, courtesy, humility, gentleness, respect.

Note: *Cheek* also means either side of the face below the eye.

Examples: She has healthy rosy *cheeks*.
They are dancing *cheek* to *cheek*.

CHEERFUL

S: genial, happy, jolly, merry, jovial, pleasant, lively, cheery, sunny, jocund, gay.

A: cheerless, joyless, dejected, unhappy, doleful, sorrowful, mournful, glum, dreary, dismal.

CHARM (Verb)

S: fascinate, attract, please, delight, influence, entice, enchant, entrance, enrapture, allure, captivate, bewitch, ravish, tempt, lure, seduce, beguile, enthral, thrill.

A: repel, repulse, rebuff, snub, disgust, deter, disturb, irritate, annoy, alarm, frighten, terrify.

COMFORTABLE

S: cosy, snug, pleasant, pleasing, pleasurable, satisfied.

A: uncomfortable, disagreeable, dissatisfied, disturbed, displeasing, irritating, miserable, wretched, troubled, cheerless.

COMPLETE (Adj)

S: whole, thorough, total, entire, full, perfect, exhausive, consummate.

A: incomplete, imperfect, partial, unfinished, uncompleted, unaccomplished, deficient, skimpy, sketchy.

CORDIAL

S: sincere, friendly, earnest, warm, hearty, ardent, heartfelt, amiable, affable.

A: unfriendly, insincere, cold, distant, formal, reserved.

COURAGE

S: bravery, boldness, valour, heroism, fearlessness, intrepidity, nerve, gallantry, pluck, fortitude, daring.

A: cowardice, timidity, pusillanimity, fear, funk.

CURIOUS

S: inquisitive, inquiring, prying, strange, unusual, nosey, meddlesome.

A: incurious, uninquiring, uninquisitive, uninterested, unconcerned, indifferent, common, usual.

CORRECT (Adj)

S: accurate, proper, exact, precise, right, true, regular, perfect.

A: incorrect, improper, inexact, wrong, untrue, irregular, imperfect.

Words Beginning With D

DAFT

S: silly, crazy, irrational, foolish, unreasonable, reckless, insane, imbecile, lumpish.

A: sane, sound, sensible, deft, rational, reasonable.

DAINTY

S: pretty, neat, delicate, refined, tasty, delicious, fastidious, elegant, toothsome, exquisite, cute, tasteful, palatable.

A: inelegant, coarse, vulgar, rough, crude, rude, nasty, dirty.

DEEP

S: abstruse, profound, intense, learned, sagacious, extreme, devious, vivid, submerged, bottomless, unfathomable, abysmal, mysterious, knotty, astute, recondite, intricate.

A: shallow, apparent, familiar, artless, commonplace, ordinary, trite, naive, superficial, cursory, simple, banal.

DELIGHT

S: joy, pleasure, rapture, ecstasy, enjoyment, bliss, gratification, gusto, comfort.

A: displeasure, discomfort, sorrow, distress, misery, anguish, suffering, agony, woe, despair, depression.

DETRIMENTAL

S: harmful, injurious, hurtful, pernicious, damaging, noxious.

A: good, beneficial, valuable, useful, profitable, harmless, inoffensive, unobnoxious.

DIFFICULT

S: hard, troublesome, perplexing, tough, laborious, irksome, toilsome, arduous, knotty, burdensome, uphill, herculean, enigmatic.

A: easy, uncomplicated, intelligible, lucid, plain, simple, facile, manageable, tractable, elementary, rudimentary.

DILIGENT

S: industrious, laborious, hard-working, attentive, assiduous, observant, mindful, vigilant, watchful, wakeful, careful.

A: careless, heedless, inattentive, indifferent, unobservant, unmindful.

DISHONEST

S: untrustworthy, false, fraudulent, deceitful, crooked, tricky, deceptive, treacherous, unjust, unfair, unreliable.

A: trustworthy, reliable, fair, just, candid, frank, sincere, upright, truthful, veracious, honest.

DOCILE

S: pliant, tractable, amenable, teachable, yielding, compliant, tame, submissive, gentle, unresisting, dutiful, passive, acquiescent, unassertive, manageable, governable, obsequious.

A: obstinate, stubborn, intractable, self-willed, dogged, defiant, insolent, resistant, resisting, obdurate, disobedient, wilful, uncompromising, unyielding, refractory, recalcitrant.

DOUBTFUL

S: questionable, uncertain, unsure, unlikely, improbable, disputable, debatable, dubious, controversial, fishy, moot, ambiguous.

A: certain, sure, probable, indisputable, unquestionable, positive, absolute, definite, clear, unmistakable, reliable, trustworthy, undoubted, undeniable, indubitable.

DROLL

S: amusing, laughable, funny, comic, sarcastic, whimsical, comical, odd, queer, farcical, ludicrous, ridiculous, absurd, diverting, rompish.

A: sad, lamentable, lugubrious, tragic, painful, dolorous, hurtful, distressing, grievous, woeful, rueful, mournful, deplorable, touching.

DULL

S: stupid, boring, monotonous, foolish, unintelligent, cheerless, gloomy, uninteresting, spiritless, blunt, doltish, sad, stolid, dismal, dowdy, drab, unfashionable, insensible.

A: sensible, cheerful, bright, intelligent, clever, lively, animated, brilliant, sharp, talented, jolly, merry, joyful, gay, jocund, energetic, keen, active, intense, brisk, lively, trenchant, rousing.

Words Beginning With E

EAGER

S: ardent, earnest, zealous, keen, fervent, fervid, vehement, intent, agog, avid, excited, impatient, curious, anxious, enthusiastic, wistful, hearty, cordial, desirous.

A: indifferent, disinterested, cool, loath, unconcerned, apathetic, reluctant, unwilling, disinclined.

EFFICIENT

S: capable, able, competent, gifted, effective, effectual, efficacious, skilful, proficient, talented, intelligent, adept.

A: inefficient, incompetent, ineffectual, unskilled, inexpert.

ELIGIBLE

S: fit, suitable, desirable, worthy, qualified, acceptable, right.

A: unfit, unsuitable, unworthy, unacceptable, undesirable, unqualified.

EMPHEMERAL

S: short-lived, transitory, transient, fleeting, momentary, fugitive, evanescent, fugacious, temporary.

A: eternal, perpetual, perennial, permanent, intransient, lifelong, everlasting, long-lived, prolonged, protracted.

ENORMOUS

S: immense, gigantic, colossal, huge, vast, gargantuan, monstrous, prodigious, stupendous, plentiful, plenteous, copious.

A: trivial, insignificant, ordinary, average, small, little, tiny, diminutive.

ENOUGH

S: plenty, ample, sufficient, abundant, adequate.

A: insufficient, inadequate, meagre, scanty, deficient, scant, jejune, skimpy.

ENTHUSIASM

S: verve, ardour, zeal, fervour, fanaticism.

A: apathy, indifference, detachment, ennui, unconcern, lethargy, weariness, exhaustion, lassitude, languor.

EXPERT (Adj)

S: adept, skilled, adroit, proficient, skilful, deft, dexterous, versed, accomplished.

A: inexpert, unskilful, unskilled, maladroit, clumsy, lungling, unqualified, raw, inexperienced, green, incompetent.

Words Beginning With F

FACE (V)

S: confront, oppose, defy, meet, encounter, resist.

A: avoid, shun, elude, avert, eschew.

FAITHFUL

S: loyal, trustworthy, conscientious, true, accurate, devoted, exact, reliable, staunch, steadfast, constant, dependable, compliant.

A: disloyal, untrustworthy, inaccurate, inexact, unreliable, unfaithful, treacherous, undependable, untrue, fickle.

FICKLE

S: inconstant, disloyal, unfaithful, capricious, impulsive, unpredictable, changeable, unstable, variable, vacillating, wavering, fanciful, whimsical, mutable, irresolute, erratic, unreliable, fitful.

A: steady, steadfast, unchangeable, unwavering, constant, loyal, faithful, reliable, dependable, stable, immutable, invariable.

FIT (Adj)

A: suitable, appropriate, proper, advantageous, sound, well, meet, becoming, fitting, qualified, apt, apposite, decent, decorous, congruent, congruous, concordant, harmonious, eligible.

A: unfit, unsuitable, unbecoming, disadvantageous, unwell, indecent, indecorous, improper, inappropriate, inapt, incongruent, ineligible.

FOOLISH

S: silly, stupid, unwise, ridiculous, absurd, asinine, imbecile, indiscreet, irrational, idiotic, brainless, senseless, nonsensical, witless, preposterous, inane, fatuous, imprudent, inconsistent, illogical, laughable, paradoxical, dotty.

A: wise, sane, prudent, discreet, sound, sensible, rational, sagacious, judicious, sage.

Note: Each of the following words means *foolish person.*

FRIENDLY

S: kindly, pleasantly, amicable, cordial, hearty, warm-hearted, affable, genial, well-inclined, good-tempered, amiable, favourable, pleasing, sociable, companionable, nice, neighbourly, benevolent, well-disposed.

A: hostile, unsociable, unfavourable, unfriendly, adverse, inimical, antagonistic, distant, reserved, cool, ill-inclined, ill-disposed, resistant, opposed.

FUNDAMENTAL

S: basic, primary, essential, cardinal, indispensable, original, rudimentary, elementary, radical, most important, prime, chief.

A: secondary, subordinate, minor, inferior, resultant, second-rate, subsidiary.

FUNNY

S: amusing, jocular, jocose, laughable, eccentric, absurd, droll, comical, comic, playful, ludicrous, farcical, humorous, ridiculous, odd, queer, diverting, strange.

A: sad, serious, solemn, sober, sedate, staid, grave, sorrowful, mournful.

Words Beginning With G

GARRULOUS

S: talkative, chatty, verbose, loquacious, communicative, glib, voluble, prolix, wordy, long-winded, diffuse, profuse, discussive, rambling, circumlocutory, maundering, periphrastic.

A: laconic, reticent, silent, taciturn, uncommunicative, terse, reserved, short-spoken.

GENUINE

S: authentic, sound, true, real, pure, veritable, unadulterated, unalloyed, unaffected, natural, factual, actual, legitimate, undistorted, tangible, valid, sterling.

A: sham, spurious, fictitious, artificial, adulterated, alloyed, impure, apocryphal, untrue, fallacious, unsound, invalid.

GIFTED

S: talented, intelligent, sagacious, competent, wise, able, proficient, efficient, capable, shrewd, inventive, skilful, ingenious, experienced.

A: foolish, doltish, silly, stupid, idiotic.

GLORIOUS

S: famous, beautiful, splendid, magnificent, enjoyable, pleasant, grand, exalted, lofty, majestic, sublime, noble, bright, radiant, renowned.

A: base, ignoble, low, ordinary, ridiculous.

GOOD (N)

S: benefit, profit, advantage, virtue, boon, weal, prosperity, blessing, gain, welfare, righteousness, merit.

A: harm, injury, corruption, wickedness, depravity, detriment, disadvantage, ill, calamity, loss, evil, curse.

GRACEFUL

S: elegant, pleasing in style and attitude, polite, considerate, comely, beautiful, attractive, lithe, lissom, svelte, sylphlike, willowy.

A: ungainly, awkward, lumbering, uncouth, ill-mannered, not refined.

GRAND

S: august, exalted, stately, splendid, majestic, lofty, superb, imposing, dignified, noble, princely, magnificent, big, pompous, gorgeous, sublime, impressive.

A: mean, common, insignificant, secondary, inferior, unimportant, little, undignified, unimposing, petty, paltry, beggarly, lowly.

GRIM

S: fearful, stern, fierce, ruthless, horrible, determined, strong-willed, horrid, repellent, frightful, ghastly, gristly, gloomy, severe, unrelenting, unpleasant, depressing, determined, repulsive, dingy, drab, savage, appalling, ferocious, ugly, sullen, hideous.

A: handsome, pretty, graceful, elegant, gentle, gracious, friendly, humane, benign, mild, docile, attractive.

GRUFF

S: rough, surly, blunt, harsh, rude.

A: affable, courteous, mild, smooth.

Words Beginning With H

HARMFUL

S: detrimental, pernicious, prejudicial, deleterious, injurious, noxious, hurtful, mischievous, obnoxious, inauspicious, oppressive, baneful, baleful, menacing, malignant, unhealthful, vitiated, damaging.

A: helpful, profitable, beneficial, advantageous, harmless, useful, favourable, good, salutary, healthful, inoffensive, unobnoxious.

HARMONIOUS

S: congruous, concordant, uniform, proportioned,

consistent, tuneful, melodious, sweet-sounding, agreeable, friendly, amicable, cordial.

A: unfriendly, hostile, unfavourable, adverse, opposing, opposed, antagonistic, contrary, discordant, conflicting, inconsistent.

HARSH

S: rough, stern, cruel, severe, blunt, coarse, gruff, discordant, raucous, hoarse, rugged, severe, shrill, strident, austere, acrimonious, ungenial, sharp, sour, ungracious, brutal, heartless.

A: gentle, mild, smooth, soft, melodious.

HEALTHY

S: robust, strong, vigorous, lusty, hearty, sound, well, hygienic, salubrious, wholesome, salutary, bracing, invigorating, harmless, healthful, hale and hearty, inoffensive, laudable, moral.

A: diseased, delicate, infirm, injurious, frail, noxious, sick, ailing, ill, sick.

HEARTY

S: warm, earnest, sincere, heartfelt, cordial, sound, ardent, friendly, enthusiastic, cheerful, healthy, fervent, fervid.

A: cool, reserved, taciturn, insincere.

HONEST

S: frank, sincere, direct, fairly earned, truthful, upright, virtuous, right, sincere, genuine, trustworthy.

A: dishonest, untrustworthy, tricky, deceitful, fraudulent, insincere.

HONOUR (N)

S: privilege, probity, integrity, glory, distinction, great respect, glory, dignity, reverence, grandeur, high-mindedness, eminence, renown, fame.

A: dishonour, disrespect, contempt, irreverence, disgrace, degradation, slight, infamy, perfidy, treachery, improbity, scorn, disdain.

HUMOROUS

S: droll, amusing, ludicrous, funny, jocular, merry, comic, jocose, waggish, farcical.

A: solemn, serious, sober, grave, composed, sedate, dignified.

Words Beginning With I

IDLE

S: indolent, lazy, inactive, unemployed, useless, unoccupied, slothful, futile.

A: active, busy, occupied, working, industrious, employed.

INDUSTRIOUS

S: diligent, hard-working, laborious, assiduous, sedulous.

A: lethargic, inactive, apathetic, lazy, idle, indolent, slothful, torpid, sluggish, shiftless, slack, lax, supine.

IMPORTANT

S: significant, valuable, weighty, influential, momentous, prominent, material, essential, remarkable, eventful.

A: insignificant, unimportant, petty, trivial, mean, secondary, minor, uninfluential, worthless, valueless, immaterial, inferior.

INGENIOUS

S: adroit, clever, dexterous, quick-witted, skilful, talented, smart, bright, sharp, adept, original, inventive, expert, intelligent.

A: unskilled, dull, foolish, clumsy, awkward, stupid, unskilful, inexpert, maladroit, incompetent, inexperienced, unconversant, ungainly.

INGENUOUS

S: innocent, open, candid, frank, sincere, straightforward, truthful, artless, honest, naive, simple, trusting, unaffected, outspoken.

A: insincere, reserved, sly, wily, contrived, disingenuous, mean, pretentious, sham, affected, priggish.

INFINITE

S: boundless, endless, unlimited, unbounded, limitless, immeasurable, interminable, stupendous, eternal, immense, vast, incalculable, numberless, countless, bottomless, unfathomable, inexhaustible, indefinite, perpetual.

A: finite, limited, restricted, bounded, conditioned, confined, definite, determinate, circumscribed.

INTELLIGENT

S: brainy, clever, bright, brilliant, keen, sagacious, quick-witted, discerning, sharp, shrewd, astute, canny, perspicacious, perceptive, nimble, well-informed, enlightened.

A: foolish, doltish, dull, stupid, unintelligent, stolid, obtuse, silly, inane.

INTEGRITY

S: honesty, probity, uprightness, rectitude, truthfulness, sincerity, trustworthiness, fairness, wholeness, completeness, oneness, totality, entirety, indivisibility.

A: dishonesty, duplicity, unfairness, deceit, fraud, improbity.

IRRITABLE

S: peevish, touchy, irascible, testy, short-tempered, fretful, splenetic, petulant, grumpy, pettish, snappish, choleric, peppery, churlish, cantankerous, fractious, crabbed.

A: calm, composed, agreeable, gracious, cheerful, genial, good-natured, blithe, jaunty, buoyant, lively, animated.

Words Beginning With J

JEALOUS

S: envious, invidious, suspicious, resentful, covetous, jaundiced, distrustful, apprehensive, intolerant.

A: unenvious, unjealous, tolerant, liberal, genial, indifferent, unsuspecting.

JOLLY

S: genial, jovial, jubilant, lively, gay, joyful, merry, mirthful, cheerful, light-hearted, jocular, jocund, blithe.

A: cheerless, joyless, sad, mournful, gloomy, morose, sullen, lugubrious, sorrowful, melancholy, dismal, unhappy.

JUST

S: fair, honest, proper, right, reasonable, well-founded, deserved, impartial, true, upright, exact, precise, proportioned, normal.

A: unfair, unjust, improper, unreasonable, partial, untrue, inexact, abnormal, ill-proportioned, prejudiced, biased.

Words Beginning With K

KEEN

S: acute, sharp, penetrating, astute, clever, cunning, quick, shrewd, wily, eager, enthusiastic, intense, deep, strong, cutting, ardent, nippy, avid, fervent.

A: indifferent, blunt, dull, languid, indifferent, cool, careless, half-hearted, unconcerned, lukewarm, impervious, insouciant.

KIND (Adj)

S: friendly, gentle, mild, obliging, benign, lenient, helpful, sympathetic, favourable, benevolent, amiable, good-natured, cordial, courteous, gracious, warm-hearted, humane, compassionate, generous, philanthropic.

A: unfriendly, unfavourable, discourteous, unkind, harsh, severe, hard, callous, cruel, inhumane.

KNOWLEDGE

S: understanding, learning, information, instruction, acquaintance, cognition, cognizance, awareness, comprehension, apprehension, consciousness, familiarity, ken, enlightenment, experience, attainments, scholarship, education.

A: ignorance, nescience, illiteracy, incomprehension, inexperience, unawareness

Words Beginning With L

LABORIOUS

S: diligent, hard-working, industrious, toilsome, ledious, tiresome, irksome, arduous, assiduous, wearisome, strenuous, painstaking, uphill.

A: easy, light, feasible, indiligent, lazy, indolent, simple, idle.

LACONIC

S: curt, terse, concise, pithy, short, brief, succinct, crisp, compendious, compact.

A: lengthy, prolix, wordy, circumlocutory, verbose, discursive, long-winded, rambling, roundabout, copious, diffuse.

LAX

S: negligent, careless, remiss, sluggish, inattentive, neglectful, heedless, vague, desultory, unmethodical, loose, slack, relaxed.

A: careful, meticulous, attentive, methodical, severe, strict, heedful, regardful, cautious, prudent, discreet.

LESSEN

S: shorten, abate, curtail, decrease, reduce, diminish, abridge, mitigate, contract, deduct, subtract, shrink, allenuate.

A: increase, enlarge, augment, extend, expand, grow, amplify, enhance, magnify.

LIVELY

S: high-spirited, vigorous, energetic, active, animated, brisk, bright, blithe, frolicsome, merry, playful, spirited, forceful, sprightly, vivacious, joyous, joyful, gay.

A: dull, listless, insipid, vapid, inactive, uninteresting, depressed, languid, torpid, apathetic, indifferent, sluggish, dejected, joyless, cheerless, unlively, spiritless.

LOGICAL

S: cogent, convincing, sound, valid, effective, reasonable, natural, rational, sane, relevant.

A: illogical, invalid, ineffective, unreasonable, unnatural, irrational, insane, irrelevant, fallacious.

Words Beginning With M

MADDEN

S: infuriate, enrage, incense, derange, craze, anger, offend, displease, embitter, exasperate, rankle, affront, irritate, provoke, nettle, inflame, annoy.

A: placate, pacify, soothe, calm, assuage, appease, mollify.

MALICIOUS

S: spiteful, malignant, malevolent, evil-minded, hostile, rancorous, virulent, wicked, malign, pernicious, vicious, harmful, maleficent, ill-disposed, ill-intentioned.

A: benign, kind, good-natured, benevolent, cordial, unselfish, sympathetic, gracious, well-intentioned, humane, warm-hearted, affectionate.

MASTERLY

S: skilful, adept, deft, dexterous, expert, skilled, consummate, perfect, masterful, dominating.

A: unskilled, maladroit, clumsy, inexpert.

METHODICAL

S: orderly, logical, systematic, regular, procedural, planned, arranged, tidy.

A: disorderly, illogical, irregular, unsystematic, unmethodical, untidy, desultory, unarranged, disarranged, sloppy, chaotic, anarchical.

MODEST

S: moderate, inexpensive, not showy or splendid in appearance, not vain or boastful, shy, bashful, humble, meek, reserved, unassuming, unpretentious, diffident, unobtrusive, coy.

A: immodest, showy or splendid in appearance, vain, boastful, ostentatious, pretentious, proud, arrogant, bold, conceited, haughty, disdainful, pert, imperious, domineering, priggish, smug, self-satisfied, egotistic, self-important.

MOMENTOUS

S: important, prominent, significant, weighty, material, pressing, influential, grave, consequential, serious, notable, solemn, memorable, remarkable.

A: unimportant, immaterial, inconsequential, insignificant, mean, petty, trivial, slight, niggling, trifling.

Words Beginning With N

NATURAL

S: innate, inherent, original, normal, spontaneous, unaffected, characteristic, typical, native, unstudied, inborn, naive, ingenuous, inbred, ingrained, usual, intrinsic.

A: unnatural, abnormal, artificial, affected, forced, irregular, unusual, inconsistent, fictitious.

NECESSARY

S: requisite, needful, essential, inevitable, unavoidable, indispensable.

A: unnecessary, optional, unessential, dispensable, voluntary, discretional, casual.

NICE

S: pleasant, agreeable, friendly, kind, fine, subtle, respectable, scrupulous, dainty, attractive, fastidious, tasteful, delicate, choosy, refined, palatable, delectable, pleasing, pleasurable.

A: disagreeable, coarse, unscrupulous, rough, nasty, rueful, mournful, woeful, deplorable, distressing.

NIMBLE

S: agile, sharp, active, brisk, lively, spry, quick.

A: slow, sluggish, clumsy, inert, lazy, indolent, awkward, slothful.

NOVICE

S: beginner, tyro, neophyte, apprentice, greenhorn, learner, acolyte, rookie.

A: expert, adept, master, teacher, trainer, instructor.

Words Beginning With O

OBEDIENT

S: observant, dutiful, complying, compliant, loyal, faithful, devoted, fractable, docile, submissive, pliable, pliant, yielding.

A: disloyal, unfaithful, intractable, uncomplying, uncompliant, unruly, unsubmissive, refractory, resisting, contumacious, recalcitrant.

OBSTINATE

S: stubborn, obdurate, dogged, tenacious, persistent, insistent, headstrong, pertinacious, unyielding, determined, self-willed, wilful, resolute.

A: irresolute, subservient, yielding, submissive, amenable, wavering.

OFFENSIVE (Adj)

S: insulting, annoying, disgusting, repulsive, aggressive, distasteful, foul, aggressive, obnoxious, nasty.

A: pleasant, defensive, inoffensive, harmless, blameless, unaggressive, innocuous.

OWN (V)

S: possess, confess, admit, avow, acknowledge, have, hold, concede.

A: deny, disclaim, disavow, renounce, disown, abjure, abandon.

Words Beginning With P

PEEVISH

S: irritable, touchy, testy, tetchy, irascible, fretful, bad-tempered, crabbed, pettish, petulant, snappish, waspish, fractious, hotheaded, crabby, churlish.

A: affable, genial, good-natured, good-tempered, pleasant, cordial, hearty, jolly, soft-spoken, polite, urbane.

PERFECT (Adj)

S: complete, excellent, ideal, exact, precise, total, absolute, thorough, faultless, indefective, indeficient, immaculate, impeccable, sound, spotless, entire, utter, consummate.

A: imperfect, incomplete, inexact, deficient, faulty, unsound, deformed, impaired, blemished, crude.

PLEASANT

S: enjoyable, polite and friendly, pleasurable, agreeable, pleasing, delectable, palatable, delightful, cheerful, delicious, jocular, merry.

A: unpleasant, disagreeable, unlively, lugubrious, dismal, sad, mournful, offensive, unpleasing, disgusting, obnoxious, nasty.

PLENTIFUL

S: ample, abundant, copious, profuse, plenteous, prolific, bounteous, bountiful, lavish.

A: scanty, meagre, limited, skimpy, insufficient, sparing, scarce, deficient, rare.

POMPOUS

S: self-important, ostentatious, high-flown, bombastic, grandiose, arrogant, haughty, grand, imposing, lofty, magnificent, majestic, stately, sublime, dignified, showy, pretentious, assuming, turgid, magniloquent.

A: unassuming, plain-mannered, unpretending, modest, unobtrusive, humble-minded, unpretentious, bashful, coy.

PRECISE

S: exact, accurate, definite, correct, punctitious, fastidious, particular, proper.

A: inexact, inaccurate, indefinite, incorrect, improper, vague, ambiguous, rough, circumlocutory.

PREPOSSESSING

S: attractive, charming, taking, alluring, engaging, winning, appealing, winsome.

A: unattractive, repulsive, ugly, unprepossessing, ill-looking.

PREPOSTEROUS

S: outrageous, absurd, unreasonable, ridiculous, foolish, silly, stupid, inconsistent, irrational, nonsensical, laughable, idiotic, illogical, ludicrous.

A: consistent, reasonable, rational, logical, sensible, sound, just, fair, right, moderate.

PRINCIPAL (Adj)

S: chief, main, foremost, prime, leading, most important, pre-eminent, outstanding, excellent, conspicuous, highest, first-rate, cardinal, fundamental, primary, paramount, supreme, predominant.

A: minor, inferior, subordinate, secondary, auxiliary, subsidiary.

PUSHY

S: aggressive, offensive, forceful, belligerent, bold, impudent, rude, disrespectful, insolent, self-assertive.

A: cowardly, timid, defensive.

Words Beginning With Q

QUESTIONABLE

S: doubtful, uncertain, suspicious, dubious, disputable, debatable, arguable, fishy, controversial.

A: certain, indisputable, obvious, evident, unquestionable, sure.

QUICKEN

S: hasten, hurry, speed, accelerate, refresh, animate, rush, expedite.

A: retard, slacken, moderate, curb, shorten, slow, relax, delay, impede, hinder, obstruct.

QUIET (Adj)

S: calm, peaceful, serene, hushed, silent, modest, restrained, subdued, gentle, unostentatious, restful, relaxed, leisurely, unhurried, reposeful, tranquil, quiescent, unobtrusive, passive, undisturbed, motionless, still, mild, modest.

A: loud, agitated, disturbed, perturbed, noisy.

QUIET (N)

S: calm, calmness, hush, peace, repose, rest, silence, stillness, tranquility, serenity, quiescence, quietude.

A: agitation, disturbance, uproar, noise, din, noisiness, loudness, tumult, excitement, turmoil, commotion, unrest

Words Beginning With R

RAPID

S: speedy, quick, swift, fast, prompt, expeditious, hasty, hurried.

A: slow, sluggish, slack, tardy, leisurely, gradual, languid.

REASONABLE

S: sensible, logical, moderate, tolerable, acceptable, average, sound, fair, rational; inexpensive, sober, temperate.

A: unreasonable, absurd, unfair, illogical, irrational, intolerable, immoderate, expensive, senseless, preposterous, ridiculous. silly, excessive, obstinate.

REGULAR

S: proper, systematic, symetrical, normal, usual, habitual, constant, orderly, steady, methodical, consistent.

A: irregular, improper, abnormal, unusual, disorderly, inconstant, desultory, unmethodical, changeable, erratic, sporadic.

REMARKABLE

S: unusual, exceptional, august, impressive, extraordinary, uncommon, splendid, singular, notable, noteworthy, striking, distinguished, wonderful, famous, prominent, conspicuous, imposing.

A: ordinary, average, inconspicuous, normal, usual, common, customary, undistinguished.

RESPONSIBLE

S: answerable, trustworthy, dependable, accountable, liable, chargeable, reliable.

A: irresponsible, untrustworthy, undependable, unreliable, unaccountable, unanswerable.

RICH

S: wealthy, affluent, prosperous, opulent, nourishing, abundant, ample, fruitful, fertile, luxuriant, vivid, bountiful, sumptuous, gorgeous, sonorous, well-to-do, plentiful, fecund, well-heeled, productive, wholesome, nutritious.

A: poor, needy, penniless, beggarly, indigent, destitute, barren, sterile, unfruitful, unproductive, impecunious, hard up, necessitous.

Words Beginning With S

SCHOOL (V)

S: train, teach, direct, lead, guide, educate, instruct, control, discipline, inform, enlighten, tutor.

A: misdirect, mislead, misguide, deceive, delude.

SCRUPULOUS

S: absolutely honest, extremely careful and thorough, paying great attention to details, exact, meticulous, punctitious, upright, moral, conscientious, veracious, truthful, right-minded, high-principled.

A: dishonest, deceitful, tricky, fraudulent, unscrupulous, careless, unprincipled, conscienceless, knavish.

SILLY

S: foolish, doltish, indiscreet, stupid, unwise, childish, inane, fatuous, senseless, absurd, ridiculous, idiotic, nonsensical, irrational, preposterous, outrageous, imprudent.

A: wise, prudent, rational, sane, discreet, sound, intelligent, sensible, sapient, sagacious, discerning, perspicacious, brainy, brilliant, well-advised, judicious, astute, shrewd.

SLY

S: foxy, wily, crafty, cunning, deceitful, secretive, furtive, roguish, mischievous, stealthy, underhand, surreptitious.

A: open, frank, candid, ingenuous, sincere, artless.

SOFTEN

S: mollify, soothe, ease, calm, comfort, quiet, temper, moderate, mitigate, abate, allay, alleviate, assuage, diminish, lessen, extenuate, relieve.

A: harden, stiffen, augment, irritate, increase, aggravate, worsen, enhance, heighten, intensify, infuriate, indurate.

SUITABLE

S: appropriate, proper, fitting, right, becoming, apposite, eligible, seemly, apt, meet, decorous, seasonable.

A: unsuitable, improper, unbecoming, inapt, indecorous, unseemly, ineligible, inappropriate, inapposite.

Words Beginning With T

TEDIOUS

S: boring, tiresome, wearisome, irksome, monotonous, dreary, uninteresting, dull, humdrum, drab.

A: interesting, amusing, entertaining, exciting, delightful, brisk.

TERRIBLE

S: horrible, alarming, fearful, shocking, frightful awesome, appalling, dreadful, terrifying, frightening, formidable, terrific, horrid, terrible. fearsome.

A: pleasing, encouraging, safe, secure, joyous informidable, unastounding.

TOLERABLE

S: endurable, bearable, passable, sufferable, acceptable.

A: intolerable, unbearable, unacceptable, unendurable.

TOTALLY

S: fully, wholly, completely, entirely, absolutely, thoroughly, perfectly, utterly.

A: partially, partly, incompletely, somewhat.

TRUE

S: accurate, actual, unerring, correct, authentic, exact, real, veracious, constant, faithful, loyal, genuine, precise, veritable, reliable, rightful, sincere, factual, legitimate.

A: untrue, inaccurate, incorrect, inexact, unreal, unfaithful, disloyal, unreliable, insincere, false, spurious, fictitious, erroneous, inconstant, fickle, fallacious, apocryphal.

Words Beginning With U

UNASSUMING

S: modest, reserved, retiring, humble, diffident, bashful, shy, coy, unpretentious, unostentatious.

A: arrogant, boastful, haughty, proud, vain, immodest, pretentious, ostentatious, pert, vainglorious, imperious, smug, priggish, domineering.

URBANE

S: suave, affable, polite, civil, courteous, refined, well-bred, well-mannered, accomplished, sophisticated, courtly, amiable.

A: uncivil, uncouth, rude, ill-mannered, discourteous, impolite, boorish, impertinent.

UTTER (Adj)

S: complete, entire, thorough, full, whole, perfect, absolute, sheer, total, downwright, consummate, arrant.

A: incomplete, imperfect, partial, meagre, lacking, wanting, deficient, sketchy, skimpy.

Words Beginning With V

VALID

S: binding, sound, legal, logical, effective, cogent, operative, weighty, well-grounded, just.

A: invalid, illegal, illogical, unjust, unsound, ineffective, null and void, inoperative.

VANITY

S: pride, egotism, arrogance, conceit, immodesty, self-esteem, smugness, priggishness, vainglory, boasting, boast, bombast, bluster, brag, rodomontade.

A: modesty, humility, meekness, simplicity, unostentatiousness.

VIGOROUS

S: energetic, active, strong, potent, powerful, mighty, forceful, animated, lively, spirited, sprightly, brisk, vivacious, intense.

A: powerless, ineffective, ineffectual, dull, feeble, unsound, impotent, flabby.

VITAL

S: essential, indispensable, necessary, basic, cardinal, paramount, energetic, lively, dynamic.

A: unessential, unimportant, dispensable, immaterial, insignificant.

Words Beginning With W

WELCOME (Adj)

S: pleasing, agreeable, acceptable, gratifying, pleasant, pleasurable.

A: unwelcome, unacceptable, disagreeable, distasteful, unpleasant, offensive, repugnant, repulsive, unpalatable.

WISE

S: prudent, sagacious, sage, learned, profound, well-advised, judicious, scholarly. well-informed, well-read, shrewd.

A: unwise, foolish, shallow, silly, stupid, inane, fatuous, injudicious, imprudent, ill-advised, doltish, uneducated, unschooled.

WRONG (Adj)

S: erroneous, incorrect, unjust, inaccurate, mistaken, faulty, untrue, unprecise, improper, bad, amiss, inappropriate, unsuitable, false, unfair, unfit.

A: right, correct, true, proper, suitable, exact, just, precise, fair, accurate.

Words Beginning With Y

YEARLING

S: youngling, colt, filly, cub, whelp, puppy.

A: elder, doyen, old-timer, veteran.

YEARN

S: desire, strongly, pine, long, hanker, grieve, mourn.

A: hate, detest, despise, loathe, dislike, abominate.

YIELDING

S: pliant, tractable, docile, submissive, compliant, flexible, soft, manageable.

A: intractable, unmanageable, awkward, stubborn obstinate, obdurate, unyielding, inflexible, hard, unruly, recalcitrant.

YOUNG

S: youthful, new, fresh, inexperienced, immature, youngish, teen-age, juvenile, adolescent, green, puerile.

A: old, elderly, experienced, aged, senior, mature, full-grown.

Words Beginning With Z

ZANY (Adj)

S: ridiculous, eccentric, amusing, ludicrous, foolish, doltish, silly, inane, fatuous, stupid, droll, funny, whimsical, dull, drab.

A: wise, intelligent, accomplished, well-informed, shrewd, brisk, active.

ZANY (N)

S: merry-andrew, buffoon, clown, madcap, fool, comedian, jester, nitwit, dunce, dolt, nincompoop, ninny, simpleton, numskull, oaf, loon, dullard, dunderhead, blockhead, goof, idiot, booby, bonehead, dunce, imbecile.

A: sage, scholar, genius, wise person, intelligent person.

ZEAL

S: enthusiasm, energy, verve, keenness, vim, vigour, heartiness, earnestness, spirit, eagerness, warmth, ardour, fervour, devotion, dash, briskness, alacrity, intensity, vehemence.

A: apathy, indifference, unconcern, ennui, detachment, coldness, torpor, torpidity.

ZEALOUS

S: eager, keen, enthusiastic, deep, strong, intense, earnest, passionate, spirited, ardent, warm, energetic, fervent, fervid, impassioned, vehement.

A: cold, apathetic, indifferent, nonchalant, calm and casual, cool.

ZENITH

S: acme, top, summit, apex, climax, vertex, culmination, peak, prime, highest point.

A: nadir, lowest point or part, base, bottom, foot.

ZEST

S: gusto, relish, enthusiasm, exhilaration, thrill, great enjoyment or excitement.

A: distaste, disrelish, dislike, insipidity.

VOCABULARY

Words Beginning With A

Abandoned
Abashed
Abdicate
Abdomen
Aberrant
Abeyance
Abhorrence
Abnegate
Abracadabra
Abridge
Abridgement
Abscess
Absentee
Abstemious
Abstinence
Abtruse
Abysmal
Abyss
Accede
Accent
Accept
Access
Accessible
Accession
Accessory
Accident
Acclaim
Acclamation
Accolade
Accommodation
Accomplice
Accordance
Accost
Accrue
Accumulate
Accurate
Accuracy
Accusation
Achieve
Achievement
Acknowledge
Acme
Acolyte
Acquaint
Acquiesce
Acquire
Acquisition
Acquit

Acquittal
Acronym
Across
Acumen
Adage
Addendum
Addle
Adept
Adhere
Adieu
Adequate
Admissible
Adolescent
Adolescence
Adumbrate
Adventitious
Adventure
Adversary
Aegis
Aesthetic
Aesthete
Affable
Affiance
Affirm
Affluence
Affray
Afield
Aggrandise
Aggregate
Aggression
Aggrieved
Agile
Agoraphobia
Agreeable
Aide-memoire
Aisle
Albumen
Alfresco
Alien
Alienate
Allergy
Alleviate
Allusion
Amanuensis
Amalgamate
Amateur
Ambassador

Ambidextrous
Amour
Amorous
Ambiguous
Ambivalent
Amiable
Amicable
Analogous
Analogue
Ancient
Animosity
Anniversary
Anomalous
Anonymous
Anorexia
Antecedent
Anxiety
Anxious
Apiece
Apostle
Appal
Appalled
Apparent
Argument
Arrant
Assay
Ascend
Ascertain
Ascetic
Ascrib
Assassin
Assault
Assign
Atrocious
Auction
Audacious
Audible
Audience
Augment
Auspicious
Austere
Authentic
Autobiography
Autocracy
Autonomous
Autumn
Axiom

Words Beginning With B

Babble
Bachelor
Badge
Balderdash
Balmy
Bamboozle
Banquet
Batch
Battalion
Batter
Batty
Bawdy
Bawl
Beguile
Belief
Believe
Beneficent
Bereave
Beseech
Biosterous
Blasphemou
Blossom
Bludgeon
Blurt
Bonanza
Borrow
Bosom
Bouquet
Brassiere
Brawl
Breadth
Brief
Brochure
Bruise
Budge
Budget
Buffoon
Bumtious
Bumpkin
Buoyant
Bureaucracy
Buttress
Buxom

Words Beginning With C

Cache
Cabbage
Cadge
Calendar
Calf
Callous
Calm
Calumny
Campaign
Cancellation
Canny
Cantankerous
Capricious
Captious
Cartoon
Catalogue
Cauliflower
Causal
Cautious
Chagrin
Chancellor
Chaos
Charisma
Charlatan
Chauffeur
Chauvinist
Chef
Chequered
Chicanery
Chivalrous
Chivvy
Chronological
Circumlocution
Circumstantial
Clamour
Clandestine
Claptrap
Clause
Claustrophobia
Cliche
Clientele
Climacteric
Clique
Clutch

Codger
Coercion
Collage
Colleague
Colleen
Collision
Colloquial
Collusion
Cogent
Colossal
Column
Come-uppance
Commensurate
Commission
Committee
Commodious
Communique
Compassionate
Compendious
Complementary
Complimentary
Complexion
Comprehensible
Concatenation
Conceive
Conceit
Conception
Concupiscence
Condemn
Condign
Congregation
Congruent
Congruous
Conquest
Conscience
Conscientious
Conscious
Consensus
Consign
Consequential
Consignment
Conspicuous
Constituency
Contagious
Contemptible
Continuous

Contumacious
Conundrum
Convenient
Coquette
Corrigendum
Credentials
Criterion
Critique
Cuisine
Courteous
Courtesy
Courtly

Words Beginning With D

Dabble
Damn
Daunt
Dawn
Dearth
Debonair
Deceit
Deceive
Deficient
Deign
Deity
Delight
Delusive
Demagogue
Demeanour
Dementia
Demur
Demure
Descend
Design
Devour
Devout
Dialogue
Differentiate
Dilemma
Dipsomaniac
Discern
Disguise
Dislodge
Disquiet
Distraught
Dodge
Dodgy
Dolour
Dough
Doughty
Draught
Dubiety
Dummy
Duologue
Dyspepsia

Words Beginning With E

Eavesdrop
Eccentric
Echelon
Eclat
Edge
Edgy
Eerie
Effete
Efficacious
Egotist
Elocution
Eloquent
Embarrass
Embezzle
Enamoured
Encomium
Encyclopedia
Ennui
Ephemeral
Epilogue
Epistle
Epitaph
Epithet
Erratum
Erroneous
Etiquette
Euphemism
Euphoria
Exaggerate
Exceed
Exemplary
Exhaust
Explosion
Exposure
Exquisite
Extant
Extempore
Extension
Extenuate
Extinguish
Extravagant
Extrinsic
Extrovert
Exuberant
Exude
Exult

Words Beginning With F

Fabulous
Facade
Facetious
Fallacious
Fallible
Fascinate
Fasten
Fastidious
Fatigue
Favouritism
Feasible
Feature
Feign
Felicitous
Ferocious
Fervour
Fetching
Fiancee
Fiasco
Finesse
Flabbergast
Flamboyant
Flaunt
Flavour
Flibbertigibbet
Flippant
Flourish
Folly
Formidable
Foreign
Fortitude
Fortunate
Fraças
Fraud
Fraught
Fright
Frivolous
Fuddy-duddy
Fudge
Fulfil
Fulsome
Fulminate
Fussy
Futile
Funk
Fusty

Words Beginning With G

Gabble
Gaggle
Gaiety
Gallant
Garrulous
Gauche
Gawky
Gazette
Germane
Gesticulate
Gesture
Ghastly
Gibberish
Gigantic
Giggle
Gimmic
Gingerly
Glamour
Glossary
Glutton
Goad
Gobble
Goggle
Gorgeous
Gourmand
Gourmet
Gracious
Grandeur
Grape-vine
Grandiloquent
Grapple
Gratuitous
Greenhorn
Gregarious
Grievance
Grieve
Grief
Grievous
Grimace
Groggy
Grotesque
Grouch
Grubby
Grouse
Grudge
Gruesome
Grumpy
Guarantee
Guffaw
Guile
Guilty
Guise
Gullible
Gusto
Guzzle

Words Beginning With H

Hackneyed
Haggard
Haggle
Hagridden
Hallucination
Hangdog
Hanky-panky
Haphazard
Hapless
Haranque
Harbour
Harlot
Harry
Hassle
Hasten
Hatch
Haughty
Haunt
Hauteur
Haven

Hearten
Hedge
Hedonism
Heighten
Heinous
Helter-skelter
Hen-party
Henpecked
Herculean
Heyday
Heterogeneous
Hierarchy
Higgledy-piggledy
Histrionic
Hitch
Hobble
Hobnob
Hocus-pocus
Hodge-podge
Hoity-toity
Homogeneous
Homograph
Homonym
Homophone
Honorarium
Honorary
Honourable
Hoodwink
Homicide
Homogeneous
Hooey
Horrendous
Horrible
Horrid
Horrific
Hotch-potch
Hoyden
Hubbub
Hubby
Huddle
Hugger-mugger
Hullabaloo
Humdinger
Humdrum
Humorous
Hurly-burly
Hussy
Hustle
Hydrophobia
Hymn
Hyperbole
Hypochondria
Hypocrisy

Words Beginning With I

Idiocy
Idiosyncrasy
Ignoramus
Ignorant
Illegal
Illegible
Illegitimate
Illicit
Illiterate
Illogical
Illusion
Illustrate
Imbecile
Immaculate
Immanent
Immaterial
Immature
Immeasurable
Immemorial
Immense
Imminent
Immobile
Immoderate
Immodest
Immoral
Immovable
Immune
Impalpable
Impartial
Impassable
Impatient
Impeccable
Impede
Impel
Impending
Imperious
Imperishable
Impertinent
Impetuous
Impiety
Impish
Implement
Implicate
Implicit
Imposing
Impressive
Impropriety
Imprudent
Impulsive
Inaccurate
Inadequate
Inane
Inappropriate
Inaugural
Inauspicious
Incoherent
Incompetent
Incorrigible
Incredulous
Indigenous
Indigent
Indignant
Indisposed
Indolent
Indomitable
Indulge
Ineffable
Inefficient
Influential
Ingrained
Innate
Innumerable
Inordinate
Insane
Insipid
Insolent
Instigate
Integrity
Intimidate
Intractable
Intrepid
Intrique
Introvert
Invariably
Iota
Introvert
Irritate
Irritable
Isthmus
Itemize
Itinerant
Itinerary

Words Beginning With J

Jab
Jabber
Jade
Jam-packed
Jargon
Jaundice
Jaunt
Jaunty
Jealous
Jeer
Jejune
Jeremiad
Jest
Jiffy
Jiggery-pokery
Jilt
Jitter
Jocose
Jocular
Jocund
Jolly
Jostle
Judder
Juvenile
Juxtapose
Juggernaut
Jumble
Juncture

Words Beginning With K

Kaleidoscopic
Keel
Keepsake
Ken
Kickback
Kindred
Kleptomania
Knack
Knave
Knick-knack
Kowtow
Kudos

Words Beginning With L

Labial
Laborious
Lack-lustre
Lackadaisical
Laconic
Lady-killer
Laggard
Lambaste
Languish
Largesse
Lascivious
Latent
Laudable
Layabout
Laxative
Leer
Legible
Leisure
Lethargy
Lesbian
Lewd
Liaison
Libertine
Licentious
Lieu
Limbo
Lissom
Listen
Locale
Locution
Lodging
Loggerheads
Loony
Loophole
Loquacious

Lucid
Lucrative
Lugubrious
Luscious
Luxurious

Words Beginning With M

Madcap
Madden
Magnate
Magnificent
Magniloquent
Malevolent
Malign
Mammoth
Manifesto
Marital
Matricide
Mature
Meagre
Meddle
Medieval
Martinet
Medley
Meek
Megalomania
Melodorous
Melee
Memento
Memorandum
Mendacious
Meretricious
Meritorious
Meticulous
Mettle
Mien
Milieu
Miscellaneous
Mischief
Mischievous
Misogynist
Missive
Mollycoddle
Momentous
Momentary
Monologue
Monotheism
Morale
Mordant
Moribund
Mosque
Motley
Mundane
Myriad
Mysterious
Mystecism
Mystical
Mystique
Myth

Words Beginning With N

Nab
Nadir
Naff
Nag
Naive
Namby-pamby
Nap
Nark
Nascent
Nasty
Natter
Natty
Naughty
Nebulous
Nefarious
Negligee
Nestle
Nexus
Nibble
Nicety
Nich
Niff
Nifty
Nigard
Niggle
Niggling
Nincompoop
Ninny
Nippy
Nitwit
Nitty-gritty
Nix
Nobble
Noddle
Nosh
Nonce
Nonchalant
Nosey
Novice
Noxious
Nubile
Nuance
Nub
Nudge
Nugatory
Nugget
Numskull
Nuptial
Nuts
Nymphet
Nymphomania
Nymphomaniac

Words Beginning With O

Oaf
Obese
Obnoxious
Oblivious
Obloquy
Odious
Odour
Ominous
Omission
Omnipotent
Omnipresent
Omniscient
Omnivorous
One-upmanship
Oodles
Oomph
Ooze
Opprobrious
Optimistic
Opulent
Oration
Orgy
Oscillate
Ostensible
Ostentatious
Otiose
Oust
Outlandish
Outskirts
Outsmart
Outspoken
Outwit
Ovation
Overwhelm
Ovoid

Words Beginning With P

Paddle
Paddy
Palatable
Palatial
Palindrome
Palm
Palpable
Pamper
Pandemonium
Pander
Panegyric
Panjandrum
Panorama
Pantheism
Pap
Paragon
Paradox
Paramount
Pariah
Parlance
Parlour
Parlous
Parochial
Paroxysm
Parricide
Parrot-fashion
Parry
Parsimonious
Parvenu
Passionate
Pastime
Patriarch
Patricide
Patsy
Paucity
Pauper
Peckish
Peccadillo
Peer
Pedagogue
Pedant
Peek
Peep
Peevish
Pejorative
Pell-mell
Penurious
Penury
Pepper
Peppery
Pernicious
Persist
Perspicacious
Pesky
Pester
Petite
Pettish
Petulant
Picky
Pinafore
Pique
Plethora
Poignant
Polyandry
Pompous
Plait
Plaudit
Pluck
Plummy
Plump
Poday
Polygamy
Popinjay
Poppycock
Prattle
Precocious
Prepossessing
Prig

Prescient
Prodigy
Proficient
Prologue
Pronto
Psalm
Pseudonym
Puberty
Puckish
Pudgy
Puerile
Pugnacious
Punctillious
Puppy-love
Purloin
Putative
Pyromania
Pyromaniac

Words Beginning With Q

Quagmire
Quash
Queer
Quell
Quench
Querulous
Query
Quest
Quibble
Quicken
Quickie
Quiescent
Quilt
Quip
Quirk
Quisling
Quintessence
Quintuplet
Quiver
Quizzical

Words Beginning With R

Rabble
Racy
Raffish
Rag
Ragamuffin
Ragtag
Ramble
Ransom
Rapacious
Rapport
Rapture
Ravenous
Razzmatazz
Reign
Relieve
Relief
Replete
Retrieve
Ribald
Ridge
Rigmarole
Rinse
Risque
Rustle

Words Beginning With S

Sacrosanct
Sagacious
Salient
Sally
Salubrious
Salutary
Sardonic
Sass
Satire
Saunter
Saucy
Savvy
Scamper
Scapegoat
Scatty
Scotfree
Scurrilous
Sedate
Seduce
Sententious
Shifty
Shilly-shally
Shirty
Shiver
Shrewd
Shudder
Simper
Simpleton
Skittish
Slapdash
Slight
Slender
Slipshod
Sloppy
Slough
Slovenly
Sluggish
Smarmy
Smirk
Snigger
Solemn
Somersault
Sonorous
Sordid
Spleen
Splendour
Spontaneous
Sporadic
Spruce
Squander
Stentorian
Studious
Stupendous
Sturdy
Sultry
Surmount
Swagger
Swoon
Swoop
Syllogism

Words Beginning With T

Taboo
Tacit
Taciturn
Tangible
Tantamount
Tardy
Tarnish
Tart
Tattle
Tautology
Tedious
Teeny-bopper
Tell-tale
Temerity
Tenacious
Testy
Tetchy
Terse
Tete-a-tete
Theism
Thesaurus
Tipsy
Tiptop
Titbit
Titillate
Tittle-tattle
Tizzy
Tomboy
Tomfool
Topsy-turvy
Totter
Tractable
Trite
Triplet
Triumph
Trivet
Trogeodyte
Trollop
Truculent
Trudge
Turpitude
Twaddle
Twit
Twitter
Twosome
Tycoon
Tyke
Tyro

Words Beginning With U

Ubiquitous
Ultimate
Ulterior
Umpteen
Uncanny
Unique
Universal
Unkempt
Update
Upgrade
Uphold
Upkeep
Uplift
Uppish
Upright
Uproar
Uproot
Upset
Upstairs
Upstart
Upswing
Uptake
Uptight
Up-to-date
Urbane
Usher
Usherette
Usurp
Utilitarian
Utmost
Utter
Uxorious

Words Beginning With V

Vacillate
Vacuity
Vacuous
Vade-mecum
Vagabond
Vagary
Vagrant
Vague
Vainglory
Valet
Valetudinarian
Vamp
Vanity
Vanquish
Vary

Vaunt
Veer
Vendetta
Venerable
Ventriloquism
Venue
Veracious
Veracity
Verbatim
Verbiage
Verbose
Verge
Versatile
Verve
Vex
Vicious
Vigorous
Virago
Vital
Vivid
Vixen
Vogue
Volition
Voluble
Voluptuary
Voracious
Votary
Vouch
Vulgar
Vulnerable
Vulpine
Vulture

Words Beginning With W

Wad
Waffle
Waggle
Waif
Wardrobe
Washy
Wayward
Waggish
Wag
Wanton
Weeds
Ween
Weird
Well-nigh
Wet-nurse
Wheedle
Whet
Whey
Whisper
Whipper-snapper
Whiz-kid
Whore
Willy-nilly
Wilsome
Winsome
Wont
Woo
Wriggle
Writhe
Wiseacre
Wisecrack
Witty
Write
Wrought
Wry

Words Beginning With X

Xantippe
Xenodoctium
Xenodochy
Xenomania
Xenophobia
Xerox

Words Beginning With Y

Yack
Yacketry-yack
Yammer
Yank
Yap
Yard
Yardstick
Yarn
Yawn
Yearn
Yell
Yield
Yob
Yokel
Yoke
Yolk
Yowl
Yttrium
Yucky
Yuppie

Words Beginning With Z

Zany
Zap
Zeal
Zealous
Zealot
Zenith
Zest
Zestful
Zigzag
Zing
Zip
Zombie
Zonked
Zoophilist
Zoroastrianism
Zucchini

CLOZE TEST

Directions: *Each of the following passages contains some blank spaces, each of which has been numbered. These numbers are printed below the passage. Four or three words are suggested against each number, one of which fits the blank space appropriately. Fill in the blank spaces with the help of the suitable words.*

PASSAGE-1

The population of the country poses a ...1... economic situation, for we are not able to ...2... it by our own agricultural produce. Besides ...3... all development efforts, the problem brings ...4... to the community, to the family and the individual. To plan when population growth is ...5... is like building a house where the ground is constantly ...6... . An argument is put ...7... that our country is overpopulated. The vast potent resources of the country still lie ...8... . It is indeed a pity that our vast resources ...9... unused. If we are able to ...10..., our productive forces, even double the present population can be ...11... .

1. A. grim B. satisfactory
C. foul

2. A. maintain B. finance
C. support D. flourish

3. A. dismissing B. rejecting
C. boosting D. neutralising

4. A. difficulty B. distress
C. relief D. pleasure

5. A. encouraged B. increased
C. checked D. unchecked

6. A. futile B. flat
C. fertile D. flooded

7. A. down B. up
C. through D. forward

8. A. uncontrolled B. dormant
C. untapped

9. A. lie B. appear
C. stay

10. A. bridle B. harness
C. stem

11. A. supported B. encouraged
C. enhanced

PASSAGE-2

It is neither the size nor the length of life which makes man ...**1**... . The growth of mind and the intellect is ...**2**... in porportion to the growth of the human body. The man may ...**3**... physically the stature of a giant, but he may remain ...**4**... a dwarf. The true worth of man ...**5**... upon his action, deed and thought. Man is not like a tree. An oak tree ...**6**... to a huge size and lives for hundreds of years, only to ...**7**... to the ground, withered, dry and a leafless ...**8**... . It is not in ...**9**... things that ...**10**... is sought.

1. A. humble B. better
C. polite

2. A. surely B. roughly
C. usually D. never

3. A. attain B. keep
C. earth D. grow

4. A. spiritually B. intellectually
C. socially D. morally

5. A. gathers B. revolves
C. lies D. depends

6. A. rises B. grows
C. lifts D. raises

7. A. dwindle B. fall
C. disappear D. short

8. A. wood B. chip
C. pole D. log

9. A. big B. lengthy
C. small D. broad

10. A. value B. interest
C. perfection

PASSAGE-3

Books are ...**1**... the most ...**2**... product of human effort. Temples ...**3**... to ruin, pictures and statues ...**4**..., but books ...**5**... . Time is of ...**6**... with great thoughts which are as fresh today ...**7**... when they first ...**8**... through their authors' minds ages ago ...**9**... was then thought and said, still speaks to us as ...**10**.... as ever from ...**11**... printed page. The only effect of time ...**12**... to sift and winnow out the bad products, for nothing in literature can ...**13**... survive which is not really good. Books introduce us ...**14**... the presence of the greatest minds that have ever lived. We hear what they said and did.

1. A. decidedly B. definitely
C. by far D. certainly

2. A. lasting B. everlasting
C. temporary D. permanent

3. A. break down B. fall
C. broken D. crumble

4. A. die B. decay
C. fade D. disappear

5. A. live B. survive
C. last D. are born

6. A. no account B. no value
C. no importance D. no significance

7. A. such B. that
C. as D. so

8. A. run B. penetrate
C. pass D. see

9. A. as B. that
C. such D. what

10. A. clearly B. vividly
C. graphically D. manifestly

11. A. the B. a
C. an D. no word

12. A. is B. had been
C. has been D. has

13. A. ever B. never
C. long D. no word

14. A. to B. into
C. with D. of

PASSAGE-4

Man is the ...**1**... of his ...**2**... fate. If he ...**3**... a proper division of his time and ...**4**... his duties accordingly, he is sure to ...**5**... and prosper in life, but if he does otherwise, he is sure to repent when it is ...**6**... and he ...**7**... drag out a miserable ...**8**... from day to day

...9... time is as culpable ...10... to commit suicide, ...11... our life is nothing ...12... the sum total of hours, days and years. Youth is the golden season of life. In youth the mind is ...13... and soft and ...14... moulded in any form we like. If we lose the morning hours of life, we ...15... repent afterwards. It ...16... the seed of life. If we sow a good seed, we shall reap a good harvest, when we ...17... .

1. A. worker B. decider C. architect D. builder
2. A. own B. good C. himself D. bad
3. A. will make B. has made C. make
4. A. will do B. does C. has done D. did
5. A. of improving B. in improving C. to improve D. improve
6. A. very late B. late C. too late
7. A. will have to B. have C. had D. will have
8. A. existence B. life C. world D. the world
9. A. for killing B. in killing C. to kill D. killing
10. A. such B. so C. therefore D. as
11. A. as B. for C. so D. such
12. A. but B. except C. excluding
13. A. flexible B. pliable C. amenable D. impressionable
14. A. will be B. has C. can be D. had
15. A. shall be B. shall C. have to D. had to
16. A. is called B. called C. will be called D. has called
17. A. have grown B. grow up C. have grown up D. grow

PASSAGE-5

Science has made an ...1... contribution to the relief of human suffering, and humanity ...2... a deep ...3... of gratitude to scientists whose ...4... and sacrifices have led to the many ...5... discoveries and inventions which have done so much to ...6... human pain and ...7... . It is indeed ...8... to calculate the ...9... of science in providing ...10... to suffering mankind. In the first place, scientific machines have, to a ...11... extent replaced human ...12... .

1. A. active B. enormous C. excessive D. intensive
2. A. offers B. feels C. owes D. acknowledges
3. A. fund B. amount C. debt
4. A. discoveries B. achievements C. successes D. labours
5. A. advantageous B. strange C. useful
6. A. disappear B. decrease C. alleviate
7. A. discomfort B. misery C. unrest D. anxiety
8. A. possible B. plausible C. impossible D. impertinent
9. A. relevance B. use C. cost D. value
10. A. rest B. peace C. relief D. comfort
11. A. large B. wide C. big D. broad
12. A. effort B. labour C. work D. enterprise

PASSAGE-6

The neglect of one half of mankind costs the world a great deal both in economic and social ...1... . A family ...2... an educated mother is, in most cases a poorer family than one in which everyone is educated and can ...3... a living. A family of the former kind may ...4... in other ways too, because the mother is ...5... to help the children in their education and training for ...6... . An educated and enlightened mother can ...8... all the difference to the ...8... fortunes. This must be ...9... true of nations with or without enlightened ...10... .

1. A. areas B. aspects
C. terms D. values

2. A. with B. of
C. without D. including

3. A. manage B. earn
C. create D. spend

4. A. prosper B. destroy
C. suffer D. fail

5. A. unable B. able
C. pleased D. qualified

6. A. life B. business
C. career D. studies

7. A. create B. cause
C. make D. mean

8. A. individual B. family
C. domestic D. personal

9. A. probably B. equally
C. remotely D. hardly

10. A. men B. citizens
C. leaders D. women

PASSAGE-7

Many a years ago, we made a ...1... with destiny, and now the time comes when we shall ...2... our pledge, not wholly or in full ...3... but very substantially. At the ...4... of the midnight hour, when the world sleeps, India will ...5... to life and freedom. A moment comes, which comes but ...6... in history, when we step ...7... from the old to the new, when an age ends, and when the ...8... of a nation, long suppressed, finds ...9... . It is fitting that at this ...10... moment we take the ...11... of ...12... to the service of India and her people and to the still larger ...13... of humanity.

At the dawn of history, India, now the biggest democracy in the world, started on her unending ...14... and trackless ...15... are filled with her striving and grandeur of her success and failures.

1. A. engagement B. pledge
C. promise D. tryst

2. A. recall B. redeem
C. review D. revive

3. A. length B. volume
C. measure D. scope

4. A. moment B. time
C. point D. stroke

5. A. awake B. come
C. change D. rally

6. A. surely B. off and on
C. rarely D. repeatedly

7. A. in B. out
C. over D. round

8. A. destiny B. fortune
C. body D. soul

9. A. fulfilment B. reward
C. utterance D. reaction

10. A. grave B. happy
C. important D. solemn

11. A. pledge B. promise
C. obligation D. requirement

12. A. decision B. dedication
C. declaration D. loyalty

13. A. cause B. defence
C. consideration D. regard

14. A. path B. road
C. quest D. way

15. A. efforts B. centuries
C. miseries D. years

PASSAGE-8

We should remember that all religions preach good ...1... in life, the ...2... of which should rest on ethics. Without the basis of morality, philosophy would remain ...3... polemics and religion meaningless and vain. Nobody can say that he is religious ...4..., he is truthful, straightforward, honest, humble and absolutely unselfish. He should be the very ...5... of love. I have always tried to ...6... in my own humble way a sense of ...7... and also the virtues of introspection and retrospection. I have always felt that by constant endeavour through thought, word and deed, one could ...8... absolute peace of mind, which will give greatest happiness to a human being ...9... of the status or position he occupies.

1. A. behaviour B. deportment
C. appearance D. conduct
2. A. basis B. foundation
C. fundamental D. ground
3. A. merely B. mere
C. simply D. only
4. A. if B. until
C. till D. unless
5. A. emblem B. sign
C. incarnation D. embodiment
6. A. practice B. practical
C. practise D. practising
7. A. attachment B. objectivity
C. detachment D. detaching
8. A. get B. procure
C. acquire D. possess
9. A. irrespectful B. irrespective
C. introspective D. prospective

PASSAGE-9

There is no gainsaying the fact that India is the greatest democracy in the world. In a ...1... of a parliamentary democracy which we have deliberately ...2... for ourselves, it is essential that we achieve our desired results by the ...3... effort of the people. We must remind ourselves constantly of the ever-present danger that democracy when it becomes merely formal would ...4... . Democracy can save itself only by a process of constant and continuous ...5... . It must not only keep its institutions free from corrupting influences but also must ...6... its forms and replenish its content in accordance ...7... the current social conditions. A deep concern for national welfare alone can make our democracy ...8... and lasting.

1. A. institution B. organisation
C. pattern D. system
2. A. moulded B. framed
C. fashioned D. distorted
3. A. together B. overall
C. total D. collective
4. A. die B. end
C. collapse D. fell
5. A. refreshing B. revival
C. survival D. renewal
6. A. see beyond B. look beyond
C. see up D. look up
7. A. in B. to
C. with D. of
8. A. meaningless B. meaningful
C. important D. purpose

PASSAGE-10

I recall the training that was ...1... us when we were young by our mothers and teachers who taught us the ...2... character, integrity and adherence to truth. It is such training given to us in our ...3... years that inspired us to contribute our mite in the cause of the nation when many of us ...4... the freedom struggle for the liberation of our country from foreign ...5... . No doubt, in the process, we had to ...6... many privations and sufferings, but we bore them cheerfully, for we were always goaded and guided by the laudable goals that were before us. That was the time when we had to make sacrifices. But today the conditions are different when the youth are ...7... themselves actively in constructive endeavours of nation-building and of winning the economic ...8... for millions and millions of our countrymen who are in the brink of starvation.

1. A. given for B. given to
C. to given D. for giving
2. A. qualities of B. virtuosity of
C. virtues of D. problems
3. A. formal B. informing
C. informative D. formative
4. A. dipped B. dipped into
C. plunged D. plunged into
5. A. yolk B. burden
C. yoke D. folk
6. A. undertake B. undertaken
C. undergo D. undergone
7. A. to engage only B. only to engage
C. engage to only D. engage only to
8. A. freedom B. liberty
C. emancipation D. release

PASSAGE-11

The vast millions of our men and women are ...**1**... for a better and fuller life. This is a challenge which our leadership has to face, and face boldly and purposefully. Time will not ...**2**... and the legitimate aspirations of our people on whose ...**3**... support will depend the success or failure of the democratic system cannot be ignored. I would ...**4**... this opportunity to appeal to all political parties not to ...**5**... the energies of the people in meaningless squabbles. The question before us today is the ...**6**... of poverty; ignorance and disease from which millions of our countrymen are suffering. This is possible only if there is ...**7**... and determined effort. We must realise that for the solution of economic problems there need not be any difference of opinion. All parties should unite in making an ...**8**... to banish poverty.

1. A. pining B. grieving
C. yearning D. desiring

2. A. stay B. await
C. halt D. wait

3. A. unbending B. inflexible
C. unflinching D. unpinching

4. A. utilise to like B. to like utilise
C. to utilise like D. like to utilise

5. A. twitter B. embitter
C. fritter D. scatter

6. A. dedication B. motivation
C. eradication D. precipitation

7. A. unity of will B. united will
C. unitary will D. will united

8. A. out-all effort B. all-out effort
C. out-all penetration D. out all drive

MORE DIFFICULT PASSAGES

PASSAGE-12

One of the greatest ...**1**... of modern times is the prevailing belief that we are more ...**2**... than our ancestors. At no other period in the history of mankind has the word *civilisation* been so often misused and ...**3**... . It is not in the abundance of ...**4**... alone that civilisation lies. Neither does it consist in the advance of scientific knowledge, however amazing it may be. The inventions and discoveries of science have ...**5**... unheard of blessings and comforts to us. But they are not civilisation. What we have failed ...**6**... is that civilisation is a special way of human behaviour, of thought and feeling. The essential quality of civilisation lies in the spirit of man, in his attitude to ...**7**... to his fellowmen and to life as a whole. Looking everywhere around us today, you will find that man has made no progress ...**8**... the dawn of history, in attitude towards his fellowmen. On all the highest pillars in the cities of the world, you will find the figure of a conqueror or a general soldier. We know ...**9**... our killers and destroyers than about our saviours and saints. The heroes of the world are the heroes of war.

1. A. allusions B. conclusions
C. seculsions D. delusions

2. A. cultured B. civilised
C. modernised D. scrutinised

3. A. interpreted B. understood
C. maljudged D. misunderstood

4. A. goods material B. material goods
C. goods D. materials

5. A. brought undoubtedly
B. doubtfully bright
C. undoubtedly brought
D. brought doubtfully

6. A. in seeing B. for seeing
C. to see D. by seeing

7. A. he B. him
C. his D. himself

8. A. for B. since
C. by D. between

9. A. more about far B. far about more
C. about more far D. for more about

PASSAGE-13

The ideal State is one where every citizen is ...**1**... to be a part of the community, to share its burdens, to put its interest before his own, to sacrifice, ...**2**... his own wishes, conveniences, time, and money to it. It is a machine of which no part is ...**3**... or inefficient: none rusted, broken or ill-fitting; in which each pulley and cog ...**4**... its full share of the load, and plays its part in the swift and smooth running ...5... . A man who evades his taxes is, so far, a bad citizen; but so is one who, in giving a vote for Parliament, thinks only of interests, or is too indifferent or lazy to vote at all: so is the bad employer whose treatment of his employees is not only a ...6... of the moral law, but adds to the social problems of the country; so are workmen who strike for some private interest, when the existence of their country is at stake: so is the man who would be useful in local government but ...7... the burden, not because he cannot, but because, he will not spare the time.

1. A. decided B. devoted
C. addicted D. determined

2. A. if necessary is B. if necessary be
C. if need is D. if need be

3. A. idle B. inessential
C. idol D. alone

4. A. takes in B. takes to
C. takes up D. takes by

5. A. as a whole B. for the whole
C. of the whole D. to the whole

6. A. breaking B. bleaching
C. breach D. impeachment

7. A. avoids B. evades
C. throws D. shoulders

PASSAGE-14

The question of ...1... may rightly be called one's ...2... own, safe from encroachment, grows most confused in the case of private ...3... . According to the democratic view, each of us may control his ...4... surroundings to a reasonable extent, only the too particular people being regarded ...5... and trouble-makers. Between one person and another a no man's land of property is assumed to exist,...6... which neither has any special control. And if we dislike the new buildings ...7... a favourite old street of ours, the sole grounds on which we are allowed to protest are those of ...8... artistic taste; through entitled to our private opinion, we can claim no sight to be consulted. The favourite old street is our only in a manner of speaking. Its architectural effect must be regarded as a public property subject to our control ...9... the municipal system alone: our personal reactions as individual citizens do not and cannot, interest this remote and ...10... authority.

1. A. that B. however
C. what D. this

2. A. undivided B. reliable
C. inalienable

3. A. amenities B. facility
C. desires D. likes

4. A. mediate B. all
C. whole D. immediate

5. A. as exception B. exception
C. freaks D. as freaks

6. A. on B. in
C. over D. through

7. A. going up along B. going up
C. up going D. coming up

8. A. personal B. partial
C. impersonal D. nominal

9. A. by B. through
C. over

10. A. firm B. known
C. cruel D. stubborn

PASSAGE-15

Success grows out of ...1... to overcome difficulties. If there ...2... no difficulties, there were ...3... no success. If there were nothing to struggle or ...4..., there would be nothing achieved. ...5... it is well, that men should be ...6... the necessity of exerting themselves. In this necessity ...7... exertion we find the chief source of ...8... advancement — the advancement of ...9... as of nations. It has led to ...10... splendid mechanical inventions and improvements of the age. It has ...11... the shipbuilder, the merchant, the manufacturer, the mechanic, the tradesman and ...12... workman. In all departments of ...13... industry, it has been the moving power. It has developed the resources of this and of other countries — the resources of the soil and the character and qualities of the man who ...14... it. It seems to be absolutely necessary for the purpose of stimulating the growth and culture of every individual. It is deeply rooted in man ...15... him ever to seek after and endeavour to realise, something better and higher than he has yet attained.

1. A. fights B. labours C. struggle D. work

2. A. were B. was C. had been D. has been

3. A. is B. was C. would be D. would

4. A compete B. compete for C. compete with D. compete in

5. A. However B. So C. Therefore D. Consequently

6. A. in B. under C. of

7. A. of B. for C. in D. to

8. A. human B. humane C. human beings D. humanity's

9. A. persons B. entities C. identities D. individuals

10. A. may of B. most of C. too many D. many

11. A. excited B. incited C. stimulated D. helped

12. A. artisan B. skilled C. adept D. adapted

13. A. producing B. production C. productive D. productively

14. A. dwell in B. dwell upon C. dwell D. dwell up

15. A. leading B. lead C. had led D. will lead

ANSWERS

Passage-1

1	2	3	4	5	6	7	8	9	10
A	C	D	B	D	D	D	C	C	B
11									
A									

Passage-2

1	2	3	4	5	6	7	8	9	10
B	D	A	B	D	B	B	A	A	D

Passage-3

1	2	3	4	5	6	7	8	9	10
D	A	D	C	C	C	C	C	D	A
11	**12**	**13**	**14**						
B	B	A	A						

Passage-4

1	2	3	4	5	6	7	8	9	10
C	A	B	B	D	C	A	A	C	D
11	**12**	**13**	**14**	**15**	**16**	**17**			
C	B	D	C	B	A	B			

Passage-5

1	2	3	4	5	6	7	8	9	10
B	C	C	D	C	C	B	D	D	D
11	**12**								
A	B								

Passage-6

1	2	3	4	5	6	7	8	9	10
C	C	B	C	A	A	C	B	B	C

Passage-7

1	2	3	4	5	6	7	8	9	10
B	B	C	D	A	A	A	D	A	D
11	**12**	**13**	**14**	**15**					
A	B	A	A	B					

Passage-8

1	2	3	4	5	6	7	8	9
D	B	B	D	D	C	C	C	B

Passage-9

1	2	3	4	5	6	7	8
D	C	D	C	D	B	C	B

Passage-10

1	2	3	4	5	6	7	8
B	C	D	D	C	C	B	A

Passage-11

1	2	3	4	5	6	7	8
C	D	C	D	C	C	B	B

Passage-12

1	2	3	4	5	6	7	8	9
D	B	D	B	C	C	D	B	D

Passage-13

1	2	3	4	5	6	7
D	D	A	C	C	C	B

Passage-14

1	2	3	4	5	6	7	8	9	10
C	C	A	D	C	C	A	C	B	D

Passage-15

1	2	3	4	5	6	7	8	9	10
C	A	C	B	B	B	A	A	B	C
11	**12**	**13**	**14**	**15**					
D	B	C	A	A					

COMPREHENSION

General Observation

Bear in mind that what I pen below are of immense import. They amply deserve to be thoroughly studied and grasped. This is indisputably one of the most important topics, so far as various competitive examinations conducted by Union Public Service Commission (UPSC), Staff Selection Commission (SSC), and many other recruitment agencies are concerned. You must take it seriously in the real sense of the term.

It goes without saying that comprehension is a very important part of General English paper. The questions on comprehension lay particular stress on understanding a given passage. You are required to read a passage and answer a few questions based on it. It must be remembered that the various comprehension questions are set solely with the objectives named below:

(a) To test your ability to detect the central idea or the focal point in the given passage.

(b) To test your ability to understand and interpret the given passage.

(c) To judge your capability to pick out the various arguments put forward by the writer for or against something.

(d) To test your accuracy and richness of vocabulary.

(e) To test your academic ability to understand the implied and the clearly and fully expressed ideas of the writer of the passage.

(f) To test, occasionally, your power of appreciating critically the views contained in the given passage.

While answering comprehension questions, you must comply with the following important points. Know it for certain that complete compliance with the following method will undoubtedly be highly valuable and useful to you in the matter of giving correct answers to the questions.

(a) First, read the whole passage attentively, carefully and quickly. Such a reading will certainly enable you to grasp the gist of the given passage as well as to remember the important details. You will get a general idea of the subject dealt with in it.

(b) Thereafter, read it for the second time, slowly but steadily, wholly concentrating your attention on the questions set below the passage. The second reading, with an eye on the questions, will help you to find out the correct answer to the given question. The extra reading will reinforce your understanding of the passage.

(c) Don't look at the questions before you have fully gone through the passage.

(d) Make it a point to study the first and the last sentence of the passage. Sometimes, the said two sentences indicate the main idea.

(e) Work out the probable meaning of new words, from the context in which they have been used.

(f) Make a due note of the mode in which the ideas have been developed in the passage.

(g) Underline and look for transitional words and phrases as an aid to comprehension.

(h) Words and phrases which are often repeated should be sought out and underlined. They are likely to give you more than an inkling of the subject matter of the passage.

(i) Verify your answers by making a reference to the material in the selection. Your particular choice should be supported by evidence.

(j) The process of elimination should be used while selecting the correct answer. Apparently incorrect choices should be discarded at the first stage. Then find evidence to support your particular choice.

(k) Questions concerning inference or deduction can best be answered by your studying the author's choice of words and his development of the main idea.

(l) Don't jump to any conclusion or decision upon a single choice as the answer before you have wholly considered all the choices.

(m) Your answers should be brief and to the point.

(n) Your answers should be, as far as possible, in your own words.

(o) Don't give your comments on the opinions expressed in the passage, unless comments are asked for. It must be borne in mind that your job is merely to comprehend the given passage, and not to quarrel with the ideas contained in it.

(p) Don't explain or elaborate any point with illustrations of your own. You must keep yourself totally close to the passage.

(q) See to it to answer the questions within the time allotted.

(r) Don't waste time on difficult questions.

(s) Before handing over the paper, you should revise it and carry out necessary corrections, if any.

Directions: *Read the following passages carefully and choose the best answer to each of the questions out of the several alternatives.*

PASSAGE-1

The group of tired dusty riders arrived at a fork in the road. Their leader immediately sprang to the ground after first throwing his rein to one of the others, and began to examine minutely the sandy track. The problem was simple; if the fleeing enemy had taken the left turning, there remained little hope of catching them, since he knew that it led back to a small settlement of native huts where they should be sheltered by the friendly inhabitants. If, on the other hand, they had branched to the right, they would have before them the open desert, not a flat expanse of sand such as they had just crossed, but a country broken by a series of ridges, behind any of which a whole army could hide.

He turned to his companions to see if he could read any solution in their faces. But they were too occupied by their aching limbs and several were taking a quick drink from the flasks which hung at their belts. He realised every minute's delay lessened their chances of overtaking their adversaries. So, with a rapid glance at the sun, he jumped once more into the saddle and with his whip indicated the way they were to go.

Questions

1. Why did the leader look at the sun?
   A. To estimate what daylight still remained
   B. He sent a silent prayer to the sun-god to show the way
   C. To estimate chances of their overtaking their adversaries
   D. To estimate their position in the desert

2. What, if any, was the difference in the nature of the terrain they had already traversed and the one lying ahead?
   A. The country-side already traversed was ups and downs
   B. There was hardly any difference as it was a vast expanse of unending desert
   C. The terrain hitherto was dusty and tiring, the road ahead led back to a habitation
   D. What they had crossed was a flat expanse of sand and what they lay ahead to the right was a series of ridges of sand

3. What difficulties did they expect if they took the branch to the right?
   A. The open desert ahead promised no oasis to shelter them at night
   B. They were absolutely in the dark about what they lay ahead of them
   C. Ahead lay a country full of ridges of sand providing cover to the fleeing enemy
   D. They would have before them the open desert obstructing pursuit

4. What was the aim of the group of riders?
   A. They were fleeing from a pursuing enemy
   B. They had a small settlement of native huts as their goal
   C. They were exploring a desert
   D. They were pursuing a fleeing enemy

5. What difficulties did the pursuers expect if they took to the left hand track?
   A. It led through a trackless expanse of unending desert
   B. It led to a settlement where the residents would surely shelter the enemy they were after
   C. The settlement it led to was hostile to them
   D. The leader anticipated a possible revolt among his followers, foot-sore, dust covered and tired as they already were.

6. Where and why did they stop?
   A. At a fork in the road to examine the sandy track for foot-prints of the fleeing enemy
   B. At the huts of some friendly inhabitants in order to rest their weary limbs
   C. At a three-way crossing where the leader wanted to study the position of the sun in the sky
   D. At a fork in the road in order to decide whether they should turn left or right

PASSAGE-2

Just as some men like to play football or cricket, so some men like to climb mountains. This is often very difficult to do so, for mountains are not just big hills. Paths are usually very steep. Some mountain sides are straight up and down, so that it may take many hours to climb as little as one hundred feet. There is always the danger that you may fall off and be killed or injured. Men talk about conquering a mountain. It is a wonderful feeling to reach the top of a mountain after climbing for hours and may be, even for days. You look down and see the whole country below you. You feel god-like. Two Italian prisoners of war escaped from a prison camp in Kenya during the war. They did not try to get back to their own country, for they knew that was impossible. Instead, they climb to the top of Mount Kenya, and then they came down again and gave themselves up. They had wanted to get that feeling of freedom that one has, after climbing a difficult mountain.

Questions

1. Some men like to climb mountains because:
   A. They know the trick of climbing
   B. They don't like to play football or cricket
   C. They want to have wonderful feeling
   D. They like to face danger
2. To climb mountains is often difficult because:
   A. mountains are big hills
   B. it consumes more time
   C. prisoners often escape from camps and battle there
   D. paths are steep and uneven
3. Mountaineering is not a very popular sport like football or cricket because:
   A. there are no spectators in this sport
   B. it may take many hours or even days
   C. not many people are prepared to risk their lives
   D. people don't want to enjoy a god-like feeling
4. It is a wonderful feeling .... . It refers to:
   A. the steep path B. the prisoners
   C. the mountain D. mountaineering

PASSAGE-3

Although he was born in a little village near the coast and had gone to school in the nearest sea-side town, Ram Mehar, was not a lover of the sea; even when walking along the sands, he was always afraid of being cut off by the tide. He was not a good swimmer, so perhaps this accounts for it.

After working for some years in Calcutta, he was transferred to a coast resort and, of course, the family outings were often made to the beach. One day his children pleaded to go out into the bay in a boat. The sun shone brightly. There was little wind and the water was calm. So Ram Mehar hired a boat and with his two children rowed out into the bay. Of course, they were tempted to go further than they had intended, past the protecting cliffs and out to the open sea. At first all went well, but when they decided to turn back they encountered difficulties. A strong breeze had sprung up and the currents here were rather treacherous.

Ram Mehar rowed very hard, but it seemed they were making little progress. The children were waving to attract the attention of the people on the beach. Just then a motor-boat appeared from the direction of the bay. Their plight had been noticed and the boat had come to their rescue.

A line was soon attached and they were towed back round the cliff to the shore. Ram Mehar's dislike of the sea was not diminished by this experience.

Questions

1. What did the children plead to be allowed to do?
   A. Climb the cliff to have a better view of the bay
   B. Go to a coast resort
   C. Go for a outing on the beach
   D. Go out into the bay in a boat
2. Ram Mehar was tempted to go farther away from the land than he had intended because:
   A. he enjoyed rowing in the bright sunshine
   B. the sea was calm, there being little wind
   C. his children wanted to go far out in the sea
   D. he encountered no danger while rowing the boat
3. What accounted for his dislike of the sea?
   A. Being not a good swimmer, he feared that he might get drowned in the sea
   B. The protruding cliffs made navigation dangerous
   C. He was accustomed to comfortable city life
   D. Many a tragedy had occurred in the past near the sea coast
4. Ram Mehar was nervous of walking along the sands because:
   A. he had no love for the sea
   B. there the sea was infested with deadly monsters
   C. he feared that tide may cut him off from the land
   D. the sea was too deep even near the coast

PASSAGE-4

The bulk of our population is poor and illiterate. Their sorry condition poses a problem. On the one hand, there is a shortage of teachers for adult education and, on the other, the adults feel shy of starting to learn at a late age and atttend classes like children. Moreover, the adult villagers have little time to spare for attending classes. The job of a farmer is very strenuous and he needs ample rest and relaxation. In addition, he finds that what is taught at adult centres of education has no bearing on his daily needs and therefore he has become cynical about adult education. It is necessary to make adult education in villages agriculture-oriented so as to make it more meaningful for the farmer. In towns and cities also, adult education needs to be made work-based. It should comprise types of system in which earning and learning go together side-by-side. Efforts should be made to discourage the tendency of the village folk to migrate to the towns!

Another aspect of the problem is the confinement of industry to cities and towns. What is called the *industrial area* is entirely the monopoly of the cities. For expansion of education and literacy in the rural areas, it is necessary that industry should be dispersed in the villages also. An important development that has taken place in the countryside is the phenomenal success of the Green Revolution.

Questions

1. What is needed for adult education in villages is that:
   A. it should be made agriculture-oriented
   B. it should be free
   C. it should be made compulsory
   D. it should be available in every village

2. The main problem in educating the adult villagers is:
   A. their financial helplessness to purchase books, etc. required for studies
   B. they hardly find time to attend classes
   C. their inability to read and write
   D. there is no room for schools in villages

3. A farmer has grown cynical about education because:
   A. what is taught in such schools is mostly of no use in his daily life
   B. there is no one in his family to look after his cultivation when he goes to attend the classes.
   C. he has no time to go to school
   D. he has no money to pay the fees for education

4. One of the main problems of adult education in the country is:
   A. poor financial condition of the people
   B. shortage of teachers for such schools
   C. shortage of school buildings
   D. want of funds with the government for such schools

PASSAGE-5

Just as it is vital for parents to live their own lives as fully as possible and to deepen their understanding of themselves to the utmost, so it is important for teachers and educators to do the same. When children go to school their teachers become, during school hours, substitutes for their parents. The children transfer to the teacher some of the feelings they have for their parents and are influenced in their turn by the personalities of the teachers. This mutual relationship is of more importance than any teaching method, and a child's ability to learn is continually hampered if the relationship is unsatisfactory. Again, if teachers really want to be educators, to help children to develop into satisfactory men and women, and not simply to *stuff them with knowledge*, they will only be really successful if they themselves have sound personalities. No amount of preaching, however well done, no principles however sound, no clever technique of mechanical aids can replace the influence of a well-developed personality.

Questions

1. Teachers will be real educators by:
   A. adopting advanced teaching methods
   B. stuffing children with knowledge
   C. developing sound personalities of their own
   D. through good teaching aid

2. The central idea of the passage is that:
   A. teachers should develop sound personalities of their own to be able to influence the children

B. informal education is better than formal education
C. there should be more research done in education
D. parents should have the right relationship with teachers of their children

3. The writer recommends to the teachers to deepen their understanding of themselves on the assumption that it:
A. will earn them a name of nation-builders
B. is their duty
C. will make them earn more
D. helps to build a well-developed personality

4. The teachers and educators are important to the children because:
A. without them they would remain ignorant
B. they help them to get jobs
C. they serve as substitutes for parents in schools
D. they preach good principles

PASSAGE-6

Once a man saw that three masons along with some labourers were constructing a temple. He observed the masons for some days and found that though the three of them were doing the same kind of work, there was a marked difference in their approach to their job.

He saw that the first mason reported for his work late, did his work half-heartedly and sluggishly, enjoyed longer respite, frequently checked the time on his wrist-watch and left the work before time.

The second mason was very punctual in arriving and leaving, and did his work methodically and conscientiously.

The third mason, however, would come before time, took little rest in the interval and often worked overtime.

The man naturally got curious and wanted to know the three masons' outlook on their work. He asked them what they were doing. The first mason tapped his protruding belly with his hand and said, *I am earning fuel for this bloody belly.* The second said, *I am constructing a building.* The third looked at the stately edifice and said, *I am building the house of God.*

Questions

1. The first mason was:
A. lazy B. sick
C. hard-working D. active

2. The first mason was concerned only with his:
A. wages B. job
C. time D. rest

3. The masons and labourers were building a:
A. club B. monastery
C. school D. temple

4. The third mason approached his work with:
A. zest B. skill
C. duty D. dedication

PASSAGE-7

Scarcity not created by war; it is a permanent characteristic of all human society and is the basis of the problem that faces, and always had faced, the human race whatever its form of organisation. It springs from the fact that the material resources of the world are limited and that our ability to make use of those resources is even more limited by our ignorance.

Everthing that we need to satisfy our wants has to be derived finally from two sources — the natural resources that are available and the human ability to make use of them. As our knowledge grows and we increase our skill, we can exploit more and more of the opportunities that nature offers to us. The increase in communications, for example, has made accessible many minerals from depths below the earth's surface that could not be reached by earlier generations. But whatever the rate of development may be, there is, at any one time, a limit to the total of what can be produced. Here and now, there is only so much of the material resources of the world accessible to us and there are only so many people capable of work and endowed with the capacities and skills that they have developed. No doubt we waste a lot by stupidity even if the very best possible use is made of all the resources we can reach, there is still a limit to what can be produced out of them, and it is out of that total that we must all satisfy our wants.

Questions

1. Some of the material resources are:
A. wasted by man's stupidity

B. neglected by man
C. accessible to man
D. stored for the future

2. The first sentence of the passage tells us that scarcity is:
A. created by war
B. caused by human beings
C. not permanent
D. present in all human societies

3. The main idea of the passage is:
A. the cause of scarcity
B. the need to work hard
C. how to overcome scarcity
D. the need to increase our knowledge

4. The cause of scarcity is:
A. limited natural resources and still more limited knowledge of how to use them
B. the limitation of man's knowledge
C. human ignorance of natural resources
D. the limitation of various natural resources

MORE DIFFICULT PASSAGES

PASSAGE-8

The great Acharyas have said that having discovered a great goal, surrender yourself to that goal and act towards it drawing your inspiration from that goal whereby you will get a new column of energy. Do not allow this energy to be dissipated in the futile memories of the past regrets or failures, nor in the imagined sorrows of the future, nor in the excitement of the present. And this bring that entire focuss into activity. That is the highest creative action in the world outside. Thereby, the individual who is till now considered most efficient, finds his way to the highest achievement and success.

This is said very easily in a second. But in order to train our mind to this attitude, it needs considerable training because we have already trained the mind wrongly to such an extent that we have become perfect in imperfections. Not knowing the art of action, we have been master artists in doing the wrong thing. The totality of activity will bring the country to a wrong end indeed.

If each one is given a car to achieve an ideal socialistic pattern and nobody knows how to drive, what would be the condition on the road? Everybody has equal right on the public road. They each car must necessarily dash against the other, and there is bound to be a jumble. This seems to be very apt pattern of life that we are heading to. Everyone of us is a vehicle. We know how to go forward. The point is that intellect is very powerful and everyone is driving, but nobody seems to know to control the mental energy and direct it properly or guide it to the proper destination.

Questions

1. Which of the following is the source of energy?
A. A column that supports a building
B. Stimulation obtained from a set aim
C. Highest creative action
D. Proper training of the mind to achieve perfection

2. Which of the following could lead to success?
A. Cherishing the memories of the past
B. Preparing oneself to face the probable sorrow of the future
C. Bringing all the energy into activity
D. Being alert about the excitement of the present

3. What is the effect of the wrong training of the mind?
A. We have become perfect in all aspects
B. Art of action too much emphasized
C. Each of us could become master artist
D. We could avoid wastage of our energy
E. None of these

4. The author's chief aim is:
A. establishment of socialistic pattern
B. the car accidents resulting from each of driving skill
C. discovery of a great goal in life
D. regulation of energy in proper direction

PASSAGE-9

In our boyhood we beheld the dying rays of that intimate sociability which was characteristic of the last generation. Neighbourly feelings were then so strong that the informal gatherings were a necessity, and those who could contribute its amenities were held in great respect. People now-a-days call on each other on business, or as a matter of social duty, but not to foregather by way of informal gatherings. They have not the time, nor are there the same intimate relations. What goings and comings we used to see, how merry were the rooms and verandahs with the hum of conversation and the snatches of laughter. The faculty our predecessors had of becoming the centre of groups and gatherings, of starting and keeping up animated and amusing gossip, has vanished. Man still come and go, but those same verandahs and rooms seem empty and deserted. In those days everything from furniture to festivity was designed to be enjoyed by the many, so that whatever of pomp or magnificence there might have been did not savour of hauteur. These appendages have since increased in quantity, but they have become unfeeling and know not the art of making high and low alike feel at home. The barebodied, the indigently clad, no longer have the right to use and occupy them, without a permit, on the strength of their smiling faces alone. Those whom we now-a-days seek to imitate in our house-building and furnishing, they have their own society, with its wide hospitality. The mischief with us is that we have lost what we had but have not the means of building up afresh on the European standard, with the result that our home-life has become joyless. We still meet for business or political purposes, but never for the pleasure of simply meeting one another. We have ceased to contrive opportunities to bring men together simply because we love our fellow-men. I can imagine nothing more ugly than this social miserliness, and, when I look back on those whose ringing laughter, coming straight from their hearts, used to lighten for us the burden of household cares, they seem to have been visitors from some other world.

Questions

1. Which of the following is social miserliness according to the author?
   A. Diminishing intimate sociability
   B. Increasing social inequality
   C. Bare-bodied, half-starved masses
   D. We don't wish to incur expenditure merely to get people together
2. Why does the author feel that the rooms and verandahs have lost their charm?
   A. The rooms and verandahs have been deserted by the people
   B. They have been crowded by gatherings of gossiping people
   C. The conversational quality our predecessors had has now vanished
   D. Unlike in the past, no facilities for arranging meetings are available
3. People whom do which of the following now would look like visitors from some other world?
   A. Eradication of poverty and establishing social equality
   B. Strengthening the ties of love and affection through recurring informal meetings
   C. Reducing the burden of household cares by extending monetary assistance
   D. Enhancing business opportunities with European countries
4. How is the meeting of people of present generations different from the meeting of the people of the past?
   A. Intimate sociability has crept in
   B. Neighbourly feelings have now been strengthened
   C. Informal gossiping is not considered ethical these days
   D. People now do not meet merely for the pleasure of meeting one another
5. The approach of the author seems to be:
   A. extremely critical about our indifference towards the past generation
   B. emphatic about the need for informal social interaction
   C. cynical about our blindly imitating the Western style
   D. pessimistic about our business and political avenues
6. Why, according to the author, has our home life become joyless?
   A. We have lost the means of building up houses on the European standards
   B. Complete imitation of the West is not possible owing to different climatic conditions
   C. We have lost interpersonal intimacy and sociability. We do not have the means to build up afresh on the European standards

D. Most people are bare-bodied and half-starved

7. Which of the following statements is definitely true in the context of the passage?
   A. Poor people in the past generation did not have the right to enjoy anything without permission
   B. We have ceased to bring people together solely for the pleasure of meeting them
   C. Dying rays of intimate sociability was the characteristic of the last generation
   D. The gap between different strata of the present society is on the increase

PASSAGE-10

A close look at the facts relating to political interference in administration shows that it is not a one-way process. There is often a nexus between power-hungry and corrupt politicians and civil servants with convenient principles. Many civil servants are only too anxious to oblige the politicians, and then cash the obligation when they need some special favour. So attitude of self-righteousness adopted by the civil service is sometimes only a war of covering their own flaws by blaming others. Every now and then some retired civil servant comes out with his memoirs, painting a glorious picture of the heights of administrative efficiency reached during his reign. There is often the suggestion that had there not been so much political interference, things would have been even more fantastic. It is not unusual for the self-styled hero to blame not only interfering politicians but also fellow civil servants who were idiots or crooks, for his failures. This attitude of smug self-satisfaction is unfortunately, developed during the years of service. Self-preservation rather than service is encouraged by our whole system of rules and procedures.

The remedy has to be drastic and quickly effected. The over-protection now granted to civil servants must end. Today to remove an erring civil servant is just not possible. And the only thing that the highest authority in the government, both in the State and at the Centre, can do is to transfer an official from one job to another. The rules for taking disciplinary action are so complicated that, in the end, the defaulting civil servant gets away, and gets his full emoluments even for the period of the disciplinary proceedings, thus making it a paid holiday for him.

The result is that the administration has become rule-oriented and not result-oriented. Action is possible against the official who takes some interest in his work, but no action is over taken against a person who does not deliver the goods. If the country is to adopt a result-oriented approach, it is necessary to link job performance with job retention.

Questions

1. The facts relating to the problem of political interference indicate that:
   A. honest bureaucrats are always being troubled by politicians
   B. politicians are often misled and trapped by civil servants
   C. politicians and civil servants co-operate to gain mutual advantages
   D. politicians and civil servants use interference as an excuse for victimising the common man

2. The attitude of self-righteousness adopted by the civil service, according to the writer:
   A. is not welcomed and supported by politicians
   B. is dishonest and conceals the facts
   C. is very difficult to maintain because of opposition
   D. does not really help the public get fair treatment

3. Civil servants, who pen their memoirs after retiring:
   A. claim that they would have achieved outstanding success if interference had not come in the way
   B. prove that constant political interference made it impossible for them to do anything properly
   C. complain that the credit for their achievement goes to dishonest politicians
   D. prove that people of inferior quality in the civil service bring about interference

4. The existing system of administration seems to encourage civil servants:
   A. to become self-styled heroes and boss over others

B. to present a glorious picture of the administration

C. to become self-centred and concerned mainly about their own gain

D. to become self-righteous and fight back against corrupt politicians

5. The problem with the present set-up needing urgent action is:

A. a lack of accountability on the part of civil servants

B. a lack of control over the power of politicians

C. neglected ideals of self-righteousness

D. complicated rules and procedures that greatly reduce efficiency

6. The main principle of the remedy proposed by the writer is that:

A. the politicians should be made accountable for all their decisions

B. the high level of protection enjoyed by civil servants should be reduced

C. the common man's right to efficient and fair administration must be protected

D. rules should be simplified, so that there is less scope for misuse

PASSAGE-11

A recent report in New York Times says that in American colleges, students of Asian origin outperform not only the minority group students but the majority Whites as well. Many of these students must be of Indian origin, and their achievement is something we can be proud of. It is unlikely that these talented youngsters will come back to India, and that is the familiar brain drain problem. However, recent statements by the nation's policy makers indicate that the perception of this issue is changing. *Brain bank* and not *brain drain* is the more appropriate idea, they suggest, since the expertise of Indians abroad is only deposited in other places and not lost.

This may be so, but this brain bank, like most of the banks, is one that primarily serves customers in its neighbourhood. The skills of the Asians now excelling in America's colleges will mainly help the USA. No matter how significant, what Non-Resident Indians do for India and what their counterparts do for other Asian counteries is only a by-product. But it is also necessary to ask, or be reminded, why Indians study more fruitfully when abroad. The Asians whose accomplishments New York Times records would have probably had a very different fate if they had studied in India. In America they found elbow room, books and facilities not available and not likely to be available here. The need to prove themselves in their new country and the competition of an international standard they faced there must have cured mental and physical laziness. But other things helping them in America can be obtained here if we achieve a change in social attitudes, especially towards youth.

We need to learn to value individuals and their unique qualities more than conformity and respectability. We need to learn the language of encouragement to add to out skill in flattery. We might also learn to be less liberal with blame and less tight-fisted with appreciation, especially to those showing signs of independence.

Questions

1. Among the many groups of students in American colleges, Asian students:

A. are often written about in newspapers like New York Times

B. are the most successful academically

C. have proved that they are as good as the Whites

D. have only a minority status like the Blacks

2. The students of Asian origin in America include:

A. a fair number from India

B. a small group from India

C. persons from India who are very proud

D. Indians who are the most hardworking of all

3. In general, the talented young Indians studying in America:

A. have a reputation for being hardworking

B. have the opportunity to contribute to India's development

C. can solve the brain drain problem because of recent changes in policy

D. will not return to pursue their careers in India

4. There is talk now of the *brain bank*. This idea:
   A. is a solution to the brain drain problem
   B. is a new problem caused partly by the brain drain
   C. is a new way of looking at the role of qualified Indians living abroad
   D. is based on a plan to utilise foreign exchange remittances to stimulate research and development

5. The brain bank has limitations like all banks in the sense that:
   A. a bank's services go mainly to those near it
   B. small neighbourhood banks are not viable in this age of multinationals
   C. only what is deposited can be withdrawn and utilised
   D. no one can be forced to put his assets in a bank

6. The author feels that what Non-Resident Indians do for India:
   A. will have many useful side-effects
   B. will not be their main interest and concern
   C. can benefit other Asian countries, as a lay-product
   D. can help American colleges be of service of the world community

ANSWERS

Passage-1

1	2	3	4	5	6
A	D	C	D	C	D

Passage-2

1	2	3	4
C	D	C	D

Passage-3

1	2	3	4
D	B	A	C

Passage-4

1	2	3	4
A	B	A	B

Passage-5

1	2	3	4
C	A	D	C

Passage-6

1	2	3	4
B	D	D	D

Passage-7

1	2	3	4
C	D	C	A

Passage-8

1	2	3	4
B	C	C	D

Passage-9

1	2	3	4	5	6	7
D	C	E	D	B	C	B

Passage-10

1	2	3	4	5	6
C	B	A	C	D	B

Passage-11

1	2	3	4	5	6
B	A	D	C	D	C

SPOT THE ERRORS

Directions: *Each of the following sentences are divided into four parts—A, B, C and D. One of the parts is incorrect. Pick out the part which is incorrect. if none of the parts is incorrect, your answer will be E, i.e., No Error.*

TYPE I

1. (A) Sita as well as Rita/(B) are playing/(C) in/(D) the room./(E) No Error.
2. (A) Many a man/(B) have/(C) been arrested/(D) by the police./(E) No Error.
3. (A) These facts have/(B) no relevance/(C) to the matter/(D) at hand/(E) No Error.
4. (A) I shall help her/(B) in need/(C) if she will be/(D) loyal to me./(E) No Error.
5. (A) I had told him yesterday/(B) that I did not/(C) find him/(D) at home./(E) No Error.
6. (A) It is/(B) as good or/(C) perhaps/(D) better than that./(E) No Error.
7. (A) I deny the/(B) allegation that/(C) less people/(D) are buying our books./(E) No Error.
8. (A) The children ran/(B) away/(C) seeing the tiger/(D) in terrible fear./(E) No Error.
9. (A) This is only/(B) the first part;/(C) the book/(D) consists four parts./(E) No Error.
10. (A) She is fond to read/(B) the jokes/(C) in/(D) this magazine./(E) No Error.
11. (A) The plane was/(B) struck/(C) by lighting and/(D) completely destroyed./(E) No Error.
12. (A) I intended to reach Patna/(B) as soon,/(C) if not/(D) sooner than you./(E) No Error.
13. (A) Passing by the/(B) damaged house,/(C) a brick from the roof/(D) fell on my head./(E) No Error.
14. (A) Nothing/(B) has or/(C) could be more unfortunate/(D) than her illness./(E) No Error.
15. (A) She congratulated me for/(B) my brilliant success/(C) in/(D) the examination./(E) No Error.
16. (A) I inquired of/(B) his/(C) why he was negligent/(D) in his studies./(E) No Error.
17. (A) He met me last year,/(B) so/(C) he must be/(D) remembering me./ (E) No Error.
18. (A) On holidays I always go/(B) for/(C) walking/(D) in the garden./ (E) No Error.
19. (A) At no circumstances/(B) should you/(C) lend him/(D) any money./(E) No Error.
20. (A) The mother as well as/(B) her two children/(C) were taken/(D) to hospital./(E) No Error.
21. (A) She can only/(B) he cured/(C) by/(D) a surgical operation./(E) No Error.
22. (A) You/(B) arrived here/(C) last evening./(D) Where are you living?/(E) No Error.
23. (A) It is a pity that/(B) the standard of/(C) our football is going down;/(D) I hope our team will lose./(E) No Error.
24. (A) The students will be/(B) giving/(C) their final examinations/(D) shortly./(E) No Error.
25. (A) I can hardly/(B) say/(C) the difference/(D) between these two things./(E) No Error.
26. (A) She is/(B) changing her dress;/(C) please don't/(D) see./(E) No Error.
27. (A) He/(B) emphasised on/(C) the point/(D) again and again./(E) No Error.
28. (A) He does his best to help/(B) the poor,/(C) but he is/(D) not communist./(E) No Error.
29. (A) I shall return/(B) the money/(C) in /(D) one day or two./(E) No Error.
30. (A) You have been looking/(B) for your book/(C) for over an hour./(D) Haven't you found yet?/(E) No Error.
31. (A) What he/(B) really wants is/(C) one/(D) glass water./(E) No Error.
32. (A) I was much annoyed/(B) by her behaviour;/(C) she did nothing/(D) but sang./(E) No Error.
33. (A) He was trying to/(B) find a place/(C) where he/(D) could had parked his car./(E) No Error.
34. (A) He has so far/(B) shown himself/(C) a quiet and/(D) well-mannered person./(E) No Error.

35. (A) She would have gone/(B) away/(C) at the time/(D) I reach home./(E) No Error.

36. (A) A student has/(B) to pass many a sleepless nights/(C) before the result is/(D) announced./ (E) No Error.

37. (A) Don't you know that/(B) I had the privilege/(C) of setting under the/(D) feet of an eminent historian./(E) No Error.

38. (A) The minister cannot do anything;/(B) there is no/(C) use/(D) see him./(E) No Error.

39. (A) If it would snow/(B) we should/(C) give up/(D) the trip./(E) No Error.

40. (A) Neither failure in the examination/(B) nor the anger/(C) of his father are/(D) going to upset him./(E) No Error.

41. (A) You are misinformed;/(B) I am neither/(C) a poet/(D) nor scientist./(E) No Error.

42. (A) She reads all/(B) the time; (C) she prefers/ (D) to read than to write./(E) No Error.

43. (A) Does this/(B) hotel give/(C) both fooding/ (D) and lodging?/(E) No Error.

44. (A) He was appointed/(B) as secretary/(C) by the members of the/(D) club./(E) No Error.

45. (A) Unless you do not work/(B) hard,/(C) you cannot/(D) pass the examination./(E) No Error.

46. (A) I have rejected/(B) your proposal;/(C) it hinders,/(D) instead of helps us./(E) No Error.

47. (A) He was shouting/(B) on the top/(C) of his voice/(D) when I slapped him./(E) No Error.

48. (A) She has told me/(B) that the committee/(C) comprises of ten members/(D) including the chairman./(E) No Error.

49. (A) While/(B) playing hockey,/(C) his both hands/(D) were injured./(E) No Error.

50. (A) I think/(B) she sang/(C) very well./(D) Is n't it?/(E) No Error.

51. (A) He is superior/(B) than you/(C) in/(D) rank in the army./(E) No Error.

52. (A) No sooner did he catch/(B) the thief/(C) when/(D) the police arrived./(E) No Error.

53. (A) I shall entreat/(B) her/(C) to consider me/ (D) as her friend./(E) No Error.

54. (A) He is sure/(B) to secure at least/(C) passable/(D) marks./(E) No Error.

55. (A) Do you know/(B) that he/(C) has sold/(D) five dozens pens? (E) No Error.

56. (A) I assure/(B) you that/(C) she cannot endure/(D) my separation./(E) No Error.

57. (A) She denied/(B) that she/(C) did not steal/ (D) the pen./(E) No Error.

58. (A) There were/(B) not less/(C) than ten girls/ (D) in the party./(E) No Error.

59. (A) She was about/(B) to leave but/(C) I prevented/(D) her to go./(E) No Error.

60. (A) Remember that such/(B) boys who/(C) play regularly/(D) enjoy sound health./(E) No Error.

61. (A) She requested me/(B) to introduce/(C) her/ (D) with my friends./(E) No Error.

62. (A) I know/(B) he is true/(C) to his/(D) words./ (E) No Error.

63. (A) I worked very hard/(B) with a view/(C) to secure/(D) a first class./(E) No Error.

64. (A) He says it is one of/(B) the worst accidents/(C) that/(D) has occurred this year./(E) No Error.

65. (A) Know it for certain/(B) that/(C) she resembles/(D) with her mother./(E) No Error.

66. (A) None of these/(B) ten girls have/(C) done the home/(D) task./(E) No Error.

TYPE II

67. (A) She took a/(B) different attitude/(C) than what he/(D) used to take./(E) No Error.

68. (A) If you would have studied/(B) the problem/(C) you would have/(D) found a solution./ (E) No Error.

69. (A) Honour/(B) as well as/(C) profit/(D) are to be gained by honest means./(E) No Error.

70. (A) Neither the critics/(B) nor the author/(C) were right/(D) about the reaction of the public./(E) No Error.

71. (A) An official should be/(B) both regular and/ (C) punctual in attendance, even though he or she/(D) are otherwise efficient./(E) No Error.

72. (A) Despite/(B) all her faults/(C) I cannot/(D) help but like her./(E) No Error.

73. (A) You can rely/(B) on my doing/(C) everything to avert/(D) a disaster./(E) No Error.

74. (A) She made four/(B) accusations against me/(C) and the latter/(D) was the most significant./(E) No Error.

75. (A) He preferred/(B) trudging through/(C) the mud/(D) than to take the road./(E) No Error.

76. (A) I told her/(B) one part only/(C) of the/(D) lengthy story./(E) No Error.

77. (A) I ordered for/(B) the books;/(C) I must/(D) accept them./(E) No Error.

78. (A) Many students/(B) often come across with/(C) terrible difficulties/(D) in learning the English language./(E) No Error.

79. (A) Thieves/(B) broke into his house/(C) last night/(D) this caused much loss./(E) No Error.

80. (A) He accepted/(B) all these tales/(C) with no sign of/(D) disbelief./(E) No Error.

81. (A) I/(B) married/(C) only her for/(D) her money./(E) No Error.

82. (A) When he was/(B) walking towards/(C) Akbar Road,/(D) he was arrested./(E) No Error.

83. (A) These organisations/(B) are worried,/(C) lest their activities/(D) may he banned by the government./(E) No Error.

84. (A) We are going/(B) to Kashmir/(C) on our/(D) forty days' summer holiday./(E) No Error.

85. (A) He is/(B) due to/(C) another two/(D) weeks' holiday./(E) No Error.

86. (A) Please tell/(B) me something/(C) about/(D) Himalayas./(E) No Error.

87. (A) Foreigners take great/(B) pleasure/(C) to remind us/(D) of our poverty./(E) No Error.

88. (A) If/(B) I was you,/(C) I would not attend/(D) the meeting./(E) No Error.

89. (A) Please believe me, I do not/(B) hardly know/(C) what happened/(D) yesterday./(E) No Error.

90. (A) What is the/(B) use of/(C) him trying/(D) to do that work?(E) No Error.

91. (A) It is rather very/(B) difficult for me/(C) to understand/(D) what he says./(E) No Error.

92. (A) The price of this article/(B) vary considerably/(C) in different parts/(C) of the country./(E) No Error.

93. (A) Ten members only/(B) attended the meeting/(C) held on Friday,/(D) the 28th April, 19.., at 4.30 p.m./(E) No Error.

94. (A) Everyone/(B) at the party/(C) was enjoying/(D) themselves. (E) No Error.

95. (A) She has an/(B) urgent work/(C) to do/(D) at home./(E) No Error.

96. (A) He quickly/(B) accustomed/(C) to this/(D) new way of life./(E) No Error.

97. (A) I shall not go into all the depressing details;/(B) suffice it to/(C) say the whole affairs/(D) was an utter disaster./(E) No Error.

98. (A) The price of/(B) my car is/(C) higher than/(D) your car./(E) No Error.

99. (A) He paid/(B) the price of/(C) the car/(D) in cheque./(E) No Error.

100. (A) She/(B) committted/(C) suicide thrice/(D) before she died./(E) No Error.

101. (A) The reason/(B) of his success/(C) is due to/(D) his hard work./(E) No Error.

102. (A) She and/(B) her sisters/(C) love each other/(D) very much./(E) No Error.

103. (A) I have set up/(B) another college/(C) with a view to/(D) compete against my rival./(E) No Error.

104. (A) As he is highly qualified and well experienced,/(B) we appointed him/(C) as general manager/(D) of the company./(E) No Error.

105. (A) They called her/(B) as a whore/(C) and this angered/(D) her much./(E) No Error.

106. (A) Her all daughters/(B) are ugly,/(C) so they cannot be/(D) married easily./(E) No Error.

107. (A) As his both hands/(B) have been injured,/(C) he cannot/(D) work properly./(E) No Error.

108. (A) You should/(B) only write/(C) on one side/(D) of the paper./(E) No Error.

109. (A) You should/(B) look at/(C) everything from/(D) their best side./(E) No Error.

110. (A) She does not/(B) talk to me but I/(C) do not care/(D) fig for her./(E) No Error.

111. (A) Your essay/(B) should not/(C) exceed more than/(D) three hundred words./(E) No Error.

112. (A) He is/(B) always/(C) making excuses/(D) to be late./(E) No Error.

113. (A) She enjoys/(B) to learn/(C) the English language as she is/(D) interested in it./(E) No Error.

114. (A) The secretary of the/(B) association/(C) was first to/(D) break the silence./(E) No Error.

TYPE III

115. (A) She said that/(B) she preferred the/(C) red gown/(D) than the white one./(E) No Error.

116. (A) I would have invited her/(B) to dinner if/(C) I had known that/(D) she is staying here tonight./(E) No Error.

117. (A) She reminded me/(B) that she has/(C) often told me/(D) not to play with fire./(E) No Error.

118. (A) I told them/(B) that one should/(C) work hard to earn/(D) his livelihood./(E) No Error.

119. (A) He had been writing/(B) the article for/(C) two hours but he still/(D) has not finished./(E) No Error.

120. (A) She looked/(B) upon me/(C) for a few moments/(D) before he spoke./(E) No Error.

121. (A) The problems are/(B) complex and/(C) has been/(D) obscured by other factors./(E) No Error.

122. (A) India need/(B) a large number/(C) of selfless and devoted/(D) political leaders./(E) No Error.

123. (A) He/(B) as well as his two sons/(C) were missing/(D) from the house./(E) No Error.

124. (A) Hardly had/(B) I left the house/(C) than it began/(D) to rain./(E) No Error.

125. (A) India is/(B) one of the/(C) leading rice producing/(D) country in the world./(E) No Error.

126. (A) A policeman/(B) together with his/(C) wife and three daughters/(D) were kidnapped by dacoits./(E) No Error.

127. (A) If I would have/(B) worked hard/(C) I would have/(D) passed the examination./(E) No Error.

128. (A) Everyone of the/(B) workers has given a day's pay/(C) as their/(D) contribution to the relief fund./(E) No Error.

129. (A) Neither the size/(B) nor the/(C) colour of the gloves/(D) were right./(E) No Error.

130. (A) Studying late/(B) at night is one of/(C) those things/(D) that makes me tired./(E) No Error.

131. (A) They were to/(B) have been married/(C) last month but had to postpone the marriage/(D) until next April./(E) No Error.

132. (A) The fact that he has/(B) rose to eminence/(C) from poverty,/(D) is highly creditable./(E) No Error.

133. (A) She could not/(B) attend the meeting/(C) because his/(D) father's serious illness./(E) No Error.

134. (A) Although the servant/(B) is a new recruited boy,/(C) his style of working/(D) is quite appreciable./(E) No Error.

135. (A) She is already/(B) as well as/(C) acquainted with these/(D) affairs as I am./(E) No Error.

136. (A) The fraud was/(B) discovered, and/(C) he was tried and/(D) imprisoned since six months./(E) No Error.

137. (A) She has a scheme/(B) of her own which,/(C) she thinks, preferable/(D) to that of any other person./(E) No Error.

138. (A) He advised his sons/(B) to not quarrel/(C) among themselves but to/(D) remain united./(E) No Error.

139. (A) In spite of his being/(B) a mere boy,/(C) he offered/(D) to fight the dacoits./(E) No Error.

140. (A) When I offered/(B) him to help/(C) which he needed, he/(D) persisted in refusing it./(E) No Error.

141. (A) She told me/(B) that she wrote/(C) a lengthy letter to her mother/(D) about her future plans./(E) No Error.

142. (A) Of the/(B) two brothers,/(C) the elder is/ (D) most intelligent./(E) No Error.

143. (A) It was/(B) him who/(C) was to blame/(D) for the accident./(E) No Error.

144. (A) This/(B) is a/(C) best book/(D) on the subject./(E) No Error.

145. (A) The train/(B) has arrived/(C) when we reached/(D) the station./(E) No Error.

146. (A) The two first/(B) to arrive were/(C) the lucky recipients/(D) of a gift./(E) No Error.

147. (A) If I would have/(B) planned more carefully,/(C) bankruptcy might have been/(D) avoided./(E) No Error.

148. (A) He was accused of/(B) embezzlement,/(C) assault and/(D) forging./(E) No Error.

149. (A) Ganges/(B) is a sacred/(C) river of the/(D) Hindus./(E) No Error.

150. (A) One of his/(B) four sons/(C) are very/(D) intelligent./(E) No Error.

151. (A) I introduced her to one/(B) of my friends/ (C) who is a writer/(D) and an artist./(E) No Error.

152. (A) I am surprised/(B) that he/(C) is working/ (D) on this job for four days./(E) No Error.

153. (A) It is a matter of great/(B) regret that owing to her illness,/(C) she could not give/(D) her examination./(E) No Error.

154. (A) It is one of/(B) those tricky/(C) questions that/(D) has two answers./(E) No Error.

155. (A) Being a rainy day,/(B) she decided/(C) not to go/(D) out of the house./(E) No Error.

156. (A) Having performed the risky act,/(B) the spectators/(C) expressed their admiration/(D) for Bhim with prolonged applause./(E) No Error.

157. (A) He/(B) has not been/(C) attending school/ (D) from last month./(E) No Error.

158. (A) Hardly did I sit/(B) on the chair/(C) when there was an/(D) explosion outside the house./ (E) No Error.

159. (A) As each year passes,/(B) the number of/ (C) tigers/(D) are increasing./(E) No Error.

160. (A) My eldest son is/(B) one of those/(C) I can always count on/(D) when in trouble./(E) No Error.

161. (A) She does not/(B) know/(C) to read/(D) Hindi./(E) No Error.

162. (A) I think that/(B) the report of the police/(C) is equally as good as/(D) the report of the magistrate./(E) No Error.

163. (A) He had a chance/(B) to invest wisely,/(C) establish his position and/(D) displaying his ability as an executive./(E) No Error.

164. (A) The four thieves/(B) decided to share/(C) the loot/(D) between themselves./(E) No Error.

165. (A) I shall begin working/(B) since the second/ (C) week of/(D) next month./(E) No Error.

TYPE IV

166. (A) They made so/(B) much noise/(C) that/(D) I cannot sleep./(E) No Error.

167. (A) I ate/(B) my food when/(C) she/(D) called on me yesterday./(E) No Error.

168. (A) The police/(B) has arrested a man/(C) on the charge of kidnapping/(D) a minor girl./(E) No Error.

169. (A) No sooner he had/(B) arrived than/(C) he was asked/(D) to leave again./(E) No Error.

170. (A) After an absent of/(B) two months she/(C) returned home/(D) this forenoon./(E) No Error.

171. (A) I saw/(B) a two years old/(C) red deer/(D) in the zoo./(E) No Error.

172. (A) The present ruler of/(B) that country/(C) is not different/(D) than his predecessors./(E) No Error.

173. (A) She/(B) is going/(C) to school/(D) regularly./(E) No Error.

174. (A) Will the students/(B) that have/(C) secured high marks/(D) be rewarded?/(E) No Error.

175. (A) The applicant/(B) being a major, (C) he is/ (D) entitled to vote./(E) No Error.

176. (A) If he has/(B) taken the/(C) pen, let/(D) her return it./(E) No Error.

177. (A) What is the most unique/(B) function that/ (C) you have ever/(D) attended?/(E) No Error.

178. (A) In our college/(B) library,/(C) the number of books/(D) is less./(E) No Error.

179. (A) He is/(B) very poor that/(C) he cannot/(D) help you./(E) No Error.

180. (A) Tell me/(B) whether/(C) you know/(D) to swim./(E) No Error.

181. (A) Neither Kamini/(B) nor Mohini were/(C) aware of the arrangements/(D) made for their stay./(E) No Error.

182. (A) No man/(B) in your troupe/(C) is as sprightly as/(D) his son./(E) No Error.

183. (A) A little/(B) did I realise how/(C) cleverly/ (D) I had been deceived./(E) No Error.

184. (A) She will be/(B) visiting me/(C) in the holi-days/(D) this summer./(E) No Error.

185. (A) They have/(B) just/(C) returned back/(D) from the meeting./(E) No Error.

186. (A) We felt that the safety of/(B) doctors and nurses/(C) of the hospital were/(D) in peril./ (E) No Error.

187. (A) Had the price control scheme/(B) been fully implemented,/(C) the economy/(D) would be on the right path./(E) No Error.

188. (A) She dislikes/(B) them sitting/(C) too far/ (D) from the table./(E) No Error.

189. (A) One girl only/(B) has done/(C) the work/ (D) properly./(E) No Error.

190. (A) It is not proper/(B) for you/(C) to call him/ (D) as a fool./(E) No Error.

191. (A) The thief/(B) took to his heels/(C) because he was afraid/(D) to be caught and beaten./(E) No Error.

192. (A) One should look/(B) for his/(C) own faults first and then/(D) those of others./(E) No Error.

193. (A) The truck which/(B) is stopped by the police/(C) contained a large number of/(D) smuggled articles./(E) No Error.

194. (A) Although it is winter,/(B) the weather in Kashmir/(C) was quite/(D) pleasant./(E) No Error.

195. (A) The lawyer asked him/(B) where had he kept his clothes/(C) before going for/(D) a dip in the river./(E) No Error.

196. (A) Unless you/(B) do not take care/(C) of your health,/(D) you will continue to suffer./ (E) No Error.

197. (A) I would have/(B) come sooner if/(C) I knew/(D) they were here./(E) No Error.

198. (A) It is no use/(B) to ask you to/(C) help him/ (D) with money./ (E) No Error.

199. (A) Four boys/(B) were quarrelling/(C) with/ (D) each other./(E) No Error.

200. (A) Contrary to earlier reports/(B) I found her to be/(C) a suave/(D) and amiable person/(E) No Error.

201. (A) She/(B) says/(C) you are/(D) a foolish./(E) No Error.

202. (A) I/(B) say/(C) she is/(D) fool./(E) No Error.

ANSWERS

1. **B:** is playing
2. **B:** has
3. **D:** in hand.
4. **C:** if she is
5. **A:** I told
6. **B:** as good as
7. **C:** less number of people
8. **C:** on seeing the tiger. This expression should be placed at the beginning of the sentence.
9. **D:** consists of four parts.
10. **A:** She is fond of reading
11. **D:** was completely destroyed.
12. **B:** as soon as
13. **A;** As I was passing

14. B: has been
15. A: She congratulated me on
16. B: him
17. A: He had met me last year
18. C: a walk
19. A: under no circumstances
20. C: was taken
21. A: She can only. In this sentence 'only' should be placed at the beginning of the sentence.
22. D: Where are you staying.
23. D: I fear our team will lose.
24. B: taking
25. B: tell
26. D: look.
27. B: emphasised
28. D: not a communist.
29. D: one or two days.
30. D: haven't you found it yet.
31. D: glass of water.
32. D: but sing.
33. D: could have parked his car.
34. B: shown himself as a
35. C: by the time
36. B: to pass many a sleepless night
37. C: at setting under the
38. D: seeing him.
39. A: If it would snows
40. C: of his father is
41. D: a scientist.
42. D: reading to writing.
43. C: boarding
44. B: secretary
45. A: Unless you work
46. D: instead of helping us.
47. B: at the top
48. C: comprises ten members
49. C: both of his hands
50. D: Didn't she?
51. B: to
52. C: than
53. D: her friend.
54. C: passing
55. D: five dozen pens.
56. D: separation from me.
57. C: stole
58. B: not fewer
59. D: her from going.
60. B: as boys who
61. D: to my friends.
62. D: word.
63. C: to securing
64. D: have occurred this year.
65. D: her mother.
66. B: ten girls has
67. C: from what he
68. A: If you had studied
69. D: is to be gained by honest means.
70. C: was right
71. D: is otherwise efficient.
72. D: help liking her.
73. B: on me for doing
74. C: and the last
75. D: to taking the road.
76. B: only one part
77. A: I ordered
78. B: often come across
79. D: and caused much loss.
80. B: all of these tales
81. C: her only for
82. A: While he was
83. D: should be banned by the government.
84. C: for our
85. B: entitled to
86. D: the Himalayas.
87. C: in reminding us
88. B: I were you,
89. A: Please believe me, I do not
90. C: his trying
91. A: It is very very
92. B: varies considerably
93. A: Only ten members
94. D: himself.
95. B: urgent piece of work
96. B: accustomed himself
97. C: say that the whole affairs
98. C: higher than that of
99. D: by cheque.
100. B: tried to commit
101. C: is
102. C: love one another
103. D: competing against my rival.
104. C: general manager
105. B: a whore

106. A: All of her daughters
107. A: As both of his hands
108. B: writing only
109. D: its best side.
110. D: a fig for her.
111. C: exceed
112. D: for being late.
113. B: learning
114. C: was the first to
115. D: to white one.
116. D: she was staying here tonight.
117. B: that she had
118. D: one's livelihood.
119. A: He has been writing
120. B: at me
121. C: have been
122. A: India needs
123. C: was missing
124. C: when it began,
125. D: countries in the world.
126. D: was kidnapped by the dacoits.
127. A: If I had
128. C: as his
129. D: was right.
130. D: that make me tired.
131. B: be married
132. B: risen to eminence
133. C: because of his
134. B: is newly recruited boy
135. B: as well
136. D: imprisoned for six months.
137. C: she thinks, is preferable
138. B: not to quarrel
139. A: In spite of being
140. B: him help
141. B: that she had written
142. D: more intelligent.
143. B: he who
144. B: is the
145. B: had arrived
146. A: The first two
147. A: If I had
148. D: forgery.
149. A: The Ganges
150. C: is very
151. D: and artist.
152. C: has been working
153. C: she could not take
154. D: have two answers.
155. A: It being a rainy day,
156. A: On his having performed the risky job,
157. D: since last month.
158. A: Hardly had I sat
159. D: is increasing.
160. C: whom I can always count
161. C: how to read
162. C: is as good as
163. D: display his ability as an executive.
164. D: among themselves.
165. B: from the second
166. D: I could not sleep.
167. A: I was eating
168. B: have arrested a man
169. A: No sooner had he
170. A: After an absence of
171. B: a two-year-old
172. D: from his predecessors.
173. B: goes
174. B: who have
175. C: is
176. D: him return it.
177. A: What is the unique
178. D: is small.
179. B: so poor that
180. D: how to swim.
181. B: nor Mohini was
182. A: No other man
183. A: Little
184. C: during holidays
185. C: returned
186. C: of the hospital was
187. D: would have been on the right path.
188. B: their sitting
189. A: Only one girl
190. D: a fool.
191. D: of being caught and beaten.
192. B: one's
193. B: was stopped by the police
194. C: is quite
195. B: where he had kept his clothes
196. B: take care
197. C: I had known
198. B: asking you to
199. D: one another.
200. A: Contrary to previous reports
201. D: a foolish person.
202. D: a fool.

SPOT CORRECT SENTENCES

Directions: *There are four sentences in each of the following questions. One of the sentences is correct, and the rest are incorrect. You are to select the correct sentence in each question.*

1. A. She is either right nor wrong.
B. She is nor right or wrong.
C. She is neither right or wrong.
D. She is neither right nor wrong.

2. A. He went to Nepal five years ago.
B. He went to Nepal five years back.
C. He went to Nepal five years before.
D. He went to Nepal five years past.

3. A. Before leaving home, it began to rain.
B. As since I was leaving home, it began to rain.
C. As I was leaving home, it began to rain.
D. When leaving home, it began to rain.

4. A. I have given up alcoholic drinks two years before.
B. I have given up alcoholic drinks two years since.
C. I have given up alcoholic drinks two years back.
D. I had given up alcoholic drinks two years ago.

5. A. I told to her to give me that book.
B. I said her to give me this book.
C. I said to her that to give me that book.
D. I asked her to give me that book.

6. A. My maternal grandmother said to me not go without having a cup of tea.
B. My maternal grandmother asked me not go without having a cup of tea.
C. My maternal grandmother asked me to go not without having a cup of tea.
D. My maternal grandmother asked me not to go without having a cup of tea.

7. A. His sister told me that he likes my new car.
B. His sister said me that she likes my new car.
C. His sister told me I like your new car.
D. His sister told me that she liked my new car.

8. A. The teacher asked me where was I going?
B. The teacher asked me where I am going.
C. The teacher asked me where I go.
D. The teacher asked me where I was going.

9. A. Your conduct admits no excuses.
B. Your conduct admit no excuse.
C. Your conduct is inexcusable.
D. Your conduct admit of no excuses.

10. A. The young woman tried on two coats and finally decided to buy the most expensive one.
B. The young woman tried on two coats and finally decided to buy the more expensive one.
C. The young woman tried on two coats and finally decided to buy the expensive one.
D. The young woman tried on coats two and finally decided to buy the very expensive one.

11. A. She is anxious about my health.
B. She is anxious of my health.
C. She is anxious for my health.
D. She is anxious with my health.

12. A. My youngest son had no difficulty with solving the problem.
B. My youngest son had no difficulty to solve the problem.
C. My youngest son had no difficulty in solving the problem.
D. My youngest son had no difficulty for solving the problem.

13. A. The plane had left before I reached the airport.
B. The plane left before I reached the airport.
C. The plane was leaving before I reached the airport.
D. The plane will leave before I reached the airport.

14. A. The four dacoits distributed the loot with themselves.
B. The four dacoits distributed the loot between themselves.
C. The four dacoits distributed the loot among themselves.

D. The four dacoits distributed the loot upon themselves.

15. A. What our country needs today is a number of selfless and competent leaders.

B. What our country need today is a number of unscrupulous leaders.

C. What our country needs today are a number of selfish leaders.

D. What our country needs today is a number of motivated leaders.

16. A. I am very sorry to learn that you lose the match yesterday.

B. I am very sorry to learn that you loosed the match yesterday.

C. I am very sorry to learn that you lost the match yesterday.

D. I am very sorry to learn that you have lost the match yesterday.

17. A. It is our bounden duty to instil a sense of responsibility into the people of the country.

B. It is our bounden duty to instigate a sense of responsibility into the people of the country.

C. It is our bounden duty to excite a sense of responsibility into the people of the country.

D. It is our bounden duty to incite a sense of responsibility into the people of the country.

18. A. He is over seventy years of age and are still alert and strong.

B. He is over seventy years of age but who is still alert and strong.

C. He is a man over seventy years of age but who is still alert and strong.

D. He is over seventy years of age, but is still alert and strong.

19. A. She told me that it is better to fail than pass by unfair means.

B. She told me it was better to fail than passing by unfair means.

C. She told whether it was better to fail than pass by unfair means.

D. She told me that it was better to fail than to pass by unfair means.

20. A. She asked me to name the capital of Nepal.

B. She asked me which is the capital of Nepal.

C. She asked me what is the capital of Nepal.

D. She told me in the capital of Nepal.

21. A. She heartily congratulated me about my splendid success in the examination.

B. She heartily congratulated me on my splendid success in the examination.

C. She heartily congratulated me for my splendid success in the examination.

D. She heartily congratulated me at my splendid success in the examination.

22. A. He replied that he will call on me tomorrow.

B. He replied that he would call on me tomorrow.

C. He had replied that he would have called on me tomorrow.

D. He replied that he will have called on me tomorrow.

23. A. I am sorry to say that she made me do the dirty job.

B. I am sorry to say that she made me to do the dirty job.

C. I am sorry to say that she would make me to do the dirty job.

D. I am sorry to say that she did me to do the dirty job.

24. A. Will you please excuse my dropping in at this untimely hour?

B. Will you please excuse me dropping at this untimely hour?

C. Will you please excuse my dropping at this untimely hour?

D. Will you please excuse my dropping by this untimely hour?

25. A. Now I must beg of your leave.

B. Now I must beg off your leave.

C. Now I must beg your leave.

D. Now I must beg leave of you.

26. A. When narrating the road accident, she was in tears.

B. As narrating the road accident, she was in tears.

C. In narrating the road accident, she was in tears.
D. When she was narrating the road accident, she was in tears.

27. A. A long period of ten years have passed since he has passed away.
B. A long period of ten years has passed since he passed away.
C. A long period of ten years passed since he has passed away.
D. A long period of ten years have passed since he had passed away.

28. A. Can you do it more quick than I?
B. Can you do it more quicker than I?
C. Can you do it more quickly than I?
D. Can you do it more quick than I can?

29. A. This coat is too small for her.
B. This coat is to small for her.
C. This coat is too much small for her.
D. This coat is much too small for her.

30. A. My boss was kind enough to grant me leave of absence for ten days.
B. My boss was enough kind to grant me leave of absence for ten days.
C. My boss was kindly enough to grant me leave of absence for ten days.
D. My boss was enough kind for granting me leave of absence for ten days.

31. A. You should work hard lest you may fail in the examination.
B. You should work hard lest you should fail in the examination.
C. You should work hard lest you might fail in the examination.
D. You should work hard lest you fail in the examination.

32. A. When entering the class-room, each of the boys kept quiet.
B. Entering the class-room, each of the boys kept quiet.
C. On entering the class-room, each of the boys kept quiet.
D. Since entering the class-room, each of the boys kept quiet.

33. A. She asked that why her son shall be punished.
B. She asked that why her son should be punished.
C. She asked why her son should be punished.
D. She asked on why her son shall be punished.

34. A. She gives me such troubles which I cannot endure them.
B. She gives me such troubles as I cannot endure them.
C. She gives on me such troubles that I cannot endure them.
D. She gives at me such troubles which I cannot endure.

35. A. I have not seen her long since.
B. I have not seen her since long.
C. I have not seen her since a long.
D. I have not seen her from a long time.

36. A. This is the same book which I lost a few weeks ago.
B. This is the same book that I lost a few weeks ago.
C. This is the same book that I lost a few weeks before.
D. This is the same book which I lost a few weeks past.

37. A. This cloth is more preferable than that.
B. This cloth is more preferable than that.
C. This cloth is more preferable to that.
D. This cloth is preferable to that.

38. A. I seldom or ever make a mistake.
B. I seldom and never make a mistake.
C. I seldom or never make a mistake.
D. I seldom that never make a mistake.

39. A. His command in the English language is very unique.
B. His command of the English language is unique.
C. His command of the English language is perfectly unique.
D. His command of the English language is totally unique.

40. A. Her speech was so halting that she stopped between each word.
B. Her speech was so halting that she stopped after each word.
C. Her speech was so halting that she has stopped each word.
D. Her speech was so halting that she was stopping between each word.

41. A. I do not know who you consider the best man of the two.
B. I do not know whom you consider to be the man of the two.
C. I do not know whom you consider better of the two.
D. I do not know who you consider as the best of the two.

42. A. Do you bathe yourself daily?
B. Do you bath yourself daily?
C. Do you bathe daily?
D. Do you daily bath?

43. A. Being a cold day, I did not go out of the house.
B. It being a cold day, I did not go out of the house.
C. Being a cold day, I have not gone out of the house.
D. It being a cold day, I had not gone out of the house.

44. A. One should do his duty honestly and efficiently.
B. One should do one's duty honestly and efficiently.
C. One should do his responsibility honestly and efficiently.
D. One should act his responsibility honestly and efficiently.

45. A. She is one of those girls who cannot control her anger.
B. She is one of those girls which cannot control her anger.
C. She is one of those girls that cannot control her anger.
D. She is one of those girls who cannot control their anger.

46. A. You should attentively listen what he says.
B. You should attentively listen to what he says.
C. You should attentively listen to what he say.
D. You should attentively listen to what he says.

47. A. If she will come, I shall certainly give her five hundred rupees.
B. If she will come, I shall certainly give with her five hundred rupees.
C. If she comes, I shall certainly give five hundred rupees upon her.
D. If she comes, I shall certainly give her five hundred rupees.

48. A. She asked me if I broke the mirror.
B. She asked me if I have broken the mirror.
C. She asked of me if I have broken the mirror.
D. She asked if I had broken the mirror.

49. A. Workers are prohibited to bring their cycles inside the factory premises.
B. Workers are prohibited from bringing their cycles inside the factory premises.
C. Workers are prohibited to bringing their cycles inside the factory premises.
D. Workers are prohibited from to bring their cycles inside the factory premises.

50. A. Do you remember the date of him leaving India for Japan?
B. Do you remember the date of his leaving India for Japan?
C. Do you remember the date from his leaving India for Japan?
D. Do you remember the date by his leaving India for Japan?

51. A. She expected to have passed in the examination.
B. She expected to have pass in the examination.
C. She expected in passing the examination.
D. She expected to pass the examination.

52. A. I have visited him four hours ago.
B. I have visited him four hours before.
C. I have visited him four hours since.
D. I visited him four hours ago.

53. A. I did not go out of the house after I wrote the letter.
B. I did not go out of the house since I wrote the letter.
C. I did not go out of the house after I had written the letter.
D. I did not go out of the house after I have written the letter.

54. A. The murderer was tried, convicted and hung.
B. The murderer was tried, convicted and was hung.
C. The murderer was tried, convicted and hunged.
D. The murderer was tried, convicted and hanged.

55. A. The sceneries of Kashmir are very beautiful.
B. The sceneries of Kashmir is very beautiful.
C. The scenery of Kashmir is very beautiful.
D. The scenery of Kashmir are very beautiful.

56. A. Unless you do not work hard, you will not achieve success in life.
B. Unless you work hard, you will not achieve success in life.
C. Unless you do not work hard, you will achieve success in life.
D. Unless you work hardly, you will not achieve success in life.

57. A. Every one of my children are intelligent and healthy.
B. Every one of my children is intelligent and healthy.
C. Every one of my childs are intelligent and healthy.
D. Every one of my childs is intelligent and healthy.

58. A. Neither of the two candidates are suitable for the job.
B. Neither of the two candidate is suitable for the job.
C. Neither of the two candidates is suitable for the job.
D. Neither of the two candidates is suit for the job.

59. A. As I am ill, so I shall not be able to attend the meeting.
B. As I am ill, so I shall not to be able to attend the meeting.
C. As I am ill, so I shall not be to able for attending the meeting.
D. As I am ill, I shall not be able to attend the meeting.

60. A. She never has and never will disobey me.
B. She never have and never will disobey me.
C. She never has disobeyed, and never will disobey me.
D. She never have disobeyed and never will disobey me.

61. A. This is the third time he broke a cup.
B. This is the third time when he broke a cup.
C. This is the third time he had broken a cup.
D. This is the third time he has broken a cup.

62. A. Let you and I be friends again.
B. Let you and myself be friend again.
C. Let you and I become friends again.
D. Let you and me be friends again.

63. A. I have come for seeing you.
B. I have come on seeing you.
C. I have came to seeing you.
D. I have come to see you.

64. A. I am true to my words.
B. I am true with my words.
C. I am true at my words.
D. I am true to my word.

65. A. She is very anxious with my health.
B. She is very anxious at my health.
C. She is very anxious about my health.
D. She is very anxious after my health.

66. A. This is one of the best books that has been published so far.
B. This is one of the best books which has been published so far.
C. This is one of the best books that have been published so far.
D. This is one of the best books which had been published so far.

67. A. She is taller than all the girls in the college.
B. She is taller then all the girls in the college.

C. She is taller than other girls in the college.
D. She is taller than all other girls in the college.

68. A. As far I am concerned, you are free to go anywhere you like.
B. As far I am concerned, you are to free go anywhere you like.
C. As far as I am concerned, you are free to go anywhere you like.
D. As far as I concerned, you are free to going anywhere you like.

69. A. He is confined to bed for about a week.
B. He was confined to bed for about a week.
C. He has been confine to bed for about a weak.
D. He has been confined to bed for about a week.

70. A. Subhash Bose was one of the greatest patriot of India.
B. Subhash Bose has been one of the greatest patriot of India.
C. Subhash Bose had been one of the greatest patriot of India.
D. Subhash Bose was one of the greatest patriots of India.

71. A. She is as good and even better than you.
B. She is as good as, or even better than, you.
C. She is as good as or even batter than you.
D. She is as good as and better than you.

72. A. They said to me that the General English paper is difficult.
B. They said me that the General English paper is difficult.
C. They said to me that the General English paper was difficult.
D. They said to me that the General English paper has been difficult.

73. A. May I have some words with you?
B. May I have a few words with you?
C. Can I have words with you?
D. May I have a word with you?

74. A. Our General Manager asked me as to why I am late.
B. Our General Manager asked me as to why am I late.
C. Our General Manager asked me why I am late.
D. Our General Manager asked me why I was late.

75. A. The story should not exceed more than five hundred words.
B. The story should not exceed than five hundred words.
C. The story should not exceed five hundred words.
D. The story should not accede five hundred words.

76. A. What is the good of him trying to do that work?
B. What is the good of his trying to do that work?
C. What the good is of him trying to do that work?
D. What is the good at his trying to do that work?

77. A. He does his best to find faults with my work.
B. He does his best in finding faults with my work.
C. He does his best to find fault with my work.
D. He does his best to find faults of my work.

78. A. This is a most unique opportunity for you to go abroad.
B. This is the most unique opportunity for you to go abroad.
C. This is a unique opportunity for you to go abroad.
D. This is a unique opportunity with you to go abroad.

79. A. Will you please say my compliments to your father?
B. Will you please say my complements to your father?
C. Will you please tell my compliments to your father?
D. Will you please pay my compliments to your father?

80. A. I always have and shall be your fast friend.
B. I always have been and shall be your fast friend.

C. I always was and shall be your fast friend.
D. I always had been and shall be your fast friend.

81. A. Tell me whether she loves you or not.
B. Tell me whether she loves you or knot.
C. Tell me whether or not she loves you.
D. Tell me whether she love you or not.

82. A. Tagore was greater than any poet.
B. Tagore was great than any poet.
C. Tagore was greater then any poet.
D. Tagore was greater than any other poet.

83. A. Going up the hill, an old temple was seen.
B. Going up to the hill, an old temple was seen.
C. On our going up the hill, an old temple was seen.
D. By going up to the hill, an old temple was seen.

84. A. The reason of her failure last time was due to her negligence.
B. The reason of her failure last time is due to her negligence.
C. Her failure last time was due to her negligence.
D. Her failure last time is on account of her negligence.

85. A. Nothing is more deplorable as dishonesty of this kind.
B. Nothing is so deplorable as dishonesty of this kind.
C. Nothing is such deplorable like dishonesty of this kind.
D. Nothing is more deplorable than dishonesty of this kind.

86. A. My cousin asked me that why did I not write to him?
B. My cousin asked me why did I not write to him?
C. My cousin asked me as to why did I not write to him?
D. My cousin asked me why I did not write to him.

87. A. She has no other ambition but only to pass the examination.
B. She has no ambition but only to pass the examination.
C. She has no ambition other than to pass the examination.
D. She has no other ambition other then to pass the examination.

88. A. If I could have worked hard, I would have passed the examination.
B. If I could work hard, I would have passed the examination.
C. If I might have worked hard, I would have passed the examination.
D. If I had worked hard, I would have passed the examination.

89. A. Four men were suspected of the crime but none of them confessed their guilt.
B. Four men were suspected of the crime but none of them accepted their guilt.
C. Four men were suspected of the crime but none of them admitted their guilt.
D. Four men were suspected of the crime, but none of them confessed his guilt.

90. A. Sita is younger to Rita but senior than her (Rita) in service.
B. Sita is younger to Rita but more senior to her (Rita) in service.
C. Sita is younger than Rita, but senior to her (Rita) in service.
D. Sita is more younger than Rita but senior to her (Rita) in service.

91. A. Tell me how are you?
B. Say me how are you?
C. Tell to me how are you?
D. Tell me how you are?

92. A. He denied that he was not a dacoit.
B. He denied that he not was a dacoit.
C. He denied he was not a dacoit.
D. He denied that he was a dacoit.

93. A. She insisted to go to Kuala Lumpur.
B. She insisted for going to Kuala Lumpur.
C. She insisted on going to Kuala Lumpur.
D. She insisted at going to Kuala Lumpur.

94. A. She gave me a chair to sit.
B. She gave me a chair for sitting.

C. She gave me a chair to be seated.
D. She gave me a chair to sit on.

95. A. He is one of the wisest persons who has ever lived.
B. He is one of the wisest persons who have ever lived.
C. He is one of the wisest persons which has ever lived.
D. He is one of the wisest persons which have ever lived.

96. A. Nobody in their senses could do such a nasty work.
B. Nobody in their senses could do such a good work.
C. Nobody in his senses could do such a nasty work.
D. Nobody in their senses could do such an excellent work.

97. A. Please tell me where is the Birla Temple?
B. Please say me where is the Birla Temple?
C. Please tell to me where is the Birla Temple?
D. Please tell me where the Birla Temple is?

98. A. They have and are still doing excellent work.
B. They have and have still doing excellent work.
C. They have and have still been doing excellent work.
D. They have done and are still doing excellent work.

99. A. All our family member have gone to Calcutta.
B. All our family member has gone to Calcutta.
C. All our family member have gone to Calcutta.
D. All the members of our family have gone to Calcutta.

100. A. Although we are living in Delhi for fifty years, we have not seen the Red Fort.
B. Although we are living in Delhi for fifty years, we had not seen the Red Fort.
C. Although we have been living in Delhi for fifty years, we have not seen the Red Fort.
D. Although we live in Delhi for fifty years, we had not seen the Red Fort.

101. A. She came to Delhi on last Sunday.
B. She came to Delhi Sunday last.
C. She came to Delhi last Sunday.
D. She came to Delhi on the last Sunday.

102. A. All the patients have been admitted and received proper attention.
B. All the patients has been admitted and received proper attention.
C. All the patients were admitted and received proper attention.
D. All the patients have been admitted, and have received proper attention.

103. A. Everyone must satisfy themselves about the truth of her statement.
B. Everyone must satisfy themselves on the truth of her statement.
C. Everyone must satisfy themselves by the truth of her statement.
D. Everyone must satisfy himself about the truth of her statement.

ANSWERS

1	2	3	4	5	6	7	8	9	10
D	A	C	D	D	D	D	D	C	B
11	**12**	**13**	**14**	**15**	**16**	**17**	**18**	**19**	**20**
A	C	A	C	A	C	A	D	D	A
21	**22**	**23**	**24**	**25**	**26**	**27**	**28**	**29**	**30**
B	B	A	A	D	D	B	C	D	A
31	**32**	**33**	**34**	**35**	**36**	**37**	**38**	**39**	**40**
B	C	C	B	B	B	D	C	B	B
41	**42**	**43**	**44**	**45**	**46**	**47**	**48**	**49**	**50**
C	C	B	B	D	D	D	D	B	B

51	52	53	54	55	56	57	58	59	60
D	D	C	D	C	B	B	C	D	C
61	**62**	**63**	**64**	**65**	**66**	**67**	**68**	**69**	**70**
D	D	D	D	C	C	D	C	D	D
71	**72**	**73**	**74**	**75**	**76**	**77**	**78**	**79**	**80**
B	C	D	D	C	B	D	C	D	B
81	**82**	**83**	**84**	**85**	**86**	**87**	**88**	**89**	**90**
C	D	C	C	D	D	C	D	D	C
91	**92**	**93**	**94**	**95**	**96**	**97**	**98**	**99**	**100**
D	D	C	D	B	C	D	D	D	C
101	**102**	**103**							
C	D	D							

PRACTICE QUESTIONS

Directions for (Qs. 1 to 30): *Each of the following sentences has been divided into three parts A, B, C. Read each sentence to find out whether there is an error in one of the parts A, B or C. No sentence has more than one error. If there is any error in any one of the parts indicate your response by the letter related to that part. If there is no mistake indicate it by 'D' which means NO ERROR.*

1. (A) Every one respects him/(B) because he is/(C) a man of parts.

2. (A) Being a very hot day/(B) we decided to go on a picnic/(C) to a far off place.

3. (A) Unless you do not listen to me/(B) I will not/(C) recommend you.

4. (A) He is one/(B) of those/(C) who does not given up.

5. (A) Me is one of/(B) the politicians who/(C) has made a mark in politics.

6. (A) I could not do this work/(B) myself so/(C) I have done it.

7. (A) He laid/(B) on the ground/(C) for some time.

8. (A) You should not/(B) think of/(C) avenging on your enemy.

9. (A) I could not find/(B) my watch/(C) no where.

10. (A) The old live with enforced leisure/(B) on fixed incomes/(C) subject to chronic illness.

11. (A) For that young man peace/(B) in the country was/(C) almost troublesome as war.

12. (A) The book is as good/(B) if not better/(C) than the older one.

13. (A) Who do/(B) you think/(C) my friend was talking to.

14. (A) He has decided/(B) to adopt a child because/(C) he had no issues.

15. (A) When he felt sad/(B) he use to play/(C) on the harmonium.

16. (A) I will not repeat the mistake/(B) done by/(C) my superiors.

17. (A) The man demonstrated/(B) himself both as a fool/(C) and a rogue.

18. (A) Do not be happy,/(B) you will have/(C) to pay dear.

19. (A) You must show me/(B) the new furnitures/(C) which you has bought yesterday.

20. (A) I have read this book last year/(B) but I do not remember/(C) its contents.

21. (A) Many a childern are/(B) naughty and endulges in/(C) monkey pranks.

22. (A) In most of the/(B) foreign countries you come/(C) across with many Indians.

23. (A) From the pavement/(B) he jumped in the car/(C) which was parked there.

24. (A) My firends have/(B) decided to go to/(C) a hill–station and enjoy.

25. (A) If all of you are determined/(B) to make a mark you would/(C) never miss them.

26. (A) I cannot tell/(B) why did not he/(C) come yesterday.

27. (A) I have visited all the tourist spots of india/ (B) and found that/(C) the sceneries of Kashmir the best.

28. (A) Since he remained/(B) in bed for a month/ (C) he complains against headache.

29. (A) There have been/(B) much improvement in the living/(C) conditions of the people.

30. (A) The doctor think that/(B) she is now enough well/(C) to leave the hospital.

Directions (Qs. 31 to 50): *A part of each of the following sentences is italicised from the answer choices which follow pick up one which can substitude the italicised part correct.*

31. It is a *general practic* of the educated people.
A. habit B. convention
C. thinking D. custom

32. He has grown quite *feeble.*
A. poor B. weak
C. strong D. rich

33. It was a *patry* sum.
A. poor B. sultry
C. unimportant D. small

34. I cannot *part with my friend.*
A. part away my friend
B. part from friend
C. part my friend
D. No change

35. Opposition hinders *instead of help* the government.
A. instead of helping
B. except of any help
C. despite the help
D. No change

36. *He did nothing but play.*
A. He did nothing except play
B. He did nothing but playing
C. He did nothing but to play
D. No change

37. *Despite of his age his skill at tennis* is good.
A. Despite his age his skill at tennis
B. Despite his age his skill of tennis
C. Despite his age his skill in tennis
D. No change

38. Take his statements *with a grain of salt.*
A. happily B. with reservations
C. in proper spirit D. exaggerated

39. I wish my bus *was not so late.*
A. were not so late
B. had not been so late
C. would not have been so late
D. No change

40. I will meet him *when he will come.*
A. while he comes
B. while he will come
C. when he comes
D. No change

41. It takes time to *eradicate* poverty.
A. finish B. control
C. uproot D. minimise

42. *Being a good suggestion* I accepted it.
A. It being a good suggestion
B. It is being a good suggestion
C. Good suggestion it being
D. No change

43. The judge acquitted *him from the charge.*
A. him by the charge
B. him of the charge
C. him the charge
D. No change

44. He stood andshouted *"please give me the another one."*
A. "please give me the other one"
B. you are requested to give the another one
C. kindly give the another one
D. No change

45. They have no *house to live.*
A. house to live in B. home to live
C. house to stay D. No change

46. *Let you and I* work together.
A. Let I and you B. Let both you and I
C. Let you and me D. No change

47. Coffee is *preferable than tea* to us.
A. preferable to tea
B. more preferable than tea

C. more preferable to tea
D. No change

48. *She prevented me to go* home.
A. She prevented me from
B. She checked me to go
C. She kept me back to go
D. No change

49. *Although you examine it carefully* you will find some flaws.
A. If you examine it carefully
B. Although you see it carefully
C. Though you examine it properly
D. No change

50. *She will inform to your brother about this.*
A. About this she will infrom your brother
B. Your brother will be informed about this by her
C. About this she will infrom to your brother
D. No change

Directions (Qs. 51 to 80): *There is a blank space in each of the following sentences. Pick up one which may complete the sentence correctly.*

51. I .....on these line before I realised my mistake.
A. worked B. was worked
C. am working D. had been working

52. I think I .....this news yesterday.
A. would read B. have read
C. read D. had read

53. They....the crime during the day.
A. committed B. performed
C. prosecuted D. disharged

54. I.....we should accept the offer.
A. will think B. would think
C. should think D. think

55. Do not shout lest....
A. he objects B. he may object
C. he should object D. he would object

56. It is difficult to say that .....
A. they should agree
B. they will agree
C. they would agree or not
D. they would agree

57. The girl .... a ruffian.
A. called the boy that
B. called the boy
C. said the boy
D. called the boy as

58. We rested.... the shade of the tree.
A. in
B. under
C. ourselves under
D. ourselves in

59. Death.....no calender.
A. olds B. maintains
C. keeps D. has

60. He picked up the coin which....on the ground.
A. lie B. lay
C. laid D. laid up

61. I....your work. Please remind me.
A. had forgotten B. forget
C. have forgotten D. forgot

62. Do not.... my hand so tightly.
A. hold B. catch
C. grab D. size

63. Nowadays she..... her drawing board to the school daily.
A. carries B. carried
C. would carry D. will carry

64. She must be ashamed.... her actions.
A. by B. at
C. of D. in

65. He admitted that he.....
A. should be at fault
B. is at fault
C. would be at fault
D. was at fault

66. They.... him of his valuable.
A. has deprived B. thieved
C. robbed D. would rob

67. No sooner did I reach there.....
A. so they left B. then they left
C. than they left D. when they left

68. He.... friends has come back.
A. along with his B. and his
C. or his D. None

69. Neither praise nor blame.... effect on him.
A. has no B. have no
C. has any D. have any

70. ..... what he says.
A. Near to B. Listen to
C. Near D. Listen

71. He told me that ..... .
A. earth revolved B. the earth revolved
C. earth revolves D. the earth revolves

72. We..... in the canal.
A. took both in the canal
B. bathed ourselves
C. bathed
D. None

73. Your success depends on your popularity.
A. of your subordinates
B. in your suborinates
C. with your subordinates
D. among your subordinates.

74. The employer waited until the workers......
A. scattered B. dispersed
C. had scattered D. had dispersed

75. His nature is such.......
A. so I cannot adjust
B. as I cannot adjust
C. which I cannot adjust
D. that I cannot adjust

76. ......has been made.
A. Every possible efforts
B. Every probable efforts
C. All possible efforts
D. All possible effort

77. Though I..... him, yet I recognised him.
A. have ever seen B. had hever seen
C. not seen D. never saw

78. Neither he nor his servants......
A. is left B. has left
C. have left D. None

79. Her nobility and virtue.....
A. deserves respect
B. claims respect
C. deserve respect
D. claim respect

80. I never have..... on my friends.
A. depended or will depend
B. depended nor will depend
C. or will depend
D. nor will depend

Directions (Qs. 81 to 97): *In each of the following questions one word in CAPITAL letters is followed by four possible synonyms. Pick up the most appropriate for each word.*

81. BENEVOLENT
A. borrower B. kind hearted
C. lender D. hard hearted

82. RECITIFY
A. specify B. to set right
C. modify D. purify

83. TAUNT
A. remark B. subdue
C. shaky D. sarcastic remark

84. QUIXOTIC
A. quiet B. serious
C. puzzling D. foolish

85. BEWAIL
A. lament B. recognise
C. take seriously D. decide

86. SPOUSE
A. to check
B. hard working officer
C. to support
D. husband or wife

87. RETRACE
A. to satisfy B. to run
C. to go back D. to pay back

88. BIGOT
A. wrong assertion
B. blind alley
C. blindly devoted to a creed
D. blind follower

89. IMPUDENT
A. insolent B. partial
C. bankrupt D. insolvent

90. QUIVER
A. playful B. restive
C. vibrate D. silence

91. PIGMY
A. dwarf B. designed
C. spotted D. related

92. FALTER
A. to speak clearly B. go unsteadily
C. to put on flesh D. None

93. DILEMA
A. stretch B. slight
C. doubt D. prayer

94. LETHAL
A. old B. modern
C. powerful D. deadly

95. IMPRINT
A. to cut down B. to decorate
C. to publish D. to fix in mind

96. MISGIVINGS
A. poor response B. wrong handling
C. apprehension D. worth giving

97. PACIFY
A. agitate B. satisfy
C. rise up D. calm down

Directions (Qs. 98 to 110): *For each of the following words in CAPITAL letters pick up correct antonym from the answer choices.*

98. DISSENT
A. renounce B. adopt
C. agree D. give

99. LAMENT
A. latent B. cry
C. hidden D. express sorrow

100. INDITE
A. run a risk B. compose a poem
C. imprint D. write

101. LINGER
A. pamper B. prosper
C. hasten D. delay

102. ENIGMATIC
A. look forward B. simple
C. puzzling D. straightforward

103. INDITE
A. absolve B. free
C. acquit D. release

104. PAUCITY
A. legality B. scarcity
C, play up D. play down

105. LAUD
A. seize B. praise
C. denounce D. patronise

106. DEFY
A. yearn
B. challenge an authority
C. firghten
D. spy

107. FROWN
A. giggle B. sneer
C. laugh D. smile

108. DENOUNCE
A. condemn B. alien
C. malign D. align

109. TEMERITY
A. strength B. weakness
C. cowardice D. courage

110. INCREDIBLE
A. understandable B. inaudible
C. unbelievable D. worthy

ANSWERS

1	**2**	**3**	**4**	**5**	**6**	**7**	**8**	**9**	**10**
C	A	A	C	C	C	A	C	C	C
11	**12**	**13**	**14**	**15**	**16**	**17**	**18**	**19**	**20**
C	A	C	C	D	B	C	C	B	A
21	**22**	**23**	**24**	**25**	**26**	**27**	**28**	**29**	**30**
A	C	B	C	C	B	C	C	A	C
31	**32**	**33**	**34**	**35**	**36**	**37**	**38**	**39**	**40**
A	B	D	B	A	B	A	B	B	C
41	**42**	**43**	**44**	**45**	**46**	**47**	**48**	**49**	**50**
C	A	B	A	A	C	A	A	A	A
51	**52**	**53**	**54**	**55**	**56**	**57**	**58**	**59**	**60**
D	B	A	D	C	C	B	A	C	B

61	62	63	64	65	66	67	68	69	70
C	A	A	C	D	C	B	A	C	B
71	**72**	**73**	**74**	**75**	**76**	**77**	**78**	**79**	**80**
D	C	C	B	B	D	B	C	B	B
81	**82**	**83**	**84**	**85**	**86**	**87**	**88**	**89**	**90**
B	B	D	D	A	D	C	C	D	C
91	**92**	**93**	**94**	**95**	**96**	**97**	**98**	**99**	**100**
A	B	C	D	D	C	D	C	D	B
101	**102**	**103**	**104**	**105**	**106**	**107**	**108**	**109**	**110**
C	D	A	B	D	B	D	A	C	C

COMPREHENSION

PASSAGE - 1

The strength of Indian Democracy lies in its tradition, in the fusion of the ideas of democracy and national independence which was the characteristic of the Indian Nationalist Movement long before independence. Although the British retained Supreme authority in India until 1947, the provincial elections of 1937 provided real exercise in democratic practice before national independence. During the Pacific war India was not overrun or seriously invaded by the Japanese and after the war was over, the transfer of power to a government of the Indian Congress Party was a peaceful one as far as Britain was concerned. By 1947 'Indianisation' had already gone far in the Indian Civil Service and Army, so that the new government could start with effective instruments of central control.

After Independence, however, India was faced with two vast problems; the first, that of economic growth from a very low level of production, and the second was that of ethnic diversity and the aspirations of sub-nationalities. The Congress leadership was more aware of the former problem than of the second. As a new political elite which had rebelled not only against the British Raj but also against India's old social order they were conscious of the need to initiate economic development and undertake social reforms, but as nationalists who had led a struggle against the alien rule on behalf of all parts of India, they took the cohesion of the Indian nation too much for granted and underestimated the centrifugal forces of ethnic division, which were bound to be accentuated rather than diminished as the popular masses were more and more drawn into politics. The Congress party was originally opposed to the idea of recognizing any division of India on a linguistic basis and preferred to retain the old provinces of British India which often cut across linguistic boundaries. However, this was later conceded as the basis for a federal 'Indian Union'. The rights granted to the States created new problems for the Central Government. The idea of making Hindi the national language of a united India was thwarted by the recalcitrance of the speakers of other impotant Indian languages, and the autonomy of the States rendered central economic planning extremely difficult. Land reforms remained under the control of the State and many large-scale economic projects required a degree of co-operation between the Central Government and one or more of the States which, it was found, was impossible to achieve. Co-ordination of policies was difficult even when the Congress Party was in power both in the States and at the Centre. When a Congress Government in Delhi was confronted with non-Congress parties in office in the States, it became much harder.

QUESTIONS

1. Why was central economic planning found to be difficult?
2. Which problems were India faced with after Independence?
3. Why was the linguistic reorganization of the States accepted?
4. According to the passage, what can be cited as an exercise in democratic practice in India before Independece?
5. Which party was originally opposed to the idea of recognizing any division of India on a linguistic basis?

PASSAGE - 2

It is difficult to imagine the extraordinary number of controls on Indian industry before 1991. Entrepreneurs needed permission to invest and could be penalized for exceeding production capacity. Even with the given investment capacity they had, entering certain areas was prohibited as these were reserved for the public sector. If they had to import anything, they required licences. To get these licences was tough, they had to persuade a bureaucrat that the item was required but even so permission was unavailable if somebody was already producing it in India. The impact of the reforms was not instantaneously and permanently wonderful. In India's case it began to show after about a year-and-a-half. After 1993 there came three years of rapid industrial growth of about 8% or so. But, in the second half of the 90s, there was a tapering of industrial growth and investment. After 1997 and the East Asian crisis there was global slowdown which had an impact on the Indian industry. But in the last few years there has been a tremendous upturn. With the rise of investment industrial growth has reached double digits or close.

However, even during the period when industrial growth was not that rapid, there is a lot of evidence that positive results of the reforms were seen. There were companies that didn't look at all internally but instead performed remarkably in the highly competitive global market. For instance, the software sector's performance was outstanding in an almost totally global market. Reliance built a world-class refinery. Tatas developed an indigenously designed car. The success of the software sector has created much higher expectations from and much higher confidence in what Indian industry can do. On the government's side it is a vindication that liberalization of both domestic and external policies, including the increased inflow of Foreign Direct Investment, has created an environment in which industry can do well, has done well and is preparing to do even better. What they need is not sops, but good quality infrastructure. For the 11th Plan an industrial growth rate of around 12% is projected. It will have methods of developing infrastructure, which will close the deficit. This can be done through increased investment in public sector for those infrastructure areas, which cannot attract private investment, and through efforts to improve private participation in different ways of public-private participation.

In the early stages of reforms, the liberalization of trade policies and a shift to a market-determined exchange rate had the effect of removing constraints on agriculture in 'terms of depressed prices. The removal of protection on industry helped to produce a more level playing field, because the earlier system was extremely unfair to agriculture. The lesson to be learnt from the reforms process is to persevere in reforming the strategic parts of the economy, which will lead to even higher growth rate. India has to do better than its current average growth rate of 8% and ensure that benefits from this higher growth go beyond industry and urban areas and extend to agriculture.

QUESTIONS

1. How did software companies deal with slow industrial growth in an open Indian economy?
2. Why did India experience a slow down in growth during the late 1990s?
3. According to the passage, what can be said about the reforms of 1991?
4. Which factor was responsible for the fall in India's growth rate in the late 1990s?
5. How did the economic reforms affect the agriculture sector?
6. What was the inpact of the flourishing Indian Software Sector?
7. Mention any restriction on India industry which was prior to 1991?
8. What does the author recommend to ensure that the industrial sector continues to perform better?
9. Why was investment by private business disallowed in certain sectors?
10. What is the author's opinion about the government's decision to liberalise the economy is 1991?

PASSAGE - 3

Though it is commonplace to say we live in a globalised world, less well understood is that globalisation is taking place in stages. In the first stage as flows of capital and goods were liberated the benefits of globalisation *e.g.*, technological advancements, flowed primarily to the developed world. As we enter the current newer age of mobility, people have begun to move across borders in great numbers in pursuit of economic security and a better life for themselves and to keep their families out of poverty. At the turn of the 20th century the United Nations estimates that approximately three per cent of the world's population is on the move, a similar scale to that witnessed in earlier eras. Growing economic inequality together with natural and man made crises prompt emigration. But this mobility has the potential to chip away at the vast inequalities that characterise our time and accelerate progress throughout the developing world. To take an example, last year migrants sent home $264 billion triple all international aid combined. The freer movement of people helps to underwrite health care, education and grass roots entrepreneurship across the developing world.

It helps to oil the global economy. When industrialised nations need to recruit nurses or software programmers developing countries are often the source. Yet, rather than look at how these gains can be harnessed to reduce poverty, governments have been slow to adapt. The result is burgeoning illegal immigration, and trafficking, social tension and intolerance, loss of faith in the government and the empowerment of criminal networks. Until a few years ago, migrants were paying exorbitant fees to send money home losing about 20% in transaction costs. Today though migrants move freely and easily thanks to easy access to low cost transport and the internet, affordable and rapidly advancing telephony and satellite television which keep them in constant touch with home. Banks easily and wirelessly transmit hard won and sometimes meagre salaries instantly to their families. The flow of people until now mostly benefited richer countries and generated worries about brain drain and the violation of migrant rights in poorer ones. Global fora represent a step in the effort to harness the power of migration to advance development and increase our knowledge of how to make the migration equation work for all. Rather than focus on the negative consequences and recriminations of exploitation by developing countries such summits provide an opportunity for all nations to come together and address these issues in a comprehensive, logical and rational way so that the benefits of migration are fully realised in both developing and industrialised countries. Countries may examine how dual citizenship laws can ease the way for migrants to play a bigger role in development by bringing their capital, knowledge and networks back home. Such efforts will usher in the third stage of globalisation where everyone can share in the world's prosperity.

QUESTIONS

1. What is the author's main objective in writing the passage?
2. What does the fact that remittance exceeded international aid illustrate?
3. According to the author why do people migrate?
4. How does the author view migration?
5. What is the objective of international fora on migration?
6. According to the passage what has facilitated migrants access to their native countries?
7. 'Governments have not fully exploited the potential benefits of migration. Is it true in the context of the passage?
8. Mention any two impacts of globalisation.

PASSAGE - 4

The US Senate's approval of an immigration Bill has been welcomed in India as well as in the IT industry in America because of the proposal to double HI-B visas for skilled foreign workers. However, the more important bit in the legislation, if approved by the House of Representatives, is the lifeline to millions of illegal immigrants in the US. Some of the key proposals in the Bill include allowing illegal immigrants, who have been in America for five years, to become legal residents by paying a certain amount in fines and back taxes.

Those who have been in the country between two and five years can go to a point of entry at the US border and file an application. There is also provision for creating a guest worker programme especially meant for farm workers. These are welcome moves to recognise the huge presence–according to some estimates 12 to 15 million–of illegal immigrants in the US and legitimising their existence. But it must be understood that the US is not considering this legislation out of a sense of altruism. The truth is that the bulk of immigrants are doing jobs that Americans simply don't want to do. They are employed in jobs that pay minimum wages and entail long working hours. But giving illegal immigrants the opportunity to become legal residents will at least ensure that they are not exploited by employers and that they are covered by social security benefits.

American legislators, however, need to go beyound this. They must recognise that the US needs trained people in various fields, particularly in schools and hospitals. India with its vast population of educated youth is a natural source of such personnel. Instead of just targeting India for its best brains, the US should open up its labour market for more school teachers, nurses and technicians from India. Compared to Mexicans, the largest component of immigrants to the US, Indians have a natural advantage in that they know English. They would also be willing to work in America's inner cities and other supposedly 'hardship' stations, Along with nuclear deals and technology transfer, the two largest English-speaking democracies must realise that they could mutually benefit from bilateral employment agreements. India, with its one-billion plus and growing population, has the potential of supplying First World nations with declining birth rates much-needed labour.

QUESTIONS

1. What is provision for an illegal immigrants in the US, who has been in America for five years?
2. India can be an effective source of man power in which sectors of USA?
3. According to some estimates how many illegal immigrants are there in the US?
4. What is the main reason behind the bulk of emmigrants in the US?
5. Which country contributes the largest number of immigrants to US?
6. In which types of jobs the illigal immigrants are employed mainly?
7. Name the immigrants country who enjoy an advantage of good communication skills in English.
8. What is the basic premise of the immigration Bill?
9. What will ensure the Bill by giving illegal immigrants the opportunity to become legal residents?
10. How can USA be benfitted by India in the author's opinion?

PASSAGE - 5

The art of effective presentation is the fruit of persistent efforts and practice. Your personality is reflected in your presentation. Adequate planning and preparation are essential for a successful presentation. A through preparation is the best antidote for nervousness. If a person is not successful in presenting his views and ideas then it will become the greatest obstacle in his career and life. People form a perception about how competent you are by how you present yourself when you stand and speak.

A successful presentation can help a person in winning orders for the company he works for. Most people who work in organizations find that their effectiveness and success depend on their ability to organize their ideas and present them effectively. Delivering your message in person provides immediate feedback that helps you clarify points and answer questions.

Oral presentations are often more persuasive. As far as possible, one should never read a presentation or memorize it. Then the presentation will lose flexibility and communication will suffer. The spoken word wields great power. Face-to-face interaction demands thinking and speaking. Anecdotes, quotations and humourous touches often make a presentation interesting. One may consult his notes frequently when he is making his presentation. This may create a feeling among listeners that the speaker has taken pains to prepare for the occasion. A positive response will be generated and the speaker will be heard with respect. Speaker's enthusiasm and confidence can influence people to accept or reject an idea in a way that a written document cannot. A presentation should be persuasive and should change the audience's attitude. The topic of the presentation must be interesting to the audience. The topic should be of interest to the speaker also otherwise he will go through the motions of making a presentation. No perfunctory approach should ever be resorted to while making a presentation. It is very important that the speaker is perceived by the audience as credible and qualified to speak about the topic. Speaker must adapt to intellectual level of the audience.

QUESTIONS

1. What is essential for a successful presentation?
2. What will happen if a person is not successful in presenting his views and ideas?
3. Which type of presentation is often more persuasive?
4. What does Face-to-face interaction demand?
5. What makes a presentation interesting?
6. In author's view what is the best antidote for nervousness?
7. What can be countered by meticulous preparation of his presentation?
8. In author's opinion which type of Topic of the presentation must be?
9. What is reflected in a presentation?
10. When will the presentation lose flexibility and communication suffer?

PASSAGE - 6

Goldman Sachs predicted that crude oil price would hit $200 and just as it appeared that alternative renewable energy had a chance of becoming an economically viable option, the international price of oil fell by over 70%. After hitting the all-time high of $147 a barrel, a month ago, crude oil fell to less than $40 a barrel. What explains this sharp decline in the international price of oil ? There has not been any major new discovery of a hitherto unknown source of oil or gas. The short answer is that the demand does not have to fall by a very sizeable quantity for the price of crude to respond as it did. In the short run, the price elasticity of demand for crude oil is very low. Conversely, in the short run, even a relatively big change in the price of oil does not immediately lower consumption. It takes months, or years, of high oil price to inculcate habits of energy conservation. World crude oil price had remained at over $60 a barrel for most of 2005-2007 without making any major dent in demand.

The long answer is more complex. The economic slowdown in the US, Europe and Asia along with dollar depreciation and commodity speculation have all had some role in the downward descent in the international price of oil. In recent years, the supply of oil has been rising but not enough to catch up with the rising demand, resulting in an almost vertical escalation in its price. The number of crude oil futures and options contracts have also increased manifold which has led to significant speculation in the oil market. In comparison, the role of the Organization of Petroleum Exporting Countries (OPEC) in fixing crude price has considerably. weakened. OPEC is often accused of operating as a cartel restricting output thus keeping prices artificially high. It did succeed in setting the price of crude during the 1970s and the first half of the 80s. But, with increased futures trading and contracts, the control of crude pricing has moved from OPEC to banks and markets that deal with futures trading and contracts. It is true that most oil exporting regions of the world have remained politically unstable fuelling speculation over the price of crude. But there is little evidence that the geopolitical uncertainties in west Asia have improved to weaken the price of oil. Threatened by the downward slide of oil price, OPEC has, in fact, announced its decision to curtail output.

However, most oil importers will heave a sigh of relief as they find their oil import bills decline except for those who bought options to import oil at prices higher than market prices. Exporting nations, on the other hand, will see their economic prosperity slip. Relatively low price of crude is also bad news for investments in alternative renewable energy that cannot compete with cheaper and non-renewable sources of energy.

QUESTIONS

1. What factor is responsible for rise in speculation in crude oil markets?
2. Which is costlier either renewable energy sources or non-renewable energy sources?
3. What has been the impact of the drop in oil prices?
4. What did result in rise in demand for crude oil?
5. When was OPEC established?
6. What was the reason behind establishing the OPEC?
7. What is the function of OPEC?
8. Today who set the oil prices to a large extent?
9. What led the alternative energy sources being considered economically feasible?
10. What does the author want to convey by citing the statistic of 2005-2007?

PASSAGE - 7

Politicians and generals talk of military strategies and manoeuvers but something completely different is needed. Stability will come only when economic opportunities exist, when youth can find jobs and support families rather than seeking their livelihood in violence. Peace can only be achieved with a withdrawal of foreign troops, sanctions and peacekeepers and the arrival of jobs, productive farms and factories, healthcare and schools. Repeatedly the fragile peace in impoverished countries has broken down because of the lack of economic follow-up. Despite promises of aid, the actual record of international aid to post war reconstruction is deficient.

Once the war ends agencies involved in post war relief efforts fail to understand how to start or restart economic development in a low income setting. They squander time, surplus aid funds and opportunities because they are not familiar with local conditions and do not understand their point of view. There are distinct phases of outside help to end a conflict. In the first phase focus is on providing food, water, shelter and medicine to refugees *i.e.*, humanitarian. In the second, emphasis is on the refugees returning home while in the last phase long term investments and strengthening of courts is the main focus.

However, once a conflict is over aid agencies sanctioned by the World Bank send study groups instead of requisite personnel. There is a gap of several years before moving from humanitarian relief to economic development. By the time such help arrives the war has restarted. It is possible to restart economic development through targeted 'quick impact' initiatives. Most economies in post conflict countries are based on agriculture. Providing free packages of seeds, fertilizers and low cost equipment quickly will ensure that former soldiers will return to their farms and establish their livelihood. But the window of opportunity closes quickly and one has to implement these measures almost immediately.

QUESTIONS

1. According to author when will stability come?
2. What will happen when economic opportunities exist?
3. Why have post conflict reconstruction efforts failed?

4. Where does the problem lie in implementing post war relief measures?
5. According to author what will prevent wars?
6. Are sanctions a means to ensure peace?
7. Where is the focus in the first phase of a war?
8. How can economic development be restarted in an impoverished country?

PASSAGE - 8

Over the past few decades, many Asian nations transformed from poverty into global competitors. From 2003 to 2007, Asian economies expanded at an average annual rate of 8.1%, triple that of advanced economies. Over the same period, inflation in Asia averaged only about 3.5%. But Asia could be facing turbulent economic times. In May, the average inflation rate throughout the region reached nearly 7%, led by spikes in oil and food prices. In India, inflation jumped to an 11.6% annual rate in June, according to the latest government figures, the highest in 13 years.

Policymakers and central bankers are forced to raise interest rates and limit credit to get inflation under control. But these same measures suppress the investment and consumption that generates growth. The combination of slowing growth and soaring inflation makes economic policy-making tricky. Inflation stirs up the middle classes because it can quickly erase years of hardwon personal gains. Inflation is cruel to the poor, because families have to spend a larger share of their meagre incomes on necessities. In the Philippines, farmers, unable to afford fuel for tractors, use water buffaloes to plough their fields.

But to avoid unrest, leaders cannot blindly adopt rigid anti-inflation measures. Voters won't hesitate to remove from office any politician who doesn't deliver the goods. So they cannot overreact to the inflation threat and scale down economic growth in the process. Developing nations need to grow quickly to create jobs and increase incomes for their large populations. With prices soaring, doing nothing is not an option. Most central banks in Asia have started raising interest rates. The Reserve Bank of India increased its benchmark rate twice last month to a six year high of 8.5%.

The challenge is especially difficult because currently, inflation is not of domestic origin. Prices are being driven higher by a global surge in oil and food prices, which individual governments can do little to control. Of course, inflation is not just a problem in Asia. World Bank President Robert Zoellick called rising food and oil prices a man-made 'catastrophe' that could quickly reverse the gains made in overcoming poverty over the past seven years. For now, though, there is more talk than action on the international front, so Asian governments are on their own.

Even though inflation throughout the region is likely to continue to rise in coming months, no one is expecting an economic calamity. According to the Asian Development Bank, Asian countries have large hard currency reserves and relatively healthy banks, and so are far better prepared to absorb external shocks than they were during the region's last recession ten years ago. Asian policymakers have learned their lessons and are more alert.

QUESTIONS

1. From 2003 to 2007, by what rate did the Asian economics expand?
2. What was the inflation rate in Asia over the same period?
3. In the context of passage mention any one anti-inflation measure which in being used by Asian countries.
4. What makes it difficult for Asian countries to control inflation?
5. Why are experts not very concerned about the impact of inflation on Asian economies?
6. What in the author's advice to politicians regarding the handling of inflation?
7. What could the impact of stringent inflation measures be?
8. Why is high economic growth necessary for developing countries?

9. Why has inflation been referred to as a 'Catastrophe'?
10. Which factor was responsible for inflation in India?

PASSAGE - 9

If you cast a thoughtful glance around you, you will become conscious of God's infinite grace. God has given us firm earth to put our feet on; He has given us oxygen enough to inhale as much of it as we like; He has created the sun to give us light and heat to illumine and warm the world; He has given us water in plenty to quench our thirst with; He has given us space enough to fly into if we can; He has created so many animals to serve us in a variety of capacities; He has given us trees and plants to provide us food, fuel and medicines; and he has given us rich soil to grow crops in.

But what is of utmost importance is the fact that he has given us our existence. We are able to avail ourselves of the universe because we exist. Had we had no existence, the whole phenomenon would have had no meaning for us.

Yet, these rich gifts of God fail to satisfy us : we want more. And we want more because we feel others have more. We want God to do for us all that we wish to happen. Should we not thank God for what he has given us even without our asking for it? I would like everyone of us to say to God every-day "God! I thank you for bringing me and my near and dear ones into existence, giving me the capacity to dream, and providing me this universe to realize my dreams in."

QUESTIONS

1. When do we become conscious of God's unlimited grace?
2. What is the purpose of animals in the world?
3. In which situation would the whole world have been rendered meaningless for us?
4. Why is man not satisfied with what he has been given by God?
5. For what does the author want to feel grateful to God?

PASSAGE - 10

Micro finance institutions aim to provide credit to the poor who have no access to commercial banks. In general, these institutions receive financial support from western donors, NGOs or commercial banks, which lend to micro finance institutions, often against below market interest rates. The micro finance institutions in turn, lend this money to domestic small companies and poor agents. The size of the loan varies but is most often small.

According to the United Nations (UN), in 2002 almost one-fifth of the world's population was living in extreme poverty, earning less than one dollar a day. In recent public debates micro finance has been mentioned as an important instrument to combat poverty. The result has been that micro finance has received a lot of attention, both from policy makers as well as in academic circles. Especially during the past 10 years, micro finance programmes have been introduced in many developing economies. Well-known examples are the Grameen Bank in Bangladesh, Banco Sol in Bolivia and Bank Rakyat in Indonesia. The Grameen Bank system of group lending (established in 1976 by Muhammad Yunus, a Bangladesh banker and economist), in.particular has been **copied** in other developing countries. Between December 1997 and December 2005 the number of micro finance institutions increased from 168 to 3,133. The number of people who received credit from these institutions rose from 13.5 million to 113.3 million during the same period.

To support the view that micro finance can be an important instrument to fight poverty, the UN declared 2005 to be the international Year of Micro credit. Recently, the attention for micro-finance and its role in reducing poverty was dramatically increased when Muhammad Yunus received the Nobel Peace prize. According to Nobel Committee, micro finance can help people to break out of poverty, which in turn is seen as an important prerequisite to establish long lasting peace. This has led to an almost euphoric attitude among policy makers and aid organizations about potential poverty reducing effects of micro credit.

QUESTIONS

1. What is the main purpose of micro finance institutions?
2. Why has micro finance been receiving a lot of consideration?
3. What is seen as a prior requirement for the establishment of long lasting peace?
4. From where do micro finance companies get their funds?
5. Why has the UN declared the the year 2005 as the Year of Micro credit?
6. In which countries micro finance programmes have been introduced in the recent past?

PASSAGE - 11

Though the Cold War has ended, selective tactics are still continuing for ensuring the military and economic dominance of developed countries. Various types of technology denial regimes are still being enforced which are now being mainly targeted against developing countries like India.

Today, we in India encounter twin problems. On one side there is a large scale strengthening of our neighbours through supply of arms and clandestine support to their nuclear and missile programmes and on the other side all efforts are being made to weaken our indigenous technology growth through control regimes and dumping of low-tech systems, accompanied with high commercial pitch in critical areas. Growth of indigenous technology and self-reliance are the only answer to the problem.

Thus in the environment around India, the number of missiles and nuclear powers are continuously increasing and destructive weapons continue to pile up around us, in spite of arms reduction treaties.

To understand the implications of various types of warfare that may affect us, we need to take a quick look at the evolution of war weaponry and the types of warfare. I am highlighting this point for the reason that in less than a century we could see change in the nature of warfare and its effects on society.

In early years of human history it was mostly direct human warfare. During the twentieth century up to about 1990, the warfare was weapon driven. The weapons used were guns, tanks, aircraft, ships, submarines and the nuclear weapons deployed on land/sea/air and also reconnaissance spacecraft. Proliferation of conventional nuclear and biological weapons was at a peak owing to the competition between the superpowers.

The next phase, in a new form, has just started from 1990 onwards. The world has graduated into economic warfare. The means used is control of market forces through high technology. The participating nations, apart from the USA, are Japan, the UK, France, Germany, certain South-East Asian countries and a few others. The driving force is the generation of wealth with certain types of economic doctrine.

The urgent issue we need to address collectively as a nation is, how do we handle the tactics of economic and military dominance in this new form coming from the backdoor? Today technology is the main driver of economic development at the national level. Therefore, we have to develop indigenous technologies to enhance our competitive edge and to generate national wealth in all segments of economy. Therefore, the need of the hour is *arm India with technology.*

QUESTIONS

1. Which are the issues of great concern that India is facing at present, according to the author?
2. Enforcement of technology denial regimes by developed countries implies which kind of tendency?
3. According to the author, is it necessary to examine how weaponry and warfare have evolved?
4. What is the most effective way to counter our major problems?

5. What, according to the author, is the solution to our problems in the international field?
6. What is the general outcome of arms reduction treaties as a whole according to the author?
7. What is the immediate problem to be collectively resolved by our country?

PASSAGE - 12

Political ploys initially hailed as masterstrokes often end up as flops. The Rs. 60,000 crore farm loan waiver announced in the budget writes off 100% of overdues of small and marginal farmers holding up to two hectares, and 25% of overdues of larger farmers. While India has enjoyed 8%-9% GDP growth for the past few years, the boom has bypassed many rural areas and farmer distress and suicides have made newspaper headlines.

Various attempts to provide relief (employment guarantee scheme, public distribution system) have had little impact, thanks to huge leakages from the government's lousy delivery systems. So, many economists think the loan waiver is a worthwhile alternative to provide relief.

However, the poorest rural folk are landless labourers, who get neither farm loans nor waivers. Half of small and marginal farmers get no 'loans from banks and depend entirely on moneylenders, and will not benefit. Besides, rural India is full of family holdings rather than individual holdings, and family holdings will typically be much larger than two hectares even for dirt-poor farmers, who will, therefore, be denied the 100% waiver. It will thus fail in both, its economic and political objectives. IRDP loans to the rural poor in the 1980s demonstrated that crooked bank officials demand bribes amounting to one-third the intended benefits. Very few of the intended beneficiaries who merited relief received it. After the last farm loan waiver in 1990, many banks went slow on fresh farm loans for some years. This waiver will similarly slow down fresh loans to deserving farmers. While overdues to cooperatives may be higher, economist Surjit Bhalla says less than 5% of farmer loans to banks are overdue *i.e.* overdues exist for only 2.25 million out of 90 million farmers. If so, then the 95% who have repaid loans will not benefit. They will be angry at being penalised for honesty.

The budget thus grossly overestimates the number of beneficiaries. It also underestimates the negative effects of the waiver-encouraging wilful defaults in future and discouraging fresh bank lending for some years. Instead of trying to reach the needy through a plethora of leaky schemes we should transfer cash directly to the needy, using new technology like biometric smart cards, which are now being used in many countries, and mobile phone bank accounts. Then benefits can go directly to phone accounts operable only by those with biometric cards, ending the massive leakages of current schemes.

The political benefits of the loan waiver have also been exaggerated since if only a small fraction of farm families benefit, and many of these have to pay bribes to get the actual benefit, will the waiver really be a massive vote-winner? Members of joint families will feel aggrieved that, despite having less than one hectare per head, their family holding is too large to qualify for the 100% waiver. All finance ministers, of the central or state governments, give away freebies in their last budgets, hoping to win electoral regards. Yet, four-fifth of all incumbent governments are voted out. This shows that beneficiaries of favours are not notably grateful, while those not so favoured may feel aggrieved, and vote for the Opposition. That seems to be why election budgets constantly fail to win elections in India and the loan waiver will not change that pattern.

QUESTIONS

1. Why do economists feel that loan waivers will benefit farmers in distress?
2. What is the author's suggestion to provide aid to farmers?
3. What was the outcome of IRDP loans to the rural poor?

4. What is the author's view of the loan waiver?
5. What will be an impact of loan waivers?
6. What are the key points of budget?

PASSAGE - 13

All men by nature, desire to know. An indication of this is the delight we take in our senses: for even apart from their usefulness they are loved for themselves; and above all others, the sense of sight. For not only with a view to action, but even when we are not going to do anything, we prefer seeing (one might say) to everything else. The reason is that this, most of all the senses, makes us know and brings to light many differences between things. By nature, animals are born with the faculty of sensation, and from sensation, memory is produced in some of them, though not in others. And therefore, the former are more intelligent and apt at learning than those which cannot remember; those which are incapable of hearing sounds are intelligent though they cannot be taught, *e.g.*, the bee, and any other race of animals that may be like it; and those which besides memory, have this sense of hearing can be taught. The animals other than man live by appearances and memories and have but little of connected experience; but the human race lives also by art and reasoning. Now from memory, experience is produced in men; for the several memories of the same thing produce finally the capacity for a single experience. And experience seems pretty much like science and art, but really, science and art come to men through experience; for 'experience made art', as Polus says, 'but inexperience luck.' Now art arises, when from many notions gained by experience, one universal judgement about a class of objects is produced. For to have a judgement that when Callias was ill of this disease that did him good, and similarly, in the case of Socrates and in many individual cases, is a matter of experience; but to judge that it has done good to all persons of a certain constitution, marked off in one class, when they were ill of this disease, *e.g.*, to phlegmatic or bilious people when burning with fevers—this is a matter of art. With a view to action, experience seems in no 'respect inferior to art, and men of experience succeed even better than those who have theory without experience. (The reason is that experience is knowledge of individuals, art of universals, and actions and productions are all concerned with the individual; for the physician does not cure man, except in an incidental way, but Callias or Socrates or some other called by some such individual name, who happens to be a man. If, then, a man has the theory without the experience, and recognises the universal but does not know the individual included in this, he will often fail to cure; for it is the individual that is to be cured.) But yet we think that knowledge and understanding belong to art rather than to experience, and we suppose artists to be wiser than men of experience (which implies that wisdom depends in all cases rather on knowledge); and this because the former know the cause, but the latter do not. For men of experience know that the thing is so, but do not know why, while the others know the 'why' and the cause. Hence, we think also that the masterworkers in each craft are more honourable and know in a truer sense and are wiser than the manual workers, because they know the causes of the things that are done (we think the manual workers are like certain lifeless things which act indeed, but act without knowing what they do, as ftre burns, but while the lifeless things perform each of their functions by a natural tendency, the labourers perform them through habit); thus we view them as being wiser not in virtue of being able to act, but of having the theory for themselves and knowing the causes. And in general, it is a sign of the man who knows and of the man who does not know, that the former can teach, and therefore, we think art more truly knowledge than experience is; for artists can teach, and men of mere experience cannot. Again, we do not regard any of the senses as Wisdom; yet surely these give the most authoritative knowledge of particulars. But they do not tell us the 'why' of anything—e.g., why fire is hot; they only say that it is hot. At first, he who invented any art whatever, that went beyond the common perceptions of man was naturally admired by men, not only because there was something useful in the inventions, but because he was thought wiser and superior to the rest. But as more arts were invented, and some were directed to the necessities of life, others to recreation, the inventors of the latter were naturally always regarded as wiser than the inventors of the former, because their branches of knowledge did not aim at utility. Hence, when all such inventions were already established, the sciences which do not aim at giving pleasure or at the necessities of life were discovered, and first in the places where men first began to have leisure. This is why the mathematical arts were founded in Egypt; for there the priestly caste was allowed to be at leisure. We have said in the Ethics what the difference is between art and science and the other kindred faculties; but the point of our present discussion is this, that all men suppose what is called Wisdom to deal with the first causes and the principles of things; so that, as has been said before, the man of experience is thought to be wiser than the possessors of any sense-perception whatever, the artist wiser than the men of experience. The masterworker than the mechanic, and the theoretical kinds of knowledge to be more of the nature of Wisdom than the productive. Clearly then, Wisdom is knowledge about certain principles and causes.

QUESTIONS

1. What is the relationship between sensation and memory?
2. What is the difference between art and experience?
3. Why, according to the author, were the mathematical arts founded in Egypt?
4. What is the central idea of the passage?
5. What does experience reveal in this passage?
6. What is wisdom here?

PASSAGE - 14

We should recognise the indebtedness of the country to its farm families who toil to safeguard national food security. Loan waiver is the price we have to pay for the neglect of rural India over the past several decades. There has been a gradual decline in investment in key sectors related to agriculture such as infrastructure, marketing, post harvest technology etc. The four crore farmers whose debt is to be relieved will be eligible for institutional credit for their cultivation expenses during Kharif 2008. The challenge is to prevent them from getting into the debt trap again. For this purpose the Central and various State governments should set up an Indebted Farmers' Support Consortium, comprising scientists, Panchayat Raj officials and others relevant to assisting farmers to improve the profitability and productivity of their farms in an environmentally sustainable manner. The smaller the farm the greater is the need for marketable surplus to reduce indebtedness.

The Indebted Farmers Support Consortium should aim to get all the four crore farmers all the benefits of the government schemes such as the Rashtriya Krishi Vikas Yojana, Irrigation Benefit Programme and others. If this is done every farm family released from the debt trap should be able to produce at least an additional half tonne per hectare of food grains. This should help increase food production by about 20 million tonnes by 2008-10. At a time when global and national food stocks are dwindling and prices are rising, this will be a timely gain for our national food security. We need to ensure that the outcome of the debt waiver is enhanced farmers' income and production. The prevailing gap between potential and actual yields in the crops of rainfed areas such as pulses and oilseeds is over 200 per cent even with the necessary technologies on the shelf. We are now importing without duty large quantities of pulses and oilseeds. If helped, farmers can produce these at a lower cost.

Opportunities for assured and remunerative marketing are essential if loan waiver is not to become a recurring event leading to the destruction of the credit system. This is why the Minimum Support Price is necessary for all not just for a few crops which is the case at present. This is the single most effective step to make loan waivers history.

There is another urgent step which needs to be taken. The loan waiver does not cover those who borrow from moneylenders. It will not be possible for the government to scrutinise the veracity of such private deals but steps can be taken such as giving them Smart Cards which will entitle them to essential inputs like seeds and fertilizers. The gram sabha can be entrusted with the task of identifying these farmers so that there is transparency in the process and **elimination** of the chances for falsification and corruption. Fear of occasional misuse should not come in the way of enabling millions of poor farmers who have borrowed from informal sources if we are to achieve the goal of four per cent growth in agriculture.

QUESTIONS

1. Why does the author feel that rural India has been overlooked in the past?
2. How can small farmers avoid debt?
3. What is the objective of the Indebted Farmer's Support Consortium?
4. What does the author mean by the phrase " indebtedness of the country to its farm families"?
5. Why does the loan waiver not cover credit taken from money lenders?
6. Why is there a vast gap in actual and potential yields of crops in rainfed areas?
7. What should the aim of indebted Farmers' Support Consortium?

PASSAGE - 15

For months the old tanker, **African Queen,** lay turned over on her side, stuck fast in the sands off the coast of Maryland. She had run aground so badly that her owners had decided to leave her to her fate. It was considered impossible to refloat her and the ship began to rust and sink deeper and deeper into the sands. Men frequently came out in small boats and removed any parts that could be sold-until two men decided to attempt the impossible to float the **African Queen** once more. Both men were engineers and had no experience of ships. So, few people thought they could succeed.

The men began by studying the exact state of the **African Queen** and came to the conclusion that she would float again if air were pumped into the tanks which were now full of sea-water. A diver was sent down to examine the underside of the ship. In the cold, dark water he found an enormous hole in her side which had been torn when the ship ran aground. It was plain that nothing could be done until the hole was repaired. As no single sheet of steel would cover it, the men were obliged to order a great number of sheets which had to be joined together. For several weeks divers worked continually to close the hole. At times, the sea was so rough that it was difficult to go down; and on more than one occasion, they had to contend with sharks.

At last the hole was covered and the men began to pump the sea-water out of the ship's tanks. It seemed as if they were bound to succeed, for when the tanks were full of air, the **African Queen** began to stir in the water. The men could not understand why she still would not float until they discovered that her rudder was embedded in mud. Huge cranes were brought to haul the sunken rudder out and the ship was again afloat. By this time, the men were almost exhausted. They had worked ceaselessly for three months to save the **African Queen** and had succeeded when everyone thought they would fail. Now they stood on the bridge of the ship, tired but proud, as tugs brought the **African Queen** into the harbour.

QUESTIONS

1. Why did men frequently go out to the African Queen?
2. How did the two men propose to float the ship again?
3. What was the danger which the divers faced?
4. Due to which reason the two men felt proud?
5. What is the part of the ship used for steering?

PASSAGE - 16

Planning in India has essentially been an effort to determine the overall direction of the economy by directing public investment accordingly. It was possible to conceive of outcomes on the basis of government spending between 1947 and 1985 when the public sector made up more than half the gross domestic product. Now that is neither possible nor desirable. The private sector accounts for threefourths of the gross domestic product reducing the role of public expenditure in meeting growth targets. Besides, decades of the government occupying the commanding heights of the economy merely resulted in low rates of growth and nearly two- fifth of the population living below the poverty line till 1991.

How can planning contribute to today's economy? It should be reconceived as a think tank that works at maximising outcomes from investments in social and physical infrastructure by identifying problems of governance. Outcomes in health and education are crucial to realise the potential of our billion-plus population, while shortcomings in power and port handling facilities can hold up future growth. Where public-private partnerships involve a number of government agencies the Commission can work as a nodal body that takes a larger view of projects and ensures their smooth implementation.

Planners should aim at meeting growth targets by ensuring that markets function efficiently. They can advise the government on market-specific policies that address lack of access to information. They can identify sunrise areas in the next decade and promote research and innovation through public-private partnership. Simultaneously, planners should explore markets for products made by unskilled workers.

The Eleventh Plan aims at 9 per cent "inclusive" growth by raising investment in infrastructure from 5 per cent of GDP to 9 per cent. Of the $475 billion investment needed for infrastructure. $130-140 billion is expected to come from the private sector. Public sector enterprises are expected to raise resources internally, with the Plan proposing lower support for them. The Plan has got its priorities right by reducing support for PSEs and increasing social sector allocations. Education is a big-ticket item, with the Planning Commission earmarking Rs. 2,75,289 crores for it alone with a view to meeting the skills shortage. Sadly, health has not been given the same emphasis. But, generally speaking, we are on the right track.

QUESTIONS

1. According to author, what was the possibility during the first 38 years after India's independence?
2. Which factor is closely associated with the term 'planning' in India?
3. Which is a way to derive **maximum** out come from investment?
4. What does the author expect planners to do about the products manufactured by unskilled workers?
5. "The area of health has been given a secondary treatment", is this statement appreciated by the author?
6. What is the best explanation of the term "Sunrise areas"?

PASSAGE - 17

Hiero, King of Syracus, had commissioned from a goldsmith of the town a crown of pure gold, but, having taken delivery of the finished article, he was suspicious. There was reason to believe that the craftsman had mixed with the gold acertain amount of other metal of inferior value. But how to find out? There was no direct evidence, and it was therefore obviously a case for the learned men of the city. And who more learned than Archimedes?

The mathematician was therefore charged with the task which would nowadays be considered a simple one, but was then a matter for serious thought. Nothing known to science could be brought forward to prove fraud or otherwise on the part of the goldsmith.

It is more than probable that the human side of the problem interested Archimedes not at all, but the scientific puzzle worried him intensely. This worry pursued him everywhere he went for days, and persisted through the routine acts of his daily round.

In the normal course of that routine, he went to the public baths. We can imagine him standing at the edge of the bath tub as he prepares to enter it, absently allowing the water to flow until he cannot help noticing it. Suddenly, he splashed out of his tub. shouting at the top of his voice: "Eureka! Eureka! (I have found it! I have found it!) Without waiting, or even thinking of such a detail" as clothes, he tore out of the building and rushed through the streets of Syracuse, still shouting: "Eureka! Eureka!"

Arrived at his house, the mathematician put his newly found discovery to a practical test, and found indeed that a body plunged in a fluid loses an amount of its weight which is equal to the weight of the fluid displaced by it. With this as a starting point - as it was to prove the starting point of many subsequent discoveries of importance - Archimedes was able to tell his king how much pure gold was in his crown. Thus was the first fundamental law in hydrostatics enunciated.

Archimedes was by this time well known to his fellow townsmen, and his sometimes strange appearance and unusual actions probably met with indulgent smiles. He came from a good family; his father Pheidias was an astronomer; he was on intimate terms with, and - according to some - was even a kinsman of King Hiero himself.

QUESTIONS

1. Why could the king **not** punish the fraudulent goldsmith?
2. Why was Archimedes charged with the task of finding out if there was any impurity in the crown?
3. What was the king's suspicion?
4. Why was Archimedes curious when he was entrusted with the taks?
5. Why did Archimedes utter "Eureka! Eureka!"?

PASSAGE - 18

Politicians and generals talk of military strategies and manoeuvres but something completely different is needed. Stability will come only when economic opportunities exist, when youth can find jobs and support families rather than seeking their livelihood in violence. Peace can only be achieved with the withdrawal of foreign troops, sanctions and peacekeepers and the arrival of jobs, productive farms and factories. healthcare and schools. Repeatedly the fragile peace in impoverished countries has broken down because of the lack of economic follow-up. Despite promises of aid, the actual record of international aid to post war reconstruction is deficient.

Once the war ends agencies involved volved in post war relief efforts fail to understand how to start or restart economic development in a low income setting. They squander time, surplus aid funds and opportunities because they are not familiar with local conditions and do not understand their point of view. There are distinct phases of outside help to end a conflict. In the first phase focus is on providing food, water, shelter and medicine to refugees *i.e.,* humanitarian. In the second, emphasis is on the refugees returning home while in the last phase long term investments and strengthening of courts is the main focus.

However, once a conflict is over aid agencies sanctioned by the World Bank send study groups instead of requisite personnel. There is a gap of several years before moving from humanitarian relief to economic development. By the time, such help arrives the war has restarted. It is possible to restart economic development through targeted "quick impact" initiatives. Most economies in post conflict countries are based on agriculture. Providing free packages of seeds, fertilizers and low cost equipment quickly will ensure that former, soldiers will return to their farms and establish their livelihood. But the window of opportunity closes quickly and one has to implement these measures almost immediately.

QUESTIONS

1. Where does the problem lie in implementing post-war relief measures?
2. According to the author how can political stability be achieved?
3. How can economic development be restarted in an impoverished country?
4. What is the benefit of "quick impact" aid?
5. What was the confusion among the agencies involved in post-war relief efforts?

PASSAGE - 19

We have witnessed several disasters in recent times, some natural others man made. The frequency of such calamities has injured us and deadened our collective sensitivity, but that does not reduce the enormity of the personal tragedy of each victim's family and community. The economic loss is only secondary to the human suffering, but is also substantial. The Government whether State or Central has standardised its response. This consists of reacting late, blaming others, visits by VIPs announcing a relief package including compensation for those affected and then forgetting all about it. There seems to be little attempt at drawing lessons from each disaster, storing the knowledge for future use, long term planning for possible pre-emptive action. Preparedness for disasters thus falls short of what is possible using today's technologies.

Floods in many parts of India like the states of Bihar and Assam are a yearly phenomenon. Yet the government seems to be caught by surprise year after year. It is obvious that tarpaulins, vaccines, medicines, clothes, satellite phones, large numbers of doctors and paramedical staff etc. will be needed as will boats and buses for evacuation. This is known to all those who have combated emergencies yet the non-availability of these essential services and commodities occurs. Worse the organisational structure and mechanisms for dealing with disasters are lethargic and ill defined. The National Disaster Management Agency, set up a short time ago being a central government agency has limitations relating to infringing the jurisdiction of states. It could have aggregated and disseminated experiences and knowledge, stocked many of the essential items required in an emergency or worked with agencies to ensure sufficient stocks, but hasn't.

While the reaction to major disasters is dismal, the response to emergencies like accident is equally sad. Victime lie unattended since passers by are wary of getting caught in a labyrinthine of police and legal systems. The resulting delay in treatment converts injuries into deaths. Of late, unique and free service to provide assistance in emergency cases is operational. Emergency Management and Research Institute (EMRI) is a professionally managed operation-initiated by the vision and grant from Ramalinga Raju. The service, which is a successful example of public private partnership likely to become operational in a few states in the near future. Given the sad failure of conventional govenment organisations in handling disasters, it is time we looked at the PPP model as an alternative without the government seeking in any way to abdicate its responsibility. While the state provides the funding, private organisations will provide the drive, professionalism, competent management and output linked efficiency of a good corporate organisation. Combining the sensitivity and purpose of an NGO with private entrepreneurial drive to handle disasters together is thus a worthwhile challenge for both corporates and the government.

QUESTIONS

1. Why do by standers not help accident victims?
2. What is the author's view on the government's current reaction to natural disasters?
3. Why is there a lack of medical care at disaster sites?

4. What does the author consider "a worthwhile challenge for both corporates and the government"?
5. Which will be the likely impact/s of the public private participation model of disaster management?

PASSAGE - 20

The strength of the Indian Democracy lies in its tradition, in the fusion of the ideas of democracy and national independence which was the characteristic of the Indian Nationalist Movement long before Independence, Although the British retained supreme authority in India until 1947, the provincial elections of 1937 provided real exercise in democratic practice before national independence. During the Pacific war India was not overrun or seriously invaded by the Japanese and after the war was over, the transfer of power to a government of the Indian Congress Party was a peaceful one as far as Britain was concerned. By 1947 'Indianisation' had already gone far in the Indian Civil Service and Army, so that the new government could start with effective instruments of central control.

After Independence, however, India was faced with two vast problems; the first, that of economic growth from a very low level of production, and the second was that of ethnic diversity and the aspirations of sub nationalities. The Congress leadership was more aware of the former problem than of the second. As a new political elite which had rebelled not only against the British Raj but also against India's old social order, they were conscious of the need to initiate economic development and undertake social reforms, but as nationalist who had led a struggle against the alien rule on behalf of all parts of India, they took the cohesion of the Indian nation too much for granted and underestimated the centrifugal forces of ethnic division, which were bound to be accentuated rather than diminished as the popular masses were more and more drawn into politics. The Congress party was originally opposed to the idea of recognizing any division of India on a linguistic basis and preferred to retain the old provinces of British India which often cut across linguistic boundaries. However, this was later conceded as the basis for a federal 'Indian Union'. The rights granted to the States created new problems for the Central Government. The idea of making Hindi the national language of a united India was thwarted by the recalcitrance of the speakers of other important Indian languages, and the autonomy of the states rendered central economic planning extremely difficult. Land reforms remained under the control of the States and many large scale economic projects required a degree of cooperation between the Central Government and one or more of the States which, it was found, was impossible to achieve. Coordination of policies was difficult even when the Congress party was in power both in the states and at the Centre. When a Congress Government in Delhi was confronted with non-Congress parties in office in the States, it became much harder.

QUESTIONS

1. What was the problem which India faced with after Independence?
2. Why was central economic planning found to be difficult?
3. Why was the linguistic reorganization of the States accepted?
4. Where does the strength of the Indian Democracy lie?
5. What were the issues which appropriately realized by the Central Government?

PASSAGE - 21

Political ploys initially hailed as master-strokes often end up as flops. The Rs. 60,000 crore farm loan waiver announced in the budget writes off 100% of overdues of small and marginal farmers holding upto two hectares, and 25% of overdues of larger farmers. While India has enjoyed 8%-9% GDP growth for the past few years, the boom has bypassed many rural areas and farmer distress and suicides have made newspaper headlines. Various attempts to provide relief (employment guarantee scheme, public distribution system) have made little impact, thanks to huge leakages from the government's lousy delivery systems. So, many economists think the loan waiver is a worthwhile alternative to provide relief.

However, the poorest rural folk are landless labourers, who get neither farm loans nor waivers. Half of the small and marginal farmers get no loans from banks and depend entirely on moneylenders, and will not benefit. Besides rural India is full of the family holdings rather than individual holdings and family holdings will typically be much larger than two hectares even for dirtpoor farmers who will, therefore, be denied the 100% waiver. It will thus fail in both economic and political objectives. IRDP loans to the rural poor in the 1980s demonstrated that crooked bank officials demand bribes amounting to one-third the intended benefits. Very few of the intended beneficiaries who merited relief received it. After the last farm loan waiver will similarly slow down fresh loans to deserving farmers. While overdues to co-operatives may be higher. economist Surjit Bhalla says less than 5% of farmer loans, to banks are overdue *i.e.,* overdues exist for only 2.25 million out of 90 million farmers. If so, then the 95% who have repaid loans will not benefit. They will be angry at being penalised for honesty.

The budget thus grossly overestimates the number of beneficiaries. It also underestimates the negative effects of the waiver-encouraging wilful default in the future and discouraging fresh bank lending for some years. Instead of trying to reach the needy, through a plethora of leaky schemes we should transfer cash directly to the needy using new technology like biometric smart cards, which are now being used in many countries, and mobile phones bank accounts. Then benefits can go directly to phone accounts operable only by those with biometric cards, ending the massive leakages of current schemes.

The political benefits of the loan waiver have also been exaggerated since if only a small fraction of farm families benefit, and many of these have to pay bribes to get the actual benefit, will the waiver really be a massive vote-winner? Members of joint families will feel aggrieved that, despite having less than one hectare per head, their family holding is too large, to qualify for the 100% waiver. All finance ministers, of central or state governments, give away freebies in their last budgets. hoping to win electoral regards . Yet, four-fifth of incumbent governments are voted out. This shows that beneficiaries of favours are not notably grateful, while those not so favoured may feel aggrieved, and vote for the opposition. That seems to be why election budgets constantly fail to win elections in India and the loan waiver will not change that pattern.

QUESTIONS

1. Why do economists feel that loan waivers will benefit farmers in distress?
2. What message will the loan waiver send to farmers who have repaid loans?
3. What is the author's suggestion to provide aid to farmers?
4. What was the outcome of IRDP loans to the rural poor?
5. What are the terms of the loan waiver?
6. What is the author's view of the loan waiver?
7. According to passage, who penalises deserving farmers?
8. Which will definitely be an impact of loan waivers?
9. What impact will the loan waiver have on banks?
10. According to the author what is the government's motive in sanctioning the loan waiver?

PASSAGE - 22

On hearing the news of the massacre at Jallianwala Bagh, Udham Singh did not attend his school but took a train to Amritsar and visited the spot. There, he stood for several minutes in a trance, picked up the soil, rubbed it on his forehead and put some in a phial. He fasted that night. According to his family members he placed fresh flowers on the holy dust every morning, drawing inspiration from it. One early morning he went to the river Ravi and pledged that he would colour its waters; with the colour of his blood, to create what he called the freedom's flood. With this aim in view in 1921, he first landed in Africa. From there, he went to America to meet the Indian revolutionaries working for the liberation of the motherland.

In 1923, he landed in England. In 1928, he returned to India in response to an urgent call from Bhagat Singh. When he reached Lahore, he was detained for violation of the Arms Act. He was released after four years rigorous imprisonment. In 1935, he escaped 10 Germany by giving a slip to the police. From Berlin, he reached Paris and purchased a revolver. He kept it ready for action and managed to reach London again. Opportunity came on March 13, 1940 when Sir Michael O'Dwyer was to speak at a seminar in the Caxton Hall. As Sir Michael turned to resume his seat after the speech, Udham Singh pulled out his revolver and fired at him. Sir Michael died without a shriek. Udham Singh was arrested and produced before the court on April 2, 1940. The court passed death sentence on him and he was hanged at Pentonville Prison, London on July 3, 1940.

QUESTIONS

1. Why did Udham Singh go to America?
2. Where did Udham Singh buy the weapon which was used for killing Sir Michael?
3. What is the link between London and Sir Michael O'Dwyer?
4. Where was Udham Singh arrested and for what?
5. Why did Udham Singh return to India in 1928?

ANSWERS

Passage - 1

1. The central economic planning was found to be difficult because outonomy was given to the states in certain matters.
2. After Independence, India faced with two problems increasing the production from a very low level and ethnic diversity and the aspirations of sub-nationalities.
3. Because the States were not co-operating with the Central Government.
4. The handling over of power by the British to India.
5. The Congress Party.

Passage - 2

1. They campaigned for infra-structure development.
2. Because, initially the economic growth rate of the country was too rapid.
3. They encouraged foreign direct investment in India.
4. There was a slowdown in the global economy.
5. A system of market determined exchange rate was introduced.
6. Other companies were unable to be competitive in the global market.
7. Industrial growth had to be maintained at a certain percentage fixed by the government.
8. Ensure a combination of public and private sector involvement in developing infrastructure.
9. To protect the interests of the public sector in these sectors.
10. It was beneficial because it created confidence in the Indian economy.

Passage - 3

1. To exhort nations to make a collective effort to ensure migration results in development of all countries.

1. Migrants misuse concessions granted to them by the countries where they earn their livelihood.
3. To get very well paid jobs in developed countries and to provide for their families.
4. As a means to reduce economic inequality.
5. Devise practical steps to optimise the benefits of migration.
6. Readily available technology, advances in telecommunication, economical means of transport, affordable means of communication etc.
7. Yes. The statement in true.
8. Increased job opportunities in developed countries and encouraging movement of citizens away from their native country.

Passage - 4

1. To become a legal resident by paying a certain amount in fines and back taxes.
2. In the health and education sectors.
3. 12 to 15 million.
4. Opportunity and availability of jobs in bulk.
5. India.
6. They are doing jobs that Americans simply don't want to do. They are employed in jobs that pay minimum wages and ential long working hours.
7. Mixico and India.
8. It is a concern of the Federal Government of the USA for welfare of the mankind.
9. It will ensure that they are not exploited by employers and that they are covered by social security benefits.
10. Both the country should make a bilateral employment agreement.

Passage - 5

1. Adequate planning and preparation are essential for a successful presentation.
2. It will become the greatest obstacle in his career and life.
3. Oral presentation.
4. It demands thinking and speaking.
5. Anecdotes, quotations and humourous touches often make a presentation interesting.
6. A thorough preparation.
7. Innate stage fright of a speaker.
8. It must be of relevant interest to the audience to induce their responses.
9. Personality of a person.
10. Reading or memorizing a presentation.

Passage - 6

1. Existence of large number of oil futures and oil contracts.
2. Renewable energy sources are costlier than non-renewable ones.
3. OPEC has decided to restrict its production of oil.
4. Lack of availability of alternative renewable energy resulted in rise in demand for crude oil.
5. OPEC was established in 1970.
6. To protect the interests of oil importing countries.
7. Determining prices of crude oil.
8. Today futures trading markets set the oil prices to a large extent.
9. Exorbitant crude oil prices made alternative energy sources and attractive option.
10. If the price of oil is high for a short time it doe not necessarily results in a drop in consumption.

Passage - 7

1. Stability will come only when economic opportunities exist.
2. Youth can find jobs and support their families rather than seaking their livelihood in violence.
3. Aid organizations do not understand issues from the perspective of the poor.

4. Aid agencies fail to study the situation.
5. Providing employments to the younger generation will prevent wars.
6. No, sanctions are not a means to ensure peace.
7. On providing humanitarian aid.
8. By means of focusing on agricultural initiatives.

Passage - 8

1. At an average annual rate of 8.1%.
2. Only about 3.5%.
3. Checks on lending.
4. The problem in global in nature, not restricted to their individual countries.
5. Because the condition of Asian banks is currently both stable and strong.
6. They must focus on maintaining high economic growth rate as inflation will taper off on its own.
7. Politicians may be voted out of power.
8. To sustain their economies despite the ill effects of inflation.
9. Because our past efforts to reduce poverty will be nullified.
10. Sudden rise in prices of oil worldwide.

Passage - 9

1. When we look around thoughtfully, we become conscious of God's unlimited grace.
2. The purpose of animals in the world is to serve mankind.
3. If there had been no human being the whole world have been rendered meaningless for us.
4. The reason of dissatisfaction was his more desire.
5. For bringing him into existence, for giving him capacity to dream and for creating the universe for him to live in, is the important reason.

Passage - 10

1. To provide money to small-scale companies and poor agents who have no direct access to commercial banks.
2. It is considered as an important instrument to alleviate poverty.
3. Enabling the poor to break, out of poverty by providing them with access to credit.
4. Microfinance companies get their funds from the many banks of western countries such as Commercial banks, Non-Government officials and donors of the same countries.
5. Micro finance has become a crucial means for combating poverty.
6. Micro finance programmes have been introduced in many developing economies. Best examples are the Grameen Bank in Bangladesh, Banco Sol in Bolivia and Bank Rakyat in Indonesia.

Passage - 11

1. The role of other countries is the main concern in the form of supplying high-tech weaponry, nuclear assistance and others anti Indian activity to Indian's neighbours.
2. Exploitation of developing nations by the mightier ones.
3. To understand their implications for us.
4. The most effective way is the development of indigenous technologies to counter our major problems.
5. The solution is to eliminate dependençe on developed countries and enhancement of in-house technology.
6. They seem to have become totally defunct.
7. Eradiaction of poverty and become economically self reliant.

Passage - 12

1. Because other government relief measures have proved ineffective.

1. Loans should be disbursed directly into bank accounts of the farmer using the latest technologies.
2. It resulted in the government sanctioning thrice the amount for the current loan waiver.
3. It will have an adverse psychological impact on those who cannot avail of the waiver.
4. Family holdings will be split into individual holdings not exceeding one hectare.
5. The budget grossly overestimates the number of beneficiaries whereas it also underestimates the negative effects of the waiver-encouraging wilful defaults in future.

Passage - 13

1. When sensation is remembered, it becomes memory experience and this leads to connected experience, which in turn gives rise to reasoning.
2. Art explains the cause of things together with its effect, whereas experience gives us just the effect of things, not the cause.
3. Because the sciences which do not cater to necessities or pleasures develop only after the previous two have been invented and only then, men have time for themselves. So, was the case in Egypt where the priestly caste had ample leisure time.
4. The central idea of the passage is "What actually is 'Wisdom'?"
5. Experience seems pretty much like science and art, but really, science and art come to men through experience.
6. Wisdom is knowledge about certain principles and causes.

Passage - 14

1. Due to drop in investment in central areas related to agriculture.
2. They have to ensure that a sufficient amount of their farm product is sold.
3. It has to track farmers eligible for government schemes.
4. Citizens should be grateful to farmers and their families for the hardships borne by them to cultivate crops.
5. It is difficult to verify these contracts between farmers and money lenders.
6. The government prefers to import these crops at a lower rate.
7. The aim should be to get all the four crore farmers all the benefits of the govt. schemes such as the Rashtriya Krishi Vikas Yojana, Irrigation Benefit programme and others.

Passage - 15

1. They wanted to take part of the ship and sell them.
2. The two men propose to float the ship again by pumping air into the tanks.
3. Having to contend with sharks, was the danger which the divers faced.
4. The two men felt proud because they had succeeded when everyone thought they would fail.
5. Rudder is the part of the slip used for steering.

Passage - 16

1. As per author, the only possibility during the first 38 years after India's independence was to envision the result of economic growth with the help of Government spending.
2. An attempt to mobilise public investment to give a proper direction to economy.
3. The most effective way to derive maximum out come from investment is by exploring and recognising problems of governance.
4. The author does expect to planners to explore the market for products made by unskilled workers.
5. The given statement is not appreciated by the author in Eleventh Plan.
6. Research and innovation are the best explanation of the term "Sunrise areas".

Passage - 17

1. The king did not have concret evidence to prove the fraud that's why he could not punish the fraudulent goldsmith.
2. Archimedes was famous as the most learned man as well as mathematician. So, he was charged with the task of finding out if there was any impurity in the crown.
3. The king's suspicion was that the goldsmith had mixed a cheaper metal with gold in the crown.
4. It was a challenge to unearth scientific fact.
5. It was a spontaneous reaction of excitement due to a discovery.

Passaage - 18

1. Aid agencies fail to study the situation.
2. Providing economic opportunities, political stability can be achieved.
3. Focusing on agricultural initiatives, economic development can be restarted in an impoverished country.
4. Soldiers earn income from their farms, is the benefit of "quick impact" aid.
5. Agencies involved in post-war relief efforts fail to understand how to start or restart economic development in a low income setting.

Passage - 19

1. They are wary of cumbersome police formalities and legal systems, so bystanders do not help accident victims.
2. The author's view on the government's current reaction to natural disasters is apathetic and has not managed to handle disasters effectively.
3. Improper medical care at disaster sites is due to lock of disaster management training for medical staff.
4. Their working together to manage disasters completely keeping public interests in mind.
5. Two things are crucial—(a) aid will be effectively deployed (b) professional approach to disaster management efforts, for the public-private participation model of disaster management.

Passage - 20

1. Increasing the production from a very low level was the problem which India faced with after independence.
2. Autonomy given to the states in certain matters causes difficulty in central economical planning.
3. The linguistic reorganization of the States was accepted due to the demand of Non-congress Governments in the states.
4. The strength of the Indian Democracy lies in its tradition, in the fusion of the ideas of democracy.
5. The issues were :

   (a) Implementation of the formulated policies

   (b) A national language for the country

   (c) Centre-State relations

   (d) Ethnic diversity of the people

Passage - 21

1. As other government relief measures have proved in effective so economists feel that loan waivers will benefit farmers in distress.
2. They will be angry at being penalised for honesty.
3. Loan should be disbursed directly into bank accounts of the farmers using the latest technology.
4. Corrupt bank officials were the unintended beneficiaries of the loans.

5. The Rs. 60,000 crore loan waiver has been sanctioned for 2.25 million marginal farmers.

6. It will have an adverse psychological impact on those who cannot avail of the waiver.

7. The loan waiver penalises deserving farmers.

8. Opposition will definitely win the election.

9. Farmers will make it a habbit to default on loans.

10. To ensure they will be re-elected.

Passage - 22

1. Udham Singh went to America to meet fellow citizens working for the same cause.
2. Udham Singh bought the weapon in Paris which was used for Killing Sir Michael.
3. Udham Singh shot at Sir Michael O'Dwyer in London.
4. Udham Singh was arrested in Lahore as he was charged for possessing unlicensed arms and ammunition.
5. Udham Singh returned to India in 1928 because he was called by a revolutionary in India.

☆☆☆☆☆☆

- **LETTER WRITING**
- **PARAGRAPH WRITING**
- **REPORT WRITING**

SSC(M) Matric LPR-2

LETTERS

Issuing an Appointment Letter

Ref: MTI/PERS/046 Date: ....

Mr Ankur Kaushal
Flat No 433B
Sector 37-C
Rohini
New Delhi-110023

Dear Mr Kaushal,

Sub: *Appointment in Our Organisation*

This is in reference to the receipt of your Curriculum Vitae by our personnel department and the subsequent interview with our Managing Director.

We are pleased to inform you that you have been appointed as a "Sales Executive" in our organisation. The terms and conditions of your appointment would be as under:

(A) You would be appointed as a Sales Executive in our company. You would report for duty on .... positively before 12.00 noon.

(B) You would be entitled for a gross monthly salary of Rs. 5000/- (Rupees five thousand only) per month. In addition, you would also be entitled for an annual bonus of 8.33 per cent of your basic salary. The bonus is payable a few days before Deepawali every year.

(C) You would be provided a furnished family accommodation in the immediate vicinity of your office.

(D) You would be eligible for a paid leave of one month after the completion of twelve months of your service.

(E) You would be entitled for casual leaves for seven days in one calendar year and one earned leave after every twenty days of your presence and working in the office. In addition, you would also be entitled for sick leave for seven days in one calendar year.

(F) The company would provide free medical facilities to you and to your family. You would also be entitled for medical insurance after a period of six months from the date of joining.

(G) You are supposed to cultivate the markets for the product range of the company throughout the length and breadth of the country. For the execution of your duties and responsibilities, you would be required to conform to all the orders and instructions issued by the company to you from time to time.

(H) You can be transferred to any part of the country or even abroad for the sake o executing your responsibilities. You would be provided free family accommodation if the management takes such a decision.

(I) During the course of your employment, you would not leak any secret of the company to any outsider.

(J) This appointment letter is valid for a period of one year from the date of its issue. Upon the completion of your probation period which is twelve months from the date of you joining the firm, you would be issued a forma appointment letter.

(K) During the period of your probation, you services can be terminated without giving yo a notice or notice pay. Similarly, you can als leave the company without prior notice an would be entitled for the salary till the la day of your presence in the firm.

Please countersign the copy of this appointmer letter as a token of your acceptance and return th same to our personnel department. Please also noti the date of your joining.

Thanking you,
Yours sincerely,
for Metal Technologies India Ltd

Ashik Sinha
(Manager-Personnel)

____

I accept

Name : ______________________

Place : ______________________

Date : ______________________

Exporting Software Products to the USA

Ref: MST/002 Date: ....

M/S ABC Exports Pvt Ltd
1209, Floor 12
Stephan Avenue
Calcutta-700 004
West Bengal
KA: Mr Pradeep Chatterji (Manager-Exports)

Dear Sir,

Sub: *Export of Software Products to the USA*

This is in reference to your enquiry no ABC/SE/040 dated December 18, ..., regarding the aforesaid subject.

We take pleasure to introduce ourselves as the leading software exporters of Northern India. We have developed application software for the following vital applications :—

(A) Accounts.
(B) Inventory Control.
(C) Shares and Stocks.
(D) Sales Invoicing.
(E) Engineering Applications.

We already have a client in New Jersey for whom we have developed software in Visual Basic 5.0 and Visual C++. We are very much keen for off-shore software projects.

Further, our software development platforms include the follow-ing :—

(A) Visual Basic 5.0.
(B) HTML.
(C) Visual Java.
(D) Visual C++.
(E) Visual Foxpro.
(F) Oracle version 7.0.

Your enquiry states that you are already exporting application software to the USA. We would be pleased to be associated with you in these prestigious projects.

Our terms include irrevocable confirmed Letter of Credit payable at sight. Our software products have been accepted worldwide (through our customer in the USA). We support our products for a period of two years from the date of activation on the computers. We specialise in Internet based software application including RDBMS and HTML.

If you like our credentials, please inform us so that we could arrange your meeting with our senior software professionals. Commercial modalities could follow later.

We look forward to hear from you soon.

Thanking you,
Yours sincerely,
For Marks Software Technologies Ltd

(Rajeshwar Gupta)
Manager - Software Exports
Encl : A Brief Profile of MST

Introducing a Marketing Manager for a Region

Ref: TECH/002 Date: ....

M/S Ricardo Sales Pvt Ltd
1941, Mohan Chambers
Nariman Point
Mumbai-400 035
Maharashtra
KA: Mr Surinder Kapoor (MD)

Dear Sir,

Sub: *Appointment of Mr Sebestian Hall as Marketing Manager-West*

We are pleased to inform you that Mr Sebestian Hall has been appointed as Marketing Manager (West) by the top brass of the company. He replaces Mr Rajan Mhatre who is retiring due to ill health on March 31, ...

Mr Hall has an envious record as a marketing professional. He is an engineering graduate from the University of Roorkee. His specialisation is Instrumentation Engineering. After completion of his graduation, he went to IIM (Ahmedabad) and specialised in marketing of industrial products. Mr Hall joined M/s Meters and Instruments in .... and worked hard for developing the North Indian markets. He was based in Chandigarh during his previous assignment.

After a two-year stint as Marketing Manager with M/s Meters and Instruments, Mr Hall joined M/s

Sunflag Instruments Ltd, New Delhi, as Assistant General Manager (Marketing). Here also, he worked hard and was able to achieve all the targets set forth by his management. In fact, he exceeded his targets. He specialises in cultivating the untapped markets of industrial products. He loves to create new market niches as well as new customers for the old product ranges.

Mr Sebestian Hall belongs to Maharashtra and has a permanent residence in Goregaon (West). He was not comfortable in New Delhi as West Indians are rarely able to adjust themselves in this part of the country. Hence, he opted for the position of Marketing Manager (West) in our company. You are our most reputed and prestigious dealer in Maharashtra. Your sales expertise and his marketing finesse would certainly lead to the cultivation of markets in the field of instrumentation and control in your region.

Mr Hall would join our Mumbai office on .... He would pay you a visit immediately after taking over as the chief of marketing operations in your region. We would humbly request you to extend all possible cooperation and supply the relevant information to him. He is our key man in the Westen markets and would need your guidance for understanding the target market niches in a more lucid manner.

If you need any other information, please do let us know.

Thanking you,
Yours faithfully,
For Rockwell Instrumentation Ltd

(Ajay Kulshreshtha)
Encl.: Accounts Satement for December, ...

Your Friend Seeks Career Guidance From You

536, Milan Avenue Date: ....
Varanasi-210 004
UP

My Dearest Akhilesh,

I hope that this letter of mine finds you in the best of your health and spirits. How are you? How is dear Arun and how is our dear sister Anita? I hope uncle's acidity is better now and *Auntieji* is able to cope with her skin allergy which bothered her for quite some time.

I received your letter yesterday only. You have requested for a career guidance after completion of your commerce graduation from Kashi College of Commerce, Varanasi. I am indeed happy that you are career conscious. Every young Indian must be career conscious and must try to make a mark in his life. This would also enable him to be economically independent.

You have informed that you have scored 78 per cent marks in your Commerce graduation degree. This is a good percentage but is not sufficient for you to get admission to a prestigious institute. Now a days, the minimum cut-off percentage for post-graduate courses is 88 per cent. At least in the major metropolises, this is the norm. A prestigious course would also include M Com course from a reputed college or university. Therefore, M Com is also a good post-graduate programme to pursue for.

The next option is Chartered Accountancy. You have a good percentage in your graduation course and moreover, you have done very well in accounts. Hence, it is advisable to go ahead with this option. You can register yourself with the Institution of Chartered Accountants of India. They have offices spread throughout the country. The head office is in New Delhi. You would be told to appear in a test which would determine your eligibility for the course. The classes are held during the evening sessions though morning sessions are also available. You can also take exemption from classes and can study on your own. In that event, you would be requested to get some specialised coaching in accounts, management and mathematics. Now a days, there are many specialised tutors available for this purpose. I hope you would find good tutors in Indore as well.

Further, you would be requested to pursue articleship in a chartered accountancy firm in your city. You would be paid less but you would be exposed to the best knowledge of industrial and business accounts. You should be able to complete your course in three years. Your examination schedule would be gruelling but the fruits of labour would be very sweet.

The final option left before you is management. You can work hard for an MBA degree from the government recognised universities. Moreover, AICTE has recognised several management training institutes which offer diplomas in management. You have to polish your English language, numerical ability, test of reasoning, decision making ability and managerial skills. Admissions are done after written tests, interviews and group discussions.

You can also appear in the GMAT test which is being conducted by Educational Testing Service (ETS) , New Jersey. If you score well in this test (a score of 600 or more is desirable), then you would be eligible for admission to the MBA programmes in the USA, Canada and other nations where GMAT scores are accepted. Some Australian universities are also offereing good management courses and some of them accept GMAT scores for admission. You can contact Australian High Commision, Chanakya Puri, New Delhi in this connection.

After completion of your MBA programme, you would be eligible for the post of Management Trainee-Finance. After three years, you would be able to make it to the cadre of Assistant Manager (Finance) and finally, you could be a manager within five years from the year of your graduation from the management school. Now a days, the position of Manager (Finance) carries great respect, financial benefits and opportunities for career growth. You could work on the information supplied by me. You could even go the colleges and universities in your region or state for getting complete information.

I would suggest that you should pursue your career in accounts and finance only. An MBA degree would be ideal for you. Ask your parents, friends and teachers for arriving at a decision. Do not hesitate to write to me.

Everything is fine here. My younger brother Tarun sends you his hello and love. My parents also wish to meet you and would like you to visit us in Varanasi. Please do come whenever it is feasible. We can have detailed discussions about your career if you come to Varanasi for a week.

Please give my best regards and namaste to your parents. Give my love to Arun and Anita.

Yours loving friend,

(Suresh Malhotra)
Akhilesh Kumar Sharma
93, Central Court Lane
Indore - 400 021
Madhya Pradesh

A Letter to Prospective Customer Announcing The Commencement of Business

Ref: LKN/ML/001 Date: ....

M/s Sunder Nath Satija And Co
General Merchants and Order Suppliers
330, Tekchand Market
Khari Baoli
New Delhi - 110 006
KA: Mr Naresh Satija (Partner)

Dear Sir,

Sub: *Introduction of "Homesafe" Brand of Exclusive Electrical Appliances*

We take please to introduce ourselves as the manufacturers of household electrical products in your area. We have established our office in Bhagirath Place market. Our manufacturing facilities are located in Naveen Shahdara.

We have an experience of around twenty years in the business of electrical household products. During late ...., my father, Mr Narendra Nath Aggarwal started a small shop in electrical appliances repairs in Karol Bagh. We have come a long way since then. After establishing repair centres in Shahdara, Karol Bagh, Khan Market and Nehru Place, we planned to have vertical diversification in our line of business. So, the manufacturing of electrical appliances for household sector was a natural choice.

My brother, Mr Sharad Aggarwal, has been associated with this business for the past eight years. Our technical expertise in repairs is well known in our target markets. We plan to repeat the same feat with our appliances as well.

We have entered the market with 'Homesafe' brand of electrical appliances. This range has already made a mark in the market as the latest and energy-saver brand of quality electrical household products. Our range of appliances includes the following :—

(A) Geyser — 3 Litre/5 Litre, Instant Heating - 2 Kilo Watts

(B) Electric Iron — 650 Watts/900 Watts

(C) OTG -- 2000 Watts/3000 Watts

(D) Sandwich Toaster — Pop-up Type - 1000 Watts

We plan to expand our product range in near future. Researches are already going on.

In light of the above, we would request you to stock the 'Homesafe' brand of electrical appliances. Please note that all the appliances undergo stringent quality control procedures and carry the BIS approval.

We propose to enter the markets through your retail outlet. Your showroom is strategically located and would be on ideal retail centre for our products. If you can place bulk orders, the prices would be very reasonable. However, we propose to utilise your shelf space for samples of our products.

Enclosed please find the brochures and technical specification sheets of our entire product range. If you need any other information, please do let us know.

We look forward for a meeting in this regard.

Thanking you,

Yours sincerely,

(Mohit Aggarwal)

Encl: a/a

A Letter to the Editor of a Newspaper, drawing attention towards the poor water and electricity supplies in your locality

Ref : PS/EXPRESS/001/99 Date: ....

The Editor
Indian Express
Bahadur Shah Zafar Marg
New Delhi - 110 002

Respected Sir,

Sub: *Poor Condition of Water and Electricity Supply in Najafgarh Area*

I am a resident of 4324/51, Roshanpura, Najafgarh. I wish to draw the attention of the civic authorities (M/s Delhi Jal Board and M/s Delhi Vidyut Board) through the columns of your esteemed daily. I have a sanguine opinion that your reputed daily would be able to put across our grievances to the appropriate authorities.

To be sent to Press

Poor Water And Poor Supply Conditions In Najafgarh

We are the residents of Najafgarh area, New Delhi-110 076. For the past two months, we have been facing severe water and power shortages in our locality. The water supply from Municipal Corporation has been suspended w.e.f. December 15, ... The water tankers have been pressed into service for supply of drinking water to the residents. But these tankers are very irregular. The authorities of Delhi Jal Board claim that the water shortage has been created as a result of bursting of a major water carrying pipeline in Najafgarh area. Although work has been going on, yet there are no signs of immediate restoration of water supply. The residents and their families has been deprived of the basic amenity of water which has created a havoc here. Ironically, the senior officers of DJB have paid three visits in the area and have declared that the situation is under control.

Further, we have been facing acute power shortage since February 4, ... The main supply transformer has been removed from the main square of Najafgarh. Electricity supply is totally haphazard. The students need electricity for preparation in their examinations. However, there is no respite from power failures due to the callous attitude of the authorities of Delhi Vidyut Board. The authorities have made no alternative arrangements for the supply of power. Some domestic industrial units are also suffering on account of severe power shortage.

Sir, we would like to draw the attention of senior officers of Delhi Vidyut Board and Delhi Jal Board. We would request them to restore the normal supplies of water and electricity in Najafgarh area so that people could heave a sigh of relief.

Thanking you,

Yours sincerely,

(Pawan Seth)
House No 4324
Street No 51
Najafgarh
New Delhi-110 076

An Application for the Post of Accounts Assistant

Ref: RK/EMP/012 Date: ....

M/s Monita Food Products Ltd
8001, Floor 8
Saint Paul Cathedral Road
Chennai-600018
Tamil Nadu

KA: Mr Neeraj Jain (Manager Personnel and Administration)

Dear Sir,

Sub: *Appointment in Your Firm as an Accounts Assistant*

JOB CODE : MFPL/A/065

This is in reference to the advertisement issued by you in "The Hindu" dated ...., ..., regarding the post of an Accounts Assistant. I would like to be considered for the aforesaid position and submit my particulars in brief as under.

I am Narendra Rastogi, B Com (Honours), MA (Economics) and have a Diploma in Computer Applications from NIIT (Chennai). I completed my post graduation in .... and was selected by a Chartered Accountancy firm through campus interview. I joined the company for a brief period and then shifted to M/s Texprint Specialities Limited as an Accounts Assistant (Trainee) on June 18, ... I was confirmed in September, ... and was accepted as Accounts Assistant with independent charge of Excise Duty and Taxation. I have been working for this firm for the past two years and am satisfied with my job content, perks and with my work environment.

However, my home has been shifted from Mount Road to T Nagar and it is quite inconvenient for me to commute through local buses. I would like to shift to a company on Cathedral Road nearby so that I could be spared the agonies of commuting through the highly congested local transportation.

Enclose please find a copy of my Curriculum Vitae which should be able to give you the requisite information you need. If you need any other information, please do let me know. I would be pleased to furnish the same.

Thanking You,
Yours sincerely,

(Rakesh Kumar)
Encl : a/a

An Application for the Post of Sales Executive

Ref: VKS/EMP/012 Date: ....

M/s Rosch Specialities Ltd
987, Floor 9
Mansarovar Building
Nehru Place
New Delhi-110019

KA: Mr Sumeet Nangia (Manager Personnel and Administration)

Dear Sir,

Sub: *Appointment in Your Firm as Sales Executive*

JOB CODE : RSL/SALES/2004

This is in reference to the advertisement issued by you in The Hindustan Times dated March 23, ..., regarding the post of Sales Executive in your esteemed organisation. I offer my services to your organisation and would like to submit the following details in order to support my claim for the aforesaid post.

I am Vivek, BA (Fine Arts) and MA (English). I am fully computer literate and have thorough exposure to Netscape Navigator, Visual Foxpro, Visual Basic 5.0, Windows 98 as well as MS Office. I am also pursuing my Post graduate Diploma in Sales Management with ABC Institute of Management, Qutub Institutional Area, New Delhi. This diploma would be over within six months.

Sales is my only passion and result oriented behaviour is the coveted goal of my life. My father is a Sales Manager in a reputed company and I have learned a lot from him about this esteemed profession.

My speciality, as would be clear from my Curriculum Vitae, is in Fast Moving Consumer Goods. I have achieved the highest targets set forth by my management in this wonderful area of growth. I won all the sales battles with flying colours and am ready to take on more challenging assignments in future. I hope you would be able to offer me more difficult challenges in sales career.

Sir, I believe that a salesman never fails in his life. I have a successful record of sales of nearly eight years. I would like to share my experiences with you and would also like to repeat the same feat in your company as well.

My reason for a shift is rather unusual one. It would be very unfair to state that I am not satisfied with my present assignment. I am also being paid well for my sales results and the incentives are also lucrative. However, my company wants me to repeat the sales performance in Rajasthan whereas I am not prepared to go outside my home state which is Delhi.

The reasons emanate from my family background. I have a family to support and my children are too young to be left alone. My wife is also working and hence, she is not able to devote enough time to the children. Further, we are a nuclear family and there is no support from our parents who are living in a remote village of Himachal Pradesh. Hence, my contention for a shift in my job is justified.

Enclosed please find a copy of my Curriculum Vitae which should be able to give you the requisite information you need. If you need any other information, please ask. I would be pleased to furnish you with more details. Two references have also been enclosed for your scrutiny of my credentials.

Kindly accept my candidature for the aforesaid position and oblige.

Thanking You,
Yours sincerely,

(Vivek Kant Shrivastava)
Encl : a/a

References :
(A) Mr Neelkamal Khanna
General Manager - Sales
Vinico Specialities Limited
567, Munirka Commercial Complex
Munirka
New Delhi - 110 045
Phones : 692 3456, 692 8902

(B) Mr Amitabh Neelamegham
Sales Manager - North
Snacks India (P) Ltd.
708, Hemkunt Towers
89, Nehru Place
New Delhi - 110 019
Phones : 644 0987, 622 7689
E-mail : amit@hotmail.com

A Personal Letter to a Friend who is unable to make a mark in his Life

121, Vasant Apartments Date: ....
New Delhi (Monday)

My Dearest Friend Ashutosh,

I hope that this letter of mine would find you fit as a fiddle. How are you? I hope your parents are having a nice time in Shimla on account of leave and our younger brother Sachin must be busy preparing hard for his first year examinations. He would certainly heave a sigh of relief when he is through. Oh! What a pleasant feeling after the examinations are over. I felt the same way when I completed my Computer Diploma examinations. You know Ashu, we have to be in touch with the latest technologies in order to be successful in this mad race of life! And the same is true for you and Sachin as well.

I received your letter a week ago. It was a picture of depression and lost hopes. You informed me that you received a compartment in your BA (Final) examinations in English. Further, you were not able to get any job whereas your classmates had bagfuls of opportunities. And finally, you failed miserably while learning computers. It is not at all surprising. Every individual faces some problem or the other in his career and life. These adversities teach us to be more tough so that we could achieve our goals. Let us analyse your problem step by step and then, we could devise some solutions for the same.

Firstly, you failed in your English examination. It was not at all surprising as you wasted your time in disco parties and night clubs. You were busy in having fun whereas your classmates slogged for achieving their targets. So far as I know, you have an excellent command over English language. And you could have easily made it to the top ten bracket in your class. I have seen your Detailed Marks Sheet which shows that you have done extremely well in other subjects. Therefore, the entire reponsibility of this academic fiasco lies with you. You should now work hard for the compartment examination in English. I know that you are capable and would be able to refurbish your image as a studious and hardworking person.

Secondly, you were not able to get a job. My dear, this is not a problem. I have talked to my uncle in Kanpur. You would be able to get the job of a Sales Executive in Kanpur itself. Moreover, your prospective employer would also be able to give you free evenings for your Diploma in Computer Applications. I rang up my uncle as soon as I received your letter. He called me back with the good news that you would be accommodated. Can you ask for anything more?

And finally, you have not been able to learn computers. My dear, this is the era of total computerisation. Internet is knocking at our doors. Every office in all the metropolises has been computerised. All production, marketing and accounts functions have been made more efficient through computers. Information Technology (IT) is the new buzzword for the next century. And you would be surprised to know that computers are quite easy to learn. Just try yourself once! You would fall in love with computers. I have also talked to my uncle in this regard. He would be able to help you in understanding computers and Internet operations. His office assistant, Mr Rajat Kumar Roy, would be able to give you basic tips on Windows 98, E-mail and Internet operations. But for that purpose, you would have to show interest in computers. You can talk to my uncle (Mr N K Singh) so that he could do the needful. His number (of Kanpur residence) is 657890. I am sure you would get in touch with him soon.

Adversity teaches a lot. You would also learn to be a better individual after you come out of your present crises. You are a brave boy and would not yield to pressures of life. I hope that this letter of mine would change your thinking. You must have a positive approach towards everything in life. Difficult times require perseverance, self-control and commitment to objectives. Keep going !!

Please do let me know when you would be able to pay me a visit in Delhi. I am eager to meet you. And please give my best wishes and *Namaste* to your parents whenever they are back from their tour. I do miss Sachin. It would be excellent if he could also accompany you during your Delhi visit. Why do not you plan a visit after his examinations? Please do write to me in this connection.

Till we meet again....

Yours loving friend,

(Rajeshwar Prasad Singh)

Mr Ashutosh Saxena
House No 56
Street No 16
Ali Ganj
Kanpur-208 002 (UP)

A Letter to your Cousin Giving him an Advice on a Serious Family Dispute

House No 65
Street 8
Kashmere Gate
Delhi - 110 006

Date: ....

My Dearest Nilofer,

I received your loving letter yesterday only (i.e., January 27th). I was indeed delighted to learn that you had topped in your BA (Honours) examinations. I am really proud of you. You are an intelligent student and would certainly make a mark in your chosen field.

You also gave me a shocking news that your uncle and father had a serious property dispute. Your grandfather had a shop in Chandani Chowk area which is the bone of contention. My dear! you know that property disputes cannot be settled in a day or two. However, I can extend a few suggestions as my uncle is a reputed estate agent of Moradabad and I have learned a lot from him in this field.

According to your letter, your father has two more brothers and your grandfather had the shop in his name. There was no will made by your grandfather. This makes the situation quite difficult. As your grandfather has expired, your father and both uncles would have to go to the court where they must file an application for the legal settlement of the disputed property. Please note that you would have to present the death certificate in the court and your father as well as your uncles would have to testify that there was no will made by your grandfather.

The court would then issue notice for the disposal of the shop in Chandani Chowk area. The proceeds of this sale would be divided equally among the grandchildren. It is the law of the land that if the grandparent does not leave a will (or does not allocate the property rights to the successor of his choice), then the property is divided among his or her grandchildren. In your case, the proceeds of the sale of the disputed shop would be divided among the grandchildren in equal proportions and the entire procedure would be supervised by the court or by the authority (or the lawyer) designated by the court.

I would suggest that you should appoint a senior counsel in Moradabad for the early settement of this dispute. This should take six months to settle. My father has informed me that Mr Surendra Nath Tyagi is a well known counsel of Moradabad and is an expert in such cases. His phone number of Moradabad is 46303. I am not aware about his address. But you can do this homework. The rest could be taken care of by your father.

Give my hello and love to Namrata and love to younger brother Manoj. I miss them a lot. I would come to Moradabad during summer vacations. We plan to go to Nainital and would stay with you for a couple of days. Do wait for me.

Till we meet again....

Yours loving friend,

(Ruchita Saxena)

Ms Nilofer Khan
Bungalow No 88
Street No 4
Brass Market Road
Moradabad-244 005 (UP)

A Letter to your Father Giving the Details of your Visit to Mumbai

Flat No 56 B   Date: ....
Floor 2, Street 5
Near Cooper Hospital
JVPD Scheme
Mumbai - 400 046
Maharashtra

Respected Father,

Pranam!

I write this letter to you from the residence of my host Mr Rajesh Chauhan. I hope that you, dearest mother and Shwetlana are enjoying themselves in the winter of Delhi. I do miss them a lot. However, I am here on a mission and this mission must be accomplished.

Dearest father, as planned by you, I arrived in Mumbai in the morning of January 8 and was received very well by the family members of Mr Chauhan. However, Mr Chauhan was not able to receive me at the Mumbai Central railway station on account of his meeting with the directors of his company.

In JVPD Scheme residental area, I am very comfortable. I have been allotted a separate room. As soon as I arrived here, I got down to work. You wanted me to locate vendors for our latest showroom of readymade garments in New Delhi. I must state that Mumbai is a paradise of textiles goods. I was amazed by the variety of jeans and T-shirts which are available in abundance.

I travelled to Nariman Point and also tried to develop vendors from Tank Bunder area. I have to get a major breakthrough in Ghatkoper area as the suppliers are keen on supply on a cash-down basis. They do not want to trust a new buyer from Delhi as they have had bad experiences during the past. Mr Chauhan would accompany me day after tomarrow and would introduce me to some garments manufacturers. He knows almost all of them.

Further, the shirts for the male executives are being manufactured by fourteen major vendors. Some of them have been exporting these shirts to The UAF and Singapore. They have got irrevocable confirmed Letters of Credit which are payable at sight. I offered to open a revolving LC through a Mumbai bank and they have happily agreed to supply the material in bulk. Infact, they want to send their goods to Delhi markets and are looking for suitable channels. Their shirts have the usual 65-35 blend but executives in Mumbai prefer 80-20 blends as moisture contents are quite higher in this city.

Female garments also have a rich variety and hues. I visited Akbar's Alley yesterday and found that the female garments section was full of customers. Suits, dupattas and sarees are also in demand besides the usual long flowing skirts, midis and jeans. Girls and women also prefer cotton rich fabrics as they are quite comfortable when they wear this variety in the moist weather of Mumbai.

The corporate vendors have high price tags even on the bulk supplies. If they do not change their price or delivery terms, what should I do? I asked Mr Chauhan and his son Nilesh in this connection. Nilesh is already in this business and is doing well. He told me that instead of small vendors with relaxed commercial terms and lower prices, we should locate quality conscious vendors with slightly higher prices but with total commitment to quality. You are very well aware that Delhiites are very quality conscious. Hence, I think I should follow the advice of Nilesh. What is your opinion?

A major corporate vendor has already been supplying to the reputed shops of NOIDA and is keen on supplying to us. But I need approval from you. His full-sleeve shirt (of 80-20 blend) would cost us Rs 125 per piece. The 65-35 blend would cost us Rs 140 per piece. Bulk supplies are available. These are FOB Mumbai prices. The party would help us in getting cheap transit insurance. They also know some good transporters who would be able to deliver the goods within seven days of despatch from Mumbai at our Delhi godown.

My research is yet not complete. I have collected some quotations but I find the prices to be on a higher side. The negotiations are on. Mr Chauhan would also take me to some reputed textile mills and exporters. He is a really busy man. Nilesh also is too busy to talk to. But their family members are very nice and they take adequate care of my needs.

Please do write to me in response to this letter. I have purchsed some garments for you, mother and Ashima. I would buy more in the days to come. I would also be keen to purchase a stereo component system if you could kindly allow me.

Give my love to mother and Ashima. I miss them a lot.

Yours loving son,

(Akshat Kapoor)
Shri N K Kapoor
Bungalow No 18
Street 1
Sainik Farm Lane
New Delhi 110 067

A Letter to your Friend Explaining the Current Economic Scenario of India

Room No 18 Date: ....
Boys' Hostel II
I I T Campus
New Delhi

Dearest Milind,

It is nice to write to the most adorable friend in the world. I miss you a lot. How are you? How is the weather at Nainital? I am indeed tempted to pay you a visit but I have a tough examinations and practicals schedule ahead. May be, after the examinations are over, I could pay you a visit. Let us hope for the best.

I received your nicely written letter yesterday only. I was impressed that you had taken part in the trekking expedition during the first week of May, ... It must have been a thrilling experience for you and for the members of your team. You have not written to me about your experiences of the expedition. Please do write to me. I would also be keen to have such type of excursion once I am through with my examinations.

My dear! You informed me that you are going to appear in the interview of State Bank Probationery Officer's Examination. You have an interview scheduled for June 25th, ... And you want a complete brushup about the economic condition of our country. Well, I would be more than pleased to offer you some facts and figures which are as follows.

Indian economy is undergoing a painful transformation. We conducted nuclear tests during May, ... and the heat of the tests could still be felt. The USA and her allies in the West have imposed tough economic sanctions against us. This has brought our economic growth rate to almost a standstill value. These are not good signs. However, the only silver lining in the dark clouds is that Resurgent India Bonds issued by State Bank of India have been able to fetch US $ 4.16 billion from the NRIs settled abroad - a matter of pride for the Indians. It is also amazing that most of the contributions (50 per cent) towards these bonds were from Indians settled in the Gulf countries. Indians settled in Europe and the USA could contribute only 15 per cent each. This amply demonstrates the fact that the ordinary artisans and labourers settled in the Gulf nations love India and her culture more than the NRIs settled in the West.

Further, the economic growth rate is slightly over 5 per cent per annum. This is not a healthy figure. The BJP-led coalition government in New Delhi has promised a growth rate of slightly above 7 per cent per annum. But this target seems a distant dream keeping in mind the following indicators :—

(A) The exports are showing a downward trend whereas the imports are up. The net foreign exchange reserves would be depleted on account of this trend. The oil pool import costs the nation dearly. But with the launching of new premium and ordinary brands of four wheelers (cars) and two wheelers (four stroke engine scooters), petrol comsumption is going to increase. Rise in the prices could not have a detrimental impact on the consumption as has been envisaged by the government.

(B) The output of farm sector has been low during the past few years. This trend would have to be reversed keeping in mind the rising population in the urban centres as well as in the rural areas of the country. Population control measures have proved to be ineffective and the reduced farm output could lead to serious troubles in the long run including a severe shortage of foodgrains and blackmarketing of the agricultural and farm products. Already, the prices of onions, potatoes and tomatoes had reached an all time high during the months of June and July, ... The ordinary citizen of this nation wondered whether he would be able to sustain his family during such type of crisis.

(C) Industrial output has been very low and the core sectors are not performing according to the desired targets. The slump in international markets and a fall in exports are responsible for this gloomy outlook. Add to it, the unstable scenario created by an unstable government installed at the centre. The BJP has been carrying on with the help of thirteen party coalition and the moods of the constituents resemble those of a chamelion. Anything could happen during the months to come because some factions of the ruling coalition have withdrawn their support.

The businessman is afraid to make investments in the industry keeping in view the unstable government at the centre. This has led to a halt in the industrial and economic activities. There is no generation of new jobs and no fresh projects are being promoted by the government either. This trend must not continue for long as the social unrest would manifest itself in the form of strikes, demands for the revision of payscales, violence by the students and the unemployed and even a national level upheaval against economic exploitation.

The teachers have refused to accept the revised payscales offered by the government and are bent upon asking for more. The students of Delhi University are on an indefinite strike and there are no teaching sessions.

(D) The stock markets have crashed to the lowest depths during June-August .... period. The Indian Rupee had reached a value of Rs 42 and higher against the US Dollar which is the most dismal record so far. There are no fresh share issues and the primary markets are not alive. The secondary markets are also waiting for fresh buyers. The foreign investors have withdrawn in the wake of economic sanctions, low industrial and farm productions and finally, because of the unstable government in the centre. There is also an indirect impact of the consistent downslide of the stock markets of Hongkong, Singapore and Japan. However, it is being stated by the experts that our economic conditions are still better than those of most of the nations of Orient.

My dear! Keeping these indicators in mind, I would like to opine that we are going through tough economic times. The situation is not going to improve within days or months. The European and American economies are also going through a lean phase. Recession has taken its toll around the world. This hour of crisis requires political stability at the centres, fresh investments in the infrastructure sectors and projects, more agricultural output and above all, the lifting of economic sanctions by the USA and her Western allies. The months to follow would be very hectic for the economic analysts of this country.

Please give my *Namaste* and regards to your parents. Give my love to Rahul and Pooja. I would pay a visit to Nainital during my summer vacations in June. I would be with you in the second week of June as my last practical examination is due on June 9, ...

Rest is fine. Please do write to me about your interview.

Your best friend,

(Kailash Chopra)
Mr Milind Sharma
House No 56
Upper Ridge Road
Talli Tal
Nainital-232004 (UP)

Claim of dues from a Party on Account of Demurrage

Ref: RTC/HMSL/089 Date: ....
M/s Hot Mix Specialities Limited
78, Rockfort Avenue
Shakespeare Sarani
Calcutta-600090
West Bengal
KA: Mr Hitenbhai Shah (Manager Accounts and Finance)

Dear Sir,

Sub: *Credit of Rs 4506.77 on Account of Demurrage Charges at M/s Golden Roadlines Ltd (New Delhi)*

REF : Our Bill No 345 Dated December 18, ...
Against Your PO No HMSL/009 Dated December 12, ...

This is in reference to the telephonic discussions the undersigned had with you in the morning of January 3, ... I pray that the new year may bring you peace, happiness and prosperity. I also wish for deeper association between the two firms. Your good wishes for the happy new year are gratefully accepted and reciprocated.

As discussed over phone, we sent a consignment of cotton yarn (789 bales) vide the aforesaid bill and through Truck (Tata) number UP 10 B 8905 (belonging to M/s Golden Transport Ltd) on December 18, ... The truck reached their godown at Kashmere Gate on December 25, ... Your purchase officer Mr Sanjay was informed about the arrival of your consignment in the morning of December 26, ... But nobody has arrived from your office till date for claiming the aforesaid consignment.

In the meanwhile, the transport company has sent us a letter and has claimed the demurrage charges worth Rs 4506.77 (up to 04.01. ......) because the consignment was on "To Pay" basis. Obviously, if nobody from your office was willing to claim the goods, then the transporter had to contact us for demurrage charges.

We would therefore, request that your New Delhi office may please be informed about the arrival of the said consignment and the demurrage charges may please be paid to the transporter.

Further, the transporter is also claiming an amount of Rs 18,700 towards the freight charges (from our works at Indore to their transit godown at New Delhi). This payment was discussed in advance with you on December 10, ... vide a telephonic discussion. This payment may please be made to the transporter and the aforesaid consignment may please be got released.

Thanking you,

Yours faithfully,

for Rolland Textile Company Limited

(Suresh Mehta)

Marketing Manager-North

Encl : The original letter of transporter claiming demurrage charges.

A Letter to your Friend Informing him about the Latest Trends in Music

Flat No 56, Floor 4 Date: ....
Minto Apartments
Khar (West)
Mumbai - 400 056
Maharashtra

My Dearest Akanksha,

Hello!

I hope that you would be fine in Simla.You must be enjoying your holidays in Simla. I also hope that your mother and brother Sunny must be with you. Mumbai has no climate to be proud of. We are wet throughout the year. Shimla must be a place to live and enjoy. I do hope that respected Uncle and your sister Nisha must be joininmg you soon in Simla. Give my love to all of them.

You know that I am a music lover. I appreciate good classical and Western music from around the globe. And you too have been bitten by the music bug. We share a common platform in this context. Please do write to me about the latest on music front in Simla and in Delhi when you go back.

But my dear, I have been hearing some strange voices in Mumbai. It is unpleasant to note that some Indian singers have benn copying the Western tunes in a shameless manner and then making them grand hits in term of sales. We have a much richer music and instruments in our land. Then why this dirty shift? I could not understand the "teen bend" for this hoarse and unkind music.

You know very well that I have great respect and appreciation for the Great Muhammed Rafi and the ever-thrilling Kishore Kumar. These doyens of music are unequalled. Pundit Ravishankar is the *Sitar* maestro and Amjad Ali Khan has captivated his audiences with his *Sarod* so many times. I am a real fan of the enchanting music of Jagjit Singh and Ghulam Ali. The *Ghazals* rendered by them in their latest albums are simply fantastic and take you into a different world altogether.

It is so strange that Menhdi Hassan is not in news. He has got the best voice in this circuit but he is no longer heard. The marketing of these singers is also a big business and may be, Menhdi Hassan could be a victim of the free market system.

I was telling you about the stale, copy-cat and dull music from the locals. I have never liked it. The Hindi pop music scene is bereft of a good singer. I have never attended a Hindi pop music concert for ages. It is not that I do not like Hindi pop. Hindi is my mother tongue and I love my land above everything else. But I cannot accept garbage for my soul. Similarly, the current Western pop songs fail to impress. The veneer of musical and media gloss fails to protect the hidden failures in the production of numbers which are awful in terms of music, lyrics, beat and overall presentation.

My dear, I do not know what has happened to the tastes of the youth. They have adopted rustic and unpleasant tunes and have sidelined *Ghazals*, *Nazams* and classical music. Our nation is proud of our musical heritage. But are the youth thinking in terms of these lines? I think we should organise a musical conference for the youth and must discuss the issue seriously. What is your opinion?

I have purchased some CDs and cassettes. I think I should send those to you. I have also purchsed a new CD player with FM tuner. The FM programmes are stange. They always broadcast half of the songs and skilfully eliminate the other half of all of them. Why, may I know? The mad rush for money would affect all of us. If we listen to half of the song, we would never be 'complete' as the curiosity and lust for the other half song would get deeply embedded in our minds. This would affect our personalities and we would end up as half-baked individuals; we would like to leave everything mid-way as there is no direction or an urge to complete the task.

When you would be back in Delhi? Please do write to me about your visit to Simla as well. I would like to listen to new music by Yanni. He is a master player and captivates his audiences through his fine orchestra. There is a trend towards music without words now a days. And I like it. I would send you CDs of some Western Classics (Instrumentals).

Please give my *Namaste* to respected *Uncle Ji* and *Auntie Ji*. I would love to have my dear sisters in Mumbai. You can come during the autum break in September. Please do let me know whether you are coming. I would make the necessary arrangements for your arrival and stay.

Goodbye till we meet.......

Yours loving friend,

(Christina Thomas)

Ms Akanksha Chaturvedi
Station - Simla
Room No 709, Floor 7
Hotel Bremen Residency Manor
Upper Mall
Simla
Himachal Pradesh

A Covering Letter for an Export Consignment

Ref : CEI/COMP/034 Date : 18.04.

M/s Sulaiman Import Trading Co
567, Floor 5
Traders House
Jalan Sultan Ismail
Kualalumpur - 60 340
Malaysia

KA : Mr Mohammed Ali (Managing Director)

Dear Sir,

Sub: *Export Consignment No 3 Vide Your Order No 345 Dated 18.01 and Under Your LC No 67090 Dated 26.01 Opened at Hongkong Bank, Kualalumpur*

This is in continuation of the supply of the computer systems against the aforesaid LC. We are pleased to send another consignment of the Pentium 333 PCs as per schedule mentioned in your aforementioned Purchase Order.

The despatch details are as follows:

(A) COMMERCIAL INFORMATION

Your PO No. : 345 Dated 18.01. ......
Your LC No. : 67090 Dated 26.01. ......
LC Type : Revolving
Consignment No. : Seven
Our Invoice No. : CEI/COMP/034/7 Dated 15.04. ......
Invoice Value : US $ 18,400
Insurance Amount : US $ 1,100

(B) PRODUCT DESCRIPTION

Product Name : Pentium 333 Based PCs

— Intel Pentium Mother Board 333 MHz
— 4.3 GB SCSI HDD (Quantum)
— 1.44 MB FDD (Sony)
— 2 Serial and 2 Parallel Ports
— Windows Based Keyboard (Riticomp)
— 250 Watts SMPS (Microtek)
— VGA Card (Vintron)
— 14" VGA Colour Monitor (Microtek)
- Mouse (Logitech)

Product Quantity : 100 PCs

Product Packaging - Each PC System has been packed in Corrugated Seven-ply Special Packaging Paper and contains all the parts in semi-knockdown stage. All the parts have been adequately packed along with the stuffing paper and good packaging material to prevent damage during transit.

Product Packaging Details - Each Package has a slip which has been numbered from HTR001 to HTR100. The product description has been mentioned on each packaging slip. The packaging slip has been pasted on the top of each box. Th ntire consignment has been packed in Blue Container of Hanjin Carriers Ltd and is bearing number HC-0098769.

(C) DESPATCH DETAILS

Transportation : Hanjin Carriers Ltd vide their ship "Great Voyage."
Date of Departure : 16.04. ...... (10.30 Hours) Off Nhava Sheva Port (Mumbai)
Expected Date of Arrival : 29.04. ......
Destination Port : Singapore

Please find the goods in order and inform vid

E-mail address cei@aolonline.com. Please also send confirmation of receipt of goods at Singapore port through courier.

If in doubt, ask.

Thanking you,
Yours faithfully,
For CEI Computers Ltd

(Roger Winston)
Manager - International Marketing (Orient)

Encl :
(a) Invoice
(b) Quality Control Certificate
(c) Certificate Of Origin of Goods
(d) Despatch Slip
(e) Packaging Details

A Mortgage Agreement

Ref : XYZ/PQR/MORT/001 Date: ....

MORTGAGE AGREEMENT

This indenture has been made and entered into on this 25th Day of May, ... between Mr Stephan Stallone, resident of No 456, Texas Avenue, Kentucky, hereinafter known as the party of the First Part and Mr George Nile Swenson, resident of Flat No 65, Floor 12, Woodview Apartments, Capitol Highway, Washington DC, hereinafter known as the party of the Second Part

Thus witnesseth that the party of the First Part for and in consideration of US $ 47,689 (United States Dollars forty seven thousand and six hundred and eighty nine only), in hand paid — the receipt of which is hereby acknowledged vide receipt No 2456 dated 25th Day of May, ... with Mr Henry Fergusan as the witness of the cash transaction — does hereby grant, sell, convey and confirm unto the party of the Second Part, his heirs and assignees forever, all the singular and tl e following property whose details have been mentioned below.

Flat No 4590, Floor 34, Stringer Building, Hampshire Avenue, New York, NY 60 778 owned lawfully by party of the First Part under Municipal Authority's Registration No 456789902 dated January 12, ... and maintained by party of the First part including the payment of all the corporation, electricity, water, house tax and any other dues which may have been imposed by the designated authority on such a property from time to time.

Provided always that this mortgage is upon the express condition that if the said Mr Stephan Stallone (the party of the First Part) shall pay to Mr George Nile Swenson (the party of the Second Part) a sum of US $ 47,689 (United States Dollars forty thousand and six hundred and eighty nine only), then the aforesaid transfer shall be treated as null and void and of no effect.

And that in case of non-payment of the said debt as well as the interest at the rate of 3% (three per cent) per month amounting to an interest rate of 36% pa (thirty six per cent per annum) within two years of the loan, then the party of the Second Part shall have the full authorisation to legally occupy the premises of the aforesaid property of the party of the First Part. The party of the Second Part shall also be legally authorised to sell the aforesaid property at a public or private auction. The proceeds of the sale so effected shall be used by the party of the Second Part for clearing the debt taken by the party of the First Part after deducting all the expenses that may be involved for the sale of the aforesaid property.

If the sales proceeds of the aforesaid property fail to satisfy the debt obligation of the party of the First Part towards the party of the Second Part, then the balance of the debt, the interest, the costs and other related or connected payments shall be paid by the party of the First Part to the party of the Second Part for making up the deficiency.

In the presence of the witness, therefore, I hereunto agree to abide by the terms of agreement of this mortgage agreement which is signed by me without any coercion or compulsion.

____

Stephan Stallone
459, Texas Avenue
Kentucky 56789

Date : Time : Place :

In the presence of the witness, therefore, I hereunto agree to abide by the terms of agreement of th mortgage agreement which is signed by me witho any coercion and compulsion.

George Nile Swenson
Flat No 65, Floor 12
Woodview Apartments
Capitol Highway
Washington DC-45680
Date: Time: Place:

WITNESS

Witnesseth therefore, that the aforesaid mortgage agreement was signed in my presence and the amount of US $ 47,689 (United States Dollars forty seven thousand and six hundred and eight nine only) was transferred from the party of the Second Part to the party of the First Part in my presence.

Signed, sealed and delivered in my presence under the seal of the appropriate designated court to the party of the First Part, the party of the Second Part and to the appropriate designated court.

Henry Fergusan
Bungalow No 78
Diplomatic Enclave
Washington DC-45689
Date: Time: Place:

Notary's Signature Stamp of Court

A Dissolution Deed

Ref: XYZ/PQR/MORT/001 Date: ....

DISSOLUTION DEED

This dissolution deed is made on this Fifteen Day of January, ... between :

(a) Mr Rajendra Kumar Taneja, S/o Mr Ram Tirath Taneja, r/o K-45, DDA Flats, Phase II, Mayapuri, New Delhi-110078 (hereinafter, referred to as the First Party); and

(b) Mr Animesh Gupta, S/o Mr Amolak Ram Gupta, r/o W-23, Greater Kailash II, New Delhi-110065 (hereinafter, referred to as the Second Party).

Whereas, the aforesaid, the First party and the Second Party to this deed, were carrying out the business under the name of M/s Milano Cosmetics at the address H-119, Industrial Sheds, Okhla Industrial Area, Phase II, New Delhi-110020 with effect from 15.12. .... vide their partnership deed executed on 15.12. ....

And whereas, due to the present economic trends of the international export markets and also, due to the labour strike which affected the operations of the business seriously from 29.03. .... to 04.04 .... the First party and the Second Party have finally decided to dissolve the aforesaid partnership on this Fifteenth Day of January, ...

And whereas it is deemed expedient by the First Party and the Second Party to state the terms and conditions of the dissolution for future reference and record so that there may arise no disagreement, discord or dispute with respect to the dissolved partnership, the First Party and the Second Party, jointly, with mutual consent and without any coercion, do hereby agree and confirm :

(a) that the aforesaid partnership is hereby acknowledged to be dissolved on this Fifteenth Day of January, ..., with the mutual consent of the First Party and the Second Party;

(b) that the complete financial accounting statements of the partnership in question upto the period of 15.01........, have been completed. The Trading and Manufacturing Account, The Trial Balance, The Profit and Loss Account statement, the assets and liabilities of the First Party and the Second Party and The Balance Sheet as on 15.01. .... have been got prepared through M/s R.K. Kuckreja and Co. (Chartered Accountants), 56, Deshbandhu Gupta Road, Karol Bagh, New Delhi-110005. And the aforesaid Chartered Accountancy firm has also drawn the list of debtors and creditors of the partnership upto the last day of partnership which is 15.01. ..... . The entire statement of account have been submitted in triplicate, duly admitted and signed by the First Party, the Second Party and the Chartered Accountancy Firm;

(c) that the aforesaid parties to this deed have assessed the divisible assets, liabilities and profits of the partnership firm and according to the signed, confirmed and authenticated Statement of Accounts prepared by the Chartered Accountancy firm and the list of the assets, liabilities and profit or loss has been described as under :

(c1) that the total assets of the firm after valuation by the government approved valuer Mr Ram Pratap Ahuja are of the value of Rs 2,56,789 (Indian Rupees two lakh, fifty six thousand, seven hundred and eighty nine only);

(c2) that the total liabilities of the firm after calcualtions by the Chartered Accountancy firm are of the value of Rs 49,789 (Indian Rupees forty nine thousand, seven hundred and eighty nine only); and

(c3) that the total profits of the firm after calculation by the Chartered Accountancy firm are of the value of Rs 28,900 (Indian Rupees twenty eight thousand and nine hundred only).

(d) that the full and final settlement of accounts of the firm is as under:

(d1) the assets of the firm are hereby sold to Mr Akhilesh Kumar Nagpal r/o 68, Sunlight Colony, Ring Road, New Delhi - 110 090 for a consideration of Rs 2,56,789 (Indian Rupees two lakh, fifty six thousand and seven hundred and eighty nine only). The sale deed to this effect has been signed, confirmed and approved by the First Party, the Second Party, the designated court and the witnesses to the sale.

(d2) The calculation of the final payments is as under:

The sales proceeds from the sale of assets of the firm	= 2,56,789
Less, The liabiliteis of the firm	= 49,789
Nett Balance	= 2,07,000
Add Nett Profits After Taxes	= 28,900
Total Amount	= 2,35,900
Less The Fee of Chartered Accountancy Firm	= 12,000
Less The Fee of the Government Approved Valuer	= 2,000
Less The Court Fees	= 1,400
	15,400
Nett Amount to Be Divided Among the First Party and the Second Party	= 2,20,500

The partnership percentage of the First Party	= 60 %
The partnership percentage of the Second Party	= 40 %
The First Party shall get = 2,20,500 x 0.6	= 1,32,300
The Second Party shall get = 2,20,500 x 0.4	= 88,200

(e) that neither of the parties shall use the name "M/s Milano Cosmetics" in their future businesses;

(f) that all the calculations regarding sales tax, income tax and other legal taxes as well as their documentation, filing with the appropriate authority and completion of all other formalities have been taken care of by the Chartered Accountants and that nothing is due to the State on this account; and

(g) that this dissolution deed shall be duly registered with all the government and court authorities at the joint expenses of the both the First party and the Second Party and for which they have already deposited the court fee in advance.

In witness thereof of the parties, who have signed this dissolution deed on this Fifteenth Day of January ...., the aforesaid deed is called upon to be in legal force with immediate effect and the First Party and the Second Party are to be compensated after deduction of all the expenses and liabilities as mentioned above.

Rajendra Kumar Taneja The First Party	Animesh Gupta The Second Party
Authorised Signatory for M/s R.K. Kuckreja & Co Chartered Accountants	Ram Pratap Ahuja Approved Valuer
Sunil Kumar Mehta 56, Kaveri Apartments Patparganj Delhi - 110 092	Milind Gupta 883, Block 56-B Paschim Vihar New Delhi - 110

Date: January 15, ...
Time: 12:40 PM
Venue: The Delhi High Court
Patiala House

Introducing an Old Product Range to a New Customer

REF : SEPL/PRDT/009 Date: ....

M/s Sunflag Chemicals Ltd
405, Fourth Floor
Punwani Chambers
Nariman Point
Mumbai - 400 045
Maharashtra
KA : Mr Sanjay Nagrath (Managing Director)

Dear Sir,

SUB: *Our Range of 'Stanley' Exhaust Fans for Your Firm*

We take pleasure to introduce ourselves as the leading manufacturers and distributors of 'Stanley' brand Exhaust Fans in Western India. We have been manufacturing this versatile range for the past thirty years and have established ourselves on account of high quality of our products.

We had a very humble beginning during the late sixties when we started manufacturing 15-inch exhaust fans for the domestic markets of Mumbai. We expanded our operations in entire Maharashtra and today, we are supplying our range to all the parts of the country. We have also been able to export our product range to some African nations including Kenya and Nigeria.

Our customers include the reputed chemical engineering industries like Dextor Starch And Chemicals Ltd, Matador Chemicals Private Ltd and Reliable Petrochemicals Ltd. Our annual turnover has reached Rs 70 million mark and we are likely to reach the coveted figure of Rs 100 million by the end of the current fiscal year.

We have the most modern manufacturing plant in Bhayander and are supported by 250 professionals which include engineers, technicians, office staff and hardcore marketing professionals.

We are using 99.9 per cent pure electrolytic copper wire (manufactured by M/s Furukawa Company Ltd of Japan) for the fan windings. We have been manufacturing fans at the speed of 900 RPM and 1440 RPM.

Further, our fans are completely rust-proof and waterproof and are ideal for all types of industrial premises including chemical engineering industries.

The 'Stanley' Exhaust Fan range includes the following :

(A) Stanley Super - 9-inch Exhaust Fan
Blade Size - 9 Inches
Speed - 900 RPM
Support - Bushes
Price - Rs 425/- per Pc
Excise Duty - Included
Sales Tax - Extra

(B) Stanley Super - 12-inch Exhaust Fan
Blade Size - 12 Inches
Speed - 900 RPM
Support - Bearings (Nachi Japan)
Price - Rs 730/- per Pc
Excise Duty - Included
Sales Tax - Extra

(C) Stanley Super - 15-inch Exhaust Fan
Blade Size - 15 Inches
Speed - 1440 RPM
Support - Bearings (Nachi Japan)
Price - Rs 1240/- per Pc
Excise Duty - Included
Sales Tax - Extra

(D) Stanley Super - 18-inch Exhaust Fan
Blade Size - 18 Inches
Speed - 900 RPM
Support - Bearings
Price - Rs 1500/- per Pc
Excise Duty - Included
Sales Tax - Extra

All the exhaust fans are manufactured according to BIS norms and carry a guarantee of replacement of one year from the date of purchase. We also undertake special projects for meeting the exhaust air requirements in chemical industries like yours. We undertake these projects on a turnkey basis.

Enclosed please find our technical catalogue, an introduction to the company, the photocopy of the certificate from BIS for our range of exhaust fans and the list of our valuable customers vide Annexures I,II,III and IV respectively. We hope that you would find the same in order. If you have any query, please do let us know.

We await your response so that we could depute

our senior marketing executive for paying you a visit.

Thanking you,

Yours sincerely,

For Stanley Electric Private Ltd

(Kailash Aggarwal)

Director Marketing

Encl :

Annexure I - Technical Catalogue

Annexure II - An Introduction to Stanley

Annexure III - Photocopy of BIS Certification

Annexure IV - List of Our Valued Clients

Introducing New Product Range to an Old Customer

REF : ZEL/RTM/009 DATE : ....

M/s Reliable Textile Mills Ltd

Opposite Tivoli Building

705, Peddar Road

Mumbai - 400 056

Maharashtra

KA : Mr Ashim Poddar (Managing Director)

Dear Sir,

Sub: *Our Latest Range Of INFOSTAR Pentium Computers, Peripherals And Software*

This is in reference to the visit of our Sales Manager, Mr Sanjay Nagrath, last week in connection with our new product range of computer systems for your intricate computing requirements.

As already explained by Mr Nagrath, we have entered the computer hardware business with effect from January 15, ... For this purpose, we have promoted a new division in our firm which would be rightly called the Information Technology Division (ITD). The boom in the information technology sector prompted us to diversify into computer hardware and software. We have been supplying chemicals to you for your textile mills for the past ten years. The latest range of computers would also fascinate you and would enable you to handle your information technology related problems in a more efiicient manner.

Although we have entered this most vital and fastest growing sector only a month ago, yet we have been able to achieve major breakthrough in this area with supplies to M/s Sachtel Textiles Limited, Calcutta (Pentium 333 MHZ), M/s ABC Exports Limited (software solutions for exports) and M/s Naina Speciality Chemicals Ltd (Pentium 233 MHz computer system with printer and scanner).

We have christened our product range as **INFOSTAR** and we hope that you would support it with your kind patronage.The list of our satisfied customers is increasing. We would like to give you a brief overview of our product range so that you could also get the maximum benefit from the information technology revolution.

We have the most modern assembly facilities in Pune and are also supported by 50 hardware engineers, software professionals and sales staff.

Our **INFOSTAR** range of state-of-the-art computer systems and software solutions is as follows:

(A) **INFOSTAR PENTIUM RANGE**

- Pentium 233 and 333 MHZ Motherboard (INTEL/AMD)
- RAM - 32 MB upto 128 MB (SIMM)
- 4.3 GB SCSI Hard Disk Drive
- 1.44 MB Floppy Disk Drive (Sony)
- CD-ROM Drive 40 x (CREATIVE - 650 MB) with remote
- Two Serial and Two Parallel Ports
- 14 Inches VGA Colour Monitor
- VGA Card
- 200 Watt SMPS

(B) **INFOSTAR Brand Peripherals**

- Desk Jet Printer
- Dot Matrix Printer (80 Column and 132 Column)
- Modem 33.6 KBPS
- Laser Printer 7P
- Power Cases (Tower Models) (200 W, 250 W)
- Monitor (VGA Black and White and VGA Colour)

(C) **INFOSTAR Brand Software Products**

- INFOSTAR Accountant (For Single User and for LAN Systems)
- INFOSTAR Inventory Controller
- INFOSTAR Invoicing System
- INFOSTAR Management Audit System

Our product range is compatible with latest hardware norms and technologies in vogue. We are manufacturing and assembling our products in Pune under the supervision of foreign trained hardware engineers. Our computers and peripherals are IBM compatible. Our software products are also compatible with the latest software norms and have been developed keeping in mind the latest requirements of accountancy, payroll, invoicing and management audit.

Enclosed please find our technical catalogue, an introduction to our new business, the photocopy of the certificate from M/s Intel Corporation and the list of our valuable customers vide Annexures I,II,III and IV respectively. We hope you would find the same in order. If you have any query, please do let us know.

We would expect that you would extend the same patronage to our new product range as you have beeen extending a valuable and long term support to our chemicals and dyes for the last ten years. We assure you that we would also be able to give you the best products and after-sales service as we have already been giving in respect of our range of chemicals.

We await your response so that we could depute our senior marketing executive for paying you a visit.

Thanking you,
Yours faithfully,
For Zenith Engineers Limited,

(Jaideep Sardesai)
Director Marketing
Encl :

Annexure I - Technical Catalogue –
Annexure II - An Introduction to **INFOSTAR** Range of IT Products
Annexure III - Photocopy of certificate from M/s Intel Corporation
Annexure IV - List of our valued clients

Claim of Commission on Account of Sale of Goods from the Manufacturers

Ref : MGS/MSPL/1890 Date : 30.07. ....

M/s Modern Speciality Products Ltd
B-46, First Floor
South Extension Part I
New Delhi - 110 048
KA : Mr Amar Singh Chawla (Proprietor)

Dear Sir,

Sub: *Commission Payable for Period Ending 30.06. ....*

We would like to draw your kind attention to the commission payble account which remains unsettled because of laxity on your part. We have already sent the details vide our letter no MGS/MSPL/1808 dated 10.07. .... This letter was sent through our Mr Ramakant when he paid you a visit for accounts reconciliation for the fiscal year ending on March 31, ...

We are appending herewith the commission payable account for the year ending 30.06. .... for your perusal and record (as already discussed by Mr Ramakant, the commision percentage is 10 per cent on the sales price).

Commission Payable Account as on 30.06.1999

S No	Item Supplied	Qty	Rate	Amount (Rs)	Commission Payable (Rs)
1.	T-Shirts (105 cms)	2300	175	4,02,500	40,250
2.	Diaries	180	270	48,600	4,860
3.	Fancy Watch (T30)	300	220	66,000	6,600
4.	Gold-plated Cutlery	6 sets	1,200	7,200	720
5.	Recorded CDs	800	275	2,00,000	20,000
	Total			7,24,300	72,430

Nett Amount payable for Quarter I (period 01.04. .... to 30.06. .... = Rs 72,430/- (Rupees Seventy two thousand and four hundred and thirty only).

As per the commercial terms settled with you, the commision on sales for a particular transaction must be realised by us within the first week of the next quarter. This is the first time that the payment of commission on sales realised has been delayed because of no reason.

We would therefore, request you to kindly issue the aforesaid payment at your earliest and oblige. If you want to have any clarification, please do let us know. Mr Ramakant would be able to explain the statement of accounts in this regard.

Thanking you,
Your faithfully,
for Maxima Gift Shop

(Geetika Aggarwal)
Partner
Encl: Accounts Statement (Transaction-wise) For Sales Commision Receivable.

A Letter from a Distributor to the Manufacturer Complaining about the Defects in Products and the Resulting Loss in Business

Ref : KL/FPL/1890 | Date: ....

M/s Flow Plast Limited
H-77, Second Floor
Maya Industrial Estate Part II
Indore - 400 008
Madhya Pradesh

KA : Mr Surendra Kumar Chhabria
(Managing Director)

Dear Sir,

Sub: *Defective Goods and the Resulting Loss to Our Business*

This is in reference to the despatch of your suitcases and Vanity Bags supplied by you vide your Bill No FPL/5678 Dated .... and the visit of your Production Manager Mr V K Kamat on ...., ...

With regret, we inform you that the entire consignment of suitcases, Vanity bags, Briefcases and other moulded items was defective. The goods were loaded at our godown on ...., ... and were shifted to our showroom in Connaught Place on ...., ..., for the purpose of sale. Our quality control inspector, Mr Sharma, found three defective Vanity Bags in the godown and these items were not despatched to the showroom. Totally unaware of the quality of the goods, which is normally excellent, the quality control inspector sent all the pieces to the showroom as there was an immediate demand for the same in the showroom.

However, the reality was bitter when all the packages were opened in the showroom by our sales staff. Most of the products were without locks and keys. Nearly 50 per cent of the g were found cracked on the top (it could be du the usage of wrong or defective moulding at y end). Some of the metallic parts were worn out rusted.

The loss in terms of business and the setback to our reputation was tremendous. Our salesmen could not sell any of the new arrivals on account of the defects in these goods. In fact, so embarassing the situation was that each piece chosen by the sales staff proved to be having some defect or the other which disappointed the customer. Many of our valued and old customers left the showroom in disgust as they could not digest the bare fact that we could stock such a shoddy item.

Our showroom has a reputaion for stocking quality products, decent treatment with the customers and an efficient after-sales service. This incident has given a blow to our reputation. In fact, the meeting of our directors has endorsed a serious action on this account which could possibly include a cancellation of the distributorship of your range of luggage. This agony is unbearable as our customers and our image are highly dear and pious to us.

We would therefore, request for immediate despatch of the fresh stock against our old order No 412 Dated .... We are despatching the entire lot received vide this order as 90 per cent of the goods have been found to be rejected. The transportation would be to your account and as such, the said consignment would be sent on "To Pay" basis.

We are appending herewith the itemwise description of the defects in the goods received :

	QC Report	
Our Order No 412	Our Order Date	QC Report No 345
Your Bill No FPL/5678	Your Bill Date	QC Report Date 20.01.1999
Tested By Ram Pal Sharma	Tested on	Status Rejected Lot

S.No Item Supplied	Qty	Defects Noticed
(1) Office Brief Case	100	Cracks on the Tops of 80 % Items
(2) Vanity Bags	130	Defective Locks and Rusted Metallic Parts
(3) Suitcase (Large)	30	Handles Missing, Inner Packings Torn, Blow Holes
(4) Leather Bags	108	All Bags had Scratches and Blots
Total	368	

All Items rejected by Our QC Department

QC Superior   QC Manager   GM

If similar incidents are repeated in future, the management would be forced to take a serios action. We would therefore, request for an immediate despatch of fresh stocks and a serious inquiry into the cause of this unfortunate incident at your end.

Thanking you,
Your faithfully,
for Karishma Luggage Distributors (P) Ltd,

(Mahesh Chandra Gupta)
Director - Technical

A Soothing Letter to the Distributor who Found Defects In The Products and Suffered

Ref : FPL/KL/1890   Date: ....
M/s Karishma Luggage Distributors (P) Ltd
M-66, Near Rivoli Cinema
Connaught Circus
New Delhi 110 001
KA : Mr Mahesh Chandra Gupta
(Director - Technical)

Dear Sir,

Sub: *Defective Goods Supplied By Us*

This is in reference to the despatch of our suitcases and Vanity Bags supplied by you vide our Bill No FPL/5678 Dated 12.01. ...... and the subsequent visit of our Production Manager Mr V K Kamat on January 31. ....

It was indeed sad to note that 90 per cent of the aforeasaid consignment was found to be defective. Normally, our QC department is quite vigilant and there are no compromises on the quality front. However, the production lot of the aforesaid assignment was not handled well as the quality control inspector was on leave for four days. In his absence, there was nobody who could have taken care of the testing of the aforesaid lot.

The case of defective die was investigated by me personally on the production floor. The defect was not in the die but in the tool which held the die in position on the machine. As the die was loosely fitted, the entire production lot developed cracks and defects.

Further, the rusted locks and iron parts were examined by us for another production lot as well. Your judgement was very much correct and we appreciate your keen sense for quality. The vendor had supplied poor quality — and badly electroplated — locks and levers. We have already changed that vendor and have started procuring the spares for locks and lever mechanisms from another reputed vendor.

It was again sad to note that freshly packed pieces were found to be cracked and defective. Normally, the packing department also carries out some routine tests. But this production lot escaped the attention of the packing department as well. We have taken a serious note of this issue and the real culprits of this episode would be brought to book soon.

Further, as per your letter, the loss in terms of business reputation and sales revenue seems to be of serious proportions. We have decided to offset this trend in your local markets through the following measures :—

(A) We would advertise in the local and regional newspapers for the benefit of your customers that the production lots were defective and that they are free to return the defective luggage without any deductions. This advertisement would be at nil cost to you.

(B) The customers would be offered to buy good quality luggage at 20 per cent discount from your showroom. This would boost your sagging sales. We would supply goods at 30 per cent discount to you and as such, you stand to earn 10 per cent on the list price as against 7.5 per cent during the routine sales.

(C) We have discussed the case with our advertising agency. The agency plans to start a campaign on radio, television and in the print media for the promotion of a new brand of our range of luggage. This new range — manufactured on imported machines and with the help of German technolgy — would carry new looks for the new millennium and would have some fascinating features. The customer would be able to review his thinking about our defective products and your showroom due to this media blitzkreig. The campaign begins on March 18, ...

We have taken some stringent measures at our end and the brief description has been appended below:

Your Order No	Your Order Date	Your QC Report No
412	31.12.	345
Our Bill No	Our Bill Date	Our QC Report Date
FPL/5678	12.01.	20.01. ......
Tested By	Tested on	Status
Ram Pal Sharma	20.01.	Rejected Lot

S.No Item Supplied	Defects Noticed	Remedial Measure
(1) Office Brief Case	Cracks on the Tops of 80 % Items	Fitted New Die
(2) Vanity Bags	Defe tive Lock. And Rusted Metallic Parts	Vendor of locks and Parts changed
(3) Suitcase Large	Handles Missing, Inner Packagings Torn, Blow Holes	Packaging Department Re-shuffled
(4) Leather Bags	All Bags Had Scratches and Blots	QC Made Altert

We hope that this action plan would eliminate all possible defects in our product range on account of quality. We would like to continue our commercial transactions for many years to come. A few incidents like the aforesaid should not spoil our successful partnership.

We hope you do not contemplate a punitive measure due to this episode. On behalf of my comapny, I apologise to you for any inconvenience caused to you on account of the defective supply of goods. This shall never happen again in future.

Thanking you,
Your faithfully,
for Flow Plast Limited,

(Surendra Kumar Chhabria)
Managing Director

A Letter to A Retailer announcing price Revision and giving reason for the same

Ref.: PQRS/XYZ/001 Date: ....
M/S XYZ and Company
1913, Floor 19
Airport Road
Thane
Maharashtra
KA : Mr Suraj Thapar (Director)

Dear Sir,

Sub: *Revision of Prices of Our Product Range*

This is to inform you that the prices of our 'Natraj' Brand Radio Sets have been increased with effect from 01.02. .... The details of revision of the prices are as under :—

(A) Natraj Medium Wave Radio set - Rs 400/-
(B) Natraj Medium Wave/FM Radio set - Rs 740/-
(C) Natraj Cassette recorder with Radio - Rs 1,240/-
(D) Natraj Cassette Recorder with FM Radio - Rs 1,650/-

Please note that this represents a 10 per cent increase over the previous price list. Further, please note that sales tax would be charged extra as applicable. The union budget (....... - ....) would be declared by the end of February .... New sales tax rates or excise duties levies would be decided for the financial year .... - .... in this budget. The increase in prices — proposed by us — was inevitable because of a steep hike in import duty or electronic components. This price was declared by union government on 8-1-.... We regret the incovenience cause to you on account of this price increase.

Thanking You,

Yours faithfully,

for PQRS Private Ltd,

(Sunil Taneja)

Manager - Marketing

Encl : Latest Price List

A Letter to a vendor asking for timely supplies of goods

Ref: MPL/SPPL/004 Date:

M/s Sharda Ply Products Ltd

1920, Floor 19

Raheja Chambers

Nariman Point

Mumbai - 400 068

Maharashtra

K A : Mr Sunil Tondon (Marketing Manager)

Dear Sir,

Sub: *Supply of Plywood*

This is in reference to the latest consignment of plywood received by us on April 28, ...

I would like to draw your attention to the delayed supply of ply-wood. Please note that the aforesaid consignment of goods were supposed to reach us, latest by April 15, ... However, this consignment has been received after a delay of 13 days. Similarly, the despatches against previous purchase orders have also been delayed during the recent past. This is a serious issue and deserves your immediate attention. It must be pointed out here that the delayed supply of raw materials from your end leads to a total disruption of production schedule at our end. Therefore, we are not able to make our furniture according to our production schedules.

It may further be noted that this issue was raised by our Manager (Purchase) when he paid you a visit on March 28, ... We regret to note that the same trend is being repeated time and again. This is causing a great inconvience to our valued customers and hence, to our business.

We therefore, request you to please look into the matter and to streamline the supply of plywood from your end. Please note that if erratic supply of goods continues from your end, then we would be forced to locate another vendor for this raw material.

Thanking you,

For Modern Products Ltd

(Rohit Khanna)

Deputy General Manager - Purchase

A Letter to a trading house asking for quotations of products

Ref : LTC/MPL/018 Date: ....

M/S Mahendra Plastics Ltd

2890, Street 10

Shakespere Sarani

Calcutta - 700 223

West Bengal

K A: Mr Sushil Chatterji (Manager-Marketing)

Dear Sir,

Sub: *Sourcing of high quality Toys For Our Customer in the USA.*

We take pleasure to introduce ourselves as a leading exporters of Fast Moving Customer Goods (FMCGs) to Europe and the USA. Our annual turnover exceeds US $ 2.8 million.

One of our valued customers in the USA has expressed his interest in purchasing the following products from a reputed Indian vendor :—

(a) Plastic Tricycle for children aged 3 years
(b) Colourful Blocks for children aged 3 years
(c) Battery powered cars, animals and other toys for children upto 6 years
(d) Plastic trays, plates and kitchen toys for female children upto the age of 7 years.

We plan to buy one large container for export to the USA. We would need high quality samples from your end for getting approval from the customer. The sample submitted by you shall be free of cost to us and shall not be returned.

Please send us a complete profile of your company,

export orders handled, if any, entire product range, your current price list and the prices of the items described for the purpose of export. Please note that we would not be able to process your correspondence if your response does not include two samples for each catagory of products. Your response should reach our office latest by July 20, ...

Thanking you,
For Leo Toy Company

(Gaurav Taneja)
Manager - Vendor Development

An Offer for Sole Distributorship

Ref : TT/MD/045 Date:...........
M/s Modern Distributors
6709, Kucha Ali Sher
Khari Baoli
Delhi - 110 006
K A : Mr Sureshbhai (Proprietor)

Dear Sir,

Sub: *Offer of Sole Distributorship of Our Range of Spices*

This is in reference to your letter no MD/56/008 dated January 2, ... and your subsequent visit to our office on January 10, ..., regarding the aforesaid.

Keeping in mind your vast experience in the field of spices trade as well your market reputation, we are pleased to offer you the sole distributorship of our range of spices for the entire Delhi state. The terms and conditions of the distributorship would be as follows :—

(A) You would be appointed as the distributor for the entire state of Delhi and the sale of our product range would be done by you within the state limits of Delhi.

(B) You would appoint the retailers for the distribution of our range of spices at a cost to you and you would also settle the commercial terms and conditions with them keeping in mind the broad guidelines which have been described in detail as follows.

(C) The company would supply you the follwing products :—

(C1) TT Brand Garam Masala.
(C2) TT Brand Degi Mirch.
(C3) TT Brand Chane Masala.
(C4) TT Brand Coriander Powder.
(C5) TT Brand Black Pepper (Ground).

All the products are available in 50 gm, 100 gm and 250 gm packings for the convenience of our customers. Please note that our 100 gm and 250 gm packings are more in demand than the 50 gm packings on account of lower cost per unit of the product. But you would be free to explore the markets for the 50 gm packings as well.

(D) You would supply the products to your retailers at a cost to you and the company would not be responsible for distribution to your retailers. Similarly, the collection of payments from your retailers would also be your responsibility.

(E) In no case, shall your retailers resort to the sale of spurious spices alongwith the sale of TT brand of spices. They are free to sell any other reputed brand of spices but if they are also selling the sub-standard spices along with the TT brand of products, you would cancel the retailership of the party with immediate effect. The objective is to isolate the TT brand of products from sub-standard and spurious products.

(F) Although your retailers would be allowed to sell any other brand of spices, yet you would not be allowed to be the sole distributor of any brand of spices. If you wish to opt out, you would be required to give a notice of at least three months in advance to the company. The stocks already with you would either be sold off by you or would be lifted by the company before the final culmination of the distributorship contract. The stocks lifted by the company would be sold off by the company through its other channels. The payment would be made to you after these leftover stocks have been sold off.

(G) You would be required to pay Rs. 1,00,000 (Rupees one lakh only) as the earnest money.

This amount would be in the form of a Bank Draft and drawn in favour of M/s TT Spice Products Private Limited. This amount is refundable if you wish to opt out of the distributorship. The payment would be made however, only after the deduction of all the liabilities, if any, to the company.

(H) The commercial terms and conditions of the distributorship are as follows :—

(H1) You would be entitled for a discount of 40% on the sale price of all the products of TT brand.

(H2) Your retailers would be entitled to a discount of 20% on the sale price of all the products of TT brand.

(H3) The company would deliver the product at your Khari Baoli godown at nil cost to you. The unloading costs would be to your account.

(H4) All the sundry costs regarding transportation, handling and delivery to your retailers in the entire territory of Delhi state would be to your account. You can chalk out the terms and conditions with your retailers at your convenience.

(H5) The goods would be delivered to you after you place an order on us through telephone or through a message delivered by hand or by courier.

(H6) The goods would be delivered by the comapny at its cost to your godown within seven days from the receipt of the order.

(H5) The goods would be delivered to you after you place an order on telephone or through a message delivered by hand or by courier.

(H6) The goods would be delivered by the comapny at its cost to your godown within seven days from the receipt of the order.

(H5) The authorised representative of the comapny would collect the payments on the seventh day of every month. If that day is a holiday, then the day before the holiday (ie, the sixth day) would be deemed to be the payment collection day.

(H6) If the requisite payments for the previous month are not realised (in the form of a cheque), then an interest at the rate of 3% (flat) would be charged and your account would be debited with the same after duly informing you about the details.

(H7) The accounts reconciliation as well as the stocks reconciliation would be carried out on September 25 of every year and on March 22 of every year in order to clarify the accounts or to eliminate the accounting anomalies, if any.

If the terms and conditions mentioned above suit you, please inform us about your consent and meet us personally. We would be pleased to accept you in our operations as the major channel partner.

Thanking you,

Yours faithfully,

for TT Spice Products Private Ltd

(Kailash Aggarwal)

Director - Marketing

A Letter to a Customer Asking for the Immediate Clearance of a Dishonoured Cheque

Ref : SPL/DRM/0456 Date : . .

M/s D.R. Marketing Limited

560, Floor 8

Lohar Chawl

Mumbai - 400 078

Maharashtra

K A: Mr R K Kulkarni (Director - Finance and Accounts)

Dear Sir,

Sub: *Your Dishonoured Cheque No 567034 Dated ... .*

We regret to inform you that the aforesaid cheque has been dishonoured by your bank M/s Syndicate

Bank, Lohar Chawl on account of lack of funds in your CC Account.

We have taken a serious note of this issue. You should recall that another cheque issued by you was dishonoured by your bank during December, ... , on account of lack of sufficient funds in your CC account. During that time period, our payments to our vendors were affected adversely and funds circulation was also hit. It is a pity to note that the same incident has been repeated within a period of one month.

We would therefore, request you to either issue a fresh cheque in lieu of the dishonoured cheque or inform us when we could present the same in our bank.

We would also request you to kindly avoid such incidents in future as this could affect our future transactions. We, however, extend full cooperation in this regard in case the financial problems at your end could be sorted out within a period of three months.

We would always strive for building long lasting relationships despite the problems faced by us.

Thanking you,
for Speciality Products Limited,

(Ramakant Sahai)
Marketing Director - West

A Soothing Letter to a Party which Suffered on Account of your Dishonoured Cheque

Ref : DRM/SPL/23 Date: ....

M/s Speciality Products Limited
12-A, Tardeo - Thane Road
Pune - 423 098
Maharashtra
K A: Mr Ramakant Sahai (Marketing Director - West)

Dear Sir,

Sub: *Our Dishonoured Cheque No. 567034 Dated 11.03. ....*

We are in receipt of your letter no SPL/DRM/0456 dated March 23, ... and have noted the contents therein.

We are really concerned that the aforesaid cheque has been dishonoured by our bank M/s Syndicate Bank, Lohar Chawl on account of lack of funds in our CC Account. Another cheque issued by you was dishonoured by our bank during December, ... on account of lack of sufficient funds in our account. That was the lean period of business and shortage of funds was inevitable. However, the second case of dishonoured cheque was totally unexpected. We have sufficient funds in our CC Account and there should have been no problem in clearing the aforementioned cheque.

We are looking into the matter and are getting in touch with M/s Syndicate Bank, Lohar Chawl, Mumbai. In all probability, your cheque was presented a bit earlier than the presentation of the draft in our bank which was meant for clearing this cheque.

Kindly present this cheque in your bank as soon as you receive this letter. The requisite amount has been deposited in our account so that your cheque could be honoured this time.

We assure you that such incidents would not be repeated in future. The concerned official and our bank have already been briefed in this regard.

Thanking you,
for D R Marketing Limited

(R K Kulkarni)
Director - Finance and Accounts

A letter to the Editor, *The Hindustan Times*, Kasturba Gandhi Marg, New Delhi - 110 001, about the growing importance of commercial art as career option

Ref : SS/HT/001 Date: ....

The Editor
The Hindustan Times
Kasturba Gandhi Marg
New Delhi - 110 001

Dear Sir,

Sub: *Career Options in Commercial Arts*

I want to draw your kind attention towards a change in career trends during the new millennium. I hope you would allow it to be published in the columns of your esteemed daily on Sunday.

To be sent to Press

Career Options in Commercial Arts

The next century has opened fresh career options before the youth. The young students and graduates are no longer in the conventional careers of Engineering, Medicine, Law or Architecture. They have opened their minds for more lucarative and creative careers which were side-lined earlier in favour of the mainstream career options. Commercial art is a vast discipline. Commercial artist can be of two types. The first catagory is of creative planning professionals. Art director, visualiser, copywriter, editor and senior artist fall under this catagory. These professionals are creative and their knowledge bases are highly sophisticated. These professionals make millions if they find right work environments.

The second catagory is of creative execution professionals. Junior artists, draftsmen, junior editors and artwork makers fall under this catagory. These professionals are not creative but they help in the consolidation of creativity of professionals from the first catagory. They are more technology oriented.

The creative people could be arts, science , engineering or management graduates. Even an arts or a commerce graduate could take up commercial arts as a career. All the commercial artists are essentially connected to media. They are trained at institutes of mass communication, creativity, advertising, cinema and other institutes which are connected with media.

The shift towards commercial arts was obvious because our institutes had already churned a lot of engineering, medicine, accounting, management and law professionals. Because of this glut, these professionals could not find lucrative jobs or satisfying careers in the markets. Hence, commercial artists were the obvious choices of the companies in the wake of rising exposure of their products and services through media. In fact, every firm wants to be promoted. Media help in efficient and quick promotion. And commercial artists make up the soul of media. The shift towards commercial arts as a career option is therefore, justified.

Thanking you,
Yours faithfully,

(Shashi Sahai)
56, Floor 4
Regarpura
Karol Bagh
New Delhi - 110 005

A letter to your friend Informing him about the Ill-effects of Drugs

789, Palace Building
Court Road
Allahabad - 345 890
Uttar Pradesh
July 12, ...

My Dearest Friend Mithilesh,

I received your telephonic message a few hours ago. I was not at home and hence, I could not talk to you about a very serious matter. How are you? And how are my dearest *Uncle Ji* and *Auntie Ji*? Give my Namaste to them. And I hope that our sweet little sister Namrata must have done well in her Class VIII examinations. Do write to me about her health.

Dear Mithilesh! Perhaps you could recall that when we were school-going boys, we had a friend named Rajat. We used to go for movies quite often. I hope you would be able to recall. It is a tragedy that Rajat has expired after a prolonged illness at the age of eighteen years. Rajat was a very good friend of mine. I knew his parents and brother very well. They informed me that he died due to the ill-effects of drugs.

My dear! This tragedy is unbearable for the family of Rajat. He was the eldest son of his parents. He took to drugs when he was fourteen. He started consuming smack and brown sugar and was in a bad company of drunkards and drug addicts. This bad habit took its toll. His body could not tolerate the excessive dosages of drugs during the four years of consumption. Although he was admitted in a rehabilitation clinic, yet the doctors could not save him. Therefore, the drug menace took one more toll on July 10, ...

This is a lesson for all the young boys and girls like us. Drugs have not spared anybody. In all the major and minor metroplises, drug addicts are increasing in number. Their consumption is also increasing. The popular drugs are Hashish, Brown Sugar, Smack and Heroin Besides these narcotics, students and young people also take medicines like Valium, Luminol, Mandrex and other drugs which have medicinal values. They use these medicines for the sake of fun and therefore, suffer due to their ill-effects.

Drugs work in a very strange manner. Once the boy or the girl uses it, then he or she cannot avoid it. The narcotics develop a tendency for addiction in the brain even if they are taken once by the person. They also induce a tendency for more consumption. The addict goes into a new world of fantasies and peace. This is a superficial and imaginary world because as soon as the effect of the drug is over, he finds himself in severe physical and mental pains. He is forced to consume another dose of the drug. If he is not given the injection or the puff of the drug, he could turn violent also. Drugs lead to negativistic and criminal tendencies in the minds of the individual. For the sake of his drug related needs, he becomes a drug peddler and eventually, becomes a hardcore criminal.

The same thing happened in the case of Rajat. Police arrested him twice but allowed him to be treated in the Drug Rehabilitation Centre. There were three cases of illegal drug traffic pending against him. The drug addict cannot come out of the criminal web in which he is caught on account of his drug requirements. Studies, health and family are sidelined. I would like to tell you that Rajat was an athlete and had won inter-engineering competitions. However, he was reduced to a mere skeleton due to drug intake.

A drug addict with a criminal record is a boon for the crime lords of the underworld. He is a headache for the police and a tragedy for the family. There is no escape from this evil if he is a heavy addict. But if the addiction is in a nascent stage, then the doctors are certainly able to help. You must note that the doctors too have to give mild doses of drugs to the patients in order to keep them alive. If these minor doses are not given, the craving for drugs could lead to serious problems and even death.

The treatment of such patients requires great patience, perseverance and sympathy. Many boys and girls want to come out of this evil net but are unable to do so because of a lack of moral support from the family. The police is always on the lookout for such addicts and gives them a shoddy treatment. The family, the doctors and the law-enforcing agencies must adopt positive, constructive and sympathetic attitudes towards these addicts. After all, they are mentally sick and not criminals. Their mental anomalies could be eliminated if detected at an early stage. Further, the physical problems and drug addiction could be cured through a planned programme of counselling, medicines and by support from the members of the family.

My dear! I have been shaken by the sad and painful demise of my dearest friend Rajat. Through this letter, I would like to convey to you, your friends in Delhi and to every person in your social circle that drugs must be eschewed at all costs. They could destroy the family, the society and the nation. We must avoid them for a better future.

I hope that I would be with you during the autum break. I would tell you more about this menace when we meet. Please give my *Pranam* to *Uncle Ji* and *Auntie Ji* and love to dearest Namrata.

Till we meet again ....

Yours loving friend,

(Sushil Kumar Gupta)

Mr Mithilesh Chaturvedi
4561, Street 10
Kashmere Gate
Delhi - 110 006

A letter to the Executive Editor, *The Hindu*, Chennai, about the Declining Moral Values in Indian Youth

Ref : CA/HIN/001 Date: ....

The Executive Editor
The Hindu
Cathedral Road
T Nagar
Chennai - 600 089
Tamil Nadu

Dear Sir,

Sub: *Declining Moral Values in Indian Youth*

I was very much impressed by the article by Mr Rajani Kothari about the decay of institutions in *The Hindu* dated ...., ... I was deeply impressed by the contents of this article and at the same time, I was moved by the apathetic condition of our State-run institutions. I would like to draw your kind attention towards the declining moral values in Indian youth who have been directly affected by this decay in the State-run institutions. I hope you would give them space in the esteemed columns of your daily.

TO BE SENT TO PRESS

Declining Moral Values in Indian Youth

India is a growing nation. We have a rich cultural heritage and a glorious history. But according to the current international norms, we are treated as a backward and an under-developed country. We have not been able to retain the moral values which our forefathers cherished for generations. It is true that we have to develop ourselves in terms of technology, information and modern living standards as has been done in the West. But our ancient moral and cultural value systems are much superior to those of the Western culture.

We have been following the materialistic system of the West. In this process, we have adopted the malpractices of the West. We are more modern in terms of dresses, food, entertainment, marriage and other social activities. But we are way behind in terms of spiritual and moral values. We have cable television, mobile phones, jet transport, amazing varieties of food and liquor, most modern computer systems and the finest of technologies for entertainment and leisure. But we have lost grip over family system, social norms and above all, the traditional Indian cultural milieu.

The youth of today refuses to respect its elders and teachers. The boys and girls frequently take drugs and liquor. Free sex is common in the major metropolises of India. For example, the University of Delhi is not holding any classes because of the indefinite strike of the teachers. This has proved to be a boon for the students who would be more involved in the negative and morally degrading activities. This would lead to chaos and confusion in the youth as only the best educated youth would be able to get jobs.

Another aspect of declining moral values in Indian youth is the rising hooliganism in the political platforms of the schools and colleges. Students resort to violence and monetary manipulations for amassing power and money. They are used as tools by the politicians of this country. After they have been used thoroughly, they are discarded as chaff. The students themselves are responsible for this state of affairs.

Add to it, fashion shows, beauty contests, discotheques, free movement and mixing of both the genders (on campus as well as off-campus), pornographic literature and other morally harmful inputs for the youth of today. We have dangerous concoction of evils presented to the young mind in a most fascinating form. This would send our young boys and girls on an evil path of no return. The nation would be built by the youth of today. But if the youth forgets its duties, then the nation would certainly suffer on social, political moral and economic fronts.

Every problem has a solution. In the interest of the nation, we should mould the youth of today so that they could become the responsible citizens of this country in the times to come. We do not want to state that Western culture is bad. Our only contention is that some of the negative aspects of Western culture must not be adopted in Indian context as our culture and morality have not been honed according to the highly polarised cultural norms of the West. We should adopt efficiency, logic, ability to work hard and above all, scientific thinking from the West. We must not forget our family values. The concept of nuclear family is a reality in the big cities. This is a dangerous sign for our society but we must mould our family norms so that the concept of family is not lost into oblivion.

Nobody can stop the onslaught of pornographic information through CD-ROMs, Internet and cable television. The mothers must teach the children about the right moral values and the misuse of sex in the everyday life. The students must be made aware of AIDS and other deadly diseases which could ruin their lives and careers without any hope of recovery.

The making of a character of an individual depends upon that individual and the family to which he belongs. The youth of today are sensitive, intelligent, upwardly mobile and ambitious. They would do well if they adopt the techniques of modern living by using traditional Indian values as a platform for success. And it would not be difficult for them to understand this vital aspect as their future as well as the future of the nation depends upon the moral and societal directions adopted by them.

Thanking you,
Yours faithfully,

(Catherine Miller)
Flat No 434, Floor 8
South View Apartments
Mount Road
Chennai - 600 034
Tamil Nadu

A Legal Notice

REGISTERED AD

Ref : SC/0988 Date: 29.09.1999

From
Suresh Chandra Sharma
M A, L L B
Advocate - Delhi High Court
House No 3456/18
Nirankari Satsang Colony
Rajouri Garden
New Delhi - 110 062
Phone : 570 1234

To
Shri Mahesh Kumar Kasliwal
S/o Shri Ram Chandra Kasliwal
R/o T-679, Gali Matke Wali
Kashmere Gate
Delhi - 110 006

Sub: *Legal Notice*

This legal notice is hereby given to you on behalf of my client Shri Anirudh Kumar S/o Shri Radhey Shyam Mittal and r/o 906, Jor Bagh, New Delhi-110 003 and the lawful owner of T-679, Gali Matke Wali, Kashmere Gate, Delhi - 110 006.

Through this legal notice , we bring to your kind attention the illegal occupation of house No T-679, Gali Matke Wali, Kashmere Gate, Khasra No 7, Delhi 110 006, by you on the ground of non-payment of rents for the months of June, 1999, to August, 1999.

Whereas it has been made clear vide the rent deed agreement dated 18.10.1998, that you are required to pay a monthly rent of Rs 3,000 (Rupees three thousand only) to Mr Anirudh Kumar.

And whereas you have not paid any rent for the months of June, 1999, to August, 1999 and have withheld the same without any notice or intimation to my client.

And whereas you have replied in the negative whenever my client has approached you for the payment of the same.

And whereas the electricity bill, the water bill and the house tax bill, which were to be paid by you during the period of your tenancy, have not been paid by you from June, 1999, onwards. Upon raising an objection by my client, you have misbehaved with him and have added that you would not be paying any rent or incidental expenses arising out of this tenancy. This behaviour is uncalled for and totally defies the rent agreement agreed to by you as well as the societal norms which a good citizen must follow.

Through this legal notice, served through Delhi High Court, Tees Hazari and bearing number HC/ 90080/12 Dated September 29, 1999, you are hereby informed that you must clear all the dues mentioned and defined by the rent agreement in order to continue your tenancy in the house occupied by you and owned by my client.

In the event of non-payment of the dues, you would be required to vacate the said residential premises within two months from the date of this notice. You would be required to pay all the previous rents, legal fees and other expenses till the last day of your tenancy. The amount paid by you as an advance would be utilised for the clearance of the same if you choose not to conform to the terms and conditions appended in the rent agreement.

The notice is hereby given that in the event of non-conformance with this legal notice, you would be accountable in the court of law and necessary punitive measures would be taken in order to extract the payments and pending dues from you.

You can present your viewpoint through your counsel and would be given adequte opportunity for justifying your actions. You are hereby given a period of thirty days from the date of this legal notice to submit your reply failing which, an appropriate legal action would be taken against you in the designated court.

Thanking you,
Yours sincerely,

(Suresh Chandra Sharma)
Advocate -Delhi High Court

An Annual Maintenance Contract

AGREEMENT FOR ANNUAL MAINTENANCE

(A) M/s Viniyoga Steels Ltd, Mumbai

(B) M/s Computer Services Ltd, Mumbai

This agreement is entered between M/s Viniyoga Steels Ltd, 806, Floor 8, Punwani Chambers, Nariman Point, Mumbar - 401 063 and M/s Computer Services Ltd, 421, Floor 6, JVPD Scheme, opposite Cooper Hospital, Mumbai - 400 030.

In this agrement, until or unless stated otherwise, M/s Computer Services Ltd, is here-in-after called the 'Company' and the client, whose name and address is mentioned above, is here-in-after called the 'Client.'

The Company and the Client have hereby given mutual written consent for the execution of Annual Maintenance Contract as per terms and conditions mentioned below. The Client has agreed to grant the Annual Maintenance Contract, here-in-after called the AMC, to the Company and the Company has agreed to execute the same.

This AMC is for the purpose of providing maintenance services for the computer system and its peripherals as per the configuration stated, subject to the terms and conditions that form an inseparable part of this contract.

It is also accepted by the Company and the Client that the AMC service option, once exercised, is irrevocable and unalterable to any option during the contract period.

TERMS AND CONDITIONS

M/s Computer Services Ltd shall maintain the equipment subject to terms and conditions appended below :—

(1) The rates quoted are applicable to those places where the Company has Authorised Service Centres. For those areas having no Authorized Service Centres, To and Fro Charges at actuals for travel and boarding and lodging would be borne by the Client. These charges would be payable in cash before the departure of the Service Engineer from the site of the Client.

(2) The following services would be provided by the Company to the Client under this contract during the working hours of the company :—

(A) Preventive Maintenance: This would be done periodically (six times a year) irrespective of the system requirements and complaints of the Client.

(B) On-call Maintenance: The Client can ask for troubleshooting assistance from the Company in the event of an equipment breakdown.

(3) The Company reserves the right to revise annual maintainance charges in case of any upgradation of technology in the main system or in its peripherals.

(4) This contract is renewable on expiry. All renewals are to be made before expiry. All those services rendered by the Company, which are not under AMC, would be charged as per our standard rates on per-call basis. The Company also reserves the right to revise the AMC charges at the time of renewal of the AMC or at the time when the system is moved into a new location.

(5) The Client would provide access to the system so as to enable the Service Engineers of the Company to rectify the faults and to carry out preventive maintenance.

(6) The system and its peripherals are to be used strictly in accordance with the instructions given in the User's Manual. The customer shall take utmost care of the equipment, shall house it in suitable operation-worthy conditions and shall follow such instructions on these matters from time to time as may be given by the Service Engineers of the Company.

(7) No alterations are to be made without any prior intimation to the Company. No attachments

are to be fitted or repairs or adjustments are to be carried out except those carried out by the Company. If it is deemed necessary that alterations are to be carried out by the Client, a prior written consent of the Service Engineer of the Company is a must.

(8) No equipment or part thereof shall be moved except by the Service Engineers of the Company or by a person authorised by the Company and with the prior written consent of the Company.

(9) The replaced parts become property of the company.

(10) This AMC excludes the following :—

(10A) Any work external to the system such as rectification of electrical faults, air conditioners, electrical wiring etc.

(10B) The AMC shall not cover the following:—

(10B1) Printer ribbons.

(10B2) Floppies.

(10B3) Malfunctioning due to misuse, accident, neglect or due to failure to abide by the safety recommendations on the part of the Client.

(10B4) Painting and refurnishing of the system cabinet or any other part.

(10B5) Malfunctioning due to the usage of consumables or media which are not approved by the Company.

(10B6) The component costs of the system (In case the system under contract requires replacement of components, the cost of components or spares would be to the Client's account.

(10B7) Malfunctioning due to the usage of media infected by virus (This AMC does not cover retrieval of corrupted data on a working hard disk. User is required to maintain back-ups).

(11) No part of this contract can be altered by dealers or any other person who is not authorised by the Company. In case of any such alteration, the Company cannot be held liable.

(12) The company shall not be liable for failure to perform due to *Force Majeure'*, fires, storms, earthquakes, explosions, accidents, strikes, lockouts, industrial disputes, labour troubles, transportation embargoes, imminence or existence of any state of emergency, war-like conditions, riots, inability to obtain any material or parts, refusal of licence or impositions or sanctions by the government and/or any such measures taken by the government which render it impossible for the Company to perform its obligation under this Contract.

(13) If the Client commits any breach of this contract and fails to remedy it promptly upon receiving notice from the Company, the Company reserves the right to terminate the Contract without any liability whatsoever. In case, the Client is totally disappointed by the services provided by the Company, the Company is liable to refund the Client the balance depending upon the remaining time period of contract. This amount shall be mutually agreed upon after deducting all the expenses and liabilities.

(14) This AMC shall be deemed to be located at Delhi and is valid for installed equipment at the site of the Client. However, the AMC is subject to the jurisdiction of the Delhi and New Delhi courts only.

On behalf of the Client, I __________ working for the Company/Firm called __________ in the position of __________ do hereby confirm and agree without any coercion and pressure that I agree to the terms and conditions mentioned in this AMC contract on this __________ day of __________

Name	Designation	Signatures	Date
________	________	________	________

On behalf of the Company, I __________ working for the Company/Firm called M/s Computer Services Ltd in the position of __________ do hereby confirm and agree without any coercion and pressure that I agree to the terms and conditions mentioned in this AMC contract on this __________ day of __________.

Name Designation Signatures Date

TECHNICAL SPECIFICATIONS OF THE CONTRACT

NAME OF THE CLIENT:

ADDRESS:

CONTACT PERSON:

PHONE / FAX:

MACHINE SPECS WITH PERIPHERALS:

MACHINE LOCATION:

OFFICE TIMINGS:

AUTHORIZED SERVICE CENTRE IN THE AREA:

ENGINEER/IN-CHARGE:

IN-CHARGE OF AREA:

CONTRACT STARTS ON:

CONTRACT ENDS ON:

A Written Consent/Quotation for the Supply of Goods

Ref : CPL/SPL/045 Date : 12.03.1999

M/s Super Products Ltd
No 620, Phase-I
Jia Sarai
New Delhi - 110 017
K A : Mr Amit Nagpal (Managing Director)

Dear Sir,

Sub: *Supply of 800 Kgs of Zinc Oxide on Monthly Basis*

This is in reference to the visit of your Mr Anil Nagpal (Director-Technical) to our factory on March 10, 1999 and our subsequent quotation number TPL/8700 dated March 10, 1999, regarding the aforesaid.

We are pleased to inform you that we would able to supply 800 kgs of Zinc Oxide as per the terms and conditions appended below :—

(A) Material to be Supplied : Zinc Oxide.
(B) Purity : 94 % minimum.
(C) Packing : 10-kg bags of HDPE.
(D) Quantity : 800 kgs.
(E) Supply Schedule : 10 bags of 10 kgs each every month starting from 01.04.1999.
(F) First Delivery : April 1999
(G) Last Delivery : Novermber 1999
(H) Price : Rupees 34.50 per kg.
(I) Delivery : FOB Rail From Our Factory in Coimbatore.
(J) Advance : 50 % of the Bill Amount. Balance in October 1999 before the last consignment.
(K) Transport : Material would be despatched by Rail and all the expenses related to transportation en-route would be borne by you.

Kindly issue a confirmed purchaser order to this effect and oblige. Please note that the payment must be in the form of bank draft. The delivery of the product is subject to realisation of the payment at our end.

Thanking you,
Yours faithfully,
for Continental Products Ltd,

(Sebestian Milton)
Sales Manager - North

Accounts Reconciliation with a Customer

Ref : KPL/MBSL/062 Date : 12.04.1999

M/s Metal Box Specialities Ltd
55, Phase-II
Industrial Estate
Coimbatore - 400 962
Tamil Nadu

K A : Mr P Gomes (Manager Accounts)

Dear Sir,

Sub: *Accounts Reconciliation for the Accounting Year Ending on 31.03.1999*

This is in reference to the visit of the undesigned to your office on March 25, 1999, regarding the aforesaid and your Statement of Account sent to us vide your Letter No MBSL/425 dated April 6, 1999. We are pleased to give you the details of Accounts Reconciliation Statement for the fiscal year ending on March 31, 1999, as follows:

S No	Date	Particulars	Amount Gr	Amount Dr
1.	18.09.1998	By Bill No 420 dated 18.09.1998		5000.00
2.	27.09.1998	By Bill No 605 dated 27.09.1998		725.00
3.	12.01.1999	By Bill No 719 dated 12.01.1999		2300.00
4.	11.03.1999	To Goods Returned vide Debit Note No 45 dated 11.03.1999	7000.00	
		Balance		1025.00 (Dr)

After accounts reconcilliation, the net amount due to us is Rupees 1,025 (Rupees One Thousand and Twenty Five Only).

Please send a cheque for Rupees 1,025 only towards the clearance of accounts for the financial year ending on 31.03.1999. Kindly acknowledge receipt of the same and oblige.

Thanking you,
Yours faithfully,
for Kinetic Products Ltd

(Susheel Nadkarni)
General Manager - Accounts

A Letter to a Customer Sending Consignment of Electric Motors as your Father is not in the City due to Some Work

Ref: SEPL/CCL/0234 Dated : 18.06.1999

M/s Cosmo Constructions Ltd
1912, Floor 19
Chiranjiv Towers
90, Nehru Place
New Delhi - 110 019.
K A: Mr Sushant Aggarwal (Manager Purchase)

Dear Sir,

Sub: *Supply of Electric Motors Against Your PO No CCL/836 Dated 02.02.1999.*

We are in receipt of your letter no CCL/45 dated 11.06.1999, regarding supply of electric motors.

Please note that my father, Mr Surinder Rajvansh, is out of town and as such, we would not be able to supply the entire quantity of 62 (sixty two) motors against your PO for the month of June, 1999. However, we are despatching 37 (thirty seven) motors so that your operations are not adversely affected. Please note that we have not been able to procure copper and stampings for the manufacture of the motors. My father has gone to Mumbai in order to import these products through our Import Agent based in Mumbai.

We are appending herewith the details of the 37 motors despatched on 16.06.1999 :—

(A) Product - Electric Motor
(B) Specifications - 415 V, 3 Phase AC, Class A Insulation, Frame B-14
(C) Quantity - 37 Nos
(D) Price - Rs 2,037 per pc
(E) Packing - All the motors have been packed in wooden cases and the cartons have been provided with stuffings of three-ply cardboard to ensure safe transit.
(F) Excise Duty - Included
(G) Sales Tax - 4% against form C
(H) Payment - As per PO
(I) Documents Enclosed
  (a) Invoice
  (b) QC Certificate
  (c) BIS Certificate (Photocopy)
  (d) Challan
  (e) Original GR

The goods have been despatched vide GR No 2037 dated 17.06.1999, through M/s Jaipur Golden

Transport Co on June 18, 1999. The consignment is likely to reach your godown on 28.06.1999 and has been sent on FOR basis. Regarding the short supply of the rest of the goods, my father would get in touch with you as soon as he is back.

Thanking you,
Yours faithfully,
for General Electric Pvt Ltd,

(Gautam Rajvansh)
Encl:- a/a

PARAGRAPH WRITING

1. A LITTLE ACT OF SOCIAL SERVICE

To most of the people, the very word "hospital" comes in mind with some painful and disgusting associations, though to some who some time got a new lease of life there, the hospital is a source of life and doctors and nurses are angels. I often visit the hospital for a little social service to the poor, needy and suffering patients. But my visit last Sunday will ever remain fresh in my memory. I went there in the morning as usual. But I was soon started by loud shrieks and agonising cries from the main gate. I at once rushed to that side. I saw a young boy on a stretcher covered with a cloth soaked in blood. Behind him his mother was coming presenting a hysterical figure. I learnt that the poor boy had been crushed under a truck. He was the only son of the woman who was too poor to pay for his treatment. I was immensely moved. I at once took charge of the boy. I paid his bills and got him admitted into the hospital. I, without a moment's hesitation, donated my blood to save his life, though I knew he belonged to a different religion. "Humanity is, after all, one," said I to myself. Now the boy is out of danger to the great delight of my heart.

2. THE RED CROSS *OR* HENRI DUNANT

The Red Cross is a symbol which undertakes to help the wounded soldiers and ailing human beings. Now it is known to everybody. It was started by a French man, Henri Dunant. He was a banker who saw the great human slaughter in the battle of Solferino, fought on 24th June, 1859 between the French and the Sardinians on one side and Austrians on the other. He was so much moved at the plight of the wounded soldiers that the idea of the Red Cross at once went across his mind. He arranged about three hundred volunteers from the nearly villages and helped the wounded soldiers, irrespective of their nationality, with water, bandages, etc. Since then the Red Cross Movement has spread all over the world. So far, it has helped millions of wounded soldiers and ailing people with medicines and in other ways without distinction or discrimination. Henri wrote a book in 1861 "A Memory of Solferino" which aroused the conscience of the people. He died in 1910. Let us be voluntary assistants in this humanitarian movement.

3. INDIA AS A NUCLEAR POWER

India has made tremendous progress since independence. Now she has become a nuclear power. She made her first nuclear explosion at Pokharan is Rajasthan in 1974. Thereafter, she went on developing her nuclear power but made no more explosion. It is again in May 1998 that she made more nuclear underground explosions, including thermo-nuclear ones, *i.e.*, hydrogen bomb. India became the sixth nuclear power but Pakistan soon became the seventh as she too made nuclear explosions in Chagai within a few days. There was a mixed reaction to these explosions within and outside the country. Certain countries, including USA and

Japan imposed sanctions against India. There has been only a limited effect of these sanctions on India. To be a nuclear power is a costly affair. A strict control and vigil has to be maintained. The development of the nuclear weapons, particularly the delivery system entails a lot of expenditure. But no price is too high for the defence of the country.

4. THE MEDIA AND THE HUMAN RIGHTS

The media can play an important role in safeguarding human rights. It was the media that brought to focus the holocaust in Rawanda and Bosnia. The media has the collective power to stir human conscience to action. Even in India, media has played an important role in this respect in the matter of custodial deaths, fake encounters, mass burials, inhuman exploitation of bonded labour by heartless contractors, satanic conditions of mental hospitals, sexual molestation of women, diabolical theft of human organs, death dance of casteist carnage as in Bihar, etc. But media has much more role to play in highlighting the extremes of poverty and exploitation when little children have to fight for a piece of bread with dogs over a garbage heap and when the opportunities for progress virtually exist only for the selected elite. Instead of focusing too much on beauty pageants, cinema stars and their dogs, as for instance, on the death of Rakha's "Pists", they should realise their duties towards the vast mass of poor masses that comprise the real society.

5. EARLY MARRIAGE

In earlier times, people were illiterate and did not know things as the proper time for marriage. Though amusing it may seem now, there was some time a deal struck between two pregnant women that if they gave birth to children of opposite sexes, the children would be married. However, ringing wedding bells of toddlers was quite common and is not quite uncommon even now among the tribals and people of lower classes who are mostly illiterate and not such conversant with the ways of the modern world. At first, there was the Sharda Act, according to which a girl below the age of 16 years and a boy below 18 couldn't be marriage. Now, according to the new marriage act, the proper minimum age for girls is 18 and for boys is 21. Like the earlier Sharda Act, the new act is also violated with impurity among several communities, even if not to that extent. The system of child marriage can be abolished only through social awakening. According to the medical specialists, the girl's uterus is not quite strong to hold the child safely before the age of 18 and thus early marriage is dangerous both for the child and the mother. Moreover, India is already over populated country and late marriage is one of the ways of solving the population problem to some extent.

6. AREN'T THE POOR THEMSELVES RESPONSIBLE FOR THEIR POVERTY?

Poor people often blame the rich people for their miserable state without realising that more than anybody else, they themselves may be responsible for their present state. They charge the rich people with having usurped their rights. That may be true in certain totalitarian, Fascist or dictatorial states, but probably not in democratic and welfare states. In a country like India, everybody has got the freedom of speech and to take up any trade or profession which should not be a nuisance to others. Everybody has equal opportunities with every one. It is admitted that those with money-power can avail themselves of more opportunities, but those comparatively less well-placed monetarily, can beat others by dint of hard work and systematic planning and will-power for which much often expertise or external help is not necessary. Even, otherwise, there are certain facilities only for the poor. For example, food subsidy alone (for the poor) for the year 1998-

99 is above Rs. 10,000 crores. There is a two tier system of rates at the Public Distribution System (PDS) ration depots—one for those above the poverty line (APL) and the others for those below it for whom there is central issue price (CIP) which is lower than the former. So, the poor must work hard and not blame others for all their ills.

7. PRIORITIES OF MODERN YOUTH

So far, it was believed that the modern youth is unconcerned with life and suspicious about future. But now, at least, in middle class and upper middle class families, the youths are quite awakened and conscious about the possibilities of their careers. In a survey conducted by the A & M-QRG-MARG in January, 1999, in Delhi, Mumbai, Calcutta and Chennai, of 25 points listed as priorities, the Career Ambition comes at the top. Parents' background/profession occupies the second place. Having a girl/boy friend is at S.No. 13 and going to pub or discos is still lower at No. 22. The modern youth is fond of branded clothes opting it at No. 3 and he loves music, opting it at No. 5. He wants a separate room for himself (No. 6) and desires Internet at home (No. 9). He has placed cellophone at No. 10. His role models are not 'dadas' or mere actors and actresses (though he opts for Shah Rukh Khan) but also Sachin Tendulkar, Amartya Sen and Arundhati Roy. He rejects smoking and drinking placing them at bottom at S. No. 24 and 25 respectively. Thus the modern youth whom the social scientists sometimes call "Generation X" or "Generation Next" or even "India's First Internet Generation" have so much positive and optimistic about them.

8. GETTING UP EARLY *OR* A TASTE OF CONVERSATIONAL HUMOUR

"When do you get up?" I asked my bosom friend, Mukand. "On the first crowing of the cock," replied he. "How horrible! You're so primitive! Why don't you keep an alarm clock by your side?" I asked. "Oh, why should I bother about clocks even during holidays? I keep a clock beside me only during examination," replied he, while taking a turn in his bed. "But supposing you don't hear the first crowing of the cock?" said I. "Then I don't get up. The call which I hear first will be the first one for me," he replied confidently. "Then why haven't you got up so far? The sun has risen high in the sky and the cock must have crowed many times?" I asked. "No, I'm hearing the first crowing of the cock right now and I'm just getting up," answered he smilingly. "Oh! You humorous one ever!" said I, returning the smile. "Yes, of course, Spice of life!" Was his oral missive, while eyeing me obliquely.

9. UNION IS STRENGTH *OR* UNITED WE STAND, DIVIDED WE FALL

"Union is strength" and "United we stand, divided we fall," are the synonymous sayings which are true to life. In a house where all the members of the family are united, there is peace and an atmosphere of security and rapid and determined progress. A nation which remains united even at the oddest hour in history, comes out triumphant at last. Otherwise, it is bound to fall a prey to slavery, as happened with India when the notorious betrayal by Jai Chand took place. The Britishers established their kingdom in India by attacking one ruler after the other. Had the Indian rulers helped one another, there would have been no British rule in India. Even afterwards, they played the Hindus and the Muslims against each other and ruled by this policy of "divide and rule" by bringing about a communal division. Let us, the Indians of all communities, religions, regions and castes remain united to safeguard the security and sovereignty of our motherland and ensure its rapid progress.

10. THOSE WHO LIVE IN GLASS HOUSES SHOULD NOT THROW STONES AT OTHERS

It is very easy to criticise others, but very difficult to show something achieved. There is a story of the painter who put one of his paintings at a cross with the direction: 'Cross the Mistakes." The next day, he found the whole picture was smeared with crosses. Now, he fixed the direction: "Correct the Mistakes. "The next day, he found that none of the mistake had been corrected. So, it is very easy to pick holes in others. As human beings, we must realise that we are all having faults of different kinds. Instead of finding fault with others, we should apply the principle of introspection to ourselves and make efforts to correct our own faults. Just think of a smoker advising a young man not to smoke, a gambler advising his children not to gamble. If a man has his own weaknesses, how can he take others to task for their weaknesses? One who insults others, should first try to understand that he too can be insulted. So, why not have a sober outlook of mutual respect and help and cooperation?

11. NOTHING SUCCEEDS LIKE SUCCESS *OR* EVERYBODY SALUTES THE RISING SUN

This proverb means that when a person is successful in a venture, everybody is all praise for him. The person who fails in life is condemned and depreciated by one and all. Nobody just pauses to ponder over the fact that the two persons may be having different circumstances to pass through. It is wrongly believed that in all cases, man is the maker of his own destiny. There is a general tendency among the common people to follow others like sheep. If a shopkeeper succeeds in alluring a number of customers to his side, many more are likely to follow suit, ignoring in general the quality of his goods and if once he succeeds, he can rule the roost and even improve upon the quality of his goods if he is careful. In Thomas Hardy's novels, fate and chance are the main thing. Even if Shakespeare believes that character is destiny, solutions to so many problems even in his dreams lie in happenings.

12. BETTER ALONE THAN IN BAD COMPANY

"Man is a social animal," says Aristotle, one of the greatest philosophers of the world. It is also said, "A man who lives alone, must either be a beast or a God." As human beings we are bound to live in company only, man being a gregarious animal. The earliest men lived in tribes and clans. Then grew the family and society. The emergence of nations is only a recent phenomenon. But, unfortunately, sometimes in life, man is surrounded by such people who have a dubious reputation and are hall-bent to lead him on a wrong path. Despite all one's remonstrances, things may not taper off to any progressional or salubrious end with the result that man must either fall in line with others, however suspicious their credentials, or fend for oneself alone. The same counsel in such an eventuality is shun, had company whatever the price or "Better alone than in bad company."

13. TOO MANY COOKS SPOIL THE BROTH *OR* SO MANY MENS' RESPONSIBILITY IS NO MAN'S RESPONSIBILITY

If we want to do anything efficiently, we must entrust the completion of its different components to different persons who should be considered responsible for the job entrusted to them. A joint responsibility is meaningless, since in that case, we can't know about the shirker and the whole project comes to nought. If the duty of man is fixed to do a particular job, he can get the assistance of others who he trusts and considers helpful, but overall responsibility will be his own and in this way, even if he is to supervise an enterprise, he will supervise it most diligently. This will on the one hand be a good method of avoiding waste and on the other hand a guarantee against the duplication of a particular which is the other name of waste and delay.

14. LOVE BEGETS LOVE *OR* ONE GOOD TURN DESERVES ANOTHER

It is a fallacious assumption to believe that all human beings are bad. We know there is a divine spark in everybody. Basically, every man is a good man. Only some circumstances or external impressions or experiences make him an evil person. Therefore, to believe that if you do a good turn, you will not get a positive response, is illogical. Even ferocious animals are said to respond to the gestures of love and alliance. We know the story of the lion and the mouse. That may be just an academic exercise. But we know for certain how animals like dogs, cats, cows, horses and even tigers and lions grow friendly to a loving man. In the Jungle Book, the boy Mougli who grews among animals, is rightly loved by them.

15. THERE ARE MORE THINGS IN HEAVEN AND EARTH THAN ARE FOUND IN PHILOSOPHY

In his most popular play, Hamlet, Shakespeare says, "There are more things in heaven and earth, Horatio, than are found in your philosophy". It simply means that we, in spite of all our knowledge, are unable to find all the mysteries of life and this universe. In modern times, science has made a tremendous progress, still man cannot boast of having acquired all the knowledge in this universe. Knowledge is a depthless ocean, which the deeper we go, the deeper it seems to become. The frontiers of space are infinite and the farther the man tries to explore them, the farther they seem to move away. This is true of all branches of knowledge. Even the greatest sages and scholars have admitted that they can't reach the end of knowledge.

16. WE ARE SUCH STUFF AS DREAMS ARE MADE OF

This famous line occurs in Shakespeare's fascinating romance "Tempest." It is very easy for us, the Indians, to comprehend the significance of this proverbial line. All our scriptures declare that what we see is not real. It may be just a mirage, *i.e.*, "maya". Reality may be hidden behind the veneer of this crust we know as all the visible and palpable things. We, the human beings, may be actually different from what we seen to be, even to ourselves. Our scriptures declare that human life is just a play in which we are mere actors and actresses. Or it is just a dream. Whatever we are doing or seeing, is just part of that dream. A dream is never real and, sooner or later, it comes to an end. So, our life will come to an end. A time will come when even this world, this universe itself will come to an end. So, we are nothing different from the stuffs fit for a dream.

17. KNOW THYSELF

The famous Greek philosopher who is sometimes believed to be the wisest man of the world, said, "know thyself." The same thing appears in many of our religious scriptures which enjoin upon us to realise God, realise ourselves or realise our real origin. When Lord Krishna says about the identity of souls in the. Gita as all of the souls, having been a part of the same original Supreme Soul, he simply talks of the same thing. When Swami Ram Tirath claimed, "I'm Brahamasmi", *i.e.*, I'm Brahman or God, he was only talking about the human soul. We have different colours and shapes of bodies and may be belonging to different races, geographical regions and religions, yet intrinsically, we are one, being the sparks of the same Divine Soul. That is why we should try to know ourselves.

18. MANKIND IS ONE

There are the famous words of Sri Guru Gobind Singh, the tenth Guru of the Sikhs who sacrificed everything, including all his family, for the betterment and dignity of man. "No Men Are Foreign" is a famous poem by an English poet. The human beings living in different parts of the world have the same physical limbs and organs. All of them feel appetite and thirst and pain if they are hurt. They enjoy fine weather and are tormented by excessive heat and pain. People in all countries need crops for food and they have feelings and emotions and sympathy with their young ones and friends. So, notwithstanding the disperate colours which are the result of geographical conditions and different religious faiths which are also because of certain circumstantial happenings, fundamentally all are equal and mankind is one. Any feeling of ill-will and animosity, malice or hatred is unwarranted and is, in fact, an insult of one's own self.

19. MORE THINGS ARE WROUGHT BY PRAYER THAN THIS WILD WORLD DREAMS OF

In these off quoted lines, Tennyson, the renowned Victorian poet, says that prayer can do miracles, the people do not know the real value of prayer. W.B. Yeats, the most famous poet of the twentieth century believed that apart from individual human minds, there is a super-mind which interlinks all the human minds. Thus an idea emerging in one mind can flow over to another mind when the two are at the same contemplative level or wavelength. Yeats believed in a particular "System" of the universe. Whether prayer by one man for the good of the other or oneself can solidly do anything or not, may be disputed, yet the fact remains that prayer infuses in man tranquillity, self-confidence and will to do good and ameliorative deeds.

20. TO STRIVE, TO SEEK, TO FIND AND NOT TO YIELD

Alfred Tennyson's most well-known poem, "Ulysses" concludes with the line, " To strive, to seek, to find and not to yield." This is the determination of the Trojan hero and it applies in equal measure to the modern man who has a scientific spirit in him. Modern man has an infinite thirst for knowledge. He has already made innumerable discoveries and inventions, but his curiosity for new vistas of knowledge is overwhelming. He does not know the meaning of resting on his oars. The line also expresses man's dauntless determination for achieving the toughest tasks, for attaining the unattainable. Man's explorations of the poles, reaching the Everest and the moon, crossing the sea channels like the English Channel and the Palk Straight and breaking of the atom, cloning and incredible discoveries and inventions in medicine and other fields are all the result of his indefatigable will to win and conquer nature.

REPORT WRITING

1. Write a report on twin failure of India's space research programme.

REPORT

The country faced a great disappointment in the month of July, 2006, when the maiden test fire of Agni-III and launch of INSAT-4C failed within a period of two days. Agni-III, the indigenous intermediate range ballistic missile, developed a snag immediately after take off and fell into the sea off Orissa coast on July 9 while INSAT-4C, India's heaviest communication satellite so far, blasted off on July 10 from the new launch pad at the Satish Dhawan Space Centre.

It was the first launch of *Agni-III,* the most sophisticated product of the Integrated Guided Missile Development Programme, that has been started way back in 1983. Originally, the missile was scheduled to be launched in November 2004, but was postponed for one reason or the other. However, the successful launch and testing of this missile was extremely important for the country, as it would be capable of carrying conventional and nuclear warheads, with the capability of striking the targets accurately deep inside China. DRDO put down the problem to design failure.

Agni-III missible was designed to carry nuclear and conventional warheads with a payload ranging from 600 kg to 1,800 kg, including decoys and other anti-ballistic counter measures and to have very high level of accuracy with smaller warheads of 200 to 300 kg. Earlier, we already had successfully test fired the smaller versions of Agni-III, the Agni-I (short range) and Agni-II (intermediate range) in 1989 and August 2004 respectively.

INSAT-4C was the second satellite of INSAT-4 series. It was intended to be India's latest and ultra modern communication satellite. It was launched by a Geosynchronous Satellite Launch Vehicle (GSLV) from Satish Dhawan Space Centre at Sriharikota, about 80 km from Chennai. The preparations to launch 2,168 kg satellite, the heaviest in its category, were termed as 'satisfactory' by G. Madhavan Nair, Chairman ISRO, one day prior to its launch. Even a rehearsal was successfully conducted.

The GSLV is a three-stage vehicle, 49 metre long and 414 tonnes heavy, and its successful launch would have put India in global launch vehicle market. First stage of the GSLV (GS1) was S-125 Solid Motor with 138 tonnes of solid propellants and four strap-on motors, each with 22 tonnes hypergolic liquid propellants. The second stage (GS2) had a Lower Adapter with 39 tonnes of hypergolic liquid propellants. Third and final stage (GS3), having Upper Stub Adapter and Equipment, was designed to be a cryogenic stage with 12.6 tonnes of liquid oxygen and liquid hydrogen. This was the first launch of GSLV from Rs 350 crore launch pad, which was commissioned in May, 2005.

Successful launch of INSAT-4C would have increased the capability of Direct-to-Home (DTH) television services, meterological imaging, video picture transmission, digital pictures for improved mapping of the sub-continent and digital satellite news gathering. It would have also provided space for National Informatics Centre's VSAT connectivity. Its applications would have allowed connectivity to 100 channels and many villages would have got connected to the cable television.

Successive failures, of GSLV and *Agni-III* were major setbacks to the Indian scientists and have dragged the two programmes back by a few years. Though occassional failures are experienced in space programmes of all the countries and these should not be taken seriously, yet the concerned programme of the country has for sure taken a serious beating at present.

The Ministry of Defence has ordered a probe into the causes of failure of *Agni-III,* the Department of Space has also begun to examine its processes and subprocesses. Even after early failures of ASLV and PSLV rockets, the ISRO managed to learn from its failures and emerged more determined and succeeded later.

2. Write a report how Panchayti Raj System was established in India.

REPORT

Decentralisation of power from the centre to the provincial governments was started by Lord Mayo in 1870. Some important subjects including education, medical services and roads were transferred to the provincial governments. To carry on Mayo's initiatives, Lord Ripon took some bold steps to ensure that the administrative power reaches the grassroots. His 1882 resolution called for the development of Local Boards with some effective power and suitable sources of finance. His resolution also made provision for the establishment of Taluka Boards or District Boards in the rural areas. Due to this fact, Ripon is considered as the father of the local government in India.

After the independence, the newly elected Government sponsored the programme of Community Development to fulfil the objectives of local self-government and the then Prime Minister, Pandit Jawahar lal Nehru inaugurated the Community Development Programme (CDP) on the birth anniversary of Mahatma Gandhi on 2nd October in 1952. On October 2, 1953 a network of National Extension Services (NES) for rural development was created. In January 1956 a study team of Community Development and National Extension Services headed by Shri Balwant Rai Mehta was appointed to review the working of the two schemes.

The Balwant Rai Mehta Committee recommended the establishment of Panchayati Raj on the principle of 'democratic decentralisation'. The scheme envisaged a three-tier system of local self-government with *Panchayats* at the village level, *Panchayat Samitis* at the block level and *Zila Parishads* at the district level. Each tier was to be organically linked to the next higher tier by indirect elections. Direct election was envisaged only for the Panchayats at the village level.

As per the Balwant Rai Mehta Committee scheme Panchayati Raj was launched in Nagaur district of Rajasthan on 2nd October, 1959. Andhra Pradesh and many other state governments followed Rajasthan. The structure of Panchayati Raj, however, differed in different states. During 1965-85 Panchayati Raj system began to decline in its development and working. In 1977, the Janata Party Government tried to revive the PRIs and appointed Ashok Mehta Committee to enquire into the causes of decline in the working of Panchayati Raj and suggest measure to strengthen the PRIs.

The Ashok Mehta Committee suggested a minor change in the Balwant Rai Mehta scheme. The three-tier system of PRIs was to be replaced by a two-tier i.e., one Zila Parishad at the district level and Mandal Panchayat (consisting of a number of villages) below it. The Committee also recommended the creation of Nyaya Panchayat.

However, the recommendation of the Ashok Mehta Committee could not be implemented owing to the disintegration of the Janata Government in 1980. No progress was made for the next 5 years or so. During the Rajiv Gandhi era, two new Committees were again appointed. These were G.V.K. Rao Committee in 1985 and L.M. Singhvi Committee in 1986. Taking the views of these Committees, the government decided to amend the Constitution. This amendment was made by the Lok Sabha in December 1992, by the Rajya Sabha in December 1993, and after being ratified by 17 state Assemblies, it came to be known as the Constitution (Amendment) Act, 1993. And finally it came into force w.e.f. 1994.

The functions assigned to panchayats may be classified as obligatory, discretionary and transferred functions and include: providing civic amenities, infrastructural facilities and developmental activities. Broadly, the functions may be described as: public works (construction and maintenance of roads, drinking water, pumps, wells, street lights), health and sanitation (construction and maintenance of lavatories, control of epidemic, maintenance of burial grounds, cleaning of roads, tanks, ponds and drains), agriculture and animal husbandry (distribution of improved seeds and pesticides, planning for increasing agricultural production, improving cattle breeding, arranging cattle fair, development of poultry and fishing), uplifting the weaker sections (arranging for their education, cultural activities and residential houses); and some miscellaneous works (meeting calamities, encouraging and strengthening cottage industries, strengthening cooperative societies, development of forests, welfare of women and children, and adult education programmes) etc.

3. Write a report on International Terrorism.

REPORT

Terrorism is the philosophy of intimidation of a race, Caste or Creed or a nation by waging clandestine operation or proxy war or by unleashing havoc among the targeted people. Unlike all other 'isms' terrorism is the concept of death and destruction.

The word terror got notoriety during the french revolution where the autocrat, king had unleashed 'the reign of terror' upon his opponents and revolutionary organisations. In the twentieth century, this philosophy had been adopted by the freedom fighters. In those countries where the movement for independence against the oppressive ruling class gained momentum. Either during the french revolution or the Bolṣhevik revolution in Russia or struggle for independence in India. Militant groups and organisation cropped up to take up the struggle on aggressive and retaliatory manner these freedom fighters had been involved in bombing, killing and ambushing the ruling class or establishment.

India had been familiar with militant activities for long as Bhagat Singh and his likes gained tremendous support for their acts. However, in free India militancy started during 60s when Naxalite movement was initiated by 'Charu Majumdar'. But the terrorism which started in the Punjab is late 70s and early 80s shook the national integrity.

Militancy in the Punjab grew for the separatist intentions and the idea of Khalistan' was carved out by the intellectual NRIs of USA and Canada but the chief protagonist was Bhindrawale. Indira Gandhi took two tough stance as Indian Army wiped out the militancy from the soil of the Punjab.

Kashmir was quiet then, though this beautiful state has been the bone of Contention between India and Pakistan since independence. Pakistan was never happy with the accession of Kashmir into India; it waged war in 1948 and 1965 but on both occassions was convincingly defeated. Hence, it started proxy war by fomenting terrorism in the valley which still continues. On the International level terrorism got unprecedented notoriety when twin towers were destroyed, believed tò be by the Al-Qaida terrorists apart from various bombing and kidnapping incidents across the world. Israel-Palestine conflict has been escalated by the terrorist and counter terrorist acts of Hamas group and state terrorism respectively.

India has also been the worst sufferers of terrorism. The bomb blast in Mumbai and grenade attack in J&K apart from hundreds of thousand of casualties in Kashmir for the past two decades.

Terrorism is a kind of madness as fidayeen' groups, in the name of religion or a cause, explode themselves into pieces along with the target to highlight or inculcate fear among the masses and it works as a psychological terror among the people as the danger of unknown explosion looms large like Acheles, sword.

Militancy in North-eastern states have also been posing threat to the integrity of India. When the state is constantly involved in fighting terrorists it just has to sideline other major issues from its priority list. And more, the army is never trained to deal with such situations as chances of innocent people being killed is likely to generate hostilities against the army.

However, terrorism must be crushed with full force as if unchecked it can hold the whole nation at ransom. However high and noble the cause of the terrorism may be but the practical manifestation of this philosophy through killing, bomb explosion, kidnapping etc. will never be accepted in a democratic world. This hi-tech era where access of communication has become fast, easy and feasible chances of destructive activities will increase manifold with the defeat on the practical plain the very philosophy of terrorism must be defeated by spreading human rights, democratic forms and human values.

4. Write a report on the effect of global warming

REPORT

Global warming is a severe climate changes that has been taking place on the earth whereby it continues to warm and hot summer days are getting hotter because of it. On average the globe will get warmer and receive more precipitation the various regions of the world shall experience bigger climatic changes and huge environmental impacts which ultimately will seriously disrupt our lives. Some of the most serious consequences of global warming are : rise in the sea level, prolonged heat waves and droughts which shall result in more and more conflicts for water resources and wide spread escalation of infectious diseases. Global warming will threaten our existence, health, natural habitats, forests, wetlands and even cities. Besides, severe changes in the natural environment which are being explicit by mountain glaciers are receding, 40 per cent loss of thickness in the arctic icepack during the past four decades causes behaviourial changes in plants and animals.

Global warming is a very serious problem for rising temperatures will effect every walk of our life.

Changes in rainfall and plant distribution which affected the migratory routes, feeding behaviours and mating habits of many birds. Warmer water temperatures might lead to major changes in the ocean currents which might change its direction. The result will be the disruption of entire marineco system. Due to the warming of arctic region huge amount of Methane which is now frozen under the ocean shall escape into the air with the continuous melting of the region. This will cause a vicious cycle as methane is a green house gas that traps heat in the atmosphere and the added emissions might increase the warming process.

Global warming is the direct result of human activities that emit heat trapping gases and particles into the air: the burning of fossil fuels such as coal, gas and oil and deforestation, and human adventures is helping the clean environment gets polluted. The NRDC-2005 report shows that the rising temperatures would mean more summer time smog, increase in pollen levels which will result in more asthma attack and lungs related diseases. That the human induced global warming is no hidden facts as since the beginning of the twentieth century the mean surface temperature of the earth has increased by about 1.1°F and the global warming in the twentieth century has been far greater than at any time during the six hundred years. However, the most serious aspect was that the 1990s recorded seven of the ten warmest years in the twentieth century with 1998 being the hottest year due to El Ninos effect.

A global awareness on this issue is a must. Policy makers, leaders, scientists and the general masses must have scientific information on global warming, its serious impacts and the practical solutions. To start with, reduction of emitting heat trapping gases like carbondioxide, carbon monoxide, methane and nitrous oxide and by curbing our consumption of fossil fuels and protection of the forests. In fact a careful long term planning and strategy that shall reduce human vulnerability to global warming or to mitigate its impact must be taken on the global level. By the use of renewable energy technologies and the use of clean cars that would seen on the alternative fuels and the complete stoppage of deforestation can help provide a viable solution. And of course a stern law to prohibit and punish the transgressors can also work. This is the time to take action else the human existence will face the most dangerous phase ahead.
